Holocaust Memory in the Digital Mediascape

Holocaust Memory in the Digital Mediascape

Authored by

Jennifer V. Evans, Meghan Lundrigan, and Erica Fagen

BLOOMSBURY ACADEMIC

LONDON • NEW YORK • OXFORD • NEW DELHI • SYDNEY

BLOOMSBURY ACADEMIC
Bloomsbury Publishing Plc, 50 Bedford Square, London, WC1B 3DP, UK
Bloomsbury Publishing Inc, 1385 Broadway, New York, NY 10018, USA
Bloomsbury Publishing Ireland, 29 Earlsfort Terrace, Dublin 2, D02 AY28, Ireland

BLOOMSBURY, BLOOMSBURY ACADEMIC and the Diana logo
are trademarks of Bloomsbury Publishing Plc

First published in Great Britain 2024
This paperback edition published 2025

Cover image: © MICHAEL KAPPELER/AFP/Getty Images

A catalogue record for this book is available from the British Library.

A catalog record for this book is available from the Library of Congress.

ISBN: HB: 978-1-4742-7177-6
       PB: 978-1-3503-2532-6
       ePDF: 978-1-4742-7178-3
       eBook: 978-1-4742-7179-0

Typeset by Integra Software Services Pvt. Ltd.

For product safety related questions contact productsafety@bloomsbury.com.

To find out more about our authors and books visit www.bloomsbury.com
and sign up for our newsletters.

Contents

Figures

Acknowledgments

This book is the result of a multi-year collaboration that began its life at Carleton University, while Meghan Lundrigan and Erica Fagen were students in the Public History graduate program under the supervision of Jennifer Evans. In so many respects, that program, its excellent instructors, and students played a central role in shaping the ideas that came to gel here. David Dean, Shawn Graham, Jim Opp, Audra Diptée, and John Walsh have each, in their own way, pushed our thinking on the importance of critical public-facing scholarship around memory, identity, and community. Carleton's History Department has nurtured this thinking both critically and creatively through a commitment to new and different ways of practicing the craft. This spirit of scholarly innovation, grounded in the sources, has helped us develop ideas around a topic that once seemed so outlandish to those in the field as to receive snickers whenever we mentioned them. We benefitted too from a strong circle of German history students, and now colleagues, who also made this a joyous and nurturing place to test out boundaries and work. Special thanks go out to Jane Freeland, Sean Eedy, and Emmanuel Hogg and all those students who have come in the wake of them. Christine Whitehouse, a powerhouse of a human being, will always be in our hearts and missed beyond words. She accompanied us on this journey for the most part; she laughed with us, read with us, and made us all better scholars and people.

We were fortunate to have received helpful feedback from audiences at crucial junctures, including a generous and receptive audience at the National Conference for Public History in Nashville, TN, where we first dipped our toe in formally. The smaller group discussion at the Memory Studies Association annual conference in Madrid was similarly instructive, especially thoughts shared by Fabian Virchow. Janet Ward kindly invited us to present our work at the University of Oklahoma and in a seminar on fascism and neofascism at the German Studies Association. Cynthia Miller-Idriss and Jessica Davis have lent insight from their respective corners of the web. Meghan Lundrigan presented her research-in-progress at Lessons and Legacies, as part of the European Summer Institute on the Holocaust and Jewish Civilization at Royal Holloway, the Holocaust Educational Foundation's Israel Research and Study trip, and as part of the German Studies Association Digital Humanities Network in San Diego, while Jennifer Evans thanks Tim Cole and Simone Gigliotti for inviting her to present as part of the noontime roundtable on digital memory at Lessons and Legacies. Erica Fagen presented her research-in-progress to the Trans-Atlantic Summer Institute in Bayreuth, Germany and Minneapolis, MN, and at the National Council for Public History in Indianapolis, IN. She would like to thank Yagmur Karakaya and Amanda Tewes for their comments and insights as fellow scholars on collective memory and popular culture.

This research began as part of a Social Science Humanities Research Council of Canada (SSHRC) grant on civil society opposition in the digital age and doctoral support came from that same body. It was built out with subsequent funding from the Department of Canadian Heritage, Carleton's own I-Cureus, the Jean Monnet Centre for EU Studies, and new SSHRC funding on online hate and connective memory in the Canadian and comparative mediascapes. Thanks to David Cranswick and Matthew Dodd for their work on the Hate 2.0 Project and to Christiane Wilke and Josh Greenberg for their early collaborations. We owe much to the indefatigable Brandon Rigato and the team of student researchers that form part of the SSHRC-supported Populist Publics project, including Sarina MacGillivray for her particularly good work on the Anne Frank YouTube channel. Many thanks are owed to Nicholas Surges for his fast and sure indexing of this volume. Merlyna Lim and Sandra Robinson have nudged us to think capaciously about digital publics, far rights, and online activism in ways that have sharpened this project's aims and interdisciplinary ambition. Thanks to Dean Pauline Rankin of Carleton's Faculty of Arts and Social Science, a champion of our project from early days, and to Rhodri Mogford at Bloomsbury for his faith and patience.

We would like to thank those closest to us for keeping us motivated and on task, even when things looked bleak. This includes Jason Bennett, Gillian and Ken Bennett, Kellen Wadden, Rosemary and Paul Lundrigan, Sarah Powers, Patrice Beaudoin, Claire Berger and Alvin Fagen, Danielle Fagen, and Ben Fagen.

It is not insignificant to us that this book was conceptualized and written on the unceded and occupied territory of the Anishnaabe and Kanien'kehá:ka nations. These lands were a site for storytelling for hundreds of years and remain so to this day. We would like to thank them for giving us a place to share and nurture our research, our stories, on Holocaust memory. Although our project engages with the ways that memories of genocide and atrocity shape post–Second World War Germany, we are well aware as Canadians that the violent disruptions of racial thinking, genocide, and colonization are not relics of the past; they still hold a firm place both online and offline, challenging how this country wrestles with its national story. Our hope in writing this book is to provide some tangible ideas for where we all might go from here, as the challenge of white supremacy continues to influence twenty-first-century hearts and minds in increasingly dangerous ways.

Introduction

This book was several years in the making. Whenever we opened a chapter in Dropbox, we were met by a jaunty circular photo in the margin of the last author to access the material. If one of us squirreled away some time for revising, the others knew about it instantly through push notifications to our desktop. We were connected intellectually through our shared interest in social media and memory and bound to the archival and synchronization affordances of cloud storage. While we were tethered to each other digitally and to the arguments unfolding in the book, the past we were writing about was increasingly becoming unmoored. As our writing progressed, so too did our Instagram and Flickr archives grow as people continued to add images to their personal collections. Facebook posts accumulated one after the next while the Twitterstream sped on at its incessant pace. At the same time that the sources multiplied in number, the opposite happened too. Several online groups came and went, their digital footprint erased, altered, or differently curated. Others were outlawed and blacklisted. Some domains simply expired, their URLs reclaimed or rendered defunct. The march of time brought other interpretive challenges too. Where digital sources were once either ignored outright or deemed untrustworthy for historical claims making, museums and memorial sites now developed comprehensive social media strategies to engage their publics online. This connective turn, as Andrew Hoskins has called the growth, legitimacy, and pervasiveness of digital commemorative content, has brought a shift away from the era of the witness to the era of the user.[1] It has forced a radical rethink of what memory is, what it does, and how historians should go about understanding it.[2] Our book is part of that rethinking.

In what follows, we offer an overview of the different ways in which historians might explore networked sources to better understand how memory workers, state actors, and everyday citizens use digital media to engage with and represent the past. Drawing insights from scholars of media and communications, memory studies, and visual culture, we argue that the challenges of working with social media should not inhibit us from plumbing these sources for what they reveal about how memory is forged, how it circulates and gels in particular moments in time. To do so, we argue, requires a platform-specific, mixed-method approach that underscores the uniqueness of the medium in delimiting what is sayable in this space, how audiences are imagined and reached, and how authority manifests in the first place. It isn't enough to cherry pick a few images from Instagram to underscore a point. Social media affordances including the idiosyncrasies of platform curation, the virtual mobilities of networked interaction, the involvement of algorithms in pushing certain ideas over others, and the associational logics that engender particular emotional or affective responses need to be brought to bear on the hows and whys users appeal to history to understand change over time. This book argues that the digital public sphere, or more precisely, the different digital publics called into being in and through interactive media, is not separate from their analog counterparts. Yet, fundamental differences exist not just in the conditions that undergird digital memory formation, but in how social media platforms themselves call into being specific connective memories of the past. A critical appreciation of the appeal, use, and function of the different platforms is essential if we are to fully understand their capacities both for the challenges they present to how memories form and for their usefulness in the struggle to remember in the first place.

Media and Memory

The proliferation of digital technology has caused a seismic shift in how we think about memory, including what it is made up of and does, but also where it resides including the spaces and places of memory formation itself. Since the 2000s, scholars have taken up the question of its impact in memory studies, especially around how digital affordances challenge "personal, generational, and public memory."[3] Existing definitions of collective memory no longer seemed to fit the specific ways in which representations of the past circulate and are constructed through digital forms of communication, archiving, and source production.[4] While there were concerns that mediated memory might trivialize representations of the Holocaust, communications scholars reminded their humanist colleagues that media has always suffused all aspects of life.[5] What was needed were new frameworks for understanding virtual Holocaust and post-Holocaust memory, especially when generated at the hands of users, beyond the reach of museum practitioners, professors, and institutional knowledge.[6]

Whether we like it or not, the pervasiveness of connectivity means more and more people "embody, create and are emplaced within digital memories."[7] The trick is to learn how to navigate the terrain mindfully, together with the various co-curators of the past.

If digital culture has changed how we think about memory, so too has it impacted where memory happens. Insofar as mediatization has revealed connective memory's personal, portable, and transmissible nature, no longer may we speak as easily about physical *lieux de mémoires*, places like monuments where national memories take root.[8] In effect, the shift away from sites of memory to processes of remembering and forgetting has reinforced memory's fluid cultural dynamics.[9] This opens the door to memory's inter- and transmedia workings, including its diachronic aspects, and remediation. As memory scholars Astrid Erll, Ann Rigney, and others have shown, in the digital age, memory transgresses borders and genres; it is increasingly on the move.[10]

Memory's locative nature makes it ever more difficult to pin down.[11] Globalization provides an added wrinkle as memory "spills over and seeps through" the nation, recasting the national and transnational politically as well as symbolically. As it does, it ushers forth new ways of expressing belonging and connectedness on local, national, and global scales.[12] Although these early commentators on the mobility and pervasiveness of connective media were not always media studies specialists, owing to their work and others, the field of memory studies has coalesced into a vibrant, dedicated space for the study of memory's representational axioms in the digital age. Drawing from across disciplines, memory has, in effect, taken the digital turn.

If the digital turn did not come easy for memory scholars, it was even more challenging for historians. Social data, the name given to sources that online users actively create and share in social media fora and networks—including biographical data; images; texts; locational data; shared, altered, and reposted commentaries; posts; and links—offer a rich repository of information about how people understand their world. Yet few historians know how to tap into it robustly beyond the occasional screen capture, tweet, or meme. This is both because datasets are infrequently housed in brick-and-mortar archives or museums, and we are hesitant, maybe even skeptical of creating our own source base. That this information is also often proprietary is certainly another complicating factor, since digital data is only accessible as long as the platform that houses it remains in service and accessible. Platforms can shut down access at any time or restrict largescale scraping, staunching efforts at data crawling. Connective memory is thus distinct from other forms of memory in terms of access and composition, which is fundamentally mediated by the socio-economic forces that underpin its creation and use.

Unlike other forms of memory, there is also murkiness to connective memory by virtue of the fact that it is transmedial, made up of a broad array of texts, images, and practices, pushed along a network, and operationalized by a range of agents, many of whom are unseen. At once personal and public, subjective and shared, these vast networks create a sense of intimacy and belonging by "signal(ing) an affective link to the past."[13] But that past is not singular; in the post-broadcast era, not only is memory situational but it is shared and interactive, forged through a strange and sometimes disruptive mélange of connectivities, networks, and representations.[14] Sometimes termed a "memory ecology," this "melting pot of intersecting and colliding mediated remembrances" is different from what came before. Unlike legacy and broadcast media which is univocal and perhaps even unidirectional, digital media's array of vectors has "greyed memory" according to Hoskins and Halstead, rendering it shapeless and more diffuse.[15]

Part of this grayness is caused by sheer abundance. Despite its shifting and ephemeral nature, digital culture flows all around us in public and in private, in our homes and offices, connecting us in unique if curious ways as participants, analysts, and observers of historical memory formation in real time. As much as digital culture disrupts the spaces of memory creation and research, the ever-growing corpus of social data challenges our ability to contain the past in the past. Data affords us the extraordinary possibility of knowing ever more minute details about how people live their lives.[16] Yet, how to capture the dataflows, to say nothing of how to determine what is signal and what is noise remains elusive. With more and more people curating themselves for public consumption, generating in the process massive, evolving digital footprints, the traditional tools of historical research seem woefully ill-suited to capturing memory's limitless scale.[17] Amidst the mass proliferation of technologies and media, where memory seems everywhere and nowhere at once, the task becomes how to find a suitable way in.

Archives and Memory Activism

The issue historians face, then, is disciplinary as much as it is methodological. Social data forces us to think anew about what history itself is and how we can go about interpreting the forms it takes in these new media constellations. This raises another challenge: digital archives are not catalogued in a way that is familiar to most historians.[18] In traditional archives, the archivist is responsible for accessioning what is deemed important to a city, organization, or nation's history. Today's digital repositories have bypassed the role of the curator in determining what is culturally significant. The sheer abundance of digital resources has meant that everyday people remain keenly enmeshed in the history making process, in radically new ways than before. Although not formal memory activists in the sense articulated by Yifat Gutman and Jenny Wüstenberg, they nevertheless play an augmented role in the creation of public memory.[19] They locate, curate, sort, narrate, tag, tweet, comment upon, and interpret—as well as create—masses of historical data, much of it more readily available to the general public through the click of a mouse than through a trip to the library. This has widened the gap between official memories and vernacular ones. In effect, digitization has created two media and memory cultures, "one formalized, institutionalized, regimented (including online); the other more emergent, confrontational, yet fragmented."[20] Indeed, the digital turn challenges what constitutes the past and where evidence of it might be found. It simultaneously creates fertile ground for what media scholar Jean Burgess has called "vernacular creativity," that is, memory making as a mass practice.[21] As we will show in this book, this raises the stakes for how we might capture the "memory of the multitude" by turning our attention to the "the who, what, when, and why of remembering."[22]

When placed side by side with earlier modes of representation, especially around emotion-laden topics as mass violence, total war, and the Holocaust, we can't help but appreciate the two-fold challenge posed by the increasingly individualistic and situational memories of the crowd over the common touchstones of the collective. Holocaust memory came of age in the analog era through memoirs, testimonies, photography, film, and museum collections. In media and memory scholar Wulf Kansteiner's view, how historians and museum workers have gone about engaging digital culture has yet to showcase the kind of sensitivity and self-reflexivity historians like Saul Friedlander called for years ago, when he broached the matter of a subjective turn, one that required historians to search for individual stories of victims as the prisms through which to understand and impart the moral lessons of the Shoah.[23] It would seem the shifting and fleeting terrain of digital culture flies in the face of the measured, sober, and considered approach of Holocaust memory. By some estimations, they are entirely at cross-purposes, with social media memory formations often viewed as suspect, vapid, illegitimate, and even dangerous.[24]

This is an oversimplification. Digital tools have made possible extraordinary new ways of seeing and experiencing Holocaust memory from the use of ARC-GIS to provide a new spatial sense of ghetto and camp architecture to big data visualization of entire museum and archive collections. These approaches at remediating the Holocaust challenge us to be "bigger and bolder" with our digital humanities methodologies and collaborations.[25] In Kansteiner's view, visualization, remediation, and digital witnessing pose great possibilities for teaching new lessons about the Shoah so long as they don't replicate the fascination of fascism itself with order, structure, and visual pleasure. He goes on to warn that the excitement around these methods and models might actually reinforce a culture of elitism among Holocaust and genocide scholars who inadvertently trade on the awe of what big data can do.[26] He reminds us that the tremendous potential of big data approaches present no guarantee that scholarly approaches to digital culture, mediated by networks and machines, will somehow become "a collectively organized, self-reflexive process of balanced remembering and forgetting."[27] Although emergent digital technologies, and here he mentions the transhuman hologram project of the University of Southern California's Shoah Foundation and Yad Vashem's interactive learning modules, present intriguing opportunities for institutions intent on retaining some control over the messaging, social media remains bound to the capriciousness of the "consumers' desire to engage with history on their own terms and according to their own narrative/aesthetic preferences."[28] Viewed a bit more optimistically, as his sometime collaborator Claudio Fogu notes, digital memory poses critical but productive ethical and epistemological challenges for how we might understand the confrontation of Holocaust memory and historical writing with digital forms of representation and meaning making.[29]

Memorial Legacies

This book takes up this tension not with the history of Holocaust memory directly but with the problem of aftermath, that is with the legacy of mass violence and atrocity after the Shoah. We are particularly attuned to the sensitivities around online commemoration as a mass practice, and the productive potential of social technology for creating new interpellations with this violent history. Our focus is on Germany but we cast our net wider still, to capture by way of select platform-specific case studies the fluidities and points of convergence in post-1945 connective memory formations beyond the nation as well. Ours are not totalizing claims about the scope of memory politics in Germany *tout court*. Rather, we are interested in uncovering the ways in which digital culture might serve as a site of ethical possibility and working through, where people come to see their own lives as implicated in and entangled with the histories and traumas of others.[30]

The challenge in historicizing connective memory goes beyond the fact that the source base is constantly moving. Another wrinkle is the mystery of participatory media's technological bearings themselves, which sometimes leads to skepticism around memory making as a mass practice. This book seeks to meet these challenges head on by drawing insight from across disciplines to help us better understand what networked textual, tabular, and image data archives reveal about the history and legacy of the Second World War primarily in Germany but also beyond its borders. Its guiding purpose is to demonstrate how we might harness social media to write more fulsome histories of commemoration, curation, and memory activism in the participatory public sphere.

As scholars of public history, social technology, and memory, we are interested too in how different media platforms shape the way we visualize the past. How is an image-based medium like Instagram different from microblogging sites like Facebook and Twitter? How do they impact the ways in which users frame their experiences visiting Auschwitz or their outrage at the sight of neo-Nazi marches in Dresden? And how is this taken up by their specific audiences, several generations removed from the event? As with analog media, the answers to these questions are not as simple as they might appear. Alongside the complexities of postwar remembering and forgetting, mediation is key. Taking the example of photography, an image's meaning is often presumed to be straightforward and transparent. It documents an event, freezes a moment in time, and captures an action or a sentiment for posterity. But how a photo shapes what may be seen in the first place is rarely so obvious. In fact, it is the product of complex negotiations between the photographer and sitting subject. Changes in tone are achieved through emulsion and development, the way chemical residues render on paper (or through filters and pixilation in digital images). This contours the emotional resonance of an image. How the image is rendered can occasion different responses in the viewer. In this sense, photography is agentic; it structures ways of seeing and knowing between what the technology makes discernable and what it is taken to mean, depending on how a photograph is produced, and where, how, and when it is circulated and displayed.[31] Although an image constructs a set of viewing relations, what we see is ultimately subjective.

As many scholars have shown, this has broad implications for the role images play in political judgment, ethics, and claims making to say nothing of speaking to difficult histories of violence, many of which have been written out of official accounts.[32]

Visual sources in mobile photo-sharing platforms might be analyzed according to the visual methodologies used in assessing analog images including emplacement, framing, semiology, discourse and content analysis, and read for subject and self-formation, emotionality, and the visual performance of the past.[33] Taken individually, we must linger over the choice of particular filters to enhance mood. Going a step further, we could analyze how users annotate images with superimpose dialogue and stickers, how they select hashtags to help string together what is depicted as part of a larger network of images linked across the network according to theme, and moments when they set particular geo-markers or locate an image in physical space. Instagram also contains textual information like paratexts in a photoalbum that shape the image's meaning. In other words, there are many different ways into social media visuality.

Yet user-generated content, data, and metadata are also only discernable in the first place because platform applications and the network drive us to certain profiles from within the stream of users. In some instances, scholars have been able to achieve a more wide-lens approach by harvesting large image datasets with platform-specific programming interfaces. The Instagram API, until removed from public use in 2018, allowed for the large-scale harvesting of image sets according to geo-marker or hashtag. This rendered it possible for scholars like Lev Manovich to visualize datasets of multiple thousands of images of cities like Tokyo, Singapore, Tel Aviv, and New York for aggregated spatial patterns that chart change over time in numbers of uploaded images.[34] Although we can use Python to harvest bits and bobs, it isn't robust; often, researchers must resort to screen capturing and analyzing individual images, which removes the possibility of large-scale overviews.

Digital images are different in other ways. Taken and shared in large numbers, they are more transitory than analog images, which, owing to processing and development, were often more carefully and selectively shot and in smaller batches. Mass reproduction does not necessarily mean digital images are meaningful for users. Camera phone images linked to social media accounts like Instagram, Tumblr, or Flickr turn into a kind of "visual currency for social interaction" emphasizing shared sentiment, feelings, and experiences over the objects on display themselves. As a form of communication, the visuals sometimes even supplant text itself. Personal photography, shared digitally, has emerged as a kind of memory device at the intersection of self-expression, personal narration, memory, and identity.[35]

Finally, beyond the actual analysis of photography as an image and networked text there is the matter of image sharing as a mass practice and the challenge this poses to collective memory formation. Just as photography holds great democratizing potential as an instrument of everyday expression, where everyone can be an artist or documentarian and speak truth to power, it also ushers in a more diversified—some might say fractured—public sphere (sometimes called networked publics by media scholars), where, for better but also for worse, alternative sources of authority and expertise take root.[36] The personal memories captured by photography and circulated in social media serve as an important prism into cultural memory—or connective memory if we emphasize the network side of things. But the foregrounding of countless numbers of individual commentaries and memories cannot encapsulate a single collective memory, at least not in the sense articulated by Maurice Halbwachs, who argued already in 1925 that common or shared experiences of class, family, and generation were still destabilized by individual remembrances.[37] Drawing on Halbwachs, Jan and Aleida Assmann argue that cultural memory is perhaps the better term for what vernacular memories might forge, since it allows for a better understanding of the interplay between behaviors and experiences that gain traction, meaning, and purpose through complex practices of interaction and ritualization between individuals, institutions, and wider society. Our argument goes further still in placing the relationship of texts, images, and the network in constant interpellation, as a core feature of post-1945 connective memory.

The Blackbox Effect

We might be forgiven for our inability to fully grasp how technology shapes what and how we know. Although we take full advantage of ease of use, we are far removed from the logics of how this happens, be it how algorithmic enclaves form or how ideas and users jump platforms, and which thoughts stick or become sutured to others along the way.[38] One problem is what science and technology scholar Bruno Latour has called technology's blackbox effect, that is, that the ubiquitousness of the technology masks its complexity.[39] We use Facebook, Instagram, TikTok, and Twitter so we believe we implicitly understand how it enables conversation and makes meaning happen. This has played itself out in other ways too. Among media and communications scholars, the algorithmic turn of the 2010s has witnessed an overemphasis on algorithms, filter bubbles, and echo chambers as the drivers of hate speech, mis- and disinformation, and in and out-group identity such that the dynamic relationship between user and tech has taken second place to a kind of technological determinism.[40] For historians, the issues are different still. Sometimes, as with photography, we might be guilty of analyzing social media sources like any other piece of evidence, without problematizing how platforms shape meaning in the first place. But it is also a matter of training, that regardless of the inroads of digital humanities and distant reading and visualization, most historians don't yet know how to handle the large and itinerate archives of social data. Harvesting, scraping, cleaning, and coding require a measure of interdisciplinary and technological knowhow that is often beyond our training. It also rests on a different kind of research practice and way of thinking about the manifestation of the past. For Facebook, one has to screenshot moment by moment because one is unable to cursor back more than six months, meaning in effect a scholar has to anticipate what is important before it actually may be. For Twitter, the issue is less about selective access and more about over-abundance as a single hashtag might yield over 100,000 tweets. To land on a single meme or image and read meaning into it without accounting in some way for the media affordances that made it stick in the first place is only half the story. Social media's impact on society is Janus-faced, to say the very least, with scholars, government, and wider society in a race to figure out how it works and what it all means. Still, it bears asking, how might we use this material to better understand how everyday people make sense of the legacies of the Holocaust and the lessons of the past?

We began this book several years ago by asking one simple question: given all that seems wrong with it, how can historians use social media for good? Our response is that despite the various ethical and methodological challenges to using these sources as windows into how contemporary society views the past, social media is a pertinent source for understanding the construction, preservation, personalization, and re-casting of memories of difficult heritage, that is sites and spaces of atrocity, perpetration, trauma, and violence.[41] It may make official history seem more transient, opening it up to more subjective interpretation, but connective memories are important sites of politicization, mobilization, and personal and collective accountability for a broad range of actors. We need a mix of qualitative and quantitative methods to get at how this works.

As difficult as it is, it is well worth the effort. Micro-archives of images on Flickr or Instagram, Facebook posts and "likes," and even Instagram selfies—sometimes in the most hallowed of spaces—provide windows into how everyday people engage with the past through complex forms of witnessing, emotion, and self-expression.[42] People use these sources to better understand their own lives in relation to events around them. As Amsterdam media scholar José van Dijck has argued about participatory media, it gives people the opportunity to "sharpen their own remembered experiences and the testimonies of others against available public versions—official documents, exhibits, textbooks, films, and so on."[43] Indeed it is impossible to think about memory formation in the contemporary age, Joanne Garde-Hansen tells us, without thinking about its connection to popular culture and interpersonal relations. These forms of cultural memory are personal acts of commemoration out of which arise larger, collective meditations on past trauma. They form in dialogue with official histories; they don't supplant them.

When Official Meets Vernacular Memory

As complex as this all is to navigate, galleries, museums, and research libraries have taken up the challenge of meeting their audience where it resides, online. The United States Holocaust Memorial Museum (USHMM), the Library of Congress, and even the New York Public Library all have Tumblr accounts and a presence on Instagram. The USHMM and Yad Vashem World Holocaust Remembrance Centre rely on several social media accounts to communicate programming, special events, educational initiatives, promote important dates and ceremonies, and showcase the architecture and exhibit halls. They make use of their own hashtags—#USHMM and #yadvashem—to ensure that all museum correspondence is easy to locate in the digital mediasphere, and they actively solicit museum visitor's participation in sharing their experiences online.[44] The Instagram archive of the Holocaust—connected through hashtags—is vast. It is a visual archive, but also an archive of visitor response, experience, emotion, and interpretation—serving to provide the wider Instagram public and the museums and memorial sites with a rich compendium of feedback and visitor engagement. This archive is participatory, meaning it actively seeks out audience engagement, and the responsibility of building an online digital and visual presence is shared with individual content creators who help to move and remediate the Holocaust and its memory in new digital spaces. We can see this at work in the @auschwitzemorial's requests that their visitors perform as both witnesses and messengers:

> It is said that 'A picture is worth a thousand words'. However we ask you to share your pictures with others and tell them about your experience of the visit. By taking and sharing pictures you became messengers who should tell others about the history of the German Nazi concentration and extermination camp and its victims. #auschwitzmemorial #auschwitz #photography #memory #instagram.[45]

Their caption demonstrates that photography, hashtags, and instant photo sharing serve as important indicators of presence, memory, and education. While visitors are urged to share their images, with proper hashtags and all, the museum does not request that the content creator ignore their own deeply personal interpretation of the memorial. Indeed, it plays a central role in how Holocaust memory is to be communicated to others, as part of the message of remembrance. Many followers will never be able to physically visit Auschwitz for many reasons, but the construction of a digitized sense of Holocaust space and place on Instagram collapses this distance, allowing publics far and wide to at least engage with Auschwitz's visuality through their browsers or smartphones. As one post from the @auschwitzmemorial stated: "Like = Remember." The larger caption from the museum to its viewers and visitors actually reads: "Thank you for creating our virtual community of remembrance. Thank you for showing us that photography can also be used to commemorate the tragic history of Auschwitz." The value of Instagram to the Auschwitz-Birkenau Memorial and Museum—and to global Holocaust memory more broadly—is not unnoticed or unappreciated by the museum, its colleagues, and its followers. In fact, the museum enters into a partnership of sorts with its viewing and visitor public, with Instagram serving as the place where official and vernacular memory collide. This relationship is recognized by other memorial sites too, and by the members of the public, intent on being a participant in the act of remembering. The Neuengamme Concentration Camp Memorial (@neuengamme.memorial) praises the Auschwitz-Birkenau Memorial and Museum: "thank you for commemorating and remembering also in Social Media. Thank you for going on telling stories and helping not forgetting" while Instagram user @lordwilliamoftabunut expresses their thanks for "helping us not to forget it & allowing those that aren't able to experience it in person the opportunity to see it in such detail."

It is clear from this example how the museum views user photography circulating in Instagram, and of course, as this book will show, there are rules of engagement and preferences over what suitable Holocaust memorialization should look like. But what about how everyday people use social media to curate their own encounters with the crimes of the Third Reich? Instead of simply recognizing the usefulness of social media as spaces where institutions make and share history, from the top down, what happens when we look at social media sources and their producers and consumers from the bottom up as co-curators of historical memory, as participants in a complex negotiation of how the Holocaust and Nazi criminality should be pictured and understood?

Sources of the Self

The product of this negotiation are encounters that help materialize emotional and affective relationships between the self, the past, and one's various audiences. Although connective memory is thoroughly mediated by platform technology, artificial intelligence, and the creation of filter bubbles, feedback loops and "personal ecosystems of information" determined by algorithms, it still creates tangible opportunities for the articulation of empathetic witnessing.[46] These encounters, fraught and sometimes fleeting, offer possibilities of critical reflection and mobilization around select issues at the same time that they are tied to inherently unequal corporatist economies of knowledge production.[47] They are not, in other words, in and of themselves inherently emancipatory or even necessarily democratic. That said, the digital archive created by everyday people in their social media posts and activities can serve as prisms through which to evaluate how people relate to historical events. This is especially discernable in highly personal encounters to sites of difficult heritage—sites commemorating mass death and atrocities—which orient the subject toward the like-minded as well as against others, sedimenting crucial "networked subjectivities" that draw together personal and sometimes ideological affinities.[48] Memory is the tie that binds, turning standalone "matters of fact" into actionable "matters of concern," with particular relevance to political culture and daily life.[49] Highly personalized forms of curated commemoration form important conduits for empathetic witnessing, what Christoph Bareither calls "past presencing," which spawns "new forms of social exchange about shared relationships to difficult pasts."[50]

If memory is the ground of such encounters, the presencing of the past is actualized via emotional encounters that manifest personally before emanating out into the public where they are collectively and intersubjectively shared.[51] Emotions are agentic, as Sarah Ahmed tells us. They "do things." They "align individuals with communities—or bodily space with social space—through the very intensity of their attachments."[52] Social media texts, propelled through networks and curated in online archives, produce modes of being that shape the intelligibility and believability of violence. But not all bodies or issues or emotions garner the same degree of visibility, and so we have to think mindfully about what and whose emotions "stick" and under which conditions. In other words, we have to read social media texts as multilayered cultural texts that proffer a kind of poetic thinking in Benjamin's sense, in the spaces between subjective encounters and the objectivity of the outside world, mediating the connections between individual users and their various publics, through among other things emotion. They are sources that require qualitative analyses that take seriously things like voice, cadence, irony, and in the case of photographs image constitution as well as circulation. By paying attention to the sensorial and experiential encounters with networked images and texts, we might better understand the relationship between maker and audience, and critically, how connective memory's purposefulness and authority are produced and sustained through these layered encounters themselves. The creation of affective communities or what Sara Jones has called mediated memory communities holds the potential of involving more people as secondary witnesses to mass violence, and as a result, part of an ethical community engaged in keeping these memories alive.[53] While it is true that such affective engagements might also be self-serving "fantasies of witnessing" or worse simply exploitative, as we will show drawing on Hirsch and Landsberg, they also hold the potential of creating opportunities for meaningful, empathetic interventions.[54] The fact that social media is tricky does not nullify its usefulness as a source but it does mean we have to tread mindfully.

Here is a case in point. In a series of Instagram posts, an 11-year-old girl engages with Berlin's Memorial to Homosexuals Persecuted Under Nazism and the Peter Eisenman Memorial to the Murdered Jews of Europe across the street. In two images, we see how the subject responds to the monument's call for a highly aestheticized encounter (see Figures 1 and 2).

@gillmlo stages her own sorrow at learning about these groups and their suffering, and she does this pictorially, using light and shadow to convey the mood. She is also deeply aware of her audience, careful to display solemnity, disciplining her own body's movement to suit the space. And maybe she was trying to earn her mother's praise, just a little bit as well—who was the one taking the picture. This "bodily collision" with the memorial's aesthetics becomes socially important to the curation of connective memory through the way it lends visibility to the individual and their experiences, reminding the digital publics—once it

Figure 1 @gillmlo at Memorial to Murdered Jews of Europe. Image by Gillian Bennett.

Figure 2 @gillmlo at Memorial to Homosexuals Persecuted by the Nazis. Image by Gillian Bennett.

was shared on Instagram—that "I was here" and "it was meaningful."[55] In an enactment of place, this photograph materializes an experiential manifestation of affect and memory in the space of the two memorials.[56] When connected to other images via hashtag, it becomes part of an affective economy or archive and place of secondary witnessing. In this way, it stakes a claim in contemporary memory culture. Significant too, in 2015 when the photo was taken, a child mourned queer victims, a hard-fought happening in the history of remembering queer persecution considering other victims of the Third Reich were disregarded for so long. In other words, this simple Instagram photograph marks an important shift in memory culture more broadly. Here, the image functions on several layers of performance. The taking of the photo is a staged, physical construction or first layer, while the networking of the image acts as a second mode of networked performance embedded within the social mediascape. When taken together, it becomes an example of "integrative propaganda" with its own feeling rules— that is, a series of rituals and enactments that have as their purpose the desire to build social harmony, order, connection, and belonging in this case through the act of remembering.[57] It simultaneously reveals the long and fraught history of homophobia and exclusion that marked queer victims of the Third Reich.

Mediated Memories

This book begins with an analysis of Instagram for the way it helps create a particular Holocaust visuality or way of seeing and imagining the history and aftereffects of the Shoah. Through an analysis of select images organized by hashtag, including the use of filters and user curation and interaction with images, we argue that Holocaust visuality creates a kind of post-memory of the event itself drawing on the imagination and creativity of everyday users. Networked images and the way they capture and present Holocaust visualization become important archives of personalized encounters with the memory of Nazi crimes. We continue with networked photographic sources in Chapter 2 with a discussion of the scrapbooking site Flickr. Here, we used digital humanities tools to unearth three antifascist photojournalists in Germany, whose photographic subjects include far-right and neo-Nazi demonstrations and protests. Concentrating on the curatorial and network affordances of Flickr and bringing these to bear on the way digital photographers capture and mark protest culture and police intervention in what they choose to shoot, we argue that both the image-making and curation practices of these photographers afford us insight into how antiracist activism has unfolded around a particular set of memories ranging from Nazi to police aggression more generally. In Chapter 3, we shift the focus from static images to moving ones on YouTube, to analyze two video blogging projects that blur the boundaries between history and memory. In Chapters 4 and 5, we turn to two of the most ubiquitous microblogging sites Twitter and Facebook to explore the way in which both platforms may be mined as networked publics forged around particular historical memory constructions of the crimes and aftereffects of National Socialism. In the chapter on Twitter datasets collected over a five-year timespan from the annual neo-Nazi marches in the city of Dresden, we analyze the shifting ways in which nationalist and civil society anti-Nazi mobilizations constituted important discursive and social commemorative fields, drawing on and extending memory activism from the pre-internet age. Thinking about the role of mediatization, that is the specifical socio-historical as well as technical parameters of memory creation in on- and offline spaces, requires an approach that takes into consideration different media forms and their impact in the digital environment. In Chapter 5, we document how tricky it is to work with Facebook given the limitations of the platform in allowing access to data. In this chapter, we expose the online footprint of select populist groups with data gathered through screenshots and Facebook's own marketing programs. By cross-referencing this with qualitative and network analysis from other platforms we show the ways in which one might use Facebook data to better understand and oppose the self-styled posturing of far-right groups in the digital public sphere with a particular view toward the ways in which populist groups mobilize specters of particular pasts in the way that they frame their civilizational mission. In our conclusion, we provide a dedicated look at a site of digital activism to draw out ways in which we might actualize memory mobilizations around the lessons of historical fascism and how they help might inform civic opposition to populism, authoritarianism, and illiberalism today using social media, as it were, for good.

Conclusion

Mediated memory objects such as the texts and images that circulate in social media are crucial sources for thinking about the relationship between everyday people and the culture at large, between personal memories and public knowledge, and between lay knowledge and expertise. The archives people generate out of their own texts and images are not static. They are rich and dynamic repositories of information, always in flux. They challenge institutional authority over the past, but only if we presume that they speak for the totality of cultural memory—and this would be short-sighted. Instead, it is best to view social media memory making not as a zero-sum game. It is not a distortion or enhancement of memory, rather it is part of a cultural process played out by various agents—individuals, technologies, conventions, institutions, and so on— which we need to interpret critically. Individual actions are not wholly separate from the collective—the relationship is mutually reinforcing and reflexive. Our actions are only understandable if we see them as thoroughly mediated through digital connections and through the social institutions that give them shape. They generate conversation, focus our attention, alert us to dangers, and show us that people are engaging, thinking, and indeed remembering online as well as off. The risk in denying the importance of these layers of interpretation is the loss of those who might otherwise be made part of the process of education and change.

"Holocaust Spaces, Tourist Bodies, and Networked Memory on Instagram"

Concerns over appropriate public and digital behavior at Holocaust memorial sites have become commonplace. Instagram, the eponymous den of selfies and images of what one has had for breakfast, became inseparable from these concerns not long ago. While digital narcissism and flippancy are concerning themes that tend to appear in Holocaust memory-making practices on the platform, this chapter seeks to extend the discussion beyond the debates over appropriate types of behavior, considering the value of the Holocaust image on Instagram as a memory-making digital object. We aim to underscore how networked behaviors and images impact, shift, or confirm methods of both scholarly and popular engagement with Holocaust history and memory. Put simply: everyday people make use of Instagram to visually share their experiences encountering Holocaust memory. Historians need to develop better tools to understand just how this unfolds. Whether individuals are sharing their photos from Auschwitz, the United States Holocaust Memorial Museum (USHMM), or of the Memorial to the Murdered Jews of Europe in Berlin, Instagram highlights the human desire to capture and share these experiences—and they exist in upwards of tens of thousands. The ways the Holocaust has historically been seen, photographed, and communicated are intertwined with image making, networked visualization, and representation on Instagram. This chapter explores the notion of a common or shared digital visual Holocaust imaginary and examines its connections to individual image making as an act of curation. Taking and sharing images on Instagram results in a visual, grassroots archival space where networked Holocaust visuality and memory can

Portions of this chapter appear in Meghan Lundrigan, "People, Places, Things: Considering the Role of Visitor Photography at the United States Holocaust Memorial Museum," in *Lessons and Legacies XIV: The Holocaust in the Twenty-First Century; Relevance and Challenges in the Digital Age,* ed. Tim Cole and Simone Gigliotti (Northwestern University Press, 2020); and Meghan Lundrigan, "#Holocaust #Auschwitz: Performing Holocaust Memory on Social Media," in *A Companion to the Holocaust,* ed. Simone Gigliotti and Hilary Earl (Wiley Blackwell, 2020), 639–56.

flourish. While seemingly banal, the networked Instagram image is the product of a series of creative interventions, carefully wrought from competing narratives of Holocaust representation over time.

This curatorial quality goes beyond the image. It is borne out in the digital affordances of the network itself. Connected by hashtags and geo-markers, Instagram images are simultaneously a communicative medium, an archival impulse, and a socio-spatial, linguistic phenomenon. Hashtags make images searchable; beyond being a simple archival tool, they convey a sense of place (#auschwitz, #USHMM), aesthetics (#nofilter, #blackandwhite), and affect (#heartbreaking, #sad) and often operate as a stand-in for language when language itself breaks down (#nowords). The intersection of photography, hashtags, and visitor experience at Holocaust memorial sites relies on the Instagram image as its central source; in doing so, it tracks the trajectory and forms of Holocaust visuality on Instagram. Photos of Auschwitz, the USHMM, and the Memorial to the Murdered Jews of Europe and *Stolpersteine* certainly all contribute to a digital, user-born Holocaust visual culture; but as we show here, they also hinge on the experiences of the photographer, the choices they make about their image-crafting, and their relationship to Holocaust spaces as they document them for Instagram.

Much of the scholarly work on Holocaust memory making and preservation on social media chooses one place or space of memory as its focal point.[1] This approach has its benefits, as the camera offers different memory-making affordances depending on the space in which the photographer finds themselves. Amateur photographers or ad-hoc agents of memory are prompted by the space, place, and built structure of a site in different ways. Despite this, the aim of this chapter is to show commonalities across Holocaust memory spaces, demonstrating the ways in which Instagram images remain embedded in a larger network of memory through the hashtag. For this reason, we analyze images which were uncovered on Instagram via hashtag, offering a visual and thematic reading of the ways they contribute to pre-established Holocaust memory norms, while introducing new methods of amateur Holocaust interpretation present on the platform. This chapter first engages with the limits of Holocaust representation on Instagram, before confronting the role of the hashtag in Instagramming Holocaust memory. Then, we unpack the presence and role of the body—the body of the victim, survivor, and tourist—as a means of establishing the interconnected nature of emplacement and memory at the USHMM, the Auschwitz-Birkenau Memorial and Museum, the Memorial to the Murdered Jews of Europe (Berlin), and the ubiquitous *Stolpersteine*. Common modes of engagement with the Holocaust's representation across these varied sites demonstrate the versatility of Instagram in communicating and engaging with the Holocaust's legacy in an increasingly digitally networked world.

The Limits of (Instagram) Representation

Instagram images operate as a form of Holocaust remembrance where the digital meets the personal. The act of photography remediates the Holocaust's visual character in the realm of social media. It manifests the public's understanding of how the Holocaust, visually, should appear; from documentary footage, the construction of monuments and the development of museums, to its representation in Hollywood, the Holocaust—and its visualization—looms large in public memory. As it is understood by the public, the Holocaust is not only a timeline of events, but a network of visual symbols—which includes objects, colors, shading, saturation, places, and even sentiments. This network of visual symbols provides the amateur photographer with a framework for seeing, interpreting, capturing, and producing an image which extends the Holocaust's representation in visual culture. Photography is never solely about the visual trappings of a photograph—digital, analog, or material. Rather, the process of engaging with the physical environment through photography involves a shifting relationship between the viewer, the act of viewing, and the finalized product that emerges through viewing.[2]

Holocaust representation on Instagram is multidirectional, governed by exchanges of knowledge, expectation, and authority; these exchanges are processed by, often, an amateur photographer or visitor to a Holocaust memory site. Although for a long time now, museums, memorials, and monuments have integrated social media usage into their frameworks for education and outreach, there remains nervousness around mass practices like image-making and vernacular engagement with Holocaust themes. As Claudio Fogu, Wulf Kansteiner, and Todd Presner explain, "digital Holocaust culture is at odds with popular digital culture whose users are driven by the ability to shape content in the process of consumption."[3] While websites are nearly taken for granted as valuable professional and educational tools, and most Holocaust museums, monuments, memorials, and former concentration camps have a social media presence, there has been greater reticence about vernacular history and memory making, so much so that during COVID-19 museums opted for an even greater effort to "shape Holocaust memory in the shadow of the pandemic."[4] While heritage institutions made great use of the advent of the internet and the call to digitize to reach wider audiences—and in the early days of this phenomenon, the field lay at the intersection of Holocaust memory studies and digital history— the focus rested on trying to make content accessible beyond the spaces of the museum, research institution, or archive.[5] Although this became even more urgent in the era of fake news and rising antisemitism, tensions still remain around user-driven initiatives, like Instagram image-making.

Social media usage shifts the authority of engagement with Holocaust memory and its interpretation from institutions to individual people. Sharing a photo on Instagram raises two important and interconnected questions: who is allowed to represent the Holocaust and its memory and who creates content, and for whom? Visitors to Auschwitz, Dachau, and Neuengamme can take as many photos as they want and share as many filtered and hashtagged images on Instagram, Tumblr, or even Snapchat; school groups can edit videos which capture their experiences and upload them to YouTube; and audiences can share political opinions on Twitter under the hashtag #holocaustremembranceday or #neverforget. Despite the existence of this archive of visitor responses—which also happens to provide a wealth of interpretive data—some would prefer that the public maintain a receptive position. Anxieties about how the public actively interprets and participates in the creation and curation of Holocaust memory reflect familiar Holocaust memory politics that were present in early conversations about Holocaust representation. Despite James E. Young's assertion that "memory isn't formed in a vacuum," many scholars still fear what will happen to the memory of the Holocaust if ever more seemingly irreverent posts dominate contemporary memory discourse.[6] Aside from the plethora of archived social media sources currently available, the roles of producer and consumer of web content have collapsed. Just as images themselves are multiperspectival, the creative authority over the "digital memory of the Holocaust" rests in the hands of a great many people.

Certainly, the impetus for photography at Holocaust memory sites has its roots in tourism. Since the advent of the Holocaust museum and the age of dark tourism, visitors have found ways to mark their encounters with the Shoah. Prior to the ubiquity of smartphones and Instagram, tourist photography was an integral part of the tourist experience. "To be a tourist, it would seem," argue tourism scholars Mike Robin and David Picard, "involves taking photographs."[7] Most Holocaust images on Instagram are taken while traveling; when separated from one's spaces of everyday life, the tourist connects to a sense of the "other," providing opportunities for the tourist to consider and confront themselves and their experiences through use of a camera or smartphone.[8] A photograph from a visit to Auschwitz, the Yad Vashem Holocaust History Museum (YVHHM), or the USHMM is a visual confirmation of the visit itself. In this way, the act of engaging in Holocaust tourism has been described as a form of ritualized behavior.[9] The visitor's pilgrimage to a site of Holocaust memory can be re-transmitted as a visual event. Through amateur photography, visitors who remain only tangentially connected to the history of the space can produce what Marianne Hirsch has called post-memory.[10]

What does this archive of public tourist-based experiences mean for the memory of the Holocaust? How *should* the Holocaust be represented on social media, and how does this imagined Holocaust differ from the digital reality produced by institutional accounts and authorities? The production and replication of iconic Holocaust imagery stem from a rooted cultural understanding of what the Holocaust "should" look like—from the documentary coverage of the liberation of various concentration camps, to the circulation and recirculation of these images in archives, documentaries, and Hollywood cinema.[11] These visual referents are easy to identify in most cursory searches on Instagram, and there are many motivations which serve the act of replicating this imagery.[12] One could invoke Holocaust memory scholar James Young's memory arc, connecting it with Roland Barthes' well-known work on photography. The memory arc, which Young characterizes as the ephemeral force which demands monumentalization, functions as an impulse to remember and give memory form. It is felt by individuals who visit memorial spaces every day and does not necessarily differ from Barthes' discussion of the photographic referent. The photographic referent is, at its basis, an incomplete process for recognizing the link between the contemporary viewing body, and an inaccessible past and space.[13] This process will never be completed, because its existence depends on the gaze of the viewer. Young argues similarly about the process of memorialization:

> [T]he best way to save the monument, if it worth saving at all, is to enlarge its life and texture to include its genesis in historical time [...] Memory as represented in the monument might also be regarded as a never-to-be-completed process, animated by the forces of history bringing it into being.[14]

Though not a process of monumentalization, the digital and visual Holocaust archive should be thought of as the never-to-be-completed process described above. Considering the shifting role and aesthetics of Holocaust memory in the age of social media is a process emblematic of memory growth in an era of post-memory. Conceptually, it would benefit the historian to think of the ways in which Instagram and other social media platforms serve as spaces to give publics voice; the replicating imagery, invocation of space and place, and the manner in which the public grapples with Holocaust representation remain entrenched in a historical and visual arc of looking at and remembering the Holocaust.

As Kansteiner notes, visitors have very little control over the aesthetics and arrangements they encounter at memorial sites and museums. Instagram does allow visitors some iota of control over their own interpretation of these experiences. The platform allows visitors to "craft the images and stories with which they identify, enjoying a considerable sense of cultural power linked to the circumstance that the figures and words on the screen follow commands within split-seconds."[15] The use of framing, filters, and arrangement within their own Instagram feeds, which coincides with thoughtful consideration of the Holocaust's representation at former camps, memorials, and museums, allows the visitor/photographer to connect to a larger network of Holocaust memorialization—and to contribute to it as well. As we will describe in other chapters as well, Instagram and social media writ large straddle the digital and real world; just as the visitor experience is enmeshed in wider social and memorial structures, individual Instagram photos often hinge on the present-ness and perceptions of the photographer's body, focusing on the power of the individual visitor in relation to the structure of the hegemonic site which they are moving through. Though these Instagram images are taken at different locals and feature different filters, these micro-interventions are efforts to curate singular encounters with the museum, often within the confined space of the frame itself. While not all images taken in Holocaust spaces share in the reverent behavior espoused by the images in this chapter, these photographic acts demonstrate a consideration for these spaces as vestibules for the history and memory of the Holocaust. Through this tension, we can discern the ways that visitors to Holocaust spaces do not disregard the authority of memory, but recognize the importance of it. This recognition operates as a collaboration with the institutions, memorials, and spaces in which they find themselves—by sharing in the publicly networked act of digitized witnessing.

Hashtagging the Holocaust:
Archival Impetus in Holocaust Spaces

The hashtag allows the content creator to organize and order their experiences and memories; it also makes this content keyword searchable and available to others and is a demonstrative link between an experienced performance of memory in the physical world and its presentation and interpretation in the digital.[16] As well, it has become a useful digital and linguistic shorthand, a visual indication that an individual and their content belong to a certain group. In this way, it creates a framework for digital activism and social commentary.[17] The use of hashtags has made speech searchable in a way it never was before, allowing for the analysis of large quantities of digital text and speech, as well as the mapping of new linguistic patterns.[18] Incorporating social media usage into somber practices of remembrance is indicative of the ways in which the actions of the everyday intersect with and overlap multimodal memory performances.

Like any archive, the hashtagged Instagram archive is fraught and contingent. While the thousands of photos of Holocaust museums and memorial sites on Instagram have contributed to the increased visibility of some experiences at these sites, other visualities can remain excluded. The use of hashtags sits at the intersection of language and knowledge; put simply, to know is to hashtag—which increases the visibility of some images, tastes, and preferences over others. Likewise, hashtag "search-ability" and "find-ability" are qualities unique to the content creator and the content consumer.[19] What is more, the Instagram object itself remains deeply ephemeral; images could be removed by the photographer the next day while others might remain on Instagram in perpetuity, and therefore be easier to locate and find. It is a visual archive, but one based around visitor response, experience, and interpretation. Images and image making serves to provide the wider Instagram public and the museums and memorial sites with a rich compendium of feedback and visitor engagement, yet they are also fragmentary and sometimes piecemeal. The archive is participatory, and the responsibility of building an online digital and visual presence is shared with individual content creators who help to move and remediate the Holocaust and its memory in new digital spaces. Yet, sharing a photo is not an unconscious or whimsical act; many of these images are thoughtfully and carefully composed in dialogue with official Holocaust narratives. Such an activity demonstrates a thoughtfulness that has not been easily recorded or tracked. In this sense, the Instagram archive of the Holocaust is ephemeral but it is also rich and revealing.

The hashtag has become an essential part of Holocaust memorial museum online content creation. The USHMM, YVHHM, and the Auschwitz-Birkenau Memorial Museum rely on several social media accounts to communicate programming, special events, educational initiatives; promote important dates and ceremonies; and showcase the architecture and exhibit halls. Museum staff use tags such as #USHMM, #yadvashem, and #auschwitz to ensure that all museum correspondence and discussions with visitors are easy to locate in the digital mediasphere.[20] The Auschwitz-Birkenau Memorial Museum makes especially impressive use of the Instagram hashtag, where the tag operates as a touchstone for interacting with visitors and followers in ways that feel unique to other institutions. The museum uses its authority within the digital ecosystem to make the images of visitors more accessible to wider audiences, communicating the experiences of their visitors and followers through a lens other than their own.[21] At the time of writing, their Instagram feed features over 1,350 posts, over 126,000 followers, and an open and accessible message portal. In 2016, they shared 247 images, and their followers liked their shared images 213,312 times.[22]

On June 17, 2017, The Auschwitz-Birkenau State Museum's official Instagram profile made a request of the platform itself (Figure 3):

> Dear @instagram, over 25,000 people already follow the official account of the Auschwitz Memorial here on #instagram. We try to show that images can be a very powerful tool of remembering history. Perhaps it's time to verify this account. Thank you.[23]

The verification of the account on Instagram would grant the @auschwitzmemorial account an "official" status, allowing it to function as an authoritative site of memory on Instagram. This post was met with slight resistance—not from Instagram, but from its own virtual community of remembrance. After a discussion over the use of the term "official," one user commented on the post (responding to another user):

> The museum represent [sic] the museum grounds sure, but that is only a small fraction of Auschwitz. I think its morally unacceptable to expect to be an official account for Auschwitz. An official account for a museum should have been the correct words. You certainly do not represent the Auschwitz my family suffered in on this Instagram [sic] page, not in all of your posts so far.[24]

@craigcohenhistory's assertion that the Auschwitz that occupies his family's memory has not been represented or included in the "official" visual representation of Auschwitz on Instagram is not uncommon. There is hardly a consensus on how the Holocaust should be represented. It is also understandable that the immense crime of genocide and the wide range of victim experiences during the Holocaust cannot be encapsulated in grainy, filtered photos of barbed wire fencing or frost-ridden grounds.[25] This has somewhat to do with the difficulties of encapsulating all memorialized aspects of victim experience through photography. But mostly, it speaks to the challenges in presenting the Auschwitz the public expects to millions of Instagram followers.

The majority of @auschwitzmemorial's images are photographs that have been captured and shared with them by visitors to the camp; full credit is always paid to the photographer/visitor. This sharing is demonstrative of a fully committed conversation about the Holocaust, memory, and how it can be visualized in the twenty-first century. Therefore, both visually and chronologically, Auschwitz is important, if not the central interlocutor in this conversation. It is impossible to imagine a Holocaust visuality without the camp universe and its imprint upon public memory. The question is "why" do tourists overwhelmingly photograph Auschwitz.

The answer hinges on the distinction between the authority and solemnity of the place itself and its claim to expertise. While the Auschwitz-Birkenau Memorial Museum certainly has a claim to both, its authority as a place operates differently from the authority of the USHMM in Washington, DC, or the YVHHM, in Jerusalem. This is primarily because the grounds of the former death camp assert a spatial and symbolic urgency as the actual site at which the Nazi killings were carried out. For this reason, Auschwitz occupies a space in the public's imagination of what the Holocaust was, both as an event and as a symbol of a hate-fueled ideology. In the vernacular, Auschwitz has taken on iconic status, as representative of all camps and facilities, even though it was not the only site where Nazi killings took place. It is the symbol of the Holocaust *tout court*. When various publics picture the Holocaust, they picture Auschwitz, complete with barbed wire fences, crematoria, and gas chambers.[26] This is due to the widespread availability of Holocaust images which enlist the depiction of this particular camp, its iron gate, and the railroad leading into the facility, cementing the visual codes of Auschwitz in public memory.[27]

Media scholar Marita Sturken reinforces this notion of the ubiquitousness of certain images in public memory. Iconic images come to "us not from our individual experience but from our mediated experience of photographs, documentaries and popular culture."[28] The museum employees in charge of the Auschwitz Memorial and Museum's social media projects certainly understand this, claiming responsibility for photographic representations of the visitor experience shared on Instagram. The @auschwitzmemorial is dialogic in its Instagram strategy. As it says in response to @craigcohenhistory: "here we decided to mainly focus on showing other people photography of the Memorial as we feel there is a need to promote respectful photography as a way of commemoration."[29] Through image and history, raising awareness about the Holocaust on Instagram upholds the founding tenets of Auschwitz as a memorial and a museum. As a "Truth Site," Auschwitz "is a legible, unambiguous symbol that touches the fullness of human sensitivity."[30] Though @auschwitzmemorial delineates between its own work on social media and the work of Holocaust historians at Auschwitz, they demonstrate the weight of the multifaceted nature of Holocaust memorialization on Instagram: to impact publics through photography, and to stand at the forefront of historical truth and representation in the face of globalization.

Consider, for a moment, @auschwitzmemorial's 2019 retrospective Instagram post. In that year, when the Memorial and Museum reached over 1 million cumulative social media followers (across Instagram, Facebook, and Twitter), the museum highlighted the importance of this presence in their end-of-year Instagram post:

> We started—as the first institution of this kind in the world—with our Facebook page as we noticed that this is where the users search for the information about the history of Auschwitz, and they find different—better or worse—pages devoted to the history of the camp. So, we agreed that—as a Memorial Site—we should be present there in order to be accessible, so that people could reach us, ask questions and discover the history. A few years later we launched our accounts on Twitter and Instagram [...] The main aim of the presence of the Auschwitz Museum in social media consists in commemorating the victims and educating about the history of Auschwitz, but each of the sites represents totally different characteristics.[31]

@auschwitzmemorial navigates these waters successfully by engaging with their various publics and involving them in the Holocaust's remembrance. This point has been argued by Gemma Commane and Rebekah Potton, who state that "Instagram offers a space where the Holocaust and its victims can be remembered in the digital age via a medium that is accessible, open, and interactive."[32] By encouraging its visitors and followers to share their own experiences at Auschwitz on Instagram, @auschwitzmemorial can demonstrate to larger numbers of people that Holocaust memory can be collaborative, and that individual encounters with the Holocaust are worth sharing with the world.

But increased visibility also requires that the staff at Auschwitz maintains the vision of the "imagined Auschwitz" on Instagram. This means that the @auschwitzmemorial must employ a recognizable visual framework, one which highlights the former camp's status as a "place everyone should see." This can be complicated, for the social media management team must balance the expectations of followers who have visited the museum, those who have not, and their own educational mandate. Most frequently, @auschwitzmemorial posts photos which depict the history of the camp as visually as possible. These photos are varied, often showcasing parts of the site that are not as well known, or photos that shift the ambiance of the site, communicate visual symbolism, or engage with the spatiality of the history of Auschwitz and the history of the Holocaust itself. What is more, the Auschwitz social media team actively shares authority with their audience by engaging directly with them on Instagram, re-sharing and fully crediting their visitors' photography, and attempting to leave virtually no aspect or perspective of Auschwitz's space unrepresented on social media.

In this way, the sharing of Auschwitz photos is tied to the physical reconstruction of Auschwitz as a site of authenticity, horror, and possible reconciliation. The Auschwitz Memorial and Museum foregrounds this representation, noting:

> [...] we are left with the authenticity of the Memorial. Today, this authenticity must bear witness and speak to us so that, in the background, we can almost hear the voices of those who have fallen silent. We must all take care of this place where things happened that left an everlasting mark on our European civilization, and all human civilization. [...] Caring for this place is not exclusively an obligation to past generations, to the victims and the survivors. To a large degree, it is also an obligation towards the generations to come.[33]

According to the Museum itself, Auschwitz remains as one of the lasting, physical artifacts of the Holocaust. It is Auschwitz's undeniability as a place, and as a beacon of the authentic sublime which has helped the social media team to construct an online visual identity for the former death camp. By positioning the museum on the front lines of historical truth and reality while also encouraging visitors to engage in contemporary behaviors, @auschwitzmemorial functions as a space for education and dialogue. In this way, @auschwitzmemorial has recruited thousands of Instagram followers for the work of preserving the visual memory of the Holocaust using the tools and technologies available to the public.

The visitor to Auschwitz uses a smartphone and Instagram as platforms which give voice to their act of witnessing. Although the images themselves are site-specific, Auschwitz's iconic symbolism is made mobile through the circulation of tourist photography, which gives life to, enacts, and re-enacts the tourist performance of memory formation. Turning to the interactions between these individuals and the official Instagram account, we demonstrate that Holocaust landscapes are the stage for networked acts of post-memory that gain meaning from and simultaneously transcend the space of origins. To trace this, we focus on several things: the ways in which Holocaust memorial sites embed and exert historical and memorial authority on social media, how visitor photographs take up these injunctions, and how their photos challenge and possibly even extend institutional ways of seeing the Holocaust.

The Tourist Body and Holocaust Photography on Instagram

The presence and appropriate placement of the tourist body remain a large concern in the field of Holocaust memory culture and social media, as experienced through the tourist's lens. Indeed, the act of self-photography (or "taking a selfie") has garnered an abundance of attention in recent years.[34] A visitor to Auschwitz argues, "The only criticism is not even the fault of the people running the [Auschwitz] museum, but it's the people who take selfies, it's really not the place for that."[35] The "Auschwitz selfie" could be considered what Holocaust and performance scholar Samantha Mitschke has characterized as profane performance, working against the sacred memory performances of the guided tours.[36] However, perhaps it warrants mentioning that memory functions as an embodied act; the need to preserve the Holocaust for future generations depends on the body of the post-memory witness. Imogen Dalziel has explored the policing and surveillance of the tourist body in relation to Holocaust memory-work, describing the ways in which the performance of photography at Auschwitz brushes against institutional authority.[37] On Instagram, the Auschwitz-Birkenau State Museum has built a relationship with a dedicated community, built on conversations of the Holocaust's memory and representation, both online and offline.

The bodily presence of the victim within photographs contemporary to the Holocaust provides incontrovertible truth of the victimization of many millions of people. Increasingly, the human body has emerged as a controversial site of visual representation and Holocaust memory, with the presence of the visitor/photographer body complicating the memory of the body of the Holocaust victim. Yet the body of the victim and/or survivor is arguably the first sites of Holocaust memory, established and existing long before the preservation of the former concentration camps, or the building of memorials and museums, before Holocaust "memory" itself.[38] In the words of art historian Dora Apel, "those blue numbers, now fading, have come to mark those who bear them as history's witnesses."[39] Holocaust scholar Nicholas Chare concurs that "the number, a postmark, pinpoints a moment of arrival and indicates a period of survival [...] here the tattoo, the crude hypostatization of a bureaucratic process, is power."[40] The indelible visual marking of Jewish bodies transformed those individuals into embodied sites of historicity, having borne firsthand witness to the events of the Holocaust.[41]

The faded blue numbers have neither escaped iconicization nor representation; they function primarily as a method for invoking the embodiment of Holocaust memory.[42] Tim Cole reinforces this notion as having evolved from the media's canonization of the Holocaust and the development of its memory in relation to commercialization. He notes,

> The image of tattooed numbers has become one of several which have come to represent the 'Holocaust'. It is an image which appears not only in the movies, but also towards the end of the permanent exhibition in the United States Holocaust Memorial Museum [...] Here, opposite a pile of shoes, hangs a number of photographs of tattooed arms.[43]

The tattoo has become synonymous with victimhood, survival, and the Holocaust. Consider Figure 3, where @jolynjanis describes their image of the grid of tattooed arms as "pictures of Holocaust survivors." While a portion of the survivor body is certainly depicted, the caption here equates the survivor

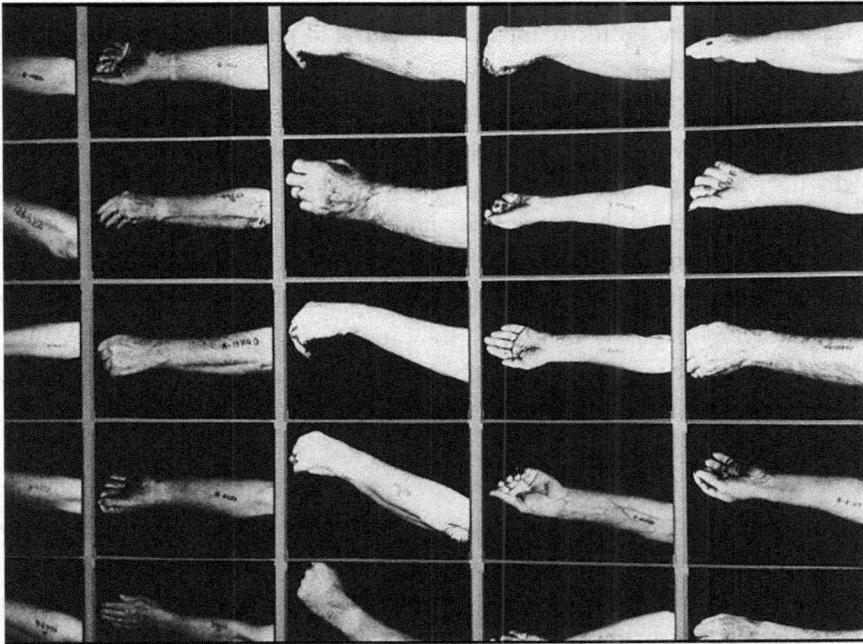

Figure 3 @jolynjanis on Instagram, "Pictures of Holocaust survivors," October 25, 2016.

body with the tattoo, which functions as a remnant of embodied Holocaust memory. Here, the tattoo is the object of the gaze, resulting in the reduction of the survivor's body to a single visual trait. @auschwitzmemorial's reminder that "behind every number there is a face, a person, a story" falls short in this image.[44] Removed from its immediate context of the USHMM, near the display of thousands of shoes from Majdanek, the viewer must rely on their own knowledge of this symbolism; in this case, the survivors in the image are seen only as representative of the Holocaust, rather than survivors of the event itself.[45]

To understand the ways in which modern bodies are created and consumed through photography, one must take into account all actors involved in the taking of a photograph, as well as their choices and interventions. Before the photography that followed the liberation of the camps, the cameras had already been turned toward victims as photography was used by Nazi officials as a form of documentation and identification. As we saw in the first chapter, the Nazis were very skilled at documenting their own rise to power, their reign, and the persecution and victimization of millions; the Auschwitz-Birkenau Memorial and Museum features over 40,000 surviving photographs of prisoners that were taken during processing alone.[46] Considering the intersection of the dearth of Holocaust atrocity images and efforts to memorialize the Holocaust visually has made the ethics of seeing the Holocaust fraught. The display of photographs which include the unidentified bodies of Holocaust victims at memorial museums has been problematized by Janina Struk, who questions why the suffering of victims through photography must exist in perpetuity in memorial museums. She notes, "they had no choice but to be photographed. Now they have no choice but to be viewed by posterity. Didn't they suffer enough the first time around?"[47] This, as argued by Susan Crane, is why understanding the photographic gaze is integral to Holocaust photography and visuality.[48] The prying eyes of the tourist, emblematic of attempts to "experience" the Holocaust, are not free from personally selfish attempts to witness one of modernity's darkest periods.

While the motivations of the photographer are not always clear, it is important to distinguish between the voyeuristic tendencies of tourism and attempts to visually represent the Holocaust through photography and social media usage. Following Julia Adeney Thomas's argument that the ethics of seeing is an ethics in *motion*, we must consider the position of the visitor/photographer's body as an ethical interrogation of the body's image in the context of Holocaust visuality. Thomas argues that "the photographs are merely stills; their ethical energy depends on us."[49] How can we understand the tourist body, in its myriad forms, within the historical trajectory of Holocaust visuality? How does it complicate our understanding that, while the Holocaust has multiple spatial components, the acts of violence were committed against actual people, whose bodies—both absent and present—remain the initial sites of Holocaust memory? While the Instagram image is used to communicate the space, place, and visual memory of the Holocaust, there is much to be said for the presence of the contemporary body in relation to Holocaust post-memory photography. Using the case of the selfie at the Memorial to the Murdered Jews of Europe as an entry point, we need to evaluate how the selfie as a photographic form has been trivialized, by embedding the selfie and the tourist body in a conversation about the presence of *all* bodies in Instagram Holocaust images. This reinforces Kate Douglas' argument that placing the visitor/photographer body within the frame of the image challenges ways we have understood the act of witnessing. Douglas explains:

> These [selfie] controversies offer a neat summary of some of the core tensions affecting the auto/biographical representations of, and by, youth: the limits of self-representation and the role of new technologies and media in enabling young people's second-person trauma witnessing and in enabling new modes of witnessing.[50]

While the selfie does not always function in tandem with traditional behavioral practices associated with witnessing, the age of new media has made it possible for millions of people to explore embodied memory making through the lens of the smartphone. This shift in authority, according to Douglas, requires us to consider and accept new forms of witnessing into memory culture, especially if such modes of witnessing are practiced by younger generations, the very individuals we wish to stand on the receiving end of this transfer of post-memory.[51] Tobias Ebbrecht-Hartmann and Lital Henig have argued that the "selfie"—whether as video or photograph—constitutes a form of self-witnessing in relation to photographing the self at Holocaust memory sites.[52] Arguably, the "Holocaust selfie" remains at the limits of post-memory Holocaust representation, but it is important to consider how its presence—and indeed, its controversy—is informed by and against traditional memorial practices in the digital age.

The presence of the body in Holocaust visuality, whether the tourist body in landscapes of post-memory, victims' bodies in evidentiary photographs, or survivor bodies, is connected to the very act of photographing, placing the body at the center of the memory-making process. Nicholas Mirzoeff has argued that self-photography remains important to the history of seeing, in that "the selfie depicts the drama of our own daily performance of ourselves in tension with our own inner emotions that may or may not be expressed as we wish."[53] Placing the body in the frame of the photograph allows for the dual performance of seeing ourselves, and also being seen. Here, art historian Hans Belting's anthropological theorization of memory as an embodied process and its connection to photography as a medium is useful.[54] Belting places the human body at the intersection of image and memory, arguing that there can be no image without the support of a vessel.[55] "Images are neither on the wall (or on the screen) nor in the head alone," he argues, "they do not *exist* by themselves, but they *happen*; they *take place* whether they are moving images (where this is so obvious) or not. They happen via transmission and perception."[56] Therefore, in the words of Elisa Serafinelli, "the human body sets itself as fundamental anthropological prototype to comprehend the relationship between images and media."[57]

If we consider the body to be a medium for the transmission of images vis-à-vis processes of memory, then it is important to consider what the presence of the visitor body in Holocaust post-memory images means in such contexts. It is necessary to remember that self-photography also signals shifting power differentials in our modern world; historically, the production of the self-portrait has operated at the intersection of class and privilege.[58] The emergence of the ubiquitous selfie demonstrates an effort on behalf of the tourist to see oneself, and to be seen in perpetuity on Instagram. Though this is closely related to the oft-argued point that to be a tourist or a visitor is to photograph, the act of inserting the tourist body pictorially within a landscape of Holocaust memory visually positions the tourist body as a receiver of memory.

Seeing and Being Seen: Selfies in Holocaust Spaces

Cultural critics have argued that the narcissistic selfie takes center stage in the frame of the image, blocking out anything important which remains in the background. Holocaust memorial scholar Irit Dekel's ethnographic analysis of observation, play, and mediation at the Memorial to the Murdered Jews of Europe firmly grounds photographic practice at the memorial as a form of individualized transfer of post-memory.[59] Arguably, amateur photography makes bodily presence in acts of Holocaust post-memory more visible. Dekel explains, "[Visitors] direct [their] interpretation and construct its materiality and legitimacy, chafing with formal visions of what it ought to do to them and in communication with the guides at the memorial."[60] However, bodily presence in sites of solemnity highlights the complex relationship between memory, landscape, space, and contemporary tourist behavior. It is therefore unsurprising that Instagram photography, the selfie, and Holocaust post-memory often find themselves at cross-purposes. Here, it is important to consider self-photography at the Memorial to the Murdered Jews of Europe as a visual act which confirms "seeing" landscapes of the Holocaust, as well as being "seen" as an integrated part of the process of post-memory.

Selfies at memorial sites further complicate the relationship between space and memorial; functioning as additional physical layers of the urban landscape, memorial landscapes embody opportunity, serving as the stage for an encounter with a memorialized past.[61] The Memorial to the Murdered Jews of Europe (hereafter referred to as the "Berlin Memorial") is no exception; since its unveiling in 2005, it has been a space of encounter, reflection, violence, and rejection. Memorials are also stages and spaces where everyday people shape their own encounters with violence, genocide, and historical memory. As we argue in this book—though the bones of the encounter remain in the ownership of the memorial, its architects, and those who maintain its spaces, its actual shape is co-curated by is co-curated by those who interact with it—and in whichever way they interact with it.

There are many ways to read the behaviors in these photographs, all entirely dependent on how the subject fashions themselves in relation to how they perceive they should be acting in such a space. This self-reflexivity ties into early anxieties over appropriate behavior within the deconstructivist memorial space. In the words of journalist Peter Rigny,

> What is allowed and not allowed at such a memorial? Is having lunch on a pillar OK? What about smoking a cigarette? When photos began appearing after the memorial's unveiling showing kids jumping from pillar to pillar, the consensus was that this was not acceptable. Such activity was seen as a desecration to such a solemn site of Holocaust memory.[62]

In 2005, Rigny's concerns were compounded with a hesitance to accept the new Berlin Holocaust Memorial in an already over-saturated memorial landscape.[63] Concerns regarding tourist behavior has also been extended to cultures of photography in the age of social media. The act of taking a selfie relies on the subject's knowledge of the space and its meaning; the subject/photographer actively chooses to represent themselves as thoughtful, playful, nervous, or however they may be feeling at that point—and these self-representations are present in the thousands of tourist images from the Berlin Holocaust Memorial. Similarly, a person's choice of photo-editing in the "post-production stage" of photo-sharing is the result of the relationship between their emotive response to the experience they are having, while also embedded in their immediate spatial context. Selfies are certainly more than what they appear; while they can be a product of an instantaneous action to share an experience, they are deceiving—duplicitous, even. This makes them no less powerful, however. The power of self-photography at the Holocaust memorial is derived from a disjunction between our perception of Holocaust imagery—that is, what we "expect to see" in imagery depicting memorialization of the Holocaust—and the reality of the image we are viewing.

If we accept that placing oneself within the frame constitutes a specific type of performance in which the photographer actively engages with the space around them, then the Holocaust image of post-memory is about being seen. By pushing against the frame of the Instagram image, memorial landscapes and their meaning are communicated through affect, catharsis, and the Holocaust as an event which overwhelms historical representation. Taking a selfie draws attention to the photographer's own presence within that frame; it draws attention away from the landscape, making the tourist/photographer's body the focus of the image. The nature of seeing and being seen in urban memorial spaces fits extremely well with the use of Instagram as a platform for self-expression; the photographer's attempts to perform bodily presence are also carried out for their digital, ephemeral Instagram audiences. The photographer wants to be viewed as present within that landscape, wishing to communicate their "there-ness" to their followers. It is perhaps unsurprising that the integration of Instagram in most aspects of everyday life has aroused concerns over the presence of the social surveillance state. However, the act of surveillance remains a double-edged sword. Mirzoeff argues that the act of surveillance is product of a "new mantra of visual subjectivity: 'I am seen and I see that I am seen.'"[64]

Figure 4 is an excellent example of the dual nature of surveillance on Instagram, demonstrating the ways in which the Berlin Holocaust Memorial continues to function as a memorial landscape that visitors can see and, in turn, be seen in. Photography at the Berlin Holocaust Memorial has become a mainstay in Berlin's urban landscape. For all the reasons explored in the previous chapter, the Berlin Holocaust Memorial is as visual as it is physical; while the

Figure 4 A photographer takes a photo of children playing at the Memorial to the Murdered Jews of Europe, Berlin. Image by Meghan Lundrigan, July 2016.

memorial is intended to invoke instability, loss, and loneliness, the thousands of photos which capture the space indicate that the memorial has become as much a visual symbol as a physical one. The movement of human bodies through the narrow pathways is an affective performance, meant to elicit an emotional response. Dekel argues that this forms the first contact phase of mediation at the memorial. She explains:

> The first challenge in visiting the memorial is its newness as means of engagement with the German past. Therefore, most critical looks at the site start with *what it is not*: it is not located in an 'authentic' site such as a former concentration camp or transportation place; it does not offer a figurative representation for what it stands for. What it stands for is at the same time clear—it is the memorial for the Murdered Jews of Europe—and unclear: Who murdered them? When? Is it dedicated to them? Given to them? What does this confusion teach us about what happens there?[65]

The visitor body within the frame populates the memorial site, demonstrating active engagement with the Holocaust memorial landscape; but the effect is also complex, drawing attention to absence through presence. In this way, the presence of the visitor's body can draw specific attention to those who are not there—the victims for whom the memorial was constructed.

Thus, the selfie remains a complex networked visual product. One need not look further than the example of Breanna Mitchell's 2014 "Auschwitz Selfie," which she tweeted after photographing herself in front of the barracks at Auschwitz.[66] Mitchell defended the selfie, explaining that she was inspired to take the photo because she had studied history with her father, who had passed away one year prior to the day. While taking a selfie at Auschwitz is not always the choice method for communicating acts of remembrance, what should have been a productive discussion regarding the fact that, in Dewey's words, "many, many people take selfies in self-evidently inappropriate places." What does it mean that it mostly manifested as a form of the active online shaming of a teenage girl?[67]

Certainly, Auschwitz is not the Berlin Holocaust Memorial, nor is it the USHMM, which has also frequently cautioned its visitors to act appropriately in the museum space. One of the complexities that digitally networked images face is that their contexts are continually shifting; what is more, the meaning of Holocaust memory transfer is still tied to the physical locations of Holocaust spaces. While the framing and taking of the photo links it physically to the space it captures, such as the built memorial landscape in Berlin, to a concentration camp in Eastern Europe, or the Yad Vashem World Holocaust Remembrance Centre in Jerusalem, the use of hashtags and sharing of the image on Instagram makes the image's context less firm.[68] What becomes of the Instagram image and its continual circulation and recirculation in a digital sphere? Recent debates over the impact of social media on Holocaust imagery have been preoccupied with the misuse and misrepresentation of memory. These are indeed pressing concerns. How, exactly, is the networked image influenced by its context, and how can we parse individual inspiration for re-contextualizing Holocaust visuality? What makes the Memorial to the Murdered Jews of Europe active is its reliance on human interaction and engagement to communicate its message of loss, disorientation, and introspection.

Berlin-based Israeli satirist Shahak Shapira's 2017 project, YOLOCAUST, showcases how contemporary tourist bodies are re-localized, changing the nature of the site-specific performance of photography at the Memorial to the Murdered Jews of Europe and embedding changing tourist visualities against archival Holocaust images. Shapira launched his project's website in February 2017 by lifting selfies from a variety of social media platforms without permission.[69]

All images repurposed by Shapira were selfies that were taken at Eisenman's Memorial to the Murdered Jews of Europe in Berlin. They feature smiling faces and silly, playful behavior—all acts which remain lightning-rods for controversy, even almost fifteen years after the unveiling of the memorial. Shapira added a new dimension to these images by splicing them together with archival photos from the Holocaust. The disturbing archival imagery features victim's bodies; when the viewer rolls their cursor over the images, the setting behind the subject would disappear, now replaced with archival footage. The photographs were no longer just selfies, or evidence of a person's time spent in Berlin; they had become examples of a complicated form of online policing, and a marker of expectation for how people are meant to behave in public spaces of solemnity.

YOLOCAUST provided a forum to question the ethics of photography, performances of Holocaust memory, and the untethered use of archival imagery in a manner that was ethically questionable. Not only were the visitors' photos collected from Instagram, Facebook, and other platforms without permission, but the artist transformed archival Holocaust imagery into spectacle in the attempt to shame the behavior of visitors to the Memorial to the Murdered Jews of Europe. It is important here to remember Hirsch's argument about the objectifying Nazi gaze when considering archival Holocaust imagery: "The subjects looking at the camera are also victims looking at soldiers whose guns helped herd them off to trains and concentration camps. As they face the camera, they are shot before they are shot."[70] Is taking a selfie at the Memorial to the Murdered Jews of Europe, an urban space which the architect believed should be encountered as the individual saw fit, the same as taking a selfie in front of Holocaust victims? The ethical argument that can be made about whether one should take a selfie at Auschwitz also applies to whether you should use archival imagery from a genocide in combination with personal (albeit public) photos to shame someone in a public forum for not experiencing a space in the same way you would.

Online responses to selfies in solemn places must also be considered critically; these perspectives form two sides of the same argument and demonstrate how complex the contemporary stakes of Holocaust memory have become in the digital age. The photographs shared on social media can help us to investigate whether public engagement with Holocaust memory has changed over time; these photographs can also help us confront more uncomfortable aspects of the conversation about Holocaust memorialization, such as the rise of selfie culture in Holocaust tourism. Most importantly, Shapira's argument is tied to a deep and complex understanding of the geographies and spatial considerations of the Holocaust, but also of genocide as a visual event.

It certainly seems Shapira wishes that all visitors to the Berlin Memorial spent their time reflecting on the graphic history of Nazi crimes, but rarely is memory work so linear and unobstructed. By linking tourist photography to archival images, Shapira suggests that visitors should think before they pose. However, the memorial was intended to be an urban memorial, constructed to be integrated into the cityscape of Berlin and supporting the continuation of city life in tandem with remembrance.[71] The space is meant to work with human interaction—in whatever form that engagement assumes. It is worth considering the words of the memorial's architect, Peter Eisenman, in his recent response to Shapira's work: "there are no dead people under my memorial."[72] Shapira's criticism and public shaming of particular modes of behavior is an attempt to invoke specific aspects of Holocaust visuality and memory in a space where that concentration camp imagery is not present.[73] Shapira's perception of Holocaust memory and memorialization is deeply tied to the visceral reaction one is expected to have while remembering the true and authentic imagery of the Holocaust.

Debates over Shapira's use of archival images and the act of splicing contemporary social media images with photographs of victims evoke the history of seeing the Holocaust in a proper way. These debates beg the question of where the Holocaust took place and what the spatial component of Holocaust memory means to contemporary conversations about geographies of the Shoah. While there are certainly no dead people under Eisenman's memorial, the memorial was constructed at the administrative center of the Nazi genocide. Meanwhile, the *Stolpersteine* are scattered across Europe, marking spaces of life which were wiped away by perpetrators, collaborators, and even bystanders and the Canadian Holocaust Monument, constructed in 2017 and the yet-to-be-built British example sit in spaces not questionably marred by their complicity in antisemitic acts of the 1930s and 1940s, but also complicit in other genocidal crimes.[74] *Where* can we say the Holocaust happened, if we wish to memorialize it in the spaces with the greatest geographical impact? What can we say the impact of the Holocaust imaginary is on the global community, of other wrongs remain forgotten? This complication sits on the same mirror's edge as Shapira's YOLOCAUST, questioning how behaviors in public and urban memorial spaces can be so policed when the landscape the memorials rest on remains ambiguous at best.

These images complicate our understanding of the memorial landscape of the Holocaust, forcing us to rethink the ways in which the public interacts with memorial spaces, and the way they are *expected* to act; the difference between the two creates interpretive dissonance. It is important to highlight the ways in which the photographer/subject chooses to represent themselves within the frame and within the memorial space is entirely dependent on their awareness of the space's provenance. The connection between the Holocaust, bodies, and death is central to the Holocaust visuality that emerged after the liberation of the camps. The aims of Shapira's project were to have visitors to Holocaust memorials imagine the bodies, destruction, and severe loss of life invoked by the memorial space in conjunction with modern attempts to access and understand the sublime in the context of Holocaust memorialization. This project rested on its ability to present the imaginable in a space where visitors are encouraged to consider the nature of the unimaginable. In this way, visitor body is embedded in the history of representing the Holocaust, bringing to light interpretive issues which have been present in Holocaust studies for decades. The sharing of the image online via Instagram is then used in an online dialogue of visual memory, eventually making up a collective. We do not believe that the act of taking a selfie at the memorial changes the meaning of the built memorial; instead, the selfie allows for individual engagement and interpretation on a very personal and singular level and carries on the conversation in a digital forum.

"Just like all of us:" Blurring Photographer and Victim Bodies

Placing the body in Holocaust visuality amounts to more than the consideration of selfies in solemn places, particularly in our highly visual, networked age. The selfie is but one representation of the visitor body on Instagram. The use of framing, filters, and arrangement within their own Instagram feeds, coinciding with thoughtful consideration of the Holocaust's representation in museums, allows the visitor/photographer to connect an individual aesthetic to a wider visual and digital Holocaust narrative. While not all images which feature the visitor/photographer's own self are beacons of appropriate behavior, these photographic acts demonstrate a consideration for the memorial space as containers and purveyors of the history and memory of the Holocaust. In many instances, through this tension, we can note the ways in which visitors to the museum do not disregard its authority. Indeed, visitors recognize its importance and seek to collaborate with the institution itself by sharing in the publicly networked act of digitized witnessing. In the ensuing photographs, the visitor exercises their own autonomy, placing their bodies as receivers of memory in various memory landscapes in Berlin, the United States, and Poland.

The presence of the visitor body is invoked in images that do not always visually *feature* an image of the photographer. It is not uncommon for visitors to Auschwitz, the USHMM, YVHHM, or JMB to use the caption to explain the physical sensations they experienced while touring these landscapes of memory and post-memory. This is an interesting distinction; the caption of the image operates as a verbal link between what is pictured, and what is felt by the photographer. Without the caption, many photos could simply depict the grounds of the camp; the addition of the photographer's perceptions, sensations, and thoughts signals to the viewer that this is not just simply a photo of Holocaust memory, but the remnant of a tourist's physical experience. These images employ Instagram as a space for describing the physical, bodily sensations felt as the visitor/photographer tours the grounds of Holocaust memorial landscapes. This type of image evokes Marianne Hirsch's argument that "[Photographs] produce affect in the viewer, speaking from the body's sensations, rather than speaking of, or representing the past."[75] The photographs which focus only on the descriptions of sensation and the physical landscapes of Holocaust memory and post-memory call into question the role of the tourist gaze in the act of taking a photo.

Instagram photographers at Auschwitz also attempt to convey embodied sensations which accompany their journey through Auschwitz, allowing their physical bodies to serve as evidence of history and memory within the space of the camp. Instagram user @leeannelouise notes "#auschwitz #concentrationcamp #holocaust #rememberthem Learnt [*sic*] about it in school, read about it and seen [*sic*] it on TV but seeing their belongings #shoes brushes and their hair that had been shaved off ... gives shivers."[76] In this instance, @leeannelouise expresses bodily discomfort in experiencing the physical remnants of the camp itself, a reaction related solely to communicating the tricky aspects of "presence" to an audience that may never experience this space. Attempts to communicate the experience of visiting Auschwitz rely on a sense of place-making connected to an "imagined Auschwitz." Instagram user @lorajayne15 echoes this sentiment, noting "Such a harrowing experience walking through the Auschwitz camp. We don't realise how lucky we are #auschwitz #horrific #poland."[77]

Raisa Galofre is a Berlin-based, Colombian-Caribbean artist. We discovered Galofre's images while scrolling through the *Stolpersteine* hashtag on Instagram—a testament to the networked Holocaust image. The images grouped under #stolpersteine featured a pair of feet, painted bronze, to match the *Stolpersteine,* standing outside a home (see Figure 5). Galofre's caption, "What

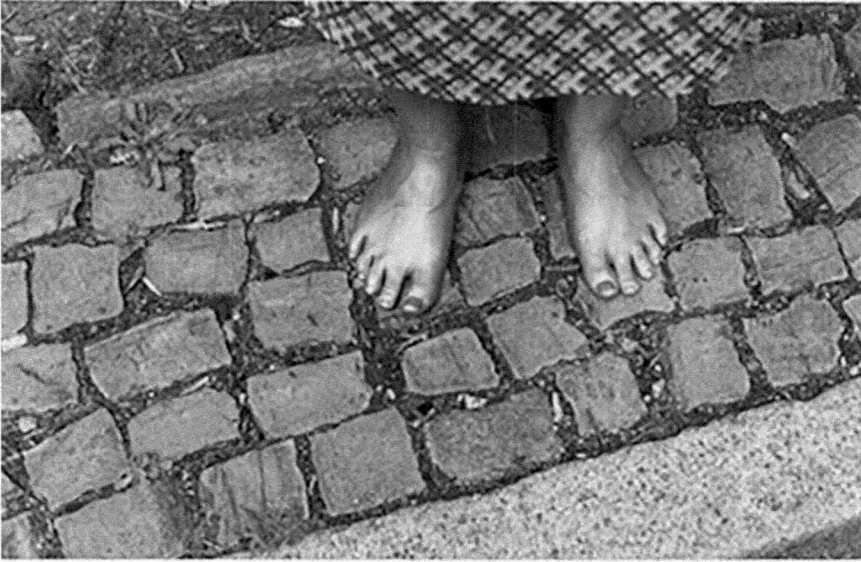

Figure 5 "If the #stolpersteine made by #gunterdemnig came to life ..." Image by artist @raisa.galofre, June 20, 2016.

if the *Stolpersteine* came to life?" belies the motivation for the photographs. Included as part of her photo collection *Heimat*, Galofre's first work explores the intersections of homeland, Germanness, and memory, all from the perspective of an immigrant. Galofre's goal when creating the work was inspired by her first few months in Germany and the things that she noticed as being integral to this Germanness.[78] The images embody magical realism and communicate the purpose of the *Stolpersteine* more plainly through the human body. Galofre's work reimbues the bronze stones with life taken from the victims, whose homes they now memorialize. By focusing on the feet, the photographer's gaze mimics that of a tourist or visitor discovering a *Stolperstein* for the first time. It forces the viewer to consider that the presence of a bronze cube is meant to invoke the absence of a person.

Building on the growing trend of photographing one's feet to capture the places they find themselves standing, the photographer's feet and a downward gaze are becoming more common in photographs of tourist sites. Instagram user @rotemzo's image complicates the tourist gaze; featuring Moshe Kadishman's *Shalekhet*, it could be considered an attempt to overwhelm the frame with representation as explored in the previous chapter.[79] However, the inclusion of the photographer's feet catches the visitor in action, actively stepping on the representative faces of roughly 10,000 victims. The exhibition is designed so that the metal of the 10,000 faces emits sound when the visitor crosses the void, embedding the cacophony in the memory of the visitor. Relying on sound and metaphor to communicate the memory of the Holocaust makes the visitor experience hard to forget, and this is communicated by @rotemzo in their image. What is more, the top-down framing which continually implicates the photographer; this framing asks a simple question of the viewer, requiring them to occupy the space of the photographer atop the many faces represented by Kadishman. This is compounded, as described by @meetmelbee, with the need to take stock of a space and consider its history. They note, in the caption of their top-down image at the USHMM: "Every once in a while my traveling toes need to stop and take in the history and emotion of a place. That is how I felt on the cobblestones from Chlodna Street in the Warsaw Ghetto."[80] For this visitor, the act of including oneself in the frame has very little to do with vanity and

Figure 6 "#thenexttimeyouseeinjustice #thinkaboutwhatyousaw #ushmm" Copyright Instagram user @danadumulescu, November 20, 2017.

narcissism, and much to do with considering their own place in relation to the past and its memory.

The portraits which line the Tower of Faces—a three-floor installation at the USHMM devoted to the victims of the Jewish community of Eisiskes, Lithuania—also feature prominently in Instagram's visual landscapes (Figure 6). The Tower of Faces extends through three floors of the museum, and visitors pass through the last third of the installation after exiting the pathway through the shoes of victims. A visitor comments: "A short walk away from the collection of shoes is the photo gallery. Above walk living, breathing people, whose shadows and shoes pass soundlessly and unknowingly [...]"[81] Here, the visitor's focus remains on the body of the tourist, rather than the body of the victim; the shadowy presence of the museum visitor and their journey from fantasies of witnessing to witness govern museum interactions.[82]

The interpretive strands of the faces of Eisiskes, the material holdings of the permanent exhibition, and the space and architecture of the USHMM are intertwined. The Tower of Faces demonstrates a combination of themes already explored in this work, such as the ways in which visitors seek to combine an affectual human connection with the material history of the Holocaust and the spatial universe of the museum itself. Tourist photographs taken of or in the Tower of Faces echo this sentiment and attempt to recreate the bodily sensations experienced when confronted by such an immense number of physical photographs. The hundreds of images rise to dizzying heights, surrounding the visitor on a narrow walkway; the tight quarters, number of other visitors, and vertical lines of this installation require that users photograph in one of three ways: with a close focus on the faces of the victims; a wide focus on the immensity of the number of victims, sometimes gazing upwards; and a close focus on the visitor engaging with the Tower, surrounded by the images of the victims of Eisiskes, as seen in Figure 4.

Instagram photos of the Tower of Faces fittingly demonstrate the life cycle of a photograph. The Tower features around 1,000 reproductions of images of Jewish life in the town, collected from over 100 families by Dr. Yaffa Eliach. Beginning their lives as physical photographs, they were captured by Yitzhak Uri Katz, along with his wife, Alte Katz, and their assistants Ben-Zion Szrejder and Rephael Lejbowicz. The images experienced a shift in space and engagement with their reproduction for the exhibit itself—transforming them from objects with a material history to replications intended for a particular though very different, context. Lastly, these images experience re-replication as either the sole subject or in the background of other peoples' images. This instance is one of many in which the material objects of the museum fade, settling into the background or flattening into two-dimensional images, synecdochic of the journeyed tourist experience.

In the latter images, the tourist body is the focal point. Each visitor is in the center of the frame, with each image capturing the active engagement with the Tower of Faces. In images featuring the tourist body, the faces are either hidden or turned away from the camera in a performance of solemnity—gazing beyond the frame, onward to something in the distance. While these photos can range from posed to candid, even the most casual photos are unintentionally staged, because the visitor/photographer is always searching for a visual moment which best expresses their experiences within the space of the museum. The memorial image is not about the victim and is no longer *entirely* about the space. Images which place the visitor body among victims of the Holocaust serve an integrative function. By featuring the tourist body or face against a surrounding tower of nameless faces, the tourist body is flattened against and into the memory pastiche that surrounds them. Certainly, this does not place the tourist body within the realm of victimhood—this much is clear, for the tourist body remains as the focal point for the viewer, the person upon whom the viewer can cast their gaze. A visitor notes, "I saw my loved ones in all the faces."[83] The presence of an identifiable person among the hundreds of unnamed victims of Eisiskes reminds the visitor, the photographer, and the viewer of what was lost: millions of identifiable people, millions of names, millions of lives lost.

The photographer positions the visitor body to be a receiver of memory, considering ethical modes of engagement with the exhibit space, the victims of Eisiskes, and visual Holocaust memory. The staging of these images reflects on the presentation of the exhibit, and the meaning of this installation within the broader museum itself. A visitor explains, "When I looked at you as you stood in line, I searched its length amongst the many faces like mine."[84] In this way, the visitor and the victim can be placed along the same organizational plane; the victim is equivocated with the visitor as anyone, a loved one, and a person, all the same.[85] In these instances, the focal point of the image is not whether the body in the frame is the body of the victim or the visitor, but rather that the image features a body at all. For many visitors to a Holocaust museum, memorial, or concentration camp, the presence of other visitor bodies or their own bodies only draws attention to the non-presence of the victim body. Visitors and photographers place their own bodies to use empathy and historical understanding to bridge between their present circumstances and the past. Instagram user @gresaismaili explains in their caption of their images from

Auschwitz, "There are no graves, no stones but ashes of million people."[86] The bodies of the victims are not present at these memorial sites, yet they are always present and are consistently invoked in visitor photographs on Instagram.

Figure 7 places the visitor's body in the space left behind by the victim's body. Instagram user @courtney_dunbar_84 shared this image, sent to her by her daughter, on Instagram in June 2018. Taken at Dachau Concentration Camp, the selfie combines the bodily presence of the visitor with the spectral presence of the victim. The reflection of the visitor in the glass assumes a ghostly quality, revealing a body that is present, but not from all angles. @courtney_dunbar_84 notes:

> [...] do you see how she fades in and melds to this prisoner's uniform? The person who wore this uniform was human ... just like Addison. This person had a family, friends, and a purpose for being ... just like all of us. This person, and the millions subject to the tyranny and barbarism of the Nazis were people just like us.[87]

Figure 7 Selfie shared by @courtney_dunbar_84, June 3, 2018.

These are the ways in which the presence of the visitor body operates as a productive form of ethical visitor photography. The images which force the visitor to consider the absence of the people for whom these spaces are memorialized demonstrate how the body continues to function as a site of memory as time continues to pass. The image of Addison (Figure 7) in the blurry and faded reflection of the prisoner uniform has the same effect as the image of the visitor against the backdrop of victim portraits at the USHMM, as well as the image of the *Stolpersteine's* feet in Galofre's work. Each of these images visually reflects @courtney_dunbar_84s admonition that "this person had a family, friends, and a purpose for being … just like all of us." This is the same call to action espoused by the USHMM: to remember the victims of the Holocaust in relation to us, to prevent future atrocity and injustice.

Conclusion

When work began on the *New Fascism Syllabus* in 2016—a multimodal, crowdsourced academic syllabus project and weblog—we were surprised by the participation of so many colleagues eager to draw lessons from the history of fascism and the Holocaust to mobilize against fake news and growing far-right activity in the United States.[88] Since working on that project, we have often revisited the role of social media in mobilizing knowledge as resistance. What does resistance look like in a mediated public sphere? Is it always 500+ academics curating public and scholarly thoughts on contemporary events through a historical lens? Or can it manifest in other ways, in other spaces, at the hands of others?

Defending social media as sites of potential good often feels like an uphill battle, especially considering how it has been instrumentalized in the service of hate. While this chapter positions Instagram as a generative space of reflection, it is certainly true that the platform has many sides—one of which is as a hotbed for conspiracy theorists, Holocaust denial, and far-right extremism.[89] In light of this, how can the forms of memory making discussed in this chapter operate as forms of resistance in the face of increasing far-right activity, both in the social mediascape and in the physical world? Does far-right resistance have a social media aesthetic? If so, how does one track, measure, and understand it and its impact? And what meaning does it hold in a world of organized forgetting?

Consider the 2018 survey conducted by the Conference on Jewish Material Claims against Germany. The survey results indicated that there was a significant lack of knowledge about the Holocaust in the United States, with 58 percent of Americans polled claiming that something like the Holocaust could happen again.[90] The survey polled Americans on a number of different topics, including whether they "knew what Auschwitz was" or could identify Auschwitz, and numbers of perceived neo-Nazis in the United States; the survey also noted that 81 percent of all Americans had never visited a Holocaust museum.[91] Since the report was released to the public (with a similar report released in Canada in early 2019), media outlets have featured many active discussions about what the results of this study can tell us about the future of Holocaust memory. Typically, upholders of Holocaust memory have been occupied with keeping that memory alive in the age of social media—and as we move further and further away from the event itself.

In some instances, the results of the Conference on Jewish Material Claims' survey are related to issues of accessibility. In many cases, not everyone will have the means to visit a Holocaust museum. Despite these accessibility issues, the use of Instagram and other social media platforms presents substantial opportunities to increase Holocaust awareness, functioning as a symbol of resistance to extremist activity in our current age. In this way, Instagram—and other social media platforms—operate as a fluid, crowdsourced visual archive for active memory making, with the potential of serving as a space of resistance for everyday people. As we have argued, Instagram has provided space for amateur commemorative photography, establishing its connections to Holocaust memory and demonstrating the power of Instagram as a valuable—and viable— stage for memory. The USHMM has certainly argued as much during their 2018 Days of Remembrance Program. They note, "Days of Remembrance programs take many forms. Choose your own way to be a part of this nationwide effort, and help us spread the word about the importance of Holocaust remembrance."[92] The USHMM's list of what counts as an act of remembrance includes, but is not limited to organizing a book or film series, creating a display, engaging one's community, and using one's social network.[93] The USHMM encourages its audience to follow the USHMM on Instagram and like their Facebook page, and take photos of remembrance events, tagging them with #daysofremembrance.

Anxiety over the aesthetics of resistance has been reduced to an anxiety over should, whether, and how the Holocaust might be represented in new and diverse media. This debate has been ever-present since the emergence of Holocaust memory politics and continues to dominate the memory of the event all these years later. As public Holocaust representation becomes more commonplace, must we choose between public engagement with Holocaust memory (albeit on social media) or a total lack of engagement? Instagram and other social media platforms have become important digital spaces where the public can share their experiences with Holocaust memory with the rest of the world. Instagram makes Holocaust memory mobile through its accessibility on one's smartphone and the use of the hashtag by its users. But, at what cost? What other ideologies does Instagram make more mobile? Besides the fact that Instagram has a deeply problematic culture of harassment, anti-Semitic and hateful content jams the signal of memory through hashtag hijacking.[94] Gavriel D. Rosenfeld has demonstrated that online cultures have been quick to trivialize the Nazi legacy through comic interpretation, reducing the horrors of National Socialism to nothing more than cat pictures and houses that resemble Hitler.[95] While you will not find any posts on Instagram tagged with "holohoax," frequently anti-Semitic, racist, and extremist content is found underneath the same hashtags that seek to condemn such activity.

Through encountering and staging place, historical narratives, aesthetics, and affect, the Instagram image remains a fluid and networked source which contributes to the development of a digital and social visual archive of Holocaust post-memory in our contemporary world. Holocaust memory currently exists in a liminal space between first-hand, experiential memory, and post-memory.[96] Apart from the overwhelming number of Holocaust tourist images on Instagram, the repeated use of the platform and its provision of space for those wishing to engage in the act of Holocaust memorialization make plain Instagram's potential as a platform for visible resistance. It is not uncommon to see Instagrammers actively connect the memory of the Holocaust as a *historical* event to current conflicts and events, such as increasing the visibility of Mexican immigrants being detained at the US border, and the debate surrounding comparisons between such activity and the construction of concentration camps during the Second World War.[97] In the midst of this debate, we frequently stumbled across Instagram posts which compared border detention photos with the historical imagery of the death camps. These images sought to raise active, contemporary awareness about Trump's family separation policies through the visual memory of the Holocaust. We found ourselves wondering: how else can social media carry the legacy of memory forward? How can substitute everyday people cultivate an aesthetic of far-right resistance in our contemporary world? Furthermore—is there a middle ground, between the violent past and hopeful future depicted on social media?

At which point does flooding of Holocaust memory imagery in the face of far-right extremism oversaturate the digital mediasphere? Sarah Harmer has argued that the Holocaust has never *not* been represented.[98] The Holocaust has always been an event grounded in visibility, making Holocaust memory on Instagram an active space for combatting far-right extremism though visual culture. Marianne Hirsch and Leo Spitzer have demonstrated through their work on incongruent images that even the way academics, museums, and publics *picture* the victims and perpetrators of the Holocaust is grounded in our understanding of how the Holocaust was initially visualized after the genocide itself.[99] Certainly, the postwar period delivered the most recognizable form of Holocaust visuality through the photos captured during the liberation of the camps. These atrocity images paved the way for how the public would continue to understand and visualize future genocides and mass violence.[100]

Memory, and the role it plays in contemporary acts of resistance, remains complicated—a process not necessarily mitigated by the fluid social media platforms of today. So often, we want memory, much like the photograph, to be a catch-all, and to operate in a myriad of situations. In *What Do Pictures Want?* W. J. T. Mitchell explored "the tendency to both over—and underestimate images, making them into 'everything' and 'nothing,' sometimes in the same breath."[101] Mitchell's comment can tell us much about the complex nature of the networked image, its function as a Holocaust memory object, and its potential for resisting current fascist movements in our contemporary world. Indeed, at face value our argument requires the Instagram image to do a great deal of heavy lifting— and optimistic heavy lifting, at that. It must understand the experience of the visitor, as seen through their camera, and conjure the difficulties of navigating the physical space of Holocaust memory. We also ask that these images help us to evaluate which histories and memories are at stake when interpretive interventions are shared on the part of the visitor. The Instagram image allows us to turn the lens back upon ourselves and the values of our contemporary memory culture. The question is not "what do pictures want?" but rather, "what do we want from pictures?"

The simple answer to this question is that we all require pictures to do different work. The Instagram image as a memory object always returns to a tension between the individual and the processes which shape what they see in front of them.[102] During this particular historical moment, we must be reminded that social media is so often not used for the playful, the curious, nor the good. These same platforms lend themselves to more nefarious activities which quickly gain ground and following. It remains to be seen whether the banality of casual hatred and prejudice, as seen through Shapira's work, is best combatted with banal memory practices.

2

"Flickr, Photojournalism, and the Digital Archive"

This chapter shifts the focus away from Holocaust memory toward the image taking, storing, and sharing practices of a small group of citizen photojournalists linked by their quest to oppose Germany's far-right. We do not know their real names. We cannot be certain where they reside. What we do know is that they form part of a nascent online community driven to document neo-Nazi demonstrations in order to mobilize purposeful opposition. Their weapon is the digital camera, the computer, and the social media photostreaming and sharing platform Flickr. Their tenacity is as great as their collection is vast, numbering over 25,000 images at the time of writing—per photographer—and growing each week. To help their photographs garner attention, they upload them to albums and link them through hashtags which allows them to be searched as a database. More so than the Instagram images, these photographs are mobile. They meander across platforms, are altered and enhanced, uploaded and downloaded, tagged, tweeted, and Facebooked. Some have even made their way into online and print publications in some of the world's most esteemed newspapers. Taken individually, and in their great number, as they are uploaded in tens, sometimes hundreds of frames, they document fleeting moments in the history of protest. When networked together, they form part of an ongoing interactive archive of anti racist memory and opposition to police violence, to polite society, and to the growing spirit of nationalism animating much of contemporary Germany. Drawing on and extending protest cultures into the digital realm, they help concretize in the mind's eye a history and aesthetics of solidarity and direct action, shedding light on the spaces and places where opposition happens, the symbols used, and audiences both targeted and reached. These online repositories of resurgent racism are proof that in the digital age, alongside museums, institutions, corporations, and media, individuals can also exhibit archive fever.[1]

What can mobile image making, sharing, and storing tell us about protest culture and activist identity in the twenty-first century? What is unique about the traffic in digitized images as a social practice and site of politicization? What can we infer from mediatized, networked image archives about the role of everyday actors in the co-curation of history, and how does it work differently on the scrapbooking blog Flickr than in other image-driven sites like Instagram? To get at these questions, we analyze the work of three activist photographers known primarily through their internet handles Boeseraltermann (angry old man in English), PM Cheung, and Thomas Rassloff to explore both the usefulness and limitations of social media for how we think about photojournalists as curators of a German post-Holocaust memory.[2] To do so requires that we focus methodologically as well as interpretively on how these sources operate both as images and also as curated texts circulating in an elaborately mediatized network that has the power to structure what and how we see and think we know.[3]

This chapter is based on data derived from a series of digital scraping and sorting tools that helped us identify potential research subjects from the mass of images circulating online. Although we initially sought to capture neo-Nazi demonstrators, topic modeling—a machine learning technique that exposes semantic structures in a text body—revealed several unanticipated surprises from our dataset.[4] It guided us to the work of these three photojournalists, whose online galleries included countless images of civil society activists alongside images of black-clad rightists. Taking our cue from the technology itself, since a good part of our argument concerns the role of digital mediation in how historical knowledge is formed, we opted to make this the focus of attention in interrogating what these images and image archives tell us about how antifascist protest is pictured in today's Germany. In the first half of the chapter, we focus on the impact of the digital turn on image making generally, including the place of opposition where on—and offline activism meet. Here, our goal is to make a methodological intervention to aid historians in periodizing what is in fact new about how participatory media has shaped photography as an aesthetic practice, site of civic engagement, and connective memory. Then, we give a brief history of neo-Nazi activity so as to historicize the work of the photographers themselves, setting their online archives against the backdrop of recent as well as historical German and European protest cultures. Finally, in exploring the work of these image makers and collectors in greater detail, we argue that these photographers are much more than simple documentarians. Their dual role as photographer/activists in real and virtual networks of creative opposition affords them the opportunity to create as well as participate in a "glocal" vision of digital protest, that is, one that melds local with global concerns and operates performatively to build emotional bonds of belonging that spur offline activism.[5] Insofar as they select certain events for posterity, shaping the terms by which protest will be visualized in the future, they are also performing vital acts of curation, influencing how local-level events will be framed by the audiences and movements coalescing around them. In thinking critically about the role social media might play in this process, which sees everyday people as simultaneous consumers, makers, and curators of memory, we argue that the ever-present place of technology, the platform, its interactive features, and the algorithms that undergird how it all works play a vital if not omnipresent part of how these images picture relationships, memories, and events anew.[6]

Photography and Connective Memory

The increased availability of cell phones with digital cameras has put memory curation, quite literally, into the hands of the people.[7] Whether uploaded from one's mobile phone or email, disseminated through RSS feeds or blogs, or circulating through groups, since its creation in 2004 by the Vancouver BC firm Ludicorp, the photosharing platform Flickr has enabled camera enthusiasts an opportunity to blend the site's database and photoalbum features in the creation of an interactive photo archive. Although it is tempting to suggest digital texts operate entirely differently than analog, digital photographs, like books, are part of an elaborate social-technological system that similarly creates and reflects information in a cycle of production, distribution, and consumption.[8] What is different are scale, scope and impact, and the role of technology itself in structuring experience. Regardless of whether they are generated by individual users, corporations, or political campaigns, the image and textual worlds of social media platforms have the power to gauge, direct, and shape public taste and popular sentiment, often in lightning speed.[9] More than simple reflections of social norms, they create and reinforce social bonds and exert agency in helping people develop "repertoires of contention" in the coordination of actions and events.[10] These feelings of connectedness are put to great use in networked publics, stitched together through online media and its platformed representational and storytelling infrastructures.[11] However, none of this happens outside of the computational logic of the algorithm, which operates without the knowledge of the user and structures what surfaces as common experience. This culture of connectivity, as José van Dijck calls it, is mediated at all times by the network and the workings of code and metadata. It has fundamentally altered how memory happens in the digital arena.[12]

There can be no doubt that participatory media has fundamentally transformed how politics happens, especially how sentiments are mobilized in online spaces.[13] And still, online activism is often mocked as ill-conceived and ineffective. Unlike collective models of social organizing, however, digital media has opened doors for connective action, where people use personal frames for contesting an action that needs to be changed.[14] It is connective insofar as it emphasizes networked-based expressions of highly personal, subjective reflections over formal group-based mobilization. Ideology still matters, but it is organized more inchoately, through the prism of the self as structured through shared practices of uploading, sharing, and liking content. In the wake of the Capitol riot, it is hard to take seriously Malcolm Gladwell's claims that social media plays little role in political organization. The revolution has indeed been tweeted, Facebooked, TikTokked, and Flickred as activists the world over clamber to the internet to voice their opposition to current issues and mount a call for change, moving between universities, home offices, coffee shops and cafés, and out into the street.[15] The challenge is finding a way to analyze how that happens.

While framing tactics are the most obvious example of changing socio-technological affordances, improvements in media production have always played pivotal roles in bringing about social change. One need only think of the function of radio and the telegraph in spreading word of revolution in Moscow.[16] Like these older media forms, social technology challenges traditional structures of opposition by exerting direct influence on political participation. Where it is different is in pace of transmission and reach. Because it creates instantaneous, networked, collaborative publics, it can mobilize opposition swifter than past technologies. Moreover, it can do this on a variety of levels simultaneously, for local, diasporic, and international audiences, all the while carving out niches—sometimes hidden or secret—for further discussion and planning. What might have the appearance of a solitary expression of outrage can quickly become multi-vocal once an image, blog, or text is linked via online systems of search, interaction, archiving, and display.[17]

As we show in Chapter 4 on Twitter, digital technologies have a spatial effect on where and how ideas take shape and how opposition happens. Thinking of social media as much as a mobile sharing practice as a tangible, material space of reflection and interaction, mobility redefines the relationship between public and private places of introspection. Looking to book scholars once more, we see that analog texts gained their meaning by migrating between and among diverse, unanticipated, and sometimes overlapping social, spatial, and communal structures. Eighteenth-century print cultures, and the imagined communities they inspired, gained traction because they linked the poster board or publishing house to the café and street, and the different publics that were found there.[18] In the internet age, the scope and pace of change are swifter and the audience more diverse and far reaching (if perhaps at times more blasé and transitory).[19] However, the medium does matter. While the telegraph connected the European colonies to the metropole and allowed news to travel 10,000 times as fast as previously imaginable, the interconnected web facilitates the sharing of data in real time.[20] In other words, in terms of scope, scale, and pace of mobilization, network society has the effect of instantiating the rapid deployment of new—if occasionally fleeting—fora in which citizen engagement might flourish.[21] If new media can subvert, alter, and transform established relationships between the individual and the crowd and between the local, national, and supranational, in an entirely different pace than that which came before, it only follows that how authority is manifested and opposed must be navigated with these differences in mind.

While gauging the pace of transmission is easy, getting at the impact of digital texts is the hard part, requiring a mix of qualitative and quantitative methods, which for social media analysis also might include machine learning, sentiment, and network analysis. This is made more challenging still with images, which, unlike conventional data, are difficult to harvest, catalogue, map, and interpret in a way that respects their (inter)textual, algorithmic, and visual workings.[22] First, there is the sheer number of them out there. In 2011, Flickr reported over 560 million uploaded photos that year alone, and the image bank has only grown since, and many of them migrate to other social media sites like Instagram and Tumblr.[23] But beyond the matter of numbers and which tools to use lurks the more vexing question of how to interpret the data they generate.

Image-based platforms like Flickr pose other challenges still. As was the case for book scholars, the advent of the digital age brought with it similar concern over the death of photography as visual culture specialists debated what photographic authenticity meant in a computer-driven world when the photograph is no longer "the index of an absolute reality."[24] There are additional obstacles at the platform level. Digital images, whether professionally taken and uploaded to Flickr or stored on a cell phone, can be deleted—or worse— supplanted by a steady stream of new ones. The ease of deletion limits the site's archiving power, at least in relation to an outside user.[25] And the flipslide, instantaneity, the constant uploading of new content, dilutes the curatorial function of the collection with the addition of ever more additives. As media theorist danah boyd [*sic*] has argued, the medium also poses serious questions around reproducibility and audience, since it cannot always be established where an image originates, or how it meanders, let alone how many people interact with it over time.[26] As if all this isn't enough cause for concern, only occasionally do people leave behind their thoughts about what they saw. Digital images—like photographs themselves—are not easily anchored.[27]

Yet despite their mobility, digital photographs are invaluable sources for historians. They carry ethical currency and weight, reflect as well as construct social norms and practices, and render events and people "thinkable" through the process of representation.[28] The symbolic work of photographs has the power to turn abstract images into meaningful events insofar as they instantiate moments of shared cultural identification and political stance taking.[29] They do this by unleashing a flurry of narratives and arguments, debate and disputation, from which movements might spring. Simply put, what these photos "mean" and what that meaning mobilizes in mediatized civic, community, and cultural spheres help manifest ideas otherwise obfuscated or hidden. How and when they are taken up into full-fledged strategies for change are determined only partly by what falls within the frame.[30] It is the network that lends traction and permanence to how—in the example here—protest is pictured and what forms civic-mindedness might take.

These three photojournalists are keenly aware of the usefulness of social technology in adding urgency to their images when they draw on Flickr to place them in reach of their intended audience. They link each other's photo streams, "tweet" their images, use common tags, and promote their photography on their individual Facebook pages. Within Flickr itself, they "favorite" each other's images, hoping that particularly striking images might be taken up by other groups or better still, by alternative and mainstream media. This is not an unrealistic expectation. As we can see in Figure 8 from an anti-Nazi demonstration in 2011, on Flickr, member pages like this one from PM Cheung forms part of a greater networked community, accessible through the use of categories, keyword tags, notes for individual photo commentary, subscriber lists, and group classification. Unlike other photo-blogging sites, Flickr's collaborative features combined with instantaneity have made it a place where amateur and professional photographers catalogue their "novel, decentralized, vision of the everyday" as part of the documentation of daily life.[31] As Jean Burgess has argued, Flickr has enabled a kind of vernacular creativity in the digitized network environment, a place that transforms photography's analog features—its aesthetic, storytelling, and documentarian impulses—through remediation.[32]

Social media not only facilitates the sense of group belonging, it allows members to refine their aesthetic and political practice (see Figure 8).

This networked collaboration goes well beyond the public act of reblogging or "liking" favorite photos. Just as the adherents of Bourdieu's amateur camera clubs critically engaged each other's skill and practice, so too do these modern-day image makers discuss practical and aesthetic matters in the so-called back channel, within the confines of private Facebook group pages, WhatsApp, and Discord.[33] It is here that these photojournalists decide which demonstrations to cover according to participant resources and work/life schedules. Social media is the glue that binds them together. It enables them to market their oeuvre while providing private space from which to strategize. Of course, as Sandra Robinson has shown in her work on how nefarious groups navigate account suspension, the affiliative assemblages fostered in encrypted back channels that allow antifascist photojournalists to organize and thrive are the same online spaces exploited by far rights, which highlights yet again the ambiguities of social media as a political space.[34]

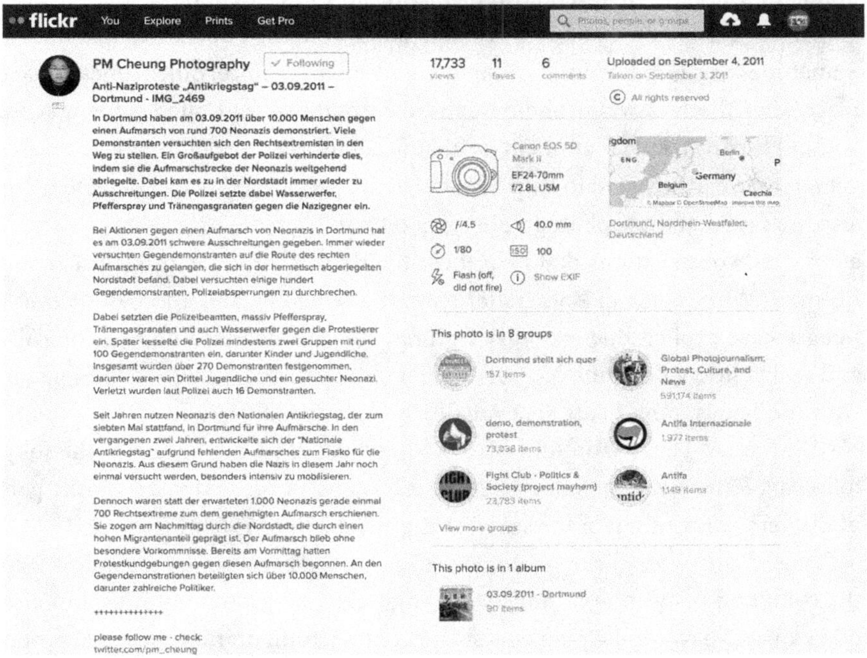

Figure 8 Anti-Naziproteste "Antikriegstag," September 3, 2011. https://www.flickr.com/photos/pm_cheung/6110669070.

Unlike 1970s New Left and student movement mimeographic reproduction and self-publishing, the taking and sharing of demonstration photographs on Flickr holds the potential to reach several audiences at once, from the local to the global. It is also an act of historical curation. The wellspring of information housed within these frames and the care with which activist participants make them available for interpretation render these image catalogues into archives of present-day political mobilization. There is craftmanship in capturing, altering, and uploading these images, learning the platform architecture and hacking the system from the inside to ensure maximum reach.[35] With established news services courting on-the-ground-images like these, demonstration photojournalism might best be understood as a highly performative visual practice that challenges the divide between fringe and mainstream media, art and politics, the exceptional and the quotidian, and—as we will argue here—institutional and everyday acts of archiving history in the making.[36]

As if following on from photography theorist Allan Sekula's 1999 photography series *Waiting for the Gas* on the G8 demonstrations in Seattle, which created a template for "anti-photojournalism" that included close-up shots from within the commons and crowd, these photographers intervene deliberately at different points in a photo's capture and remediation to draw attention to the material and historical forces that influence and shape contested social relationships.[37] Sometimes this is at the point of capture and subject choice; other times it takes place after the fact when photographs are examined and altered for upload. Although para-textual commentary that accompanies an online image creates yet another narrative arc to help historicize the people and places depicted, it is also the case that these photographers sometimes train their sights on particular actors and constellations that help them build visual arguments against recent history.[38] While some of Boeseraltermann, PM Cheung, and Thomas Rassloff's images have explicit documentary features, subjects depicted more laconically and with a heavy dose of irony carry different messaging, as we see in Figure 9, with the jaunty pink heart sign on which "love for all" is written by an anti-Nazi protester. Here, as in others in his practice, PM Cheung shows the folly, following Rancière, that police presence is somehow accepted as a requisite part of the very constitution of the social in the aftermath of 1968 (Figure 9).[39]

Viewed this way, Flickr photojournalism not only serves as a window into the evolution of twentieth- and twenty-first-century protest cultures, but also plays an active role in helping curate and contest configurations of social power via the subjectivities and practices of opposition manifest in on- and offline participatory culture. Extending the avant guard and performative impulses

PM Cheung Photography ✓ Following

Nazis blockieren - was sonst? - Magdeburg Nazifrei 2014
- 18.01.2014 - Magdeburg - IMN_8139

11,167 4 0 Uploaded on January 18, 2014
views faves comments Taken on January 18, 2014

Figure 9 "Love for All." Nazis blockieren—was sonst? Magdeburg Nazifrei, January 18, 2014. http://shorturl.at/AFY25.

of post student movement era protest into the networked, visual realm, these photojournalists tap into and extend recognizable visual cues to create narratives of opposition through the building and circulation of their online archives.[40] Further still, in casting civil opposition in a distinct visual language and register, they add aesthetic cohesiveness to an otherwise diffuse and inchoate set of messages, preparing the foundation for future social action.[41]

While it is not hard to imagine social media might serve as a likely place to analyze civic engagement, some new media scholars caution that online platforms like Flickr and even Twitter, Facebook, and Wikipedia present an unstable ground upon which to situate sustained cultural analysis. What is their concern beyond unequal access?[42] The argument is that not enough attention has been paid to the masking effect of social technology in mediating what is in fact depicted, how it is constituted, engaged with, and remembered.[43] Such skepticism of the mediated nature of digital sources is not wholly new. Indeed, it resonates with earlier concerns about the digital turn itself, when photography theorists argued that digital images could not truthfully represent an outside reality since a photo's makeup was the product of technological intervention.[44]

This need not imply nefariousness, cloak and dagger photoshopping and Stalinist-style image manipulation. However, it is well worth remembering that digital technology is not secondary to how meaning is generated online or, by extension, how our thoughts are structured, off. Insofar as it sorts what and how we see, to a great extent it creates the very conditions for social interaction in the first place. As we shall see in this photojournalist network, these relationships may be mined for the nature of social exchange, yielding interesting insight into connective sociability. Still, there is the need for a note of caution. Despite this intensely mediated set of experiences, users have very little awareness just how structured their thoughts are by the interfaces they employ. This "technological unconscious" as both Andrew Hoskins and Nigel Thrift have termed it masks the fact that we are wholly enmeshed in the digital environment in which we are situated and its role in shaping our social practices—history making included. With each click of the mouse, each glance of the eye, as witnessing turns to introspection before coalescing into knowledge, even our cognitive routines bear the hallmarks of socio-technical intervention.[45]

Despite these concerns, there can be little doubt that the digital revolution has indelibly shaped how personal and public memory is constructed and perceived. Still, how different is this from that which came before? And relatedly, how unique are the social formations called into being through these new media forms? To the first point, new media and connective cultures are "new" but they are also "old." Just as the camera obscura made manifest long-standing laws of optics dating back as early as the fifth century BCE, the rise of the internet saw significant carryover from older media forms.[46] At the same time, the advent of new technologies ushered in changes in relationships of viewership and observation, representation and audience that must be treated carefully. Here, the issue of periodization is key. The same is true about the constitution and circulation of images in social media. Like analog photography, digital images have their own unique composition and visual language. They may have a wider reach, circulating between diverse audiences along horizontal pathways, but when linked via hashtag, they are bound in a dedicated if not entirely singular conversation. When merged with similar images, they acquire the appearance of an online archive. Like the photo album that orders disparate family memories in a unified narrative, when uploaded to Flickr seemingly incongruent photographs suddenly become imbued with an organizational logic out of which individual and collective memories may stem.[47] However, just because it is mutable, we should not assume photosharing easily or inherently leads to a unified vision of the event or persons depicted.[48] This potential for "individual customization,"

Lev Manovich suggests, is but one of the core markers of difference between old and new media (he cites 5!). If users are able to change groupings and keywords willy-nilly, altering the logic and cohesiveness of the online archive, how are we to understand how meaning is formed on a foundation made of sand?[49]

Before drilling down into these questions in discussing the work of these Flickr photojournalists, it is important to consider one final point about the shift from older to newer media. New media and the relationships it engenders do not emerge out of a vacuum. Its use and impact are always already informed by culture. So too, it is safe to say that different forms of technology condition different kinds of responses from each of its audiences, whose precise reactions are similarly time bound and culturally inflected. It is certainly not the same thing to listen surreptitiously to radio frequencies in Nazi Germany, as it is to watch hacked YouTube videos in contemporary Iran. A letter to the editor in a nineteenth-century European newspaper has a different sense of immediacy than logging one's opinion in a contemporary online forum or blog. Audiences differ; impact must be differently measured; and notions of time passing, lapse, and delay reflect different social expectations and experiences. It should be no surprise to historians that these different forms of interaction, rooted in discrete social-economic and structural circumstances and structured by hardware and software, create unique dynamics of audience, reach, and resonance. That said, one cannot speak of an easy separation between old and new media as media forms are themselves remediated; that is, they incorporate the history, use, make-up, and memory of past technologies into current configurations.[50] Not only do digital platforms import and house diverse media formats from digitized photographs to sound clips, graphics, animation, and maps, but digital media recycles insofar as it repackages, revisits, recasts, and refines older forms of communication. In terms of the second point about social relationships engendered by and through divergent media structures, here too we see that creators and consumers fashion their own sense of self and identity in interpolation with these coexisting yet overlaid media forms. We see this in the technological forms themselves, but also in the thoughts they help give expression to as well as help manifest. Case in point: long before the ubiquitous "selfie," romantic painters and even modernists sought a sense of presentness through artistic production.[51] This quest for the self's endless presence, as philosopher Stanley Cavell puts it, is not dissimilar to what curators of online archives do today in seeking affirmation of presence by leaving their mark on events in our rapidly paced world.[52] Then as now, it is always transitory, always piecemeal—a work in progress. Yet, if we think of social media as a "laboratory of the self," one in which identity is forged through network allegiances in historically as well as technologically mediated publics, then there can be no question that digital media offers a different form of immediacy in chronicling time-bound claims to being.[53]

If digital texts are like Facebook relationship statuses, "complicated" cultural texts with code, what can they tell us about the work and lives of political activists and the issues at stake in contemporary protest cultures? Turning to a discussion of the three citizen photojournalists linked together by their networked visual and political practice, we argue that sources such as these are best understood as a form of civic engagement that trades in the local/global protest vernacular. Such a practice draws force and power from both historical and contemporary cultures of protest as well as the platform that mediates how we interact with it. It does this, we suggest, in two ways, reflecting the interplay between online and offline activity. On the one hand, it allows activists to break into the mass media environment while remaining true to their politics, building a sense of self around claims to professionalism in concert with others motivated by similar causes. On the other, it provides an avenue of recourse in which to comment on contemporary events and leave a digital footprint, which taken collectively forms part of a post G8 protest vernacular. This archive of online and offline oppositionality is a window into the changing form and visualization of global protest movements, showcasing the power of participatory media in harnessing "networked individualism," creating new forms of activist subjectivity and political expression that both co-opt and extend past protest cultural formations into the digital realm.[54] In this next section, our aim is not to quantify to what extent this has successfully brought about tangible change. Rather, it is to raise suggestions for how to understand user-driven mobile photographic archives as history making in the present day.

Flickr, Neo-Nazism, and Online Activism

Flickr's role as an archive is inseparable from its origins as a company and program. Coming onto the market in the last days of the internet boom, Flickr quickly became one of the largest photo sharing sites on the Web with 2 billion pictures circulating on the site by 2007 and over 6 billion by 2012.[55] Compared to the 70 million photographs housed in the Getty Foundation archive, one of the world's largest news repositories, Flickr is a tremendously rich, if largely uncharted, resource into the unfolding past.[56] While nominally a photosharing site, it also contains strong elements of social networking including microblogging and a message wall. In the intervening years, a large body of literature has developed around it, centering on its usefulness as a digital archive, its place in the articulation of memory, citizenship, and identity, and its function in the social world of amateur photography.[57] Given the platform's ease of use, cost-free membership, and abundance of storage, it is not surprising that Flickr would emerge as a go-to place for so-called altjournalism. If, as research has shown, individuals engaged in antiracist, anti-austerity movements tend to belong to shifting affinity networks and are increasingly motivated by personal calling over fixed social and cultural group identities, Flickr is an ideal launching ground for user-generated political content.[58]

Given their low cost, storage capacity, and ease of use, photosharing sites like Flickr house a disproportionately high number of images by left-leaning citizen photojournalists like the three under examination here. While government-sponsored programs might help explain the appeal of the internet in mobilizing opposition to the right, especially in a place like Germany, these photojournalists are a generation removed from those primarily targeted by such initiatives.[59] They came of age during the turbulent post-unification years, when a series of high-profile attacks against asylum seekers put the dangers of right-leaning ideas in sharp relief. But how can we know this with certainty? The answer lies in an analysis of what may be found both within and outside the frame of images captured and circulated by the photojournalists themselves. Just as far-right groups are recognizable to one another and to a wider public by a cultural symbology that extends beyond the rhetoric of racism to specific clothing brands, tattoos, hairstyles, and banner art, so too do these alternative journalists tap into established iconographic traditions surrounding the culture of civil unrest. In tackling themes like police violence and pixelating the faces of sympathizers as a kind of digital masking effect, a social media send up in defiance of the twenty-year ban on face coverings in demonstrations, these activists betray their precise ideological moorings.[60] Interestingly, our reading was confirmed when in a July 2014 interview with Thomas Rassloff he disclosed that the three had indeed cut their teeth in antifascist activism in the 1990s.[61]

Flickr makes these visual and iconographic traditions visible to the police, to opponents, and to adherents alike. However, with tens of thousands of photos in some streams, the sheer number of images defies easy categorization. In these particular photoblogs, the discerning eye is drawn to a common, oft-repeated theme. True to the long tradition out of which these photojournalists stem, including the countercultural, anti-nuclear, and student protest movements of the 1970s and 1980s and the actions of 1990s antiracist groups like the sharply named migrant activist collective Kanak Attak, their images do not simply document neo-Nazi activity and the efforts of civil society to mount an opposition. They also archive a characteristically German distrust of authority.[62] Alternative journalists the world over are eager to wedge a space away from traditional media elites for a more democratic and critical public discourse on austerity politics, immigration, and police aggression. But in Germany, with its legacy of postwar scandals over former Nazis in media, business, and government, to say nothing of recent allegations in a mass killing spree that neo-Nazi informants were paid by state coffers, this takes visual links between state aggression and the toleration of neo-Nazi encroachments on public space to a whole new level.[63]

Digital Archives

New media has afforded activist photojournalists access to a widened public sphere, while digital tools and networks have transformed how newsgathering happens. Increased media literacy has not only changed the playing field in journalism but in memory studies as well, as the explosion of personal, collective, cultural, and social memory work through "mycasting" (user generated online content) has led to a boom in new repositories of mediated and remediated visions of the past.[64] Instead of simple producers and consumers of memory, we now have "active, critical and creative citizens of media, culture, and society" with an ever-increasing appetite to produce as well as consume the online archive.[65] What in 1996 for art critic Hal Foster was polemical prognostication, by the early 2000s was reality. We live in a world where archival knowledge has burst the confines of libraries and museums.[66]

Given the power of the digital ecosystem to Flickr's representational, archival, and circulatory ambience, it only seemed right to employ digital tools in our research to help sort through the mass of images and information proliferating online. In the summer of 2012, we set out to identify potential study subjects using several scraping and sorting methodologies. Beginning with traditional academic literature reviews and note taking to garner a sense of the vernacular, we then embarked upon a quest to find out which keywords were most prescient in online discussions of the far right. To limit the focus for maximum results, we fed a series of recent newspaper reports from *Die Zeit's* "Neue deutsche Nazis" series through Voyant Tools to generate a "tag cloud" of most and least cited terms (Figures 10 and 11).[67]

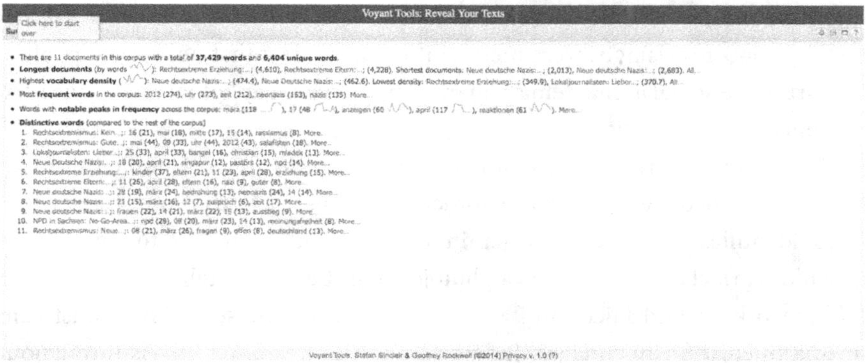

Figure 10 Keyword search, Voyant Tools.

Figure 11 Word cloud, Voyant Tools.

The end result, pretty if not entirely profound, provided us with a selection of terms to apply to our research with Flickr. Once we plugged these into the search window, we landed on several different sites, careful to limit the purview to Germany. Using the Flickr API, we scraped data from the platform using the agreed-upon keywords. Then we caught links, trends, images, and other kinds of metadata. Finally, we clipped, copied, and exported them into csv and HTML files so as to draft a chart of users ranked according to their quantitatively defined significance in the online discussion. From the fifteen users identified this way, three were chosen for their place in the ranking, their consistency in posting, the quality of their images, the size of their online archive, and the degree to which they were in communication with one another. A simple network analysis revealed a dense community of individuals, most of whom, perhaps not surprisingly, were men reinforcing the fact that networked publics, as part of the social arena, remain marked by a "cyber gap" of race, class, gender, and income stratification.[68]

Each online activist has a distinctly crafted online identity, forged through the tools available to them and afforded by extension to us. Boeseraltermann, who identifies as Christian Jäger in real life (although this too may be a pseudonym), claims to work as a photojournalist even though there is no trace of his work beyond Flickr and an erstwhile private site soliciting mainstream media interest for his images. Judging from his stream, he travels throughout Germany documenting anti-Nazi demonstrations and street rallies, while also taking snaps of subversive antifascist postering. He has "favorited" photographs by network mates Thomas Rassloff and PM Cheung, placing him in a kind of online solidarity with these two other photographers and their work.[69] With what might be considered a more overtly antifascist agenda than Boeseraltermann, PM Cheung, based in Berlin, has more links to established antifascist groups and organizations. Referred to reverently if not unproblematically as "our Chinaman" by one of the photographers, Cheung's images have had a broader scope and reach than Jäger's, and he is one of the most prolific in the network. In the years since we began analyzing his Flickr page, his photos have moved well beyond the antifascist protest niche within which they initially circulated. They have been taken up by several foundations and initiatives in Germany, including the antiracist Amadeu Antonio Foundation (which we discuss in the Facebook chapter), the Green Party affiliated Heinrich Böll Foundation, even the center right Konrad Adenauer Foundation connected to the Christian Democratic Party. If his images are any evidence, he is interested in a wide array of progressive causes from the Occupy Berlin movement to anti-nuclear, anti-globalization, and antiracist demonstrations. As might be expected, he also has a firm place in his online arcana for the yearly Dresden marches, when neo-Nazis take to the streets February 13th to call attention to the aerial bombings as a criminal human rights violation.

Cheung's aesthetic is akin to Sekula's anti-photojournalism. His photographs are rhizomatic, taken from inside the trenches, similarly capturing "the highs, the lulls, the waiting around, the flashes of violence."[70] Unlike Sekula though, he presents himself online as a committed freelancer, one who has gotten more mainstream recognition in recent years. Unlike before, now his work is represented by four image agents. He has published in *Der Spiegel* and in all the major Berlin newspapers, in addition to the weekly scene newspaper *Zitty* and the so-called anti-German *antideutsch* leftist magazine *Junge Welt*. His photographs have even surfaced in the august *Frankfurter Allgemeine Zeitung*, one of Germany's papers of record.

Of the three photographers, Cheung and the third photojournalist we uncovered, Thomas Rassloff, have the greatest claims to the title of working photojournalist.[71] Having joined Flickr in 2007, Rassloff, a Linux programer and web designer in Berlin, has built a stream of over 21,000 images, with recent photographs from Greece, Turkey, and Syria alongside more quirky, personal snapshots from a Kreuzberg neighborhood boxing tournament to an album devoted entirely to cats. He likewise posts images from demonstrations in northern Germany, with an emphasis on the provinces of the former German Democratic Republic, suggesting an affinity with this region and the specter of neo-Nazism that looms particularly large there. Identifying as a photojournalist with a specialization in architecture, landscapes, demonstrations, and conflict zone reportage, he listed no fewer than four different contact numbers on his now defunct Twitter page, one in Germany, another in Israel, Jordan, and Tunisia. On his older website, he went so far as to mention the brand name of his security apparel, giving an air of professionalism to what might be perceived as an otherwise peculiarly Spartan web presence.[72]

Rassloff gained some notice beyond Flickr when a 2013 photo he took of what was at that time the largest mass execution in besieged Aleppo was taken up by the European Pressphoto Agency. That photograph, published in *The Guardian, Time, The Times* along with another from the series in the *Boston Globe* documented the discovery of over sixty bodies, men and some youth, each killed with a single gunshot to the head. The ghastly image shows clearly that this was execution style, with hands tied behind the back. They were dumped, each a calculated distance apart, in the Qweq river that runs through the Bustan Al Qasr neighborhood of Aleppo, from the government-controlled section of the city to where most rebels at the time lived.[73] Ninety-eight bodies were pulled from the river that day. Over 200 would surface by March of that year.[74] Confirming its rhizomatic life, this single photo of what came to be called the River Massacre migrated from Rassloff's Flickr page where it was initially viewed over 300 times, to the mainstream papers via the press agency, before returning back to social media as part of an online discussion forum called *Reading the Pictures*, "a web-based, non-profit educational and publishing organization dedicated to visual culture, visual literacy and media literacy through the analysis of news, documentary and social media images."[75] In an entry labeled "I Feel It Would Be Wrong Not to Stop and Take Note of this Photo from Aleppo" dated the same day as it appeared in the mainstream press, blog owner Michael Shaw facilitated a discussion among 12 participants in the online interactive forum, some of whom have posted over 500 times on this same portal. In trying to showcase the human tragedy depicted in the photo, Shaw muses on the effect a similar photo might have had in New York City, were this taken on the High Line and not in a concrete riverbed in Syria.

This single photo's two-fold remediation reveals select features of convergence culture within this era of compulsive connectivity. For one, it shows the importance of global connectivity in how a personal image gains power through the technological and institutional affordances of Web 2.0 and journalistic news selection.[76] It provides a textbook example, too, of the way social media draws on and extends pre-digital media forms to create a sense of permanence around every day events.[77] In the case of the River Massacre photograph, one of a series of images uploaded from that killing spree, its aim was to raise awareness and provoke a sense of humanitarianism and responsibility.[78] It achieves this by serving as a witness to atrocity after the fact, in a "convergence of communication and archive."[79] In this new digital landscape, however, connectivity has blinded us to the different workings of past and present media forms and the distinctions between before and after the digital turn.[80] As Anna Reading has argued, "digital media technologies have not simply collapsed the event and its memory into one another" but "people's mediated witnessing ... is articulated, rearticulated, and disarticulated through intersecting temporalities" of what she calls "globital time," meaning the accelerated and compressed time of globalization and digitization.[81] Comparing the 1897 London Underground bombing with the July 7, 2005 attack, and the different ways they were captured by nineteenth-century news reporting versus twenty-first-century citizen journalism via mobile phones, she shows how digital media compresses time between "the *instant*, the moment of the event, and the *instances*, the repeated moments in which that instant can be communicated." The rapidity of digital witnessing, the speed a document may travel, and the way a personal record can be mass-mediated to travel not only vertically—"from eyewitness to multiple and extensive news sources—but also horizontally via the speech acts of email, blogs, and word of web" are a vastly different playing field than that which came before.[82] Rassloff's personal photoset, imagined already as a kind of "Offentlichkeitsarbeit" or public work, became part of an online archive of state intransigence and human rights abuse over two years before the world woke up to the reality of the violent civil war in Syria.[83] But it could only do so, at this quick pace, given to the technological affordances of digital culture.

Cloud technology combined with mobile devices, digital cameras, and vernacular archival platforms like Flickr allows us to capture almost everything, meaning that nearly everything is archivable and as such is external to traditional institutional forces. This new archived knowledge complicates the distinction between public and private, high and low, occupying that middle region between individual and collective. It also challenges the bricks and mortar, static view of the archive as a place or site of collective memory, and instead replaces it with digitization, data transfer, and the archive as part photostream, part database, and part repository.[84] These infinite archives, part of connective memory making, bring with them a moral imperative to act ethically in the face of all this overriding information.[85] And yet, the scale, availability, and complexity of these online image banks mean they are also well-nigh impossible to navigate despite our faith in "digitally fostered values" like open access, infinite search, and the free and unencumbered circulation of ideas.[86] If electronic media has commodified, individualized, and transformed the archive, how might images like those circulating in Flickr galvanize memory in the service of social change?[87] If we accept arguments like Wulf Kansteiner's that the more wide-reaching the medium, the harder it is that it will capture and reflect the collective memory of an ever more diversified audience, how likely is it that this evanescent and expanding archive of the present might also forge the basis of a useable past?[88] The answer lies in the symbolic work of networked antiracist photography and its place in local, national, and international chronicling of police presence and far-right extremism.

Picturing Protest

The photographs on Boeseraltermann, PM Cheung, and Thomas Rassloff's Flickr pages and linked to their Facebook and Twitter accounts bear distinct similarities, and may be read for what they tell us about their shared and evolving visual practice of picturing protest. This practice shows hallmarks of German anti-establishment thinking but is also deeply influenced by global aesthetic trends in demonstration reportage more generally. As Ulli Linke has argued, anti-establishment groups in the 1980s relied on images, memories, rhetorical strategies, and political staging to create linkages between past transgressions (the Third Reich) and current ones (in the case of her study, nuclear power and rearmament).[89] These causal frames and symbolic representations of self, community, and other drew attention to the structural inheritance of violence, forming a deliberate representational strategy aimed at underscoring their moral certitude. PM Cheung is particularly adept at using this kind of staging, with his lens firmly fixed on lines of riot police, their use of pepper spray, and their gear (Figure 12).

As this image description suggests, photos like this continue the tradition of citizen skepticism in Germany against the aggressiveness of the police. At this particular "Anti-War Day" demonstration in Dortmund on September 3, 2011, so named to draw attention to the date when the Germans invaded Poland in 1939, 700 neo-Nazis marched through a neighborhood housing a high percentage of migrants. In PM Cheung's accompanying narrative at the bottom of the image, two paragraphs long, we are told that they were met by 10,000 citizens, determined to halt or re-route the march. Intent on keeping the two sides apart, as is common practice in German demos, the police focused the bulk of their attention on the anti-Nazi protestors. Before too long, it came to blows between police and protestors and several youths were hurt with even more arrested. This image, artful in its composition with different vectors and angles in the colour version and marked by a tiny rainbow in the corner "had

Figure 12 Anti-Nazi Protest "Antikriegstag," September 3, 2011, Dortmund. https://www.flickr.com/photos/pm_cheung/6110669070.

wit" according to one viewer. Showing he pays attention to the traffic on his photoblog, Cheung's response was equally tongue in cheek: "mobile rainbow maker." These antifascist, anti-establishment visual cues and the discourse they generate picture police aggression as a strategy of persuasion, building in-group solidarity within and beyond borders and reinforcing in the process an optics built on sacrifice, emotional engagement, and commitment to the cause.[90]

Here, performance takes on double meaning. When the dramaturgy of the street demo is captured in the photograph and continued through social media, anti-Nazi protesters and their documentarian co-activists are performing their politics for a larger audience, taking their local struggle to the world stage. This happens in the civic space of the street itself, which since the nineteenth century assumed a signature place as a staging ground of political opposition and consciousness-raising.[91] But it also happens, importantly, in the domestic space of the home, where these images are uploaded, traded, and consumed by the viewing public, and all points in between via the mobile phone.[92] Although not everyone clicking through Flickr photoblogs is an equal and active participant in the dialogue, the networked trade in demo photos does open up space in these otherwise unlikely places where citizens may express their opinions, refine their ideas, and commit to increased civic engagement whether through consciousness raising or the formation of a tangible social movement.[93] To participate in the network as a producer or consumer of images is in effect to enter into a digital counterpublic sphere—to draw on Michael Warner—a place where subaltern groups may begin to forge meaningful ideas in opposition to hegemonic norms.[94] Social media does not inherently create these counterpublics; rather, it is the exchange of images and ideas that poses the possibility of turning these otherwise unlikely spaces into places from which to plan and organize.[95]

But beyond the actual spaces and actions of opposition themselves, what is captured iconographically and uploaded into the internet also suggests the need to think about how, with social media, it is not simply the network, but that which is itself trafficked, that also matters. In these images in particular, this requires a cultural analysis of the role of the absurd, humor, and the carnevalesque in digital protest politics. Anti-Nazi protestors certainly make use of diverse performative practices, drawing on a long history of visual, dramatic, and everyday strategies of opposition honed from generations of collective action, from the countercultural "happenings" of 1968ers or the candlelight protests in Eastern Europe in 1989. West German communards and members of the SDS (Students for Democratic Society) used subversive images in a variety of media—photography, posters, pornographic sketches, and film—as part of their provocatory politics.[96] Sometimes images had as much of an incendiary effect on agitators as antagonists. Films like Holger Meins's *The Making of a Molotov Cocktail* and the rape fantasies of the *Agit 883* collective were divisive and fractured the movement, suggesting that progressive "image vocabularies" could divide as well as unite.[97] These experimental visual cultural practices seeped into actual demonstration sites as well, as happenings, sit-ins, and protest spaces become stages of opposition, with protestors using all manner of devices to draw attention to the inequities of the existing power system in the search for a more authentic self.[98] Performance strategies—sometimes drawing explicit inspiration from critical theory—were strategically useful in forging a sense of solidarity and collaboration between students, artists, workers, and the unemployed.[99] Of course, differences remained but as Padraic Kenney has shown the carnival-like atmosphere of 1980s opposition in Eastern Europe allowed diverse groups to unite their voices in opposition to single-party governance.[100] Bakhtin's famous reading of the Feast of Fools celebrations for the way the laconic styles of the carnival destabilized established social hierarchies created a new way to think about collective action. In the world turned upside down atmosphere of the demonstration, where existing rules of order are suspended, new possibilities for social organization and solidarity emerge out of the melée. In theory anyway, these newly formed, collective sentiments hold the potential to transcend and change existing social, class, gender, or generational boundaries.[101] For Kenney, Eastern Europe was one such example. It was the perfect crucible of Bakhtin's carnivalesque; from among the diverse interests of environmentalist groups, peace activists, students, and workers, diverse strategies of opposition gradually coalesced into a mass movement to end Soviet-backed rule.

The carnival is subversive because it is disarming. It trades on the impression of simple pageantry much like the internet masquerades as entertainment and distraction. But the impact of insouciance cannot be underestimated online or offline. In a more recent example, Paul Routledge has shown how the antics and deliberate silliness of the roving clown brigades behind the barricades of the anti-austerity demonstrations help create "sensuous solidarities," bringing attention to their cause. Conjuring the holy fool, who was able to speak truth to power, their playful confrontation and wordplay invert the social order, revealing in the process the absurdity of the system.[102] Like the clown costumes Routledge describes, the activists in PM Cheung, Thomas Rassloff, and Boeseraltermann's photographs use both playful and subversive elements to get their message across, which the photojournalists then circulate in the digital realm. Both acts of oppositionality, the performance on the ground and the capture and circulation of the event after the fact are significant social acts. While the action in the streets challenges police authority directly, the traffic in demonstration images gives greater voice to the collective action, holding at least the potential of policitizing a larger audience beyond the confines of the event itself. Both actions form part of the political public, yet the digitized opposition transcends the physical confines of the site itself. When linked through metadata and algorithms in Flickr, these otherwise disparate protest images come together in other ways, offering up possibilities for seeing and acting on intransigence.

In Flickr, users find each other with the help of this metadata and search strings. They use the interactive features to solidify these bonds, which also facilitates the sharing of files according to common interests. Groups enable user to user communication, promote shared values around topics of interest and aesthetic practices, and link local, national, and international audiences through the click of a mouse. All three photojournalists belong to groups devoted to global protest photography. Cheung's interest in demonstration photography seems most pronounced given the wide diversity of groups he follows and that follow him back, yet it is Thomas Rassloff who has had the most reach with his photos, in terms of both reblogging and number of followers (800+ for Cheung, 12,000 for Rassloff), perhaps owing to his Syrian Civil War photography. Data scientists have culled large datasets to try and interpret sharing behavior and levels of interactivity and in-group sentiment and behavior.[103] This has yielded some sense of which images are shared, liked, and commented on. More useful are qualitative examinations of the image banks themselves. To take one example, in 2011 Cheung and Rassloff attended the same counter demonstration in Neuruppin in the northern state of Brandenburg where 500 peaceful protestors sought to stymie the march of 120 neo-Nazis. The mood their photos capture contains the unmistakable spirit of frivolity as citizens young and old gathered in the street to physically block the march. Under the catchphrase "For Tolerance and Democracy Neuruppin Remains Colourful" (Für Toleranz und Demokratie Neuruppin Bleibt Bunt), protestors donned green T-shirts and clasped orange balloons proclaiming this city was "no place for Nazis" (Kein Ort für Nazis). Each photo garnered over 500 views.[104]

While both photographers concerned themselves with the events of that day, their image archives capture different sides to the confrontation. Rassloff focuses on the protestors, young and old, seated in the street. They are photographed from different angles, sometimes smiling, taking water, checking their phones, and eating. Their humanity is on full display. His images are journalistic, documentary, without much hint of aestheticization.[105] It is clear that his interest is in civil society, including images of the various organizations that came together that day, from unions to citizen initiatives to school groups. Cheung's come at the same set of events from a different perspective. His photostream is filled with two sets of subjects, police in riot gear and the far-right marchers themselves.[106] There is occasional crossover, suggesting both men—friends it turns out—were standing in the same location while aiming the camera. This is discernible in several ways, from the angle of the photograph to the expressions on the faces of the so-called Anti Antifa Photographers that sometimes aimed their own lenses back at the men. But only Cheung takes the opportunity to focus in extensively on the police. There are other differences as well. Cheung uses a different setting, one which augments the sitting subject and blurs the background. His use of color is also more deliberate, the greens more green, the blues more blue. And he has spent considerable time with these images in postproduction, adding watermarks and blurring the faces of the same seated protestors photographed and left untouched by Rassloff. The neo-Nazis did not receive the same treatment, disclosing once again the political stance of the photographer. Interestingly, both men would be caught up in a country-wide raid in February 2013 that resulted in their cameras and computer data being seized, all with the hopes of finding a single protestor charged with violence against a police officer.[107]

While the whimsy of balloons are used in several different demonstrations from Leipzig to Neuruppin and Frankfurt, another visual strategy emerges in the placards of participants and is reflected in each of the three photojournalists' online oeuvres. Alongside the ubiquitous Hitler caricatures and reworked antifascist posters riffing on Alexander Rodchenko's famous "books" photomontage, all three photojournalists found themselves drawn to the demonstration's use of toilet humor. The choice to digitally reproduce these placards in particular, ones which evoke the German folkloric tradition of latrinalia alongside the more contemporary euphemistic meaning of "brown" as synecdoche for Nazism or "Nazis into Ploughshares," a pun on the famous "Swords into Ploughshares" East German peace movement slogan positions these photojournalists beyond simple documentarians.[108] Here, they use their photographic practice as memory devices, intervening in the visual discourse at the point of photographic capture, archiving, re-mediation, and display, aestheticizing the events so as to undermine the solemnity of right-wing ideological claims.[109]

In other words, their role is much more than participant, fellow traveler, documentarian, or enthusiast. Each is personally enmeshed in the protest actions they photograph, archive, and record. They are witnesses to the action in Israeli theater historian Freddie Rokem's sense of the word, re-animating the events orchestrated and unraveling around them. In selecting which images to capture and post, they create new narratives of the event's unfolding and meaning, provoking a response.[110] To think of these demonstrations and rallies and their reproduction in the virtual realm as remediated performance, and the photographers as participants/imagemakers/curators and witnesses, we see that Flickr photography conditions new ways of seeing police aggression and demo culture while still drawing on past iconographies. Considering, as Hassam Massum and Mark Tovey have argued, information encountered online can shape our choices, actions, and behaviors in real time, these images offer an opportunity to think about the role of networked images in the production and emergent history of perception and political consciousness.[111] The visual imaginaries, along with their travels, create conditions of possibility for activist claims making around a host of antiracist causes in a Germany still very much struggling to work through vestiges of its fraught past.

Conclusion

Despite its use of social realism, there is usefulness in thinking about the photographic practice of Boeseraltermann, PM Cheung, and Thomas Rassloff as much as a creative as a documentary endeavor. While it may be too much to see these actions as a eclipsing other forms of activism, there is little doubt that these images are an indelible part of an evolving culture of protest, whose history has yet to be fully unpacked and written.[112] What precisely is to be gained by such a methodology? First, it forces us to think critically about historical formations as unveiled as much in the present as in the past. Viewing Flickr photoalbums as an archive of purposeful oppositionality gets at this directly, fulfilling what Belinda Davis, Timothy Brown, and Lorena Anton argue marks all forms of contemporary protest, that it is, increasingly, an ongoing struggle with historical symbols in places and spaces beyond the street.[113] Second, social media texts challenge political sites and spheres of activity, linking the virtual with the real, the home with the street, recasting the role and potential at least of (semi) private acts in public realms. But in addition to creating new historical actors worthy of our attention, they also point to new agents of historical meaning making. Insofar as they visually rework the past and present meaning of protest through the circulation of images and shared participation in a network, the photographers under examination play a part in crafting a new visual theatrics of oppositionality as witnesses to and participants in the production of protest history. Third, beyond constructing spaces of creative opposition and interpretive encounter, Flickr gives photographers themselves the opportunity to refine their practice providing a context for technical and aesthetic growth. Because it enables every photographer documenting a demonstration to be—at once—part of a subjective yet global conversation, it challenges established photographic traditions and hierarchies between amateur and professional, between the supposedly detached observer and the engaged participant. As traditional media come to rely more and more on the images of lay people, these distinctions become muddier still. While these images in their great number play a not insignificant role in visualizing collective protest in the twenty-first century, we can't forget too that Flickr users themselves have the power to interact with and interpret that which is placed before them on screen.

The idea that these images are inherently political simply because they are mobile or networked or online is not our argument, although it is an assertion out there certainly, especially among the so-called cyber-utopians new media critic Evgeny Morozov takes on in much of his writing.[114] Our interest is how to think methodologically about the work of these images, how to situate them in relation to earlier forms of protest culture and photojournalism, and what they might tell us about the workings of the public sphere in this heavily mediatized age. A first step is to identify who is making them, consuming them, and circulating them, and to ask what role technology plays in the equation. A second is to ask what this might tell us about forms of demonstration culture, activist subjectivity, and opposition in the digital realm. A third is to question how distinct these formations are from what came before, if different, how, and if not, why?

Of course, there are a host of other conceptual and empirical questions begging to be asked of this material. As historians, we need to think about the everydayness of this form of documentation, its banality even. Here the sheer number of photos uploaded onto Flickr is important. What do we do when very little actually stands out, when no singular image becomes iconic? One suggestion is to interrogate Flickr and photosharing with the aid of other literatures in other fields. We've employed elements of photography and social movement theory, but one might also look more specifically still to discussions of temporality, emplotment, citizenship, and spectatorship to help get at how mobile images create conditions for civil communities of viewing beyond the sovereignty of the single photograph.[115] Another approach, one we've developed here too, is to think of other ways in via the historicization of select tropes and themes like the cultivation of irony and the carnvalesque/scatological for what they tell us about how images draw on past iconographies to help create and reinforce emotional communities and political commitment as well as moral certitude. Although the social media platform encourages the ebb and flow of documents from one medium to the next, the act of curation, archiving, and displaying photosets lends a degree of permanence to otherwise fluid social configurations like the demonstration, police intervention, and citizen counter demonstration. While it is important to map out the extent to which these images inherit what came before in terms of continental protest culture and the critique of state violence and right-wing politics so as to measure how much of this is distinctly German, one must not lose sight of the fact that these photos are mobile visual texts informed by global political and aesthetic trends. A focus on the aesthetics of opposition itself, including the role of digital photography in literally re-imaging and re-imagining protest is fruitful here since it forces us to come up with better ways of understanding what is truly different about the way social media challenges established authority while manifesting new forms of oppositionality, recasting the boundary between mainstream and alternative media, professional and amateur, the national and transnational.

Flickr photojournalism not only serves as a window into the evolution of twenty-first-century protest cultures, it creates new configurations of social power to say nothing of the subjectivities and practices of opposition that emerge through this blend of on- and offline participatory culture. It may even represent a new kind of nascent social movement, or at the very least, it lends a sense of aesthetic cohesiveness to an otherwise diffuse and often inchoate visual practice.[116] As an alternative channel of reporting, despite their flaws and shortcoming, these photographs represent an important form of collaborative claims making in emergent spaces of political expression.[117] Historians would do well to take notice, for if there is one thing that social media shows us it is that history is being made—with or without us—in the present day.

"Holocaust Vlogs and the Quest for Authenticity on YouTube"

In March 2020, Anne Frank House launched a new digital memorial initiative: the video diary of Anne Frank, uploaded to YouTube as a series of vlogs to tell Anne's story through the lens of a typical teenager in today's social media-ridden landscape. The project was met with criticism and wariness—how could something as simplistic as a video blog be used to explore Anne's story and what Anne has come to represent for public understandings of the Holocaust? The Anne Frank Video Diary project confronts several themes we have addressed thus far: social media, despite its mundane and sometimes trivial nature, is not inherently "new" media. It builds on already-trod conversations about the remediated Holocaust and its legacy. Web 2.0, regardless of its form, invites fresh conversation about the subject, bringing the history of the Holocaust to diverse audiences. The question remains, how might historians work with this kind of source and how should we gauge its effectiveness beyond its appeal?

In this chapter, we explore two of the fluid ways in which memory conception, formation, and dissemination are broadcast on YouTube, hinging on the self-reflexive genre of the vlog. We are interested in the way long-established memories of the Holocaust are re-narrativized and embodied ask what role the platform plays as a transnational pedagogical space. Despite its educational aspirations, social media's fluid, moving terrain engenders real discomfort whether in injecting fictionalizing tendencies or spectacularizing the past.[1] How suitable is the vlog format, often described as voyeuristic and narcissistic, as a vehicle for Holocaust memorialization and its engagement?[2] By comparing and contrasting two vlog-centric projects, the video diary of Anne Frank and the documentary film #Uploading_Holocaust (based around YouTube vlogs of young Israelis visiting Polish death camps), we consider the possibilities and limitations in how collective memories of victimization and suffering are rendered through the medium through the fine lines of performance, re-enactment, and re-staging in the name of authenticity. Drawing on YouTube's creative affordances to re-narrativize the past over its other uses as a commercial space of remediated mashups and archival traces, we are interested in lingering over the question of how well-suited the vlog format is for creating what Burgess and Green refer to as public and civic value by reinforcing specific memory paradigms for how to think about the Shoah.[3] First, we examine the possibilities afforded by YouTube as a place of self and memory production. Then we take up the question of vlogging specifically, as opposed to other ways in which YouTube functions as a networked, monetized, participatory space. Finally, we drill down into the tensions of diarization in the form of these two vlog projects to get at the usefulness of the medium as a site of memory making in the era of pandemic post-truth.

Broadcasting the Self

YouTube is the largest video-sharing platform in the world. It centers on the act of creating, uploading, and sharing audio-visual content. Launched in June 2005 by former PayPal employees, it was imagined as a space where people might share online content, barrier free, through a simple, easy-to-understand, interface. From these early days, it had a dual function as a repository of videos and sharing/viewing service, a space of unlimited storage and easy-to-embed links for other websites. YouTube was to be the video alternative to Flickr, a sharing platform that might integrate video into blogging sites like WordPress. It was, in other words, a far cry from the mainstream media platform it has since become, a leading player in entertainment, business, and content creation for Generation Z.[4]

Its original mandate was to serve as a "forum for people to connect, inform, and inspire others across the globe and acts as a distribution platform for original content creators and advertisers large and small."[5] It quickly surpassed expectations. By 2013, the site crowed users had uploaded over 100 hours of video every minute, some of it copyrighted. Unlike other social media platforms in operation at the time, YouTube had a broad base of support, well beyond the United States.[6] In addition to its participatory qualities, it was also an entertainment space overtaking the venerable BBC a few short years after its founding.[7] Despite its amorphousness as a global media platform, it was also a networked community, or better phrased, a series of micro-communities. A single video, its comments, and hyperlinked video responses connected thousands of people, regardless of their location. Its functionality, ease of use, and global reach catapulted it to the top of the social media ecosystem, second only to Google which acquired it in 2006 for 1.65 billion.[8]

From its inception, scholars in media and communication were keen to better understand this immense repository of visual, textual, and sociological information, a cauldron of moving texts, sound, and historical images.[9] Its large amounts of readily available material have given it the veneer of a digital archive and indeed Robert Gehl, associate professor of new media at the University of Utah, has argued that it mimics traditional collections.[10] But it deviates in important ways, too, especially in matters of accession. In an archive, the archivist labors within disciplinary and institutional power structures that dictate which sources, stories, and ultimately, which histories make it into the collection. As Cook and Schwartz note, archives and archivists exercise profound power "over memory and identity, over the fundamental ways in which society seeks evidence of what its core values are and have been, where it has come from, and where it is going."[11] While YouTube functions as a repository of visual and sociological data, without careful stewardship, it falls prey to serving as a digital *Wunderkammer*, with scores of untold—undifferentiated—curiosities inside. Others see in it the potential to rethink how knowledge over the past is constituted including where it circulates and resides. Knudsen and Stage suggest that YouTube helps actualize "the creation of a democratized memory practice."[12] Should YouTube be considered as a large mass of unorganized visual and social media, whose meaning depends entirely on the network and the user, or does this do a disservice to the new and distinct ways in which the platform functions as a repository of knowledge, albeit it in a new form?

There is a tendency to evaluate new media in opposition to what it "is not"— that is, YouTube is not television, but emulates television; is not an archive, but is similar to one; and so on. It is neither worthwhile nor beneficial to explore YouTube as a sum of its opposing parts. YouTube and its complex, shareable nature must be explored on its own terms. This includes the unique way it is involved in the making of memories, especially for a generation weaned on digital technologies as sources of knowledge and of the self. It may be useful for historians to view YouTube as an audio-visual archive whose curation depends on the user, vis-à-vis Gehl. But YouTube has also stretched beyond that analogy. As platform, cultural touchstone, and as a monetized mass entertainment medium driven by likes and subscriptions, YouTube is nowhere close to being a neutral space where information simply circulates. It is a thoroughly commodified digital field where historical narratives, even educational ones, stand cheek by jowl with fictionalized retellings and outright lies.[13] It is even more confusing when we consider YouTube not simply as an archive of pre-circulated photo montages, sound, and film clips but as a highly personalized medium that uses historical and contemporary references to diarize the self.[14] Through the "vlog"— or video blog—a user creates new content through conversational voiceovers or scripted unidirectional conversations with the presumed viewer. Vlogs emerged out of blogging, which according to David Silfry in 2007 was a practice that saw roughly 120,000 new scripts written for social media sites every single day.[15] Sharing similar characteristics to the diary, which externalized aspects of one's intimate life as an affirmation of individuality and personal taste, the vlog is a visual act of self-expression and artifact designed with the viewer in mind.[16] It stresses a person's subjective relationship with the topic under examination be that everyday life or history and memory. Drawing on theatrical metaphors used by Erving Goffmann, it is a stage upon which individuals enact their sense of themselves.[17] Vlogs have the appearance of one-way communication, but they are multidirectional, as the audience takes to the comment section to voice displeasure or solidarity with what is presented.[18] Likes and views trigger the algorithm to show a user more of the same content, which further validates certain approaches over others. In Holocaust vlogs, the result is a highly personalized and subjective engagement with the historical past, drawing on the emotions of the real and presumed audience in the present.

Although they tackle historical events, there remains an element of dramatization in the way select experiences are scripted and told for desired impact. As Michael Strangelove has argued, YouTube is a "battlefield, a contested ground where amateur videographers try to influence how events are represented and interpreted."[19] In other words, YouTube is more than a video repository, waiting for its interpretation to be bestowed upon it by casual viewers. It is a place where data assemblages shape how individuals interpolate with the past and themselves as content creators and users. Add to this that, like many of its sibling platforms, YouTube's curatorial algorithm responds to the interests, choices, and actions of the viewer, and we see that the platform both relies on the user and pre-empts their tastes and requests.

The past that vloggers construct is strung out of a vast series of networked fragments of mediated memory. For the scholar, everything that appears on YouTube—videos, playlists, responses, likes, and comments—has the potential to function as pieces of the remembered past. Of course, as Geoffrey Bowker argues, even in traditional archives, these little bits of memory do not stand in as facts but are subjected to interpretation on the part of a third-party user.[20] These potential memories are seldom eliminated from the social mediascape, except on the part of the originator. Though comments can be flagged as inappropriate, they are still available for viewing on the original page of which they were posted.

Another curious feature that interpolates between the past as it is conjured by the maker and the disposition of the contemporary viewer is the dislike count. In November 2021, YouTube removed the dislike feature from individual video pages. Yet this data is still accessible and is disclosed privately to the original content creator. Many creators have indicated that this development negatively impacts content creation on YouTube's platform because it eliminates an important aspect of YouTube's surface-level dichotomous recommendation algorithm. While seemingly benign, the loss of a "dislike" count also removes an important aspect of the platform's ecology. It prevents the audience from making small but important interventions in how certain stories are told, whether they be about style, content, or substance. Something as small as the removal of the dislike count drastically shifts how viewers and creators interact with YouTube's platform, and subsequently with history and memory making itself. While crowdsourced truth is not a replacement for expertise, for better and for worse it does go some way at least in attaching value to claims making in the digital sphere. And this can be pulled apart and critiqued.

Holocaust Education through the Vlog

Given YouTube's prominence as a video-streaming and sharing platform, it is unsurprising that the platform might be regarded as having some usefulness in reaching a broad public with the history of the Holocaust. As we've shown, there has been great take up by museum and educational institutions with digital Holocaust memory. Understanding the uniqueness of YouTube as an interactive, archival, and curatorial platform is essential if we are to unpack how Anne Frank House's recent video diary series functions as a form of Holocaust pedagogy. Alongside we contrast it with the hundreds of clips included in Sagi Bornstein and Udi Nir's #Uploading_Holocaust. While both projects are undoubtedly different, the commonalities highlight an impulse to document, interpret, and educate for future generations on a digital platform with the widest global availability.

The value of YouTube as a platform and portal for sharing and preserving the history of the Holocaust may not be readily seen. As with all social media, for very good reasons, there has been an emphasis on the nefarious usages of platforms without equal consideration of the benefits especially in terms of the civic potential of digital culture.[21] While one can make an argument for the sharing of Holocaust-related content on the platform, there are always concerns that such content does not function as part of a collective educational or memory-making process. Therefore, a two-pronged analysis driven by digital source and thematic analysis of Anne Frank's Video Diary will demonstrate the ways in which everyday audiences consume and engage with the project. Attention to the intended content of the vlogs alongside the data left behind by audiences allows us to think of YouTube comments as a bridge for understanding how that content goes over and is received. It means thinking about how the message of Anne Frank's story is staged on a platform like YouTube, within the specific affordances of the medium itself, and whether the interpretation and, ultimately, preservation of that story can find success on social media platforms.

To understand the constitution of the vlog diary, we examined the Anne Frank House's stated aims for the series and augmented that with an analysis of how the diary is emplotted visually over the course of fifteen episodes. To keep the medium's workings strictly in view, we identified select episodes and frames for further examination based around peaks in user response. Breaking the data into smaller chunks allowed us to dissect places where the creator's intentions rubbed up against audience impact.[22] To access audience responses to Anne Frank's Video Diary as a composite, we drew on a mixed set of methodologies including close and distant reading, data visualization, sentiment, content, and thematic analysis. We relied on an accessible method to harvest this data, using a script to scrape comments and export them into tabular form. Finally, we used a distant reading technique to pull out discourses at one remove through topic modeling and then did a deeper dive around the revealed themes.[23] After the data collection process, we used NVivo to analyze the sentiment and prominent themes found in the comments. The collection was modest in size, roughly 7,000 recorded comments across the first season of the series, in several different languages. As previously indicated, alone, these comments only tell half the story. Accordingly, we have paired our analysis of the comments with sources drawn from the project itself, including its promotional material and the goals and aims of the museum. We compare the Anne Frank Video with #Uploading_ Holocaust to examine the way they both mobilize civic mindedness around the memory of the Holocaust.

Political scientist Peter Dahlgren has focused attention on the way new media drives communicative and participatory practices centered on the promotion of civic values.[24] How technology creates opportunities for new civic cultures around the emotions, memories, performances, and affinities conjured through digital creation is vital if we are to think about the possibility of social media as a generative, didactic space and not merely a repressive one. While the Anne Frank House vlog series works as a re-narrativization of an established classic and is thus a remediation of an already remediated text (Anne's voice as captured through the diary and then restaged as a vlog), the Sagi Bornstein and Udi Nir documentary film and YouTube project #Uploading_Holocaust is an entirely different endeavor, composed out of YouTube films by Israeli high school students as they reflect on the Journey to Poland visits to Auschwitz. The YouTube experiment is ongoing, with over 20,000 short film vlogs uploaded to date. In the second half of the chapter, we explore whether we can consider them to be part of the same conversation about the preservation of memory in an increasingly digital age. Certainly, #Uploading_Holocaust hinges on cultures of witnessing and the diarization of the self through that act. Regardless of the differences in genre and form, it shares common themes with the Anne Frank House project, specifically around interpretation and engagement with the past and the role of the vlog format itself in narrativizing Holocaust memory.

Parasocial Relationships and Digital Witnessing in the Video Diary of Anne Frank

The Anne Frank House YouTube project is not the first vlog told from the perspective of a Holocaust victim. In 2019, Israeli media entrepreneur Mati Kochavi and his daughter, Maya, launched "Eva Stories," which tells the story of a 13-year-old Hungarian girl who died at Auschwitz in October 1944.[25] The project was intended to raise Holocaust awareness for a social media savvy generation, asking "what if a girl in the Holocaust had Instagram?" The project was heavily advertised in Israel with a billboard campaign in Tel Aviv. The project led to intense discussions regarding the role of social media in Holocaust memory. Lital Henig and Tobias Ebbrecht-Hartmann demonstrate that, while Eva Stories does not constitute a new genre of Holocaust memorialization, Instagram "allows users to become media witnesses by means of co-creating socially mediated experiences, and thereby inscribe themselves in mediated Holocaust memory."[26] We share similar arguments on the subject of social media spaces as immersive, with attempts at Holocaust memorialization on Instagram, but the social-media-as-mediated-space requires more interrogation. While our discussions of memory on Instagram, Twitter, and Facebook are certainly examples of collaborative memory making, one must question whether commenting on a YouTube video involves the same level of co-creation as those activities discussed in Chapter 1. Similarly, are those commenting on Anne's vlog entries committing to the same level of memory co-creation as that of the Israeli students in #Uploading_Holocaust?

There are key differences. Making use of Instagram as its primary platform, @eva.stories operates as a hybrid photo and video diary, complete with emoji-laden captions, spoken commentary, and shared in brief clips via Instagram's stories option.[27] In this way, the constraints of the platform greatly impact the form of the content. Anne Frank House's sole use of YouTube for the dramatization of Anne's diary lends itself primarily to longer-form video content, requiring different levels of conceptualization, particularly on the part of its videographer, young Anne Frank.[28]

At the same time that the Anne Frank House's primary directive is educational, the initiative cannot be neatly divorced from the medium's more entertainment-driven functionality. The format of the series drew on this to reach new and younger audiences with its personalized format. Filmed in 5- and 10-minute increments, they were released once every week in the spring of 2020, and viewed in over sixty countries. Frank de Horde and Tim Vloothuis of Every Media came up with the idea and the Anne Frank House lent the organization's expertise by means of reading screenplays for accuracy. It even participated with the reconstruction of the Secret Annex. The video diaries themselves rely on the cultural capital of YouTube for younger generations, specifically its power to bridge the gap between past and present. As Anne's childhood friend Jacqueline van Maarsen remarks, "by replacing the diary with a camera, young people can easily imagine themselves in that situation back then, when Anne Frank lived."[29] The interpolation between history and memory was not lost on the director of the House, Ronald Leopold, who saw eery similarities between Anne's time in hiding and the lockdown of the early Corona months.[30] He was not alone. Even *Haaretz* strayed into the world of analogies, going so far as to name Anne the latest influencer in the era of lockdown.[31] BBC commentator Standing Proud Soldier picked up on the cues, noting on April 8, 2020, "You know what? It's like we're hiding as well, from the coronavirus. Anne Frank was really brave."[32]

Entries are built around Anne's perceptions—of her life, of the goings-on in the Annex, and about the people with whom she shares her days in hiding. Narrated over the course of fifteen episodes, the episodes are accompanied by seven educational videos developed with the Anne Frank House. The pedagogical materials underscore important educational themes, drawing attention to the diary from which the vlog content is drawn, including its relevance as an historical source, while also exploring distinct themes such as discrimination and freedom.[33] Educators are encouraged to make use of the video diary series, the educational videos, and other education materials.

Tim Cole has demonstrated that it is "rather surprising that it is Anne Frank's diary which has assumed the status of 'Holocaust' text *par excellence*." He argues that "the 'Final Solution of the Jewish Question' plays a somewhat peripheral role. The 'Holocaust' is essentially the context within which the diary is written, rather than the central focus."[34] Beyond the way in which the Holocaust is depicted in the diary, there is also the matter of how her story came to be known in the first place. The Anne Frank known to most North Americans today does not owe her notoriety solely to the translation of the text to English, but rather may be linked the opening of the Broadway play in 1955 and the release of the Hollywood Film in 1959. Such productions were essential in popularizing Anne Frank as a Holocaust personality, educational tool, and commodity.[35] In other words, the popularization of the story of Anne was always a media affair.

Anne Frank's Video Diary and its sequel After the Arrest, carefully walk the line between history and entertainment, dramatic re-creation, and authenticity. The Anne Frank House is an independent organization, which has been dedicated to the preservation of the space that Anne and her family went into hiding during the Second World War. It is also the location where Anne wrote her diary.[36] The House aims to bring Anne's story to as many people as possible, to raise "awareness of the dangers of antisemitism, racism and discrimination, and the importance of freedom, equal rights and democracy."[37] The video diary project emerged from a search for a new way of sharing Anne Frank's life with younger generations.[38] Characters, locations, and events from Anne Frank's Video Diary are drawn from the *Diary of Anne Frank* letters, sharing Anne's day-to-day life, feelings, and reflections while hiding in the Secret Annex. The sequel, After the Arrest, features Anne, looking back from an indeterminate time and place to the last six months of her life in a concentration camp.

Anne begins filming herself after receiving her camera as a birthday gift; indeed, the focus of the first episode is a day in the life. Here, she introduces her parents, her sister, and the streets of her hometown. The video's tone is fun, exploratory, and expressive, lending the audience an opportunity to bond with Anne and her representation of her own life. Despite the fact that Anne begins documenting her life in 1944, her videos transcend time, forging a direct connection with contemporary viewers, regardless of when they view her vlogs. The viewer sees what Anne sees. One viewer echoes this sentiment, describing what they feel when watching Anne's vlog:

The greatest sensation that i feel while reading her diary, or watching this is that she is talking to me. Like she is writing to me, i feel that she is one of my closest friends. Sometimes i just want to talk to her, write her a letter and say how is the world outside that house. My heart gets warm every time i see anne [*sic*], she is so truly in love with every little spark of joy around her.[39]

In explaining that Anne feels like "one of my closest friends," this viewer demonstrates a key element embedded in Anne's vlog: the importance of fostering a parasocial relationship with Anne, through her front-facing lens. The proliferation and evolution of parasocial relationships in the age of social media have gained media coverage in recent years. Yet, the concept is not new. First discussed by psychologists Donald Horton and R. Richard Wohl, the term has since been applied to the relationships formed with social media personalities and influencers.[40]

By giving Anne control of the camera, she acquires agency and a sense of control over her situation, traits that come across clearly in her original diary. Anne is now a videographer, not only the camera's subject. Anna Frank House relies on this deliberate representation of Anne, highlighting its utility in an increasingly digital world:

The strength of the diary is that Anne speaks to you directly and gives you a personal and poignant glimpse into her life. We want to reach this group in the same personal and poignant way through [the] Anne Frank video diary. The video camera takes the place of the diary, yet the approach stays the same: Anne speaks to you directly and invites you into her world and her thoughts.[41]

The personal element of Anne's vlog is not lost on its audience and viewers frequently comment on how the format of the vlog creates space for an easy connection between Anne and her audience. "I discovered that project today. I can say that my experience watching it is that I am feeling close to Anne, and penalized by the situation experienced by her, her family and other people."[42] The front-facing camera creates a space for the formation of a parasocial relationship with Anne, which occurs when a viewer expresses a feeling of "knowing" the subject of the video, though they have never truly interacted with them.

Although critic and Yad Vashem lecturer Rich Brownstein laments what he calls "the selfie format" of the series as unable to match the gravitas of the diary, our evidence suggests the vlog rather successfully served the Anne Frank House in fostering intimate and meaningful parasocial relationships between Anne and the audience.[43] The audience does not truly know Anne Frank, nor is the Anne they see on YouTube the true version of her. Rather, in this context, the character of Anne in the YouTube production serves to answer a fundamental question of form and visual style—delivering a product that indicates what it might have been like if a teenage girl had access to social media during the Holocaust. By employing the vlog format, the vlog series has developed the personality of Anne-as-contemporary-influencer, all at once demonstrating that Holocaust memory and interpretation can have a place in the social mediascape. What is more, allowing Anne to take up the camera has been effective in reaching younger audiences to convey educational directives in a recognizable and relatable format.

The Audience Pushes Back

How can we understand the take up of the intended message, how it resonates with the audience, and how this feeds back into the original telling? A close and distant reading of select episodes holds some clues about how to think along with the digital affordances that make up the YouTube ecosystem. Here, digital visualization tools, when combined with more traditional historical research methods, reveal new ways to analyze sources such as social media for their usefulness in articulating Holocaust memory. To make sense of the comments on these videos, we can read them closely, annotating each comment for the kind of discourse it represents. But which ones are representative? One way to get at that is to isolate particular topics and themes that cluster around viewer interest. Using a method of distant reading to pull out discourses at one remove, we see what patterns are visible in the comment stream, and by extension, in the minds of viewers. We can also identify places where the Anne Frank House responds, underscoring the pedagogical imperatives of the project.

If we take Episode One and feed the data through a program called BERTopic, words and phrases are clustered in topic representations that may be mapped out and graphed according to frequency of use. In this episode, we see a hierarchical clustering of phrases including #5, 8, and 15 which show evidence of encouraging people how to learn more. Topic 17 on the other hand is clear hate (Figure 13).

Hierarchical Clustering

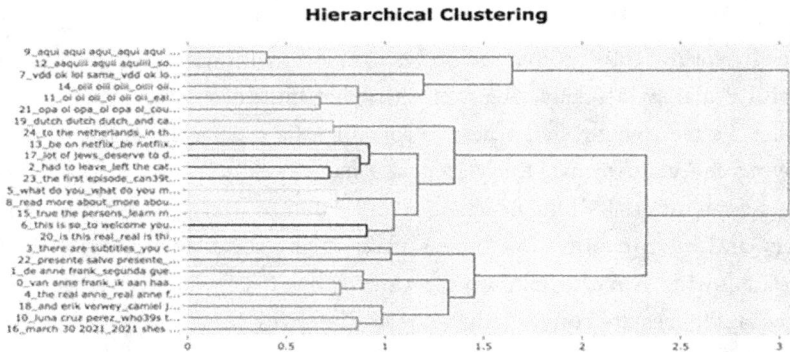

Figure 13 Hierarchical clustering of Episode 1, Anne Frank Video Diary, BERTopic.

[("lot of jews," 0.010940069619399672),
("deserve to die," 0.010940069619399672),
("love jews people," 0.010940069619399672),
("please tell me," 0.010262679271533359),
("sense that nazism," 0.006049467680161759),
("sense that nazism was," 0.006049467680161759),
("so horrible it is," 0.006049467680161759),
("so horrible it," 0.006049467680161759),
("somebodies son or," 0.006049467680161759),
("somebodies son or daughter," 0.006049467680161759)]

Figure 14 Numerical breakdown, Episode 1, Anne Frank Video Diary, BERTopic.

We are also able to see a numeric breakdown of the above references with ngram=3 as the measurement (Figure 14).

We can also plot these same topics over time to chart the ebb and flow of how these sentiments have changed. When the vlog is first posted in April 2020, there is a flurry of commentaries, then things quiet down. There is another uptick of views and comments in March 2021, possibly resulting in the peak for topic 17. Although it is impossible to surmise the precise reason behind the posts, several things happened in that same month from, a poorly phrased *Globe and Mail* article on lessons learned about lockdown from Anne to a History Channel special on the girl (Figure 15).[44]

Topics over Time

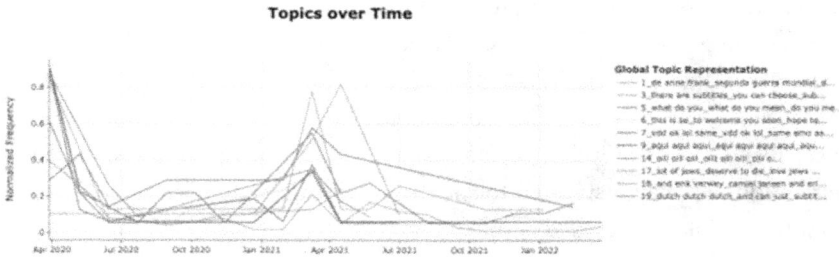

Figure 15 Topics over Time Episode 1 Anne Frank Video Diary, BERTopic.

To get an even closer look at the sentiments behind the comments themselves, we used the program NVivo. A software program, it allows us to analyze unstructured text, audio, video, and image data, isolating prominent themes and emotions. When we break down the first episode into prominent themes, we see that the form and content of the vlog clearly struck an emotional cord with viewers. In episode 1 alone, there were forty-five references (or 1.16 percent of the corpus of comments) to the quality of the production. As one commentator put it: "This series is superbly done. It is a sign of a fine production when all the actors give performances that leave you with the sense they are real people they are portraying."[45] Some comments betray the age of the respondent: "HER ACTING ! OMG THIS IS AMAZING."[46] Here, too, the question of verisimilitude comes to the fore with commentators flabbergasted that the series is so realistic: "Oh, this is such a wonderful concept. It makes me think of that if this happened in present day, Anne would most certainly would have tried to vloged [*sic*] her life. So, I think this will make Anne's story more real to the new generation."[47] Parallels to Covid lockdown were likewise laced through the comment field: "Our scenario now TOTALLY makes me empathise for these people right here. Just imagine! If being on a month's lockdown for our own good seems difficult, imagine the fate of these people, living an entire life in secret!"[48] It might also be the case that the true-to-life nature of the vlog was unsettling to some viewers. While it seems hard to imagine, there were over fifty-five coded cases of people questioning whether Anne had survived or if this portrayal was a historical document: "Is this fake or true like was this filmed fake or did Anne really film this?"[49] The number of people asking this same question by Episode 15 rose to 157 respondents or roughly 3.7 percent of commentators, suggesting the persuasiveness of the genre alongside some concern around media savviness.[50] Indeed, despite the iniquitousness of technology in the lives of generations "born digital," everyday use does not necessarily lend itself to higher level skills of critical evaluation. The informal genre of vlogging seems to lend itself to viewers seeing the representation of Anne's life as quasi historical, lived, real.[51] On one level, it seems that the makers of the series intended for verisimilitude. They instructed the actor portraying Anne to improvise and go off script. While that guided authenticity assists this version of Anne in forging an emotional connection with the viewer, the tensions related to improvisation were also things Anne Frank House had to navigate in terms of their educational interventions.

While some viewers clearly struggled with the format, believing it to be archival footage in some way, audience responses also suggest an intimate knowledge of the Anne story. As one person effused: "First of all, kudos for actually using Dutch people in this. It's refreshing to hear Anne's words known from the diary being spoken in her actual language (YES I KNOW SHE WAS BORN IN GERMANY. I KNOW)."[52] In episode 7, someone wondered "Is Anne going to speak a little English at some point? Anne wrote 1–2 sentences in English in her diary, so …?"[53] Where the Anne Frank House saw evidence of opportunity for further educational intervention, they steered viewers toward relevant historical information. This was much appreciated by viewers, who valued the connection to the historic site. One viewer gushed: "@Anne Frank House omg you replied to me this is a wish come true I never thought you would replyyyy I still can't believe it oh yeah and the actors and actresses are so talented and I am really interested in Anne frank and her diary so I hope you guys can make more series if possible!!!"[54] Fans from all across the world queried whether there would soon be versions in their own language, and some even took to the series to create educational tools of their own, like YouTuber Sehar Fatima, who used the vlog to teach English literature in her home country of Pakistan.[55] In ways other than intended, the vlog, comments, and responses from the Anne Frank House seem to have succeeded in creating an emotional community through which, it was hoped, a more nuanced—and personal—understanding of the Holocaust might be achieved.

"We feel the burden part of memory": Performing Authenticity in #Uploading_Holocaust

The video diary of Anne Frank is an example of how a social media lens—the vlog—can be applied to a pre-existing text. As Anne Frank House has indicated, and sometimes felt compelled to reiterate in its extra content, the vlog was drawn from the diary itself. It is important, however, to recognize the tension between the professional and performative aspects of the video diary. The vlog format was implemented as a tool to share a version of Anne with new audiences, and this version is very much based on public perceptions, which have shifted over time. This version of Anne is the result of many revised iterations of her. From the diary entries written by Anne herself, to the edits made by her father, multiple translations and localizations, and representations in theatre, film, television— and now, in social media—this version of Anne Frank remains highly produced and mediated. The viewer is restricted to one narrative, carefully crafted by Anne Frank House. While this narrative plays a prominent role in the global canon of Holocaust memory and serves an educational purpose by communicating the Holocaust's legacy to new generations, it showcases very different aspects of Holocaust memory than Sagi Bornstein and Udi Nir's 2016 documentary film, #Uploading_Holocaust. The Video Diary of Anne Frank is but one example of the ways the vlog format can function as an agent of Holocaust memory making and awareness. But the creative components and the medium's own affordances serve as a reminder, too, that authority over the past remains somewhat elusive, and in the hands of the audience which brings its own interpretive lens and agenda.

The provenance of #Uploading_Holocaust's component parts is different than Anne's vlog, located firmly in user experience. Their sheer accessibility demonstrates that the cultural significance of the vlog has extended beyond its initial intended form, taking root in the Holocaust memory sector. Thomas Łysak's study on the intersection of influencer culture and Holocaust vlogging dissects notions of curated visibility and self-promotion in Holocaust memory studies. While the students in #Uploading_Holocaust are not influencers per se, Łysak indicates that vlogs are a useful commemorative tool. As evidenced by the Video Diary of Anne Frank they "either encourage the audience to follow in the footsteps of an influencer or they invite viewers to empathize with a vloggers affective experience."[56] While the Video Diary of Anne Frank had a higher production budget than the #Uploading_Holocaust's student missives, vlogs remain an accessible form of communication. Along their journey through Poland, students could "film every contemporary witness, every gas chamber, and every ceremony." In this way, they produce their very own version of history, upload it on YouTube, and share it in social media.[57]

Self-framed video is easily achieved, and YouTube makes it even more sharable, particularly for younger generations. #Uploading_Holocaust addresses how accessible technologies in the hands of students allow youth to frame their own encounters with the Shoah. The smartphone and the vlog both help and hinder these students in their ability to express their thoughts, and share their experiences with classmates, educators, families, and the wider digital community. The result of Sagi Bornstein and Udi Nir's collection and interpretation of these sources presents distinct expressive themes and the methods students employed in communicating said experiences.

Bornstein and Nir's documentary is a unique digital project. Apart from being the first documentary entirely composed of existing YouTube material, it presents a historical timeline of the ways in which young Israelis have engaged with the Holocaust. Their film aptly shows audiences where the smartphone lies within the trajectory of video technology and Holocaust remembrance, which is not far removed from other hand-held recording devices. The accompanying shift has less to do with the way generations of young people have engaged with Holocaust memory, but hints more at where the focus of the camera rests. While the film does not rely entirely on footage captured by a smartphone, the footage draws attention to a particular point in the trajectory of media wherein the subject turns the camera on themselves. This performative moment underscores that the videographer and subject are no longer divisible. With the rise of the smartphone, students begin turning the camera on themselves, resulting in a marked shift in their perception of themselves both as witnesses and as curators of memory in Poland.

The documentary begins with a brief explanatory note, indicating that the journey to Poland is the initiative of Israel's Education Ministry and has served as a rite of passage for more than tens of thousands of twelfth-grade Israeli high school students since its inception.[58] The students spend a little over a week in Poland, visiting several sites of Holocaust memory, including several concentration or extermination camps, former Jewish cemeteries, synagogues, mass graves, and the Warsaw Ghetto.[59] Yet the journey to Poland begins even before the students' departure: parents, siblings, and extended family members record video messages for them, encouraging them to reflect on what they see and learn while away. The emphasis to remain present, to understand what happened in Poland, and to come back to Israel with that understanding is the key directive in these video messages. #Uploading_Holocaust pinpoints with stark specificity the ways in which easy access to technology has shaped how students engage with the spaces of Holocaust memory they encounter on while in Poland. We have identified three ways that film employs the vlog: as a vehicle of self perception, embodiment, and performance. Aspects of witnessing are present in all three forms of engagement, but to different ends.

Despite these very real differences, #Uploading_Holocaust and Anne Frank's Video Diary are composed similarly. The beginning of both the documentary and the YouTube series creates an environment of excitement. Anne has received a camera for her birthday, and she is excited to document her surroundings, her family, and her friends. #Uploading_Holocaust's initial scenes share a similar tone: the students are eager to document all aspects of the trip and were encouraged to do so by their teachers and Israel's Educational Minister. Both #Uploading_Holocaust and Anne's vlog highlight the everyday in a manner that feels befitting of their videographers. The blurred lines between performance and memory—in both Anne Frank's video diary and #Uploading_Holocaust, converge on the oft-conflicting notions of authenticity, performance, and authority. Loaded terms in the field of memory, yet despite its weight YouTube and its *nouveau* template for pared-down communication offers a chance at openness and simplicity. Anne's eye contact with the camera, the frank and open way in which she communicates the reality of her life, from the mundane to the horrifying, allows this representation of *the* Anne Frank to connect directly with the audience in both visual and visceral ways. The reading of Anne Frank's innermost thoughts does often strike a chord with audiences but seeing Anne's embodiment on one's own computer screen aids in the development of a para-social relationship with her.[60]

Where #Uploading_Holocaust and the Video Diary of Anne Frank differ is in their content and messaging. Although the actor portraying Anne was encouraged to go off-book and improvise for the camera, the Video Diary of Anne Frank was a tightly controlled educational product which aimed to communicate Anne's story in a new medium. On the other hand, the vlog lies at the center of #Uploading_Holocaust, providing students with the means for self-reflection, enmeshed in memory making. Not unlike the way that the self is digitally inscribed through vlogging, further entangling our physical lives with our digital lives, vlogging encounters with Holocaust spaces "express socio-historical agency that proves the ongoing relevance of memories from the Holocaust."[61] The act of digital inscription through vlogging extends the memory-making potential of a Holocaust memory site or Holocaust space by providing both an algorithmic and sociocultural impetus to remember. What is more, the act of filming one's own experiences, with either the intention to share with others or review on one's own, fosters a relational dialogue between the subject and space of memory. The vlogging processes in #Uploading_Holocaust aid the young filmmakers in assessing—and sometimes embracing—their own position in relation to the history and legacy of the Holocaust. In some ways, this process can be considered an exchange. The act of vlogging results in processes of self-inscription; the individual embeds themselves and their experiences into Holocaust memory frameworks, while also integrating the historical past into their own digital self.

#Uploading_Holocaust does not appear less stylized and controlled than the Video Diary of Anne Frank. Certainly, the documentary was subject to a great deal of editing and careful consideration, all which aims to develop a narrative for the audience; this cannot be ignored. Ebbrecht-Hartmann and Henig underscore that the vlogs in #Uploading_Holocaust must be viewed as appropriated private videos, which contribute to the filmmakers' narrative once all the vlogs are viewed in concert with one another.[62] Extending this thought, it is worth noting that #Uploading_Holocaust's component parts were also developed under the instruction and expectations of their peers, family members, teachers, and survivors who guide them on their journey. After all, "vloggers show that affect may be a tool for reinvigorating historical education."[63] The burden of performing authenticity, producing affective audio-visual memory products, and upholding their Israeli identity and the legacy of the Holocaust impacts the students' filmographic choices.

If the Diary of Anne Frank performs authenticity for a transnational audience, #Uploading_Holocaust pushes authenticity against notions of authority, drawing attention to how Israeli students express themselves while engaging with and struggling to understand the meaning their surroundings are imbued with. While Anne's vlog serves as a vehicle for storytelling and interpretation, #Uploading_Holocaust's vlogs open a window into the historical trajectory of the collaboration (and sometimes conflict) between Holocaust witnessing and tourism, almost always connecting space, place, and memory making. The vlog serves as a way for Anne to share her daily life with an audience beyond the lens, and the vlog also serves as a way for students—decades after Anne's death—to share their experiences confronting the Holocaust's legacy. Therefore, while the Video Diary of Anne Frank and #Uploading_Holocaust appear similar in format, they sit along a continuum of performance: Anne's performance is that of an interpretation of her own original text, played out in front of the camera lens, bestowing the burden of memory upon the viewer. Temporally removed from Anne's context, these students—many of them descendants of Holocaust victims and survivors— are impressed upon by their families, teachers, and the state of Israel itself to contend with and bear the burden of the past. As this near-constant reflection is required of them throughout their week in Poland, they are also required to rely on the tools at their disposal to understand their relationship to the history they are encountering throughout their journey.

From the beginning of their time in Poland, students affirmatively state that they must "see" the Holocaust to truly come to terms with it. "I'm serious. You must see it to understand it," states one student, being interviewed by his classmate.[64] Throughout the film, present-ness is key: "When we get there, you'll understand it all," explains one vlogger.[65] Upon arrival, encounters with concentration camps, death camps, cemeteries, ghettoes, mass graves, and ceremonies are woven into the daily activities of the high school students. In such instances, the vlog also offers brief glimpses into a variety of behaviors which do not mesh with a solemn tour of Poland. For example, before a tour of Majdanek, some students engage in a snowball fight. "As you can see, we've reached Majdanek, and there's a crazy snowstorm, and now everyone's having snowball fight ... and I understand this is the most tragic camp today," a classmate explains to his camera. "I wonder if they'll be smiling during the next three hours," he laughs.[66] Borstein and Nir weave a narrative of expectation throughout their film, teasing out the tensions between the students' quest for authenticity and their performances for friends, family, and nation. Sometimes, authenticity and reality remain at the forefront when students share their experiences visiting concentration camps or death camps alongside other visitors. "I could hardly hear the stories there were so many people," explains one student; they are less concerned with how their experience will be perceived, and instead provide commentary on the modern realities of visiting prominent dark tourist sites.[67] In other instances, authenticity and performance collide, creating a more jarring viewing experience. "There's nothing like personal stories to connect us with the journey," comments one educator after hearing a story from a student while at the Warsaw Cemetery, allowing one beat before continuing: "Now run, we are behind schedule."[68] All these exchanges are captured on the cameras of attentive students and uploaded to YouTube to share with the world.

In their effort to demonstrate that they are considering the Holocaust's legacy, many students rely on performative methods. While this includes self-framing video, some students share the frame with classmates or film the reactions of others. Apart from gaining access to individual perceptions of their own Holocaust encounters in Poland, the viewer is also granted access to the surroundings of the filmmaker. These linked video passages continuously remind the viewer that an awareness of the camera will always trigger a performance of identity in a world which is increasingly enmeshed with one's online persona. Take, for example, video footage of a student filming and photographing themselves by their great-grandfather's grave in Warsaw's biggest Jewish cemetery—complete with the most optimal pose for depicting grief.[69] The presence of a camera and the directive to document provide an opportunity for the vlog to occupy the liminal space between performance and authenticity, expectation, and reality.

Guides and educators assist the students with performative and embodied aspects of the trip, with embodiment and physical presence operating as a conduit for performative aspects of Holocaust memory. The amateur student vlog highlights "the historical past as a privileged access point, and the performance of doing memory."[70] Students board cattle cars and are famously separated into separate queues after deboarding; they are encouraged throughout these acts to reflect on what it means to be "following the paths that others took to their deaths."[71] For some students, the embodied aspect of physically visiting Holocaust spaces presents other interpretive challenges when reflecting in their vlogs. While the remaining buildings make the camp universe much more "realistic," guides struggle with conveying smells, like smoke.[72] In one section, four students sit on the tracks at an extermination camp and decide, unprompted, to perform embodied memory by trying to enact how their family members would have felt in the cold. They begin removing their clothing, vowing to try to bodily experience the cold that their ancestors would have experienced decades ago for just one minute.[73] Their performance is an embodied attempt to confront their own feelings and embed their own encounters with Holocaust memory through their physicality. This performative embodiment is met with criticism from other visitors, which is caught on camera, providing an example of the complicated ways in which young vloggers express agency in the face of the standard behavioural expectations of the visit.

Place-based Reflection as Affect

The presence of the camera forces modes of self-reflection on the students themselves, as they negotiate complicated interpolations between their own gaze and subject-position vis-à-vis past victims, the connections between the Holocaust and the establishment of Israel, and how to communicate what they have learned in a meaningful way.[74] This is a recurring theme throughout the film, more striking when contemporary footage is juxtaposed with older footage from the 1980s and 1990s, which focuses mostly on the experiences of survivors, aspects of the tours themselves, and the sites which the students visit. In older footage, less attention is paid to the feelings of the student wielding the camera. In our current day, the presence of social media and the knowledge that this video footage will be shared online add an extra layer of pressure and reinforce the need for a performance on behalf of the student. The pressure is not imagined, signifying the ways in which social media usage and patterns of performance and consumption are not relegated entirely to the digital media sphere. Versions of the self are inscribed through media usage, further enmeshing the physical world with the digital one.[75] Students are encouraged by their families, their teachers, their tour guides, and the state of Israel itself to engage with their surroundings and to—perhaps above all else—"feel." These concerns relate to their physical and social connections offline, certainly; but uploading their vlogs to YouTube embeds those pressures in the online landscape of social media. The memorialization of the Holocaust as an embodied experience is reinforced frequently throughout the film. "It bothers you that you don't [feel sad]?" one student asks of another. "Yes, I feel like something is wrong with me," he responds.[76] Another comments, after a tour of a former death camp, "It's a huge effort to really feel what it was like."[77] #Uploading_Holocaust harnesses the affective burden of memory and the emotional effort required of the students to access it to naturalize the political project of Zionism, collapsing the distance between "us" (the students) and "them" (the victims).

Reflective vlogging practices are the most easily recognizable throughout the film; personal and introspective, these moments arise when the student holding the camera considers their experiences in relation to what they have seen, and acts of self-reflection vary from student to student. Some share their expectations, and how they were or were not met upon their arrival in Poland. Many students grapple with similar roadblocks that accompany the digital witnessing of the Holocaust, bringing with them their own perceptions of the Holocaust which have been passed down by their families and their own experiences with the past. "To be honest, I was surprised that everything was in colour," notes one student, drawing attention to the ways in which prominent visual histories of the Holocaust are presented in black and white.[78] The students are constantly reminded of their emotional burdens. "We have an opportunity to feel something that we won't be able to feel later. Okay? I want you to start feeling!"[79] a guide implores in one clip. Students are urged to take stock of their feelings and inscribe them onto their experiences through documentation. Daily vlogs are the encouraged form of documentation, but students are also encouraged to share photos which represent what they have learned and what they have felt while in Poland.

In some moments, the friction between authenticity and performance can produce honest moments between students, overwhelmed with their burden of emoting. For example, a student overhears his classmate recording her vlog, reflecting on the affective difficulty she is having confronting the legacy of the Holocaust. Her classmate commiserates, stating "the only thing about Poland that makes me sad is that I can't feel anything. I try to understand but I can't feel."[80] These students are making use of video as a medium (and YouTube, as an eventual repository) to grapple with the weight of memory, and their concern over not feeling how they think they should. While the vlog of a high school student is often dismissed as glib, these portions offer the audience a peek behind the curtain of memory confrontation. This portrait of one's difficulty with difficult histories presents younger generations who are self-aware. They are aware they should be feeling something deeply, and are contending with a tension between performance, expectations, and the purported authenticity of experience. It is in these moments that students, through the lens of the camera, attempt to confront that they must uphold the memory of the Holocaust as it relates to their own Israeli identity—which is a huge undertaking, both on-camera and off.

Throughout the film, students are encouraged by and called upon by teachers to definitively explain the affective experience they have had thus far; often these reflections are poignant and honest. During a class discussion, usually occurring each evening to help students process, a student was asked to choose a photo that expresses most powerfully what she was feeling and experiencing. The student shared a photo of her friends' shadows, indicating that she feels they will "always be overshadowed by the Jews who ...." She is unable to finish the sentence, instead stating that she feels that they haunt her.[81] This pressure to feel and experience is compounded by something that many visitors to Auschwitz and other sites of Holocaust memory also experience—the fear that the modern tourism industry has diminished opportunities for reflection. One student remarked, "Actually, we went through [the gas chamber] really fast, I hardly got a chance to feel anything. We went through too fast."[82] Lamenting their inability to "feel" is one of the most common themes throughout the documentary, undergirded by anxiety; the students' encounters with Holocaust memory require them to question the way they are *supposed* to feel about everything they've seen, presented as an honest one-on-one reflection with their camera. One student explains, "I'm afraid to feel what they felt. But when I want to relate, I do it against my own will."[83] Students' contemporary encounters with the camera are not inherently dishonest; instead, it is important to view these encounters as occupying a liminal space between performance and authenticity: they know what is expected of them, but they are unsure if they are succeeding on their journey through memory. Despite being unsure, the young vloggers contribute to memory-making processes simply through the act of reflecting on their feelings and their relationship to the past: "introspective as well as enunciative modes also introduce a reflexive dimension. They preserve a moment and document an attempt to cope with the emotional and cognitive complexity of the Holocaust."[84] Though the reflective behaviors present in #Uploading_Holocaust anticipate affirmation from a future viewer on the other side of the camera, vlogging embeds the complexity of memory work in the social mediascape.

Conclusion

Even though the source material for #Uploading_Holocaust is drawn entirely from YouTube, it is telling that the documentary itself indicates that YouTube was not the impetus for this form of self-expression. The film is constructed as a thematic chronology, suggesting a historical narrative of the program itself; the clips feature participants filming and photographing long before the advent of YouTube. The documentary showcases one of our arguments rather succinctly, that YouTube serves as part of the evolution of video technology offering a content sharing tool for reflection and remediation. The action of turning the camera on oneself underscores YouTube's capacity for the historicization of engaging with sites of Holocaust memory—how audiences engaged prior to Web 2.0, and with hints of what will come after. YouTube, as a platform for sharing experiences with the Holocaust's history and its memory, continues to center on the precarious nature of "viewing the self." While the intersection of social media and Holocaust memory often repeatedly embeds voyeuristic performance in these memory contributions, performative self-reflection has become a visual style.

This visual style, examples of which are seen in the Video Diary of Anne Frank and #Uploading_Holocaust, is not always indicative of irreverent naval gazing. This new format can be used to great advantage to share Anne's experience—and the experiences of other Holocaust victims and survivors, for new generations in a format they recognize and relate to. Employing the vlog can empower younger generations to encounter difficult histories and share their experiences with their peers and the wider global community. Certainly, the age-old question of authority remains: how can those without the backing of historical training be trusted with the transmission of memory in the social mediasphere? The answer to this question is that, for the memory of the Holocaust to flourish rather than language, the newer generation must be entrusted to carry on its legacy, with whatever tools are available to them. Open dialogues and questions about the nature of memory, the role of the public in its maintenance, and the ways in which form and message shape it remain as essential to these new forms of Holocaust memory as they have in the past.

Andrew Hoskins indicates that our current media age is characterized by increased connectivity between forms, agents, and discourses of memory. This has led to unprecedented opportunities for archiving, retrieving, or interacting with the past.[85] While Ebbrecht-Hartmann argues that Holocaust memorials only began to experiment with the potential of social media for Holocaust memory in the wake of the COVID-19 pandemic, the ways in which social media—and YouTube, in particular—are used to create collaborative spaces for engagement extends further back than the last few years.[86] Today, as highlighted by Yasmin Ibrahim, sharing and narrating one's live through vlogs is an integral aspect of social media, and video-sharing platforms like YouTube.[87] Incorporating the vlog into Holocaust memory-making practices invites scholars to think critically about the ways in which individuals encounter Holocaust memory, or interpret it for the education of others. The Video Diary of Anne Frank and #Uploading_Holocaust highlight the format and visual style of a vlog in different ways, to very different ends. The Video Diary of Anne Frank remains highly stylized and produced, despite its casual and personal visual form. As Ibrahim has explained, this is an example of the ways in which vlogs function "as artefacts for the representation of the self … placing these within a historic continuum of older formats such as diaries and journals …"[88] In this context, the vlog series is building on the historical trajectory of Anne's diary as an object existing within a historical continuum, answering the question posed by Anne Frank House: itself "what if Anne Frank had a camera instead of a diary?" The answer to that question is a product which Henig and Ebbrecht-Hartmann have described as journalist and atrocity witnessing modes, which "showcase the ways in which producers consciously relate to social digital media and its ability to share personal experiences in new ways."[89] The vlog aspect of the Video Diary of Anne Frank, then, is characterized more by its visual style than its content.

#Uploading_Holocaust employs the vlog in a different fashion. While the documentary is subject to similar processes of interpretation, editing, and cinematography as the Video Diary of Anne Frank, its subjects engage in the filming of vlogs to produce a unique result. As our worlds have become increasingly entangled with digital environments, the vlogs portrayed in #Uploading_Holocaust serve to record the personal, poignant, and sometimes even mundane reactions to the individual's physical environment—spaces of Holocaust memory in Poland. In one way, Bornstein and Nir's #Uploading_Holocaust depends entirely on the existence of YouTube. When they set out to make a film which engaged with the experiences of tens of thousands of Israeli high school students' journeys through Poland, they did not expect that they would find the bulk of their material on the platform. The film explores how young Israelis confront and contemplate the memory of the Holocaust in the digital age. The beginning of #Uploading_Holocaust shares that there are over 30,000 clips on YouTube related to this annual trip. While this statistic pales in comparison to the number of followers of official Holocaust Memorial institutions (Auschwitz-Birkenau Memorial and Museum, for example, has 317,000 subscribers on YouTube alone), it nevertheless underscores the fact that a significant amount of content creation occurs beyond the real and digital confines of the museum. Just as Wikipedia has emerged as a fraught but important space where official knowledge meets the vernacular, so too is YouTube ever increasingly an important conduit of historical information.[90]

Throughout the course of writing this monograph, we have noticed that the perception of how social media should be used to commemorate and educate audiences about the Holocaust has shifted from a form of anxiety to a more reticent acceptance of the medium. This acceptance is contingent, however, less on whether there is a social media presence for Holocaust memory at all than on whether people make use of the platforms in appropriate ways—and whether they have the appropriate qualifications to do so. Holocaust memory by way of the YouTube vlog is driven by creators' direct composition and engagement with audiences on the platform. In this way, memory is the product of this negotiation. At the same time, one must also think beyond the platform, engaging the multimodal social mediascape itself. #Uploading_Holocaust shines a light on the medium's reach beyond that of its own platform, drawing attention to the ways in which the camera lens has been turned on its subjects, from the outside looking in and how this then refracts out to wider society. In either instance, what this chapter shows is that it is all the more important that scholars develop a critical apparatus to take it seriously on its own terms.

4

"Twitter, Hashtag Activism, and Remembering the Dresden Bombing Online"

Unlike other examples of carpet-bombing during the Second World War—Warsaw, Rotterdam, Coventry, London, and Hamburg—Dresden stands apart. The stuff of novels, memoirs, photojournalism, and fine art photography, it has remained in public consciousness far longer than the other campaigns, in large part due to the yearly neo-Nazi demonstrations that have marked its anniversary since the 1980s. The annual marches ensure war wounds never heal. They recast old debates anew, and with the help of Twitter, confrontations between memory activists and city officials are brought to the world in real time. The Dresden marches are a bellwether of public consciousness around the memory of mass violence and genocide.

This chapter demonstrates how mediatization has shaped post-Holocaust memory of the air war, both historically and contemporarily. It focuses on the different ways in which analog and digital technology have framed how people understand atrocity and organized dissent. Drawing on an archive of Twitter datasets, harvested since 2014 around the far-right commemorative marches every February, we argue that digital media has augmented not only the scope and tenor of the debate around the air war but also helped construct the spatial and affective relationships users attach to this historic city.[1] Analyzing tweets discursively and as part of networked, multimodal assemblages of mediatized memory making, we explore how online activity and activism recast ways in which citizens interact with the meaning of the city's fraught past. Tweets about the air war's legacy serve as shifting, moving, but nevertheless meaningful exercises in connective memory formation.

Though the memory of Dresden had been contested in the immediate aftermath, as well as throughout the decades after, the processional marches by far-right groups between 2014 and 2020 turned on a specific commemorative agenda, opposed not just in the city's physical space, but on Twitter as well.

Nationalist and anti-Nazi tweets were not the only forms of memory at work on display in the Twitter data. Our analysis reveals three different strands of Dresden memory culture that evolved in interpolation with actual spaces of confrontation on the ground during the week of demonstrations through the city center. Tweeters challenged official commemoration practices and helped renegotiate the meaning of Dresden as a both site of memory and digital *lieu de mémoire*.

As novel a practice as commemoration is on Twitter, it nevertheless draws on past aesthetics, ideologies, speech, and media forms. Yet the curatorial and algorithmic functionality of the platform means it produces different memory products and behaviors. Twitter has the unique ability to augment certain voices over others, shaping, rightly or wrongly, what user-generated content circulates, forms impressions, and gains traction as part of the digital public sphere. But there are also important limits to Twitter and the framework of online memory activism generally that nudge us to think about the impact of vernacular voices, networked publics, and the place of the bombing campaign in history and memory. Thinking about tweets as mediatized texts focuses on the dual role of Twitter as both a platform and discursive space where ideas and images are articulated, consumed, trafficked, and mobilized in a host of different ways. As we argued in the Instagram, Flickr, and YouTube chapters, it helps to recall that tweets engaging with the memory of the bombing are cultural performances linked to the symbolism of this particular place, with images and texts serving as agents in the production of specific commemorative agendas. Here, we place emphasis on the social-technical conditions that undergird how the past is made and remade in on- and offline activity to periodize the changing role of media scripts as interlocutors in the articulation of memory.[2]

Asking how platformed technology has shaped remembrance of the air war means contending with the ways the bombing campaign has been cast in media and memory. The concept of mediatization is useful here. Having gained currency in recent years, especially among communications scholars, mediatization helps describe the increasing role and importance of media forms in everyday life. Of course, all texts are mediatized, given that they are articulated and reproduced through different genres of communication. As Michael Warner has argued, each conjures an audience, even an imagined one, and in so doing constitutes a public.[3] Mediatization casts light on the changing social-technical conditions that enable sources like Tweets to make an impact in a given historical moment.[4] For the historian concerned with change over time, this melds well with our interest in investigating what Andreas Hepp calls "the interrelation between the change of media communication and sociocultural change as part of everyday communication practices, and how the change of these practices is related to a changing communicative construction of reality."[5] For example, a photograph published in a newspaper in 1920 and reproduced in another issue two decades later casts light not just on the different social contexts within which the image circulated, but also on the differing abilities of the medium itself to reach and reflect the attitudes of its publics. Were that same photograph to appear today attached to a tweet, it would speak not only to its iconic status as an image, but also to the changing makeup and structure of its audience, given twenty-first-century media affordances and the technologies that undergird them. Whether we draw our intellectual inheritance from Bourdieu or Lefebvre on the relationship of social structures and space to the media and vice versa, a focus on the material conditions of mediatization allows us to think more capaciously about the role of different sources in shaping politics, cultural practices, subjectivity, and everyday life.[6]

At the same time that digital forms of communication challenge the separation of public and private, local and global, time and place, they galvanize distinct social formations while simultaneously reflecting the changing social forces that gave them life in the first place.[7] As Piotr Celinski argues, drawing on Piaget, "culture constructs technologies, provides them with the social and symbolic base, (and) responds to expectations and capabilities of its inhabitants, whereas technology transforms these energies (...) and gives them back, changing culture" in the process.[8] Technology is no abstract driver of social change; rather, it is subject to the push and pull of the different social forces at work in each historical moment.[9] Just as media itself has indelibly changed over the last several decades, so too has its role in augmenting and amplifying certain social realities over others. "Platform society," the term José van Dijck coined to connote the immense, integrated global power of commercialized digital media to structure government, civil society, markets, and labor, has had an especially powerful reach in recent decades.[10] The reach of social media's commercial modalities, anchored in data sharing and monetization, and largely unregulated by national governments, is far more insidious than other media forms.[11] Digital communication technologies have demonstrated unparalleled powers of influence over local and national politics, political economy, governance, education, entertainment, and even health care in ways previously unimaginable. Virtually all social actors, from state and civil society institutions, to mainstream media, and everyday citizens have had little option but to reconfigure their position in the digital public sphere in this new algorithmic ecosystem.[12] Twenty-first-century memory formations are indelibly shaped by the "medial gathering and splintering of individual, social, and cultural imaginaries," which are increasingly networked, portable, and pervasive.[13] In light of these new relationships, we need to ask new questions about how memory works—and has worked—in a place like Dresden. What is different about how social media has shaped the meaning of the air war, in ways different than other points in the past?

To better understand how networked memories form through the bombing's memorialization on Twitter, we need to think about how tweets comingle with past, current, and ongoing processes of remembering and forgetting across diverse media forms over time. A tweet is not a poster or photograph, a memoir, speech, or newspaper article, though it might include these sources as metadata to supplement and reinforce an idea. Tweets are multimodal memory texts composed, sometimes at once, of several different, co-constitutive genres of writing, remembering, and representation. While they can be flippant, off-the-cuff expressions of a fleeting moment, they can also be impactful, redolent with sentiment and emotion. Some tweets are amplified by being pushed along the network and linked via retweet, while others remain static, one-time articulations lost in the tickertape of a timeline; although, in those instances they still form what Twitter analytics calls "an impression" just by being part of the living archive of ideas.[14] When harvested and analyzed together with others, they become part of a larger conversation and a window into a specific moment.

Tweets surrounding the commemorative marches in Dresden have an even more unique function. Each February, when far-right groups descend on the city with the hopes of challenging the public memory of the Second World War, the Twitter stream coalesces into a different kind of *lieu de mémoire*, a shifting digital, physical, and temporal space where users construct and reinforce competing ways of remembering German national guilt and victimhood. Tweets are not just abstract manifestations of complex technological affordances. They manifest at the intersection of real and imagined space. Tweets referencing discreet locations are geotagged, which connects them to discrete physical locations, even if the person is not actually inhabiting that space. During the Dresden marches, this grounds them simultaneously in virtual, material, communicative, and memory space.[15] They also have many different modes. Tweets can be journalistic as when activists use photojournalism and reporting to shape public debate through alternative channels like a blog. They can work as a tickertape, documenting real-time protest action, spontaneous violence, police response, and crowd dispersal. Tweets may be situational and transtemporal, linking particular issues to a variety of themes—historical as well as contemporary— through iconic language, imagery, and acts of remediation. And they coalesce into an archive, when harvested as a corpus.

The question then becomes, given these unique affordances, how does the networked public that Twitter calls into being impact and shape the way in which these memories connect with past and ongoing forms of memorialization? How does online activity shape offline actions? And, to what extent do digital contestations over German suffering interact with ongoing struggles to normalize a far-right populist reshaping of the memorial landscape? To get at this, this chapter uses a mixed-method approach. We scraped Twitter data using a Python-based harvesting method and interpreted it through a mix of keyword and critical historical analysis. We focused on tweets generated around select hashtags use during the events of February 12th to 19th of each year, between 2014 and 2020. #13Februar captures tweets from across the political spectrum. It is popular with antifascist groups and local media and memory entrepreneurs, but also contains interventions from the right. We supplemented this data with tweets from specific antifascist initiatives like #dresdennazifrei, a citizen initiative with loose connections to the left-wing party Die Linke. Similarly, we harvested data from larger, national organizations like the anti-immigration protest group #Pegida and the originally Eurosceptic #AfD or Alternative für Deutschland party. Using a variety of visualization techniques, word frequencies, social network analysis, and time and spatial mapping, we pulled out select issues for more focused qualitative research, analyzing the discourses, texts, hyperlinks, and images against this chapter's main preoccupation—the role of tweeting in the negotiation of connective memory cultures. In this way, we analyze the Twitter stream for the way it functions as a networked, activist public, where users employ distinct media tactics, repertoires, and framing devices to draw attention to the issues at hand. Our aim is to show how this space of mediation shapes how the bombing of Dresden is popularly remembered in an embattled twenty-first-century Germany, where the minimization of German war guilt forms part of the agenda of several far-right associations and political parties.

To chart change over time, our analysis begins with a review of the analog memory structures and pre-internet media forms that developed in the early aftermath of the original air raid, including how images, sentiments, and politicized memories became crystalized after the bombing. After examining the early much-contested memory of the bombing of Dresden we turn to the place of emotions in online missives to better understand what thoughts and actions are amplified, by whom, and to what end. Then, we explore the interplay of on-

and offline activity, including the use of hyperlinks and site-specific references to map how far-right and civil society re-territorialize the urban memorial landscape with the help of tweets. Our aim is to show how the twin function of Twitter helps stabilize more evanescent memories, fixing, even if momentarily, the more fluid aspects of connective memory. The impact of Twitter is profound, suggesting that digital memory formations, like those forged during the Dresden marches, have a real impact on how individuals, groups, and wider society has come to think about this moment in the history of the air war.

After the Deluge

Before Dresden could be memorialized as one of the war's great human tragedies, it was, of course, an experience. "Operation Thunderclap," the code name given to the bombing by Bomber Command, killed roughly 18,000–25,000 people on the night of February 13th to 14th and in a subsequent American-aided raid the next day. It was Fasching, the German Mardi Gras, and the few Catholic revelers in this overwhelmingly Lutheran town had visited parties and friends, welcoming in spring with revelry and fun.[16] The city's Jews, at least those fortunate to be married to Aryan partners like the philologist Viktor Klemperer, had survived the better part of the war, although the Semper Synagogue did not enjoy the same fate, having been destroyed years earlier in Kristallnacht (the Night of Broken Glass). Just after 10 PM, February 13th, the onslaught began. First, a single British Lancaster dropped a green bomb to map out the target. Several Mosquito bombers followed suit, lighting the area so that over 700 Lancasters could drop their payload—magnesium, incendiary, and blast bombs. Over the next several days, American B-17s from the 8th Air Force division would target military installations, train yards, communications and supply routes, and factories. For the RAF pilots, the attack was over in twenty minutes.[17] While they returned to their base, those on the ground came to know an unimaginable horror as streets turned into liquid tar. The firestorm drew on all available oxygen to feed its flames, creating a single inferno out of several smaller fires. The city infrastructure provided little sanctuary. Household glass melted. Lampposts bowed under the heat. The air in poorly ventilated air raid shelters turned noxious. Those who did not asphyxiate burned alive crouching in place. Even the waters of the Elbe River and the neighboring reservoirs provided no relief for those trying to flee the fires. They boiled to death in the 1,000-degree heat.

Ultimately, over 34 square kilometers of the city were incinerated, making it the most destructive of all singular wartime bombing campaigns. This dubious honor imbued it with symbolism from the very beginning. For the Allies, the targeted attack of this renowned city, the Florence on the Elbe, was meant to send a message of English and American technological mastery, to force capitulation and hasten an end to the war. The firestorm that unfolded, however, which took so much human life unleashed a maelstrom of a different sort, around Allied military conduct. In postwar memory politics, this early focus on German victimization opened the door to analogies and equivalences between the bombing deaths and those who perished in the Holocaust. It did not help that the mounds of bodies burned to prevent disease bore casual similarities to the images of corpses discovered upon liberation of the camps. The origins of the far-right fixation with Dresden as a crime against humanity may be traced back to this early reportage, both the propaganda infused reports out of Germany itself and the Allied efforts to underscore the city's importance as a military target.

Although journalism has often been disregarded in terms of its role in memory making, early news stories laid the foundation for how the Dresden bombing would be taken up in public memory for the better part of the twentieth century.[18] A full two decades before Kurt Vonnegut's *Slaughterhouse 5* brought the firestorm to an Anglo-American readership, and David Irving courted an international audience with his archival exploits, it was the foreign press that most shaped public thinking around the air war. British newspapers displayed English matter-of-factness and resolve at having survived years of raids on its own cities.[19] *New York Times* reporter Gladwin Hill provided a more pathos-laden account of smoke riddled skies and "flames (that) were seen by returning flyers 200 miles away." While the bombing had not been originally planned as a new form of warfare, explicitly targeting civilians, the scope and scale of the firestorm made it challenging to sidestep such accusations in the specific conditions of the mediatized environment of contemporary reporting. Allied news services underscored the RAF and American position that this was a campaign of targeted bombing of infrastructure and necessary to support the Soviet march westward.

If the initial accounts by the foreign press emphasized the mission over civilian misery, Goebbels's Propaganda Ministry raised the stakes. Plagued by countless reports of poor morale, Goebbels determined that the best way to maintain civilian resolve for the *Endkampf* (final struggle) was to focus on the scale of destruction. What better way to do so than by drawing on pre-existing race narratives? In an article from March 4, 1945, Reich Labour Corp leader Robert Ley reiterated the idea that the air war had been started by Jews intent on destroying German culture and values.[20] Leaning into the mythos surrounding the city, one of "Germany's most precious jewels, the peaceful, artistically precious city of Dresden," Ley sought to ignite the spirit of animosity and revenge, while propagating false statistics on the death toll.[21] The power of this civilizational frame was immense. We know from the memoirs of women in Berlin that they anticipated Soviet sexual assault because they had learned through their own media reports over the years about the violence of the German campaign on the Eastern Front.[22] Goebbels's tactic was to play to these affective communities to connect citizens to "senseless and uncalled for destruction of architecture, life, and history in Dresden." This was not difficult to accomplish. Over sixteen major cultural landmarks were destroyed in that one single night, with the eighteenth century Frauenkirche perhaps being the most recognizable as the place where Johann Sebastian Bach thanked King August III of Poland, Grand Duke of Lithuania and Elector of Saxony with a two-hour organ recital for naming him Royal Court Composer. To recast the bombing as a national tragedy, Goebbels seized on the cosmopolitan underpinnings of central European history, while simultaneously denying Germany's role in the colonial conquest of that same region.

In seeking to blame the Allies for their wanton cruelty, the German propaganda ministry benefitted from Swedish news stories which historians believe leaked information that augmented the number of dead. One such document would form the basis of Holocaust denier David Irving's argument about a higher-than-acknowledged death toll.[23] On February 17th, the *Svenska Morgenbladet* reported that upwards of 100,000 people had been killed in a city whose population had swelled from roughly 650,000 to over 2 million, given the throngs of women and children who had arrived in advance of the Red Army. A week later, another paper, the *Svenska Dagbladet,* upped that number closer to 200,000.[24] How the news cycle narrated the destruction of the city reflected the distinctiveness of Allied and German wartime experience and the expediency of an information war in the final months of the Second World War.

Picturing the Aftermath

The press was not the only medium constructing early memories of the February bombings. Photography emerged as an equally, if not more important conduit for how occupiers and occupied came to think and feel about the air war. It was through images that postwar audiences, foreign, domestic, and contemporary pictured the violence of the Second World War, selectively, as could be seen on both sides of the Iron Curtain. Photographs were, and still are, central to the process of memory making. Images create mnemonic frames that help us imagine the past. As visual anthropologist Elizabeth Edwards has argued, they "grasp time and re-materialize it" as audiences engage with them in their different sites of encounter. A photograph's "evidential force" as Roland Barthes calls it, relies not on what it pictures but what its viewers see in it at different moments in time.[25] Unlike texts or testimonies, a photograph's indexicality and ability to capture life in its perceived verisimilitude underscore the "having-been-there" of the past. This "material connection between the past and the present" embodied in the photograph is brought about by the "the witness who recognizes it."[26] It is for this reason that the photograph, even the instant, tweeted, digital image, remains embedded in the memory conflicts around Dresden.

This connection to the past is as much a corporeal encounter as one of witnessing. Images arrest moments in time, which we interpret through the senses, sight, most obviously, but also sound and touch.[27] A photograph evokes sentiment and feeling. Although it seems to isolate one moment of many, the image captures multiple layers of experiences that go beyond the singular frame.[28] These diverse textures of experience, caught in the moment, but witnessed after the fact help "temporalize the spatial," defining a place's particular meaning in the present through references to its past.[29]

It is not insignificant then, given photography's privileged place in the public imagination, that photojournalists would be among the first to capture the destruction in Dresden and other bombed-out German cities, creating in the process distinct affective responses to the air war and eventual defeat that would be taken up in collective memory. These photographs were readily available in magazines and newspapers to meet the desires of the reading public. Images were not without consequences here. The black and gray hues of early aerial photography provided foreign audiences a sense of quiet detachment, allowing readers to envision the struggle between good and evil in observable contrast without becoming mired in the optics of suffering on the ground. Embedded photojournalists like Margaret Bourke-White took photographs of bombed German cities for *Life* magazine, helping American audiences visualize retribution, while postwar German photographers adopted a more melancholic, elegiac tone.[30] For them, and in a fraction of time for the Allies too, images of rubble no longer confirmed guilt. Rather, as Stefan-Ludwig Hoffmann has argued, they became part of a photographic practice that "visually de-Nazified" the population in the eyes of the occupiers. When viewed through the lens of atrocity and triumphalism as the Cold War slowly set in, bombed-out cities engendered feelings of sympathy for the Germans.[31]

Suffering was never far from the surface of images of the aftermath of war. Ruin photography was the most wide-reaching in the postwar media landscape, with portrait and fine art photographers like August Sander and Friedrich Seidenstücker turning their lenses to the broken cityscapes of Cologne, Berlin, and of course Dresden.[32] The sheer number of photographers that descended into the ruins of Dresden meant that visual narratives from the Zero Hour would indelibly mark how Germans envisioned the air war regardless of what occupation zone they were in. Unlike the rhetoric of the far-right, which argued that there was silence around the bombing, in the 1950s Germans never "fled headlong from the past or suffered from collective amnesia."[33] The continued resurfacing of these iconic images in post-1945 memory culture ensured that the discussion of the war dead remained a core feature of memory making for the better part of the Cold War and well into the 1990s.

The images of destruction tended to fall into two genres, focused either on bodies or on the ruins themselves.[34] In the 1940s and 1950s, aftermath photographs coalesced around two narratives, one stressing suffering and the other resilience.[35] Photos commissioned by the embattled Dresden city government framed blame for the scale of destruction on the Nazi hierarchy. Contrasting the architectural destruction of the carpet bombing with the majesty of the city's earlier days, Kurt Schaarshuch's 1946 photobook *Bilddokument Dresden, 1933–1945*, with a circulation of 40,000, was even accompanied by a letter from a local city official blaming a small coterie of Nazis for the city's collective fate.[36] Schaarshuch's was not the only articulation of guilt circulating at the time. His photobook was read by a public inundated with story after story in the newspaper of the trials in Nuremberg, where high-ranking Nazi functionaries were interrogated by the Allied tribunal. And yet, by framing his photos of Dresden as a series of contrasts between how the city appeared in 1933 and again in 1945, in effect Schaarshuch elides over the Nazi years, which also has the effect of obfuscating not just the dead but that the living had supported, acquiesced to, and even upheld National Socialism along with its leaders.[37]

While the Schaarshuch photobook mirrored contemporary discourses of Nazi culpability in waging total war and genocide, other photobooks shifted the focus away from elites to everyday acts of rebuilding and survival and opened a space for talk of German victimization. This process was aided by the ways that visual narratives of death and renewal were taken up by official state memory in the emerging Cold War, especially in the nascent German Democratic Republic, founded in 1949. The hallmarks of what would become official East German memory changed only by degree over the forty-year life of the GDR. They first coalesced a few years after capitulation when local newspapers like the *Sächsische Zeitung* began publishing articles that brought back Goebbels's fixation with the city's innocence in the face of Anglo-American revanchism. Suggestions that the targeting of civilians had been a deliberate strategy, a way to demonstrate military mastery not to the Nazis but to the Soviets, were meant to humanize the Russians over the British and Americans, whom the articles argued were the true aggressors, then and even more so now.[38] In a bizarre twist of logic, the quest to make friends of enemies meant adopting Nazi-era propaganda nearly word for word.

Marita Sturken argues abstract cultural memories solidify when images are shared, reproduced, and moved through different media.[39] Following this logic, a single photo's travels from the fall of 1945 through to commemorative marches in the 2000s tell us much about mediatized memory formation from the former GDR through to today. In perhaps the most famous photobook of the bombing and its aftermath, Richard Peter's 1949 publication *Dresden. Eine Kamera klagt an* (A Camera Accuses) gave the world the iconic image of the bombed-out city as victim of a rapacious air war, viewed from the vantage of a sculpture on top of the city hall. Peter, who served as picture editor of *Zeit im Bild*, the culture magazine of record in the Soviet occupation zone and later in the socialist republic, took hundreds of photographs of the city before and after Operation Thunderclap. Although other photographers had likewise taken footage from this very same spot, his surpassed all others in notoriety and reach, not least because of his connections to the emerging GDR state.

The photobook's power as a medium is its simplicity. And of course, it was a bonus that it had help finding an audience. *Ein Kamera klagt an*'s blend of documentary and aesthetic registers struck a chord with the city government, who jumped at the chance to publish Peter's curated photo archive of Dresden. David Crew has argued he had earlier approached the state government of Saxony with a cache of over 200 images, a ready-made archive of destruction.[40] Unlike the photo-montage experiments of the 1920s and 1930s, before Hitler had purged the Bauhaus and the experimentalism of its Dada, Constructivist, and avant-guard photographers, *Ein Kamera klagt an* had a simple message that served the growing antifascist messaging of the nascent GDR state: a visual indictment of the immorality of war at the hands of the British and American Allies.[41] Although the photobook contains many examples of the violence of the bombing campaign, the mummified corpses among the most macabre, it is the *bonitas* photo that emerged from between the covers as the most recognizable symbol of destruction. Named after the statue atop the Dresden city hall that serves as the photograph's focal point, the statue, ethereal and aloof, towers high over the devastated city, one arm outreached, guiding the viewer's eye to the ruins below. The camera is positioned slightly to the side and behind the statue, its lens trained downward, as if from the heavens below. This maneuver creates a frame that collapses primary experience and secondary witnessing, as Julia Adeney Thomas calls it. It places the viewer in the position of both participant and observer to the city's fate and rebirth alongside the photographer.[42] Accordingly, the photo works literally as well as metaphorically as an artifact of war's destruction and an allegory of man's folly. This secondary meaning is helped along by the very name of the statue itself, from the Latin for "moral goodness, benevolence, and integrity." It turns out, there were many photos taken from this precipice, but none acquired the iconic status of Peter's.[43] The inclusion of a poem in the photobook by socialist poet Max Zimmering, a Jewish emigre and fellow traveler and editor of the same *Zeit im Bild* glossy that employed Peter, cemented the memorialization of the air war as a criticism of American imperialist aggression.

The photobook, like this famed image, had many lives, each defined by the media environments in which it circulated. The book's first run was a remarkable 50,000 copies, a full 10,000 more than Schaarschuch's.[44] We know from a contemporary collector, who acquired an interest in it through another enthusiast's Instagram account, that it was given as a gift by the Dresden city council well into the 1950s. A copy Jörg Colberg acquired online still bore the ex libris mark from the library of French mime Pierre Verry, complete with a hearty Christmas greeting from the local government (Figure 16).[45]

The photobook was reprinted in 1980 and again in 1995, as unified Germany returned to the question of complicity in a new round of memory wars after the Wehrmacht Exhibition cast aspersions on myths of innocence and the German Army.[46] The subject of serious essays and blog posts, it remains one of the most sought-after pieces of ephemera among collectors. It also happens to be employed by the city of Dresden today as part of its efforts to tap into the nostalgia around the city's tragic history and draw visitors. Many people are fascinated by the image's affective qualities, the way it touches across time, inspiring loss, hope, suffering, and pain.[47] A simple Google Image search reveals that many of the photos have been digitized and reproduced in one form or other on all manner of sites, highlighting the way the photos continue to resonate decades after their creation Peter himself returned to the iconic spot over the

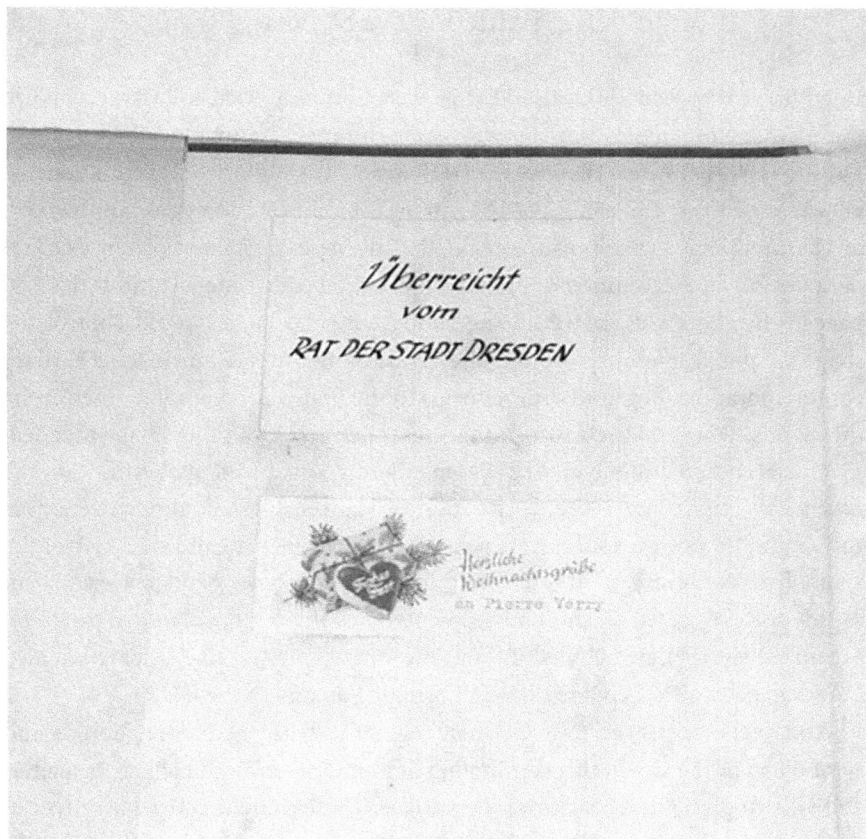

Figure 16 Jörg Colberg's copy of the 1949 edition.

years to photograph the changes to the city as it succumbed to plans for socialist architectural renewal.[48] The *bonitas* figure remained the same, which brought echoes of this earlier iteration, but the wall of ruins it once gestured to in the background was transformed into housing blocks and infill, perhaps eliciting a new form of melancholy for what was lost and will never be found again amidst the cacophony of materials and styles that made up socialist realist recovery.[49] The mediatization of the itinerant *bonitas* image created a series of emotional attachments that allowed Germans to work through their grief as a condition of defeat.[50] At the same time that it humanized the tragedy of war, however, it also created a space for the instrumentalization of a particular way of seeing the air campaign as a moral indictment of the Allies. What evoked feelings of revulsion and horror for a foreign audience also aestheticized genocide by removing the scope of Nazi crimes from view. The photo held these meanings together.

The Battle for the Streets

In addition to photobooks, the SED in East Germany tried to instrumentalize the memory of suffering in staging yearly commemorations on the streets of Dresden to promote an image of the GDR as an anti-militaristic, anti-nationalist alternative to the rapacious West Germany. Since 1955, the tenth anniversary of the bombings (which also coincided with West Germany joining NATO) national air war commemorations underscored the state's commitment to peace.[51] By the 1980s, however, the ruling elites no longer could control the shape of public memory around the Dresden bombings, once the February commemorations began to draw citizens to the Frauenkirche, sometimes in the thousands, who preferred to use the silent vigil in ways other than intended. Unofficial peace initiatives like independently organized gatherings in the *Innenstadt* (city center), the distribution of leaflets, silent commemoration or the singing of protest songs, were a reminder that the state did not control the symbolism of the street.[52] It is not insignificant that memory and peace activism of this sort, relegated to church basements once the regime clamped down on organized gatherings, bubbled up into the streets in cities like Leipzig but also Dresden, galvanizing civil society and bringing an end to the GDR.

And yet, even as the East German regime lost its grasp over the use and symbolism of the street, this comingling of memories around civilian casualties and suffering was never far from the surface. These shared victim narratives of the Nazi period, adopted into East Germany and used to differentiate the GDR from the West, became something victims of socialism might also graft onto their identities once the wall fell.[53] This sentiment even aided in the reimagination of the city in the 1990s and 2000s, as residents courted reconciliation with the city's Jewish population to rebuild the Frauenkirche and Neue Synagogue in the spirit of shared victimhood and against the plans of developers and their modernist imagination. These tropes of innocents preyed upon by Nazi aggression, victimized by English and American revanchism, further subjugated by the GDR, and disadvantaged by reunification were easy pickings for the far-right, which, also in the 1990s, began to seize the opportunity to harness the power of commemoration to serve more nefarious purposes.

Although there had existed in West Germany several far-right parties like the National Party of Germany (NPD) and die Republikaner who had moderate if not always stellar success in state elections, before 1989 most rightists allied themselves with available political parties and pushed ultra-conservative agendas within the available political system.[54] The East German state, including the secret police, turned a blind eye to neo-Nazism as a vestige of consumer capitalism, even though radical right-leaning youths were more and more visible by the 1980s, targeting queers, Jewish cemeteries, foreigners and punks in organized attacks like the famed 1987 mobbing of a concert in East Berlin's Zionkirche.[55] Perhaps owing to these different experiences, united Germany was distinct from the rest of Europe in the way far-right extremism gathered momentum beyond the parliamentary system in a series of loosely connected friendship circles (*Kameradschaften*), called groupuscules in the far-right extremism literature, whose strength was bolstered at the subcultural level.[56] These diffuse networks of the like-minded, which in 1998 the Office for the Protection of the Constitution claimed numbered around eighty in total, sometimes with as few as ten to fifteen adherents, borrowed symbols and tactics from the autonomous left scene and used cultural production—chiefly music and new media—to promote the cause of ethno-nationalism.[57] Reacting to a wave of anti-immigrant attacks on asylum houses, the German government took a proactive stance on the right and banned several of the more recognizable organizations, although this was largely symbolic considering the source of violence went further than the groups targeted. In fact, it had the opposite effect, initially driving further underground those small-scaled rhizomatic networks, which the established parties benefitted from in the long run once the bans were rescinded. With renewed vigor in the late 1990s, the NPD made it its mission to take over the streets in organized actions and demonstrations.

The commemorations in Dresden were a perfect opportunity to hone rightist praxeology (collective forms of behavior, ritual, and symbology) while tapping into long-standing tropes that held broad appeal.[58] There was cause for concern, however, so much so that a historical commission met in 2004 to put these inflated claims of civilian deaths to bed once and for all. The resulting Framework of Remembrance taken up by the City of Dresden in 2005, after much heated debate, reflects official efforts to right the wrongs of shared victimization narratives, to chart a course for a more critical self-reflexive commemoration.[59] This was challenged each February as neo-Nazis from across the country descended on the city for a week's worth of demonstrations and funeral marches through the city center. Although the inchoate nature of the far-right means that there has been debate about whether it meets the definition of a social movement, there can be no doubt that the February demonstrations were places where participants refined what it meant to belong to such a group through a "ritual affirmation of their collective identity and values, protest motives and protest goals, as well as their shared emotional understanding."[60] At the same time, these marches are also a testing grounds for civil opposition, occasionally organized around some of the very same symbols.

To take but one example, the *bonitas* photograph surfaced on demonstration posters in 2009 for both the neo-fascist NPD and on signs hoisted by members of civil society organized against them.[61] For anti-war activists intent on highlighting the corrosiveness of aerial bombing and total war, and antifascist protestors clashing with neo-Nazis in the city streets every February, analog media forms like posters, placards, chanting, marches, and barricades mobilized ritual and emotion in the service of remembering the air war a particular way. In this last decade, in addition to the vigils, marches, street skirmishes and demonstrations, activists on both sides of the political spectrum enlisted Twitter as part of these contested cultures of memory (*Erinnerungskultur*). Given the continued reach and appeal of narratives of shared victimization, how does digital connectivity around the February marches allow civil society a space of opposition to far-right extremist history claims and on what basis? To what extent did this hashtag activism, forged online and taken to the streets, materialize public memory in different ways than what came before?

Protest Cultures and Publics

As we have seen, the notion of shared victimization has proved to be quite tenacious. It outlasted the demise of the GDR, has been taken up by marketers, tourist boards, and even television producers, and helped define how everyday people thought about the bombing campaign into the 2000s.[62] Social technology adds a new wrinkle by fundamentally altering the way media, activists, and civil society meet the challenge of the far-right. But is it enough to offset revisionist forces intent on undermining a more fulsome culture of remembrance, one that recognizes, as the 2005 city ordinance on remembrance suggests that there is an obligation to "stand up against the abuse of our remembrance to play down the crimes of the National Socialist German society between 1933 and 1945?"[63] We have already seen that official memory of the air war was deeply beholden to pre-internet-era media affordances. It traveled through extensive networks, both domestic and international, and constructed in the process a textual-visual panoply of sentiments that resonated with audiences viscerally, on an emotional level. Revisionists like David Irving were able to tap into this discord, and although the myths surrounding the death toll were debunked empirically in

2004, they still circulate online, informing the annual marches and the responses to them.[64]

The role of new media in protests has received much attention in the wake of the Arab Spring, including conflagrations between ethnic minorities and government forces in several South Asian nations, the Maidan in Ukraine, Black Lives Matter, and the Capital Riot. It has spawned a dedicated literature onto how digital communication has helped and sometimes hindered activist groups to mobilize for direct action. Taking a media-specific yet culturally informed approach to protest cultures gives attention to tactics of identity building, including refining protest repertoires and the symbols that speak to the cause.[65] To think about the use of Twitter as a form of mediatization requires that we go a step further than platform-specific media practices. It means taking what Friedrich Krotz has called a more structural, "metaprocessional" approach, tying together the social and representational changes in how memories of the air war emerged through platform-specific media affordances, while also considering the changing reach and valuation of social media in the digital public sphere.[66] No analysis of media and memory can overlook how Twitter structures discursive— but also physical—protest culture and space, including the way it materializes symbols, tactics, and rhetoric in the streets and alleyways of the actual city.

As Marshall McLuhan observed already in his oft-cited book on the function of legacy media in 1964, we often overlook the quotidian and everyday when trying to understand what fires social change. In focusing on the obvious, we fail to see the unintended consequences of innovations all around, by which he meant the structures, social as well as technological, that underpin our world. The medium that was the message—as the tirelessly cited dictum goes—was not merely the change in technology from print to film, radio to television; McLuhan also meant the cultural, historical, and even religious precedents and frames that continue to shape how we perceive our present.[67] New technologies, as Raymond Williams and Lisa Nakamura remind us, are social inventions, bound by the hallmarks, exclusions, highs and lows of culture and power.[68] The internet may serve corporatist agendas, promoting user engagement and belonging so as to drive participants to make more content which might be sold to advertisers to augment consumption. Yet despite this, digital infrastructure also creates frameworks of contestation and possibility which users take up and deploy in a variety of ways. In post-Cold War Dresden, digital frameworks shaped which structures of memory were inherited over the benchmarks of 1949, 1961, 1989, and even 2004 when the history commission tendered its report to tackle, once and for all, the matter of civilian deaths. As we will see, many of the pre-existing tropes continued to hold resonance for far-right constituents, who politicized February 13th by turning it into a day of spectacle and mourning. But they were met with a new memory culture, that coalesced in this hybrid space of on and online opposition.

What was new in 2014, when we began gathering our datasets? Perhaps most obviously, the annual processional marches were organized and opposed not just in the center of the city, but also in digital space. They were, in their very essence, hybridized affairs. Tweets were deliberately crafted to bolster civic opposition, while the marches themselves turned on a particular commemorative agenda, one based on universalizing suffering. Tweets helped introduce a new set of issues and conditions with broad ramifications for how Germans would encounter and fight the relativization of the Holocaust both in and beyond the networked public sphere. Far from relativizing the past in an evanescent and continually evolving present, Twitter posts drew explicitly on these conflicting memory cultures, bringing history to bear on the contemporary struggle for city streets.[69]

Although neo-Nazis began to infiltrate city gatherings as early as 1998, as we saw in the Flickr photoalbums, since the 2000s their numbers have risen exponentially, buoyed by an upsurge of support for the far-right AfD and the vocal criticism of several of its leaders of the place of National Socialism within German memorial culture.[70] There are no fewer than three different memorial cultures reinforced in the city's public spaces each February, with specific spatial-cultural moorings. One is from the far right, which attempts to instrumentalize the bombings. This memory culture accrues in parades through the city but is also felt at the yearly wreath-laying ceremony at the Heidefriedhof to the northeast of the city. Another is put forward by the post-2004 city, state, and federal governments, which promotes silent commemoration as a form of reconciliation with a troubled past. This culture has focused mainly on the Frauenkirche as symbol of destruction and, now that it has been reconstructed, pilgrimage and dark tourism. A third and maybe a fourth (if one factors in the splintered left) sees the myth of Dresden's beauty and innocence as obfuscating the reality that the city was also a city of perpetration, complicit in genocide. These different antifascist memorial communities coalesce in various civic initiatives that seek to both broaden and deepen the field of commemoration within and beyond these two main sites. All three of the commemorative fields rely on the internet and social media to mobilize their publics.

Every February, besides Dresdeners themselves, legions of activists travel by train into the city's central station from the surrounding state of Saxony and are often joined by delegations from other parts of Germany including Leipzig, Hamburg, Frankfurt, and Berlin. Some come from as far away as France. They gather under different banners in disparate parts of the city: some attend official commemorations at the Altmarkt square, while others march from the train station to the Theaterplatz as part of the youth and mainstream wings of the Nationaldemokratie Partei Deustchlands (NPD). Some participate in the ceremony as sitting members of city, state, and federal government, giving speeches in the reconstructed Frauenkirche transmitted outside to giant screens. Members of church groups and peace initiatives pray, light candles, and observe a moment of silence. Others form 1-kilometer-long "peace chains" around known march sites in the spirit of what federal president and preacher Joachim Gauck called a form of reflexive memory, one that brings people together in peaceful dialogue instead of locating guilt in other people's hands.[71] Antifa activists of various stripes perform sit-ins, some engaging with police while trying to block the parade route which snakes around the city street by street. Neo-Nazis still march on February 12th, the night before the attack. However, city folk have overwhelmingly supported the counter blockades over police action since 2011, when the police intercepted over 1 million mobile phone messages from anyone who had gathered in the city centre.[72]

No amount of counter protest has managed to eradicate the presence of neo-Nazis completely. A CDU-FDP initiative in the Saxon parliament in 2012 gave officials the right to curtail public assembly and free speech on February 13th and 14th if it deemed this was a threat to public safety. Although this statute has been invoked several times—much to the enjoyment of activists who claim it as a victory to limit the length of a march—it has often just caused smaller groups of right-wing activists to find new places to stage their events. Take, for example, the ceremony at the Heidefriedhof (Heath Cemetery), 9 kilometers away to the northwest of the city center. There, city council and state officials found themselves standing cheek by jowl with members of the NPD, which, alongside initiatives like "Denk Mal Fort!" or "Keep Remembering!" use the cover of commemoration to host a name reading ceremony. Wreaths were laid in honor of the victims of the "Bombenterror" with no attempt made to parse the differences between civilians and Nazi functionaries and supporters. Although the Heidefriedhof wreath laying ceremony emerged during GDR times, since 2011 half of the participants have come from the far-right.[73]

While marches, wreath laying, name ceremonies, and civil disobedience are physical manifestations of memory wars, groups on all sides of the political spectrum use Twitter to speak to the media and adherents, to organize their activities, and advance their cause. When taken together, they form an archive of sentiment, strategy, and emotion, bearing important insight into how civil society mounts symbolic and direct action to oppose the instrumentalization of memorial space by right-wing extremists. Tweeting helps create episodic publics, within the larger public sphere. Sometimes they coalesce in arranged or formalized ways, like organized action, and other times they serve as part of the more abstract public sphere, alongside the readers and viewers on site and around the world. Evidence of these publics is fragmentary in its original state. Like documents in an archive file folder, the datasets are raw assemblages of entries on an excel spread sheet. Cleaned of extraneous characters and data, they are run through network, sentiment, and visualization software to reveal complex ways in which online communication both structures and reflects anxieties on the ground around the changing memory of the air war.

Tweets broaden the spaces and tactics of memorialization away from the marches and vigils in the Altmarkt, the Frauenkirche, and the Heidefriedhof to cyberspace, and back again. The networked publics that emerge become spaces of "imagined community formation at the intersection of people, technology, and practice."[74] These spaces are not entirely new, but the technical affordances of Twitter, including searchability, shareability, spreadability, and visibility mean some tweets gain more traction than others. Some publics are more identifiable and, in a sense, more public than others—whether by design or not. The same may be said for regular social interactions, but the social media field augments, extends, and amplifies social relations in ways different from the everyday.[75] Twitter allows actors of all stripes, some disenfranchised, others emboldened to execute some influence over the mainstream public sphere, while providing "rhetorical training ground for future agitational activities aimed at other publics," although as we will see, not all voices carry the same impact and social and institutional connections still matter.[76] Just as Twitter has the power to shape and refine the communicative potential for people and their practice, ultimately it cannot contain it, as ideas born on Twitter flow across platforms and become hybridized with subaltern and mainstream media.[77] The glue that binds these publics together is memory.

Twitter exchanges are largely phatic.[78] There is a kind of digital intimacy, with texts reinforcing and extending existing social bonds.[79] Tweets might serve as a kind of log, declaration, or diary in which the user writes to mark the day.[80] Like other platforms, there is no expectation of reciprocity. People tweet to advance a personal brand or self-performance, and they also, sometimes, present themselves as tricksters, using fake names, identities, and affectations. Liking tweets serves a similar purpose, as Twitter algorithms reveal a user's preferences outside of their own personal networks. Tweets can be campy and playful, as well as solemn, earnest, and inflammatory. In short, Tweets can reflect whatever sentiment the account holder chooses. Often, Twitter users negotiate these multiple different expressions of self in the same feed targeting overlapping audiences in something known as context collapse. The selective and strategic use of hashtags helps with this process of self-presentation and audience.

Since 2009, Dresden has witnessed ever-increasing numbers of people descend on the city. In 2011, estimates suggest as many as 20,000 counter protesters were involved in demonstrating against the streams of neo-Nazis that marched under various banners including the NPD, the Youth Association of East Germany, select Kamaradschaften, the Young National Democrats, and other affiliated groups.[81] The Antifa Research Team Dresden argues that by 2014, the number of far-right leaning memory activists grew steadily from 2,000 to 7,000, a huge increase from the thirty or so that had surreptitiously tried to join the peaceful march to the Frauenkirche in 1998, carrying candles and flowers.[82] As a point of entry into the fraught debates over how best to commemorate the air war, the Twitter stream reflects these differences in political affiliation and the battle over memory in Dresden. Hashtags serve as technical filtering devices to mark the differences between "us" and "them." As a social practice of identification, they help solidify bonds within the imagined community of activists linked in the struggle on the ground or following along via computer.[83]

In our datasets, #13Februar was the prime hashtag present in tweets during the events of February 12–19th between 2014 and 2019. It was employed by mainstream media outlets, citizen journalists, civil society, as well as activists across the political spectrum. Each yearly dataset contained roughly 1,500 tweets per year from each commemoration week under that hashtag; tweets revolved entirely around the day-to-day transactions unfolding on the ground in real-time, from the moment neo-Nazis were spotted arriving at the Neustadt train station, to the skirmishes with police in the street. Activists affiliated with the *Bund der Antifaschisten*, an organization founded in 1990 during the final years of the GDR, tweeted with #dresdennazifrei, though in far fewer numbers.[84] The anti-immigration, anti-Islam #pegida movement has its own hashtag together with the #AfD. These tweets numbered in the tens of thousands, although not all of them pertained to the events that week in Dresden. Taken together, these various datasets constitute several, intertwining networked publics, some explicitly organized around oppositionality, and others negotiating in the spaces between subaltern, radical, fringe, and mainstream discourses of memory, identity, and politics. Unlike the photobooks and news reportage of the early postwar, or even the commemorative strategies of the GDR state, what Neumayer and Valtysson call the "inherent functionalities of Twitter" suggest a different set of relations feeding into memory articulation and expression in the overlapping publics of the current moment, all as a result of Twitter's technical, epistolary, and multimodal qualities.[85]

Hashtags separate out neo-Nazis and the anti-immigration far-right from other oppositional groups. Despite this, the Twitter stream can still be jumbled and mixed. #13Februar, as an example, includes tweets from across the political spectrum (Figure 17). Within several minutes between 7:55 p.m. and 7:57 p.m. on February 12th, 2014, there were no fewer than four discernably different strands of tweets. Some, like the one retweeted by @M_Z_Bri, included a post by @RadioDresden that quoted mayor Helma Orosz as saying "Wir wollen in unserer Stadt keine Nazis!/We want no Nazis in our streets!" Others, like the queer, antifascist @KapselHipster wondered out loud why Nazis were allowed to roam unencumbered through the streets ("Ich frage mich nur warum die Nazis so ungehindert durch das Herz Dresdens marschieren dürfen?/ I ask myself only why are the Nazis allowed to march so unencumbered through the streets?") which they soon followed up by questioning more directly why police seemed to target Nazi opponents with more venom than the haters themselves. Meanwhile, @zukunftsstimmen retweeted jubilantly from the far-right @gedenkmarsch_dd account lauding the "over 500 patriotic Germans (*volksstreue Deutsche*) who made it to the yearly funereal [sic] march through the Altmarkt."[86]

Although not perfect, the use of hashtags, multimodal references, and links to outside sources are just some of the tools these Twitter users have at their disposal to draw attention to the memory politics of the far-right. There are other interventions as well, some playful and performative, others more strategic. One option is to spam another group's hashtag, spreading false information about the time of a demonstration or the number of attendees of a march. Spamming engages the platform's algorithms to create echo chamber effects, augmenting the ubiquity of some ideas over others, and giving a fringe idea a better chance of getting picked up by mainstream media. The simple act of retweeting can operationalize Twitter's machine learning capacity, leading it to drive certain ideas to other users. That this may be done anonymously shows the potential and pitfalls of Twitter's "interactive, dynamic and multi-modal characteristics," which can easily pave the way for ethno-cultural notions of platformed antagonism alongside more progressive hope for change.[87]

Sheet 2

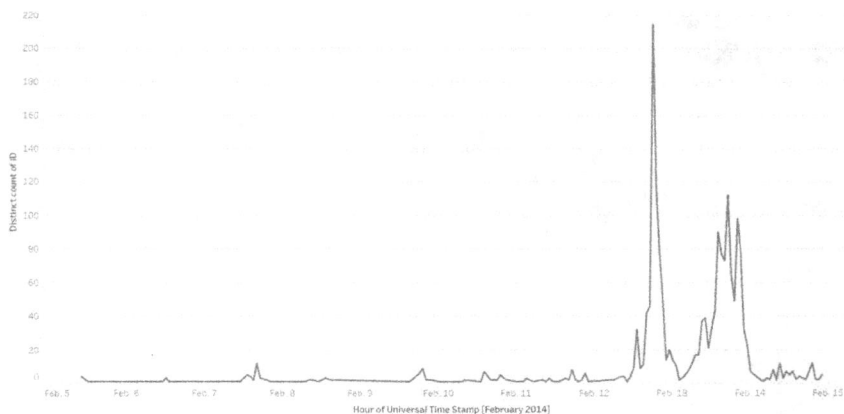

Figure 17 Tableau visualization of Twitter dataset for #13Februar, February 12, 2014.

This is one of the affordances that makes Twitter datasets particularly vexing to work with. One can never be entirely certain who is behind each handle, which is why it is helpful and important to envision each tweet as a micro-performance. Despite these challenges, visualization software presents opportunities to see patterns in the data stream. When a harvested Excel spreadsheet is fed through visualization software, one can parse the data several different ways. One is to view the dataset at a distance, for a time-series cluster of when the highest number of tweets was published. In 2014, for example, the largest spike in activity was on February 12th around 6 p.m., the usual time of the funeral fugue the night before the bombs dropped. Curiously, in 2015 there was second spike of tweets on February 15th at 4 p.m. (Figures 17 and 18). As we've argued, tweets do not stand on their own; much like the photobooks and commemorative debates of the past few decades, they must be read alongside the progression of mediatized memory. By going back over the tweets, and contrasting them with newspaper accounts and news stories, Twitter contributes to a more holistic sense of what specific issues mobilized bodies and minds during commemoration week.

In 2014, the spike was associated with the late afternoon neo-Nazi march. It was a chilly winter Wednesday. Radio Dresden, tweeting alongside the Mitteldeutscher Rundfunk (MDR) and the *Dresdner Neueste Nachrichten*, observed that over 11,000 people had formed a human chain to try and block access to the center of the city. Earlier in the day, they had also succeeded in stopping several hundred far-right activists from interrupting a service on perpetrator traces. The service was organized by the Dresden Nazifrei under the erstwhile stewardship of Silvio

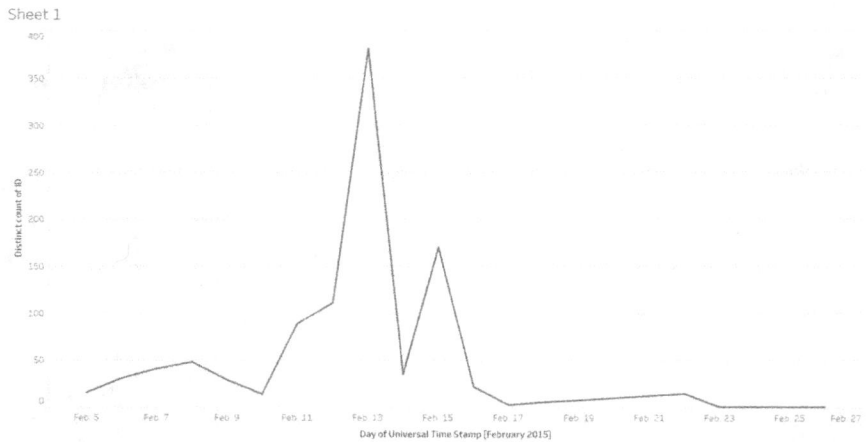

Figure 18 Tableau visualization of Twitter dataset for #13Februar, February 15, 2015.

Lang, the collection of left-affiliated activists ranging from Die Linke and the Green Party to the German Communist Party (Deutsche Kommunistische Partei), the Communist Action Collective (Kommunistisches Aktionsbündnis Dresden), and several independent other unaffiliated antifascist organizations.

Other tweets in the February 12th Twitter stream reflect the play by play of events as neo-Nazis moved through streets. An outraged classical music lover, @th_g did not mince words: "these right-wing imbeciles must leave my city right now!" Their *cri de coeur* must have hit a nerve. It was retweeted nineteen times that evening. @diefarbegrau asked the void "did someone hear a bomb at the Theaterplatz just now?" Others, like @asozialeoutput sent instructions to fellow activists to destroy leaflets passed around by march attendees, while @Motorick joked that neo-Nazis should take too many pills and save them all the trouble by overdosing.[88] Whatever the sentiment, the action of civil society was enough that night to put a stop to the planned march slated for the next day.[89] By using an ethnomethodological approach to the spikes in online activity, and then extrapolating outward to other tweets and news footage, we are able to measure the temperature of the crowd in terms of what onlookers deemed most significant. It also affords a glimpse into a disjunct simultaneity of perspectives and experiences, all expressed in and around the same moment in time.

Another way into the dataset is to search for the most active individual user based on follower count and reach, most visible tweets, and most significant retweets by number. By going back to the Excel sheets again, we can then review the original tweet content and examine any metadata attached to it, including geo-location, other media, and any images that may have been attached at the time. With enough material, spanning several years, we are also able to account for change across time, from one year's commemorations to the next, over a six-year span.

The platform's anonymity protocols allow for great fluidity and experimentalism among users, especially those who choose handles that do not reflect their real names. While news organizations, academics, politicians, and professionals tweet as themselves with reference to their institutions of affiliation, anonymous accounts are abundant on Twitter, and in this dataset this is no exception. Alongside posts from erstwhile Pirate Party member and Berlin city counsellor Oliver Helm (@riotbuddha) and Die Linke party member and the embattled future Minister-President of Thuringia @bodoramelow there are missives from @GroovyHistorian/@DresdenArt, who was one of many to retweet a photo of a quote by pacifist and anti-Nazi writer Erich Kästner emblazed on a flag outside the Semper Opera House ("An allem Unfug, der passiert, sind nicht etwa nur die Schuld, die ihn tun, sondern auch die, die ihn nicht verhindern./All the mischief that happens is the fault not only of those who commit it, but also of those who do not prevent it"). A surprising number of private persons' handles are silly and irreverent, like @Desaster77, @unzulaessig (@inadmissible) and @amusiert (@amused), which might certainly serve as covers for activism on the ground or simply reflect the long-standing internet practice of using idiosyncratic IDs that speak in opaque ways to a person's style or interest. This is indicative of the diversity of identities, political backgrounds, and views of those in our dataset, further compounding the complex memory discussions taking place online and on the ground in Dresden.

Secondary hashtags provide indication of a user's ideological moorings, which also often hinges on specific strands of memory. These hashtags are a kind of "searchable talk" that incorporates metadata into a post so that the online conversation can be more easily searchable and found.[90] It also further refines a post's meaning, making it visible in other timelines organized by theme. While both antifascists and pro-Nazi activists tweeted under #13Februar and #Dresden, a user's secondary hashtags further differentiate their posts along a political axis. Such tweets also highlight the memory framework that links personal experience of the march to the Dresden myth. #linkskriminellen (#leftistcriminals) is most obvious in its vitriol, while #thankyoubomberharris "is not anti-German, but a valid criticism of today's Germany," at least according to affirmed social democrat @TSmithRV, who tweeted with it in 2015. While posts in 2014 and 2015 show some evidence of right-leaning inflection, there is also a noticeable change in the lexicality of tweets in 2019 and 2020. In 2014, there were only occasional and oblique references to far-right qualifiers with very little traction in terms of reach or audience. By 2020, however, there is a palpable shift in the frequency and tone of hashtags trending toward the right. #propaganda and #bombenholocaust circulate alongside a sharp rise in tweets connected to the #AfD, which was nowhere in the tweet stream a few years prior, a testament to its meteoric rise in several eastern states and city councils after the migration wave of 2015.

The rise in importance of the AfD in stoking the flames of historical revisionism did not go unnoticed by the Antifa Research Team Dresden (ARTM), who waged a "solidarity-based" critique of Dresden Nazifrei citizen's initiative in 2020 for not putting a fine enough point on the far-right party's efforts to derail hard-won gains in the city's memorial policies.[91] In advance of the 75th anniversary of the bombing campaign, Dresden Nazi Frei called upon city denizens to resist, yet again, far-right attempts "to bring their rightist ideology into the street."[92] Reflecting long-festering fissures within the left, the ARTD wanted more of an emphasis on the nefarious ways in which the AfD locally had worked assiduously to disrupt the city's memorial politics, whether in agitating for a "worthy" memorial in the Altmarkt or in opening up the 2004 historical commissions' findings to new scrutiny. After all, the AfD had just invited local history buff Gerd Bürger to city hall for a discussion of the long-discredited notion that low flying American flyers had deliberately trained their guns on civilians.[93] These efforts at obfuscating the truth were not lost on several users, who took to Twitter to protest both the AfD's interventions and the inadequacies of mainstream politicians for allowing this misuse of process and history to continue unabated. En masse, users endorsed a tweet by the Dresden Cultural Bureau (@DBDresden) condemning the first year of the Heidefriedhof name reading ceremony which critics argued failed to differentiate between victims and perpetrators.[94] Indeed, the top five accounts with the most reach directed their ire at right-wing but also mainstream parties for allowing for equivalences to be made between victims (Figure 19).

One such tweet, by Michael Bergmann, from February 6, was retweeted over 100 times by February 13, 2020 (Figure 20). An independent journalist who tweets as @Bergmannblog while also writing for the left-leaning anti-German (anti-deutsch) magazine *Jungle World*, Bergmann reminded readers that it was city hall that had instituted the non-naming ceremony. He reserved the harshest words for the business-friendly chief organizer Free Democrat Holger Hase,

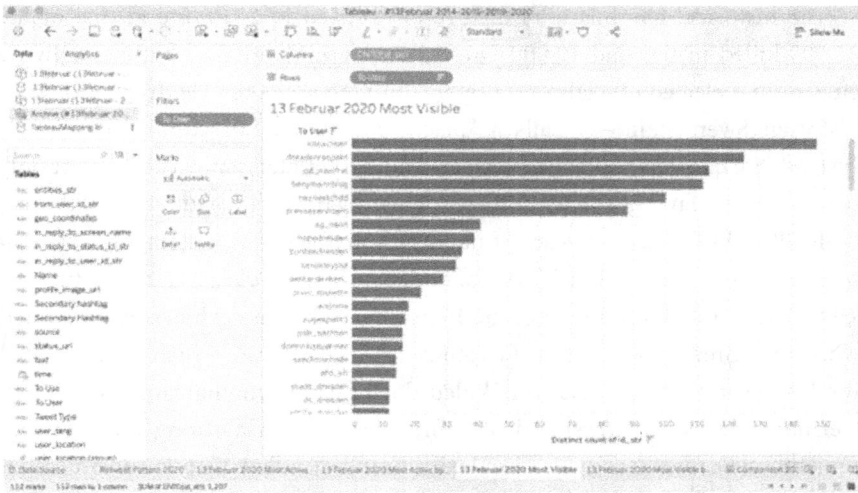

Figure 19 Tableau visualization of #13Februar dataset for Most Visible (aka tweets with the most reach), February 2020.

Michael Bergmann
@Bergmannblog

Am #13Februar sollen Namen von Bombentoten in #Dresden verlesen werden.Darunter zahlreiche NS-Täter,die zu Opfern gemacht werden.Der Hauptorganisator, Holger Hase, ist #FDP-Kreischef.Sein Kreisverband gratuliert #Kemmerich u wünscht ihm Glück u Kraft. #justsayin #dd1302

♡ 43   3:34 AM - Feb 6, 2020   ⓘ

💬 41 people are talking about this   ＞

Figure 20 Screen capture of tweet from @Bergmannblog from February 6, 2020.

whose district organization, Bergmann pointed out, had also sent well wishes to Thuringia's bumbling Thomas Kemmerich, who at the time of the tweet was amidst a scandal for opting to share power and shake hands with the AfD's hard right Holocaust minimizer Björn Höcke. Interesting to note here is that Twitter does not supersede traditional forms of memory making via print or news media, but rather it augments it.

The historical commission's final report, tabled in 2010, found that of the 25,000 killed in the raid 19,000 Dresdeners were identifiable by name, giving citizens and elected officials every opportunity to make the Heidefriedhof what historian Swen Steinberg calls a "place of learning not commemoration."[95] Instead, the choice to go ahead with an undifferentiated name reading not only played into the far-right's agenda by perpetuating the myth of universal suffering, it also flew in the face of years of nuanced, careful public history projects that opened up the memorial field to more nuance. The simple act of retweeting the @DBDresden announcement of the 19 Namen/19 Names exhibition co-curated with the Green Party-affiliated-Heinrich-Böll-Stiftung, which documented the lives of nineteen Dresdeners killed during the bombing campaign—Jews, Germans, forced laborers, and of course Nazis—sent a strong message that remembrance must recognize complexity. As independent historian and member of the *AutorInnenkollektiv Loukanikos* Henning Fischer said in an interview with *Die Zeit*, "memory must be like pain, it can't be calming."[96]

Time and Space

Tweets, and the memories they help construct, travel. They conjure new, platform-specific models for how to think about the air war and how it might be experienced both in real time on the Twitter scroll and as a representation of the recent past in the public sphere.[97] Tweets challenge the static, bounded, and knowable nature of the past via the traditional archive through the "residual abundance" of texts, the sheer mass of messages, hashtags, and hyperlinks that build on and extend collective frames of action across physical, digital, imaginary, and material spaces.[98] Social-technological interventions of this sort, the use of mobile devices, and the special geo-spatial communicative flows they instantiate turn everyday people into memory entrepreneurs, and common city streets into stages of memory contestation and construction. Locative media— media used to reference real places—shapes the stances of civil society, its practices, and its identities. It also helps create living archives as people tweet and post through their own filter what they believe should make up both the imaginative and physical memorial terrain of contemporary Dresden.[99] These interpretations collide with their own identities as civilians and protesters alike. As seen in the previous section, the memorial landscape of Dresden is not solely located within the confines of the city itself. Rather, the struggle over city space during commemoration week is a battle waged online and offline, across media both old and new, on and across different platforms.[100] Dresden's cityscape facilitates the merging of analog and digital protest and media ecologies, from shouting into a megaphone, performing a sit in to tweeting with a hyperlink to a news story, YouTube video, or photo. Commemoration week and its digital presence raises questions about who should govern and enforce the meaning of public, commemorative spaces within a shifting array of hyperconnected social and media practices that, by their very nature, remake and remodel relationships of remembering and forgetting. But, it is also a textbook example of the tensions at work in the digital networked environment where memory is made and remade "on the fly."[101] While digital practices bring new voices into view, shaking up older, more monolithic memorial and archival traditions and injecting the personal and everyday into questions of public importance, mediatized memory's future orientation, flux, and impermanence also bring uncertainties alongside innovation, especially in a media field where the circulation, storage, and veracity of digital communication are unstable, uncertain, and fleeting.

The single most important way in which the Twitter stream challenges existing memory formations is in re-territorializing Dresden's memory space. This combination of discursive and spatial reordering is a shared feature of left and right identified users, suggesting the power of Twitter in materializing vernacular forms of memory making. Not only do tweets speak to alternative sites of memory, shifting attention away from the Frauenkirche and Heidefriedhof to sites of perpetration and everyday encounters, but they also move memorialization away from past practices, such as wreath-laying and name lists, toward new ones, such as walking tours, historically informed tweets, links to news stories, and observations from the protest arena. Both forms of memorialization, old and new, have gained meaning through complex webs of communication and debate over time. Nor are they easily separated from one another; older forms of commemoration overlap with newer efforts to broaden memorial culture, and to debunk the "victim mythology" that activists claim re-centers innocence instead of the history of genocide. In this way, memorialization in the age of social media continues to build upon prior memory-making practices, rather than abandon them altogether. Differences exist in how users themselves politicize tweets, how they tap into the platform's affordances to make claims about the air war and how it should best be remembered. We see this at work in the spatial and temporal attributes of tweets, and the way algorithms shape outreach.

Geo-specific data is discernable through metadata. Metadata (data about data) is a set of descriptors and coordinates that refer to other data within a dataset like authorship, location, attributes, hyperlinks, property, and other relevant schemata. Although only 1–2 percent of location data might reliably relate to the actual place of a user, this nevertheless provides a useful index of self-characterization in relation to an event.[102] Since the Mumbai terrorist attack and Iran Uprising in 2009, Twitter dismantled its coordinate data function and put geo-referencing in the hands of users to allay concerns of privacy and surveillance. Of course, IP addresses are geo-markers of a different sort, so users are not entirely, ever, off-grid unless they take extra steps to mask location, but this is a level of analysis beyond the reach of most researchers.[103] Twitter geo-coordinates are mineable, but they are fully in the hands of the user who can set their own location parameters as they see fit. Geo-spatial references might also include references to a physical place. So, when a user mentions a street name, public square, or city, this too is swept up in the data stream. In other words, geo-data is publicly available at the discretion of the user. It grounds a tweet in a material location that is itself a constructed reality. This nevertheless provides an interesting snapshot into how users frame their purpose and activity online.

Sometimes, what goes unmentioned is the most illuminating. In 2015, the 70th anniversary of the aerial attacks, very few users in the #pegida and #AfD datasets harvested during the marching season mention Dresden by name even though the movement itself originated there not six months earlier.[104] A survey of tweets shows that February 13–15th was less significant than other days in the anti-immigration protest calendar that year (Figure 21). In 2015, the issue of relevance was a February 28th anti-Pegida march in Newcastle, UK, ostensibly because it had held the promise of expanding the movement beyond the continent. Instead of growing their numbers, the protest drew over 2,000 counter-protestors.[105] How might we explain this? Research reports from media interest groups suggest that Twitter had yet to establish itself as the go-to platform for #pegida, whose organizers gravitated initially to Facebook in the early months after its founding in October 2014.[106] Of those who did make reference to the Dresden anniversary, some, like @Pegidizer, one of the most prolific, tweeted links to news articles depicting the commemoration ceremonies as glossing over the existence of perpetrators among the honored dead.[107] This suggests that the hashtags #13Februar and #DresdenNaziFrei captured the bulk of tweets from day-to-day events on the ground, while the hashtags #pegida and #AfD were largely directed toward the broader issues of immigration and Islam in Germany and Europe. It also demonstrates that although tweets might be used to disrupt the communication and framing practices of opponents, by and large users remain siloed in their selection of hashtags and the partisan conversations these housed.

Tweets Over Time 2015

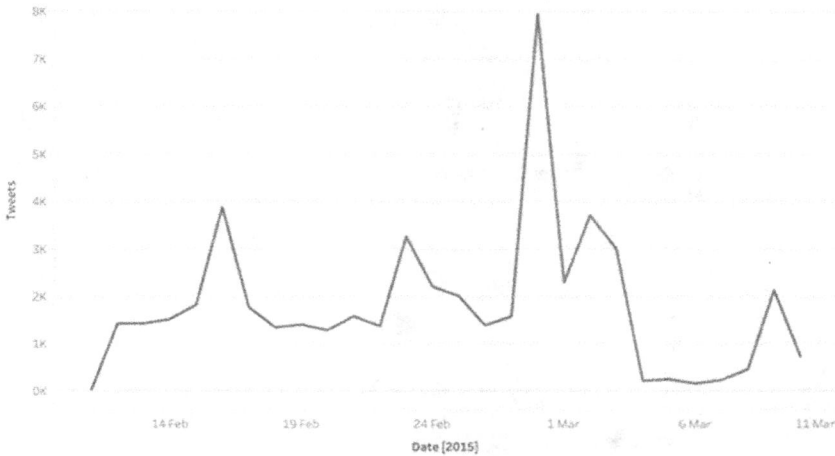

Figure 21 Tableau visualization of Tweets over Time #Pegida dataset 2015.

Beyond measuring the frequency of tweets, whether truth or invention, geo-spatial metadata provides a window into the translocal, national, and transnational character of memory-making efforts via Twitter. The modification of locational data is a qualitative intervention in the cultural and connective memory of the city, which might also be mapped and mined for change over time. As an example, in 2014, many users in #13Februar self-identified as coming from Dresden and Saxony. Berlin and Leipzig were well-represented in the dataset, as were occasional western German cities (see Figures 22 and 23).

However, users also played with place settings, whether as a matter of how they chose to present themselves online generally, or as an act of subterfuge. Some were from "deine und meine Heimat" (your homeland and mine), Earth, and Elbflorenz (Florence on the Elbe). One user's location was notably "im Bett" (in bed), while another lamented being stuck at home ("immer noch zu Hause"). While some users claimed to come from the four corners of the globe, including Tokyo, Toronto, Argentina, Peru, and Antarctica, others were only to be found wistfully "somewhere over the rainbow." One Twitterer was fortunate enough to occupy the former Hohenzollern palace in Berlin ("Schlossplatz 5 in Berlin). Similar patterns played out in the other intervening years. In the 2020 #13Februar dataset, which captured conversations during the 75th anniversary of the bombing, alongside even more denizens of planet earth, a few self-identifiers hinted at a rise in pessimism with locations like "Dresden, failed

Location 2014

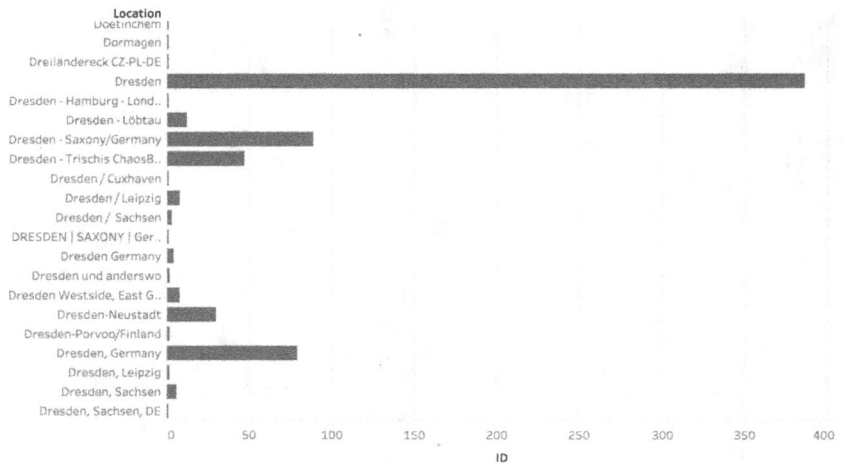

Location

Doetinchem	
Dormagen	
Dreiländereck CZ-PL-DE	
Dresden	
Dresden - Hamburg - Lond..	
Dresden - Löbtau	
Dresden - Saxony/Germany	
Dresden - Trischis ChaosB..	
Dresden / Cuxhaven	
Dresden / Leipzig	
Dresden / Sachsen	
DRESDEN	SAXONY	Ger..	
Dresden Germany	
Dresden und anderswo	
Dresden Westside, East G..	
Dresden-Neustadt	
Dresden-Porvoo/Finland	
Dresden, Germany	
Dresden, Leipzig	
Dresden, Sachsen	
Dresden, Sachsen, DE	

ID: 0   50   100   150   200   250   300   350   400

Location 2020

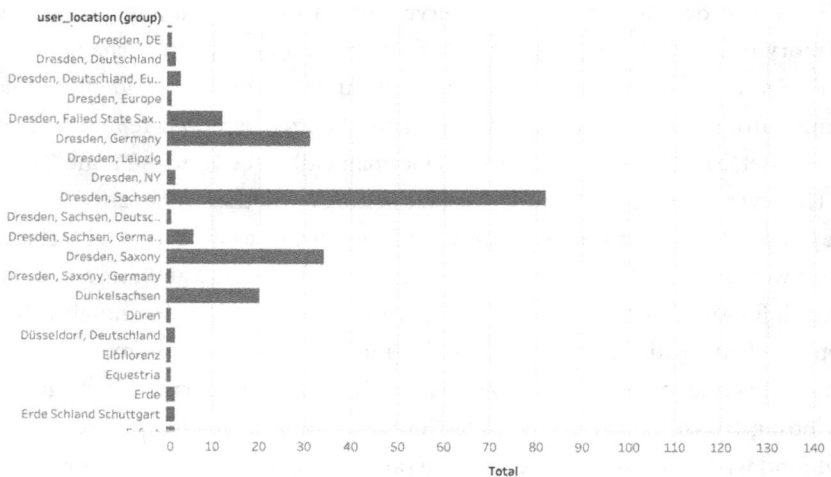

user_location (group)

Dresden, DE	
Dresden, Deutschland	
Dresden, Deutschland, Eu..	
Dresden, Europe	
Dresden, Failed State Sax..	
Dresden, Germany	
Dresden, Leipzig	
Dresden, NY	
Dresden, Sachsen	
Dresden, Sachsen, Deutsc..	
Dresden, Sachsen, Germa..	
Dresden, Saxony	
Dresden, Saxony, Germany	
Dunkelsachsen	
Düren	
Düsseldorf, Deutschland	
Elbflorenz	
Equestria	
Erde	
Erde Schland Schuttgart	

Total: 0   10   20   30   40   50   60   70   80   90   100   110   120   130   140

Figures 22 and 23 Twitter dataset #13Februar, Tableau Visualization, 2014 and 2020.

state Saxony" and "Dark Saxony" entering into the geo-locational data stream. Curiously, there were also fewer far-flung places. Visualization software allows us to see differences between user groups. Those who opted to tweet under the hashtags #13Februar and #DresdenNaziFrei overwhelmingly identified using German place markers, while datasets harvested for #pegida during the same week of commemorations either suggest users installed VPN to disrupt locational signaling, or interest was indeed generated beyond Germany.

This is especially noticeable in the 2020 dataset, where locational data for #pegida is even more playful, campy, and dubious, hinting perhaps at the radicalization of the organization, aspects of which have earned the focus of interest of the Ministry for the Protection of the Constitution.[108] While locational data is a shared fiction, it peels back the curtain and allows a peek into how individuals craft their public selves. Dresden is clearly a translocal and transnational site of memory, both in traditional and new media—especially among adherents of the global far right but also to European notions of integration—tweets from those identifying left of center are more local in character, reflecting German and Dresden-specific struggles over commemoration.

Not only do tweets serve as another way to conceptualize the spatial and discursive field of memory around the yearly events, but they also lay claim to new spaces and places of violence, suffering, and perpetration. Like the Stolpersteine ("stumbling stone") project, which asks wanderers to pause over shiny golden cobblestone references to those who once lived in these apartment blocks but perished in the Holocaust, tweets call to re-territorialize neighborhood city spaces, and to inject personal perspectives and experiences into more monolithic forms of remembering.[109] They often show evidence of a deep sense of reckoning with the past. In 2015, several users lauded the city's decision to do away with the wreath laying ceremony at the Heidefriedhof, which a few noted was one vestige of GDR times best allocated to history.[110] That year's Twitterstream was particularly steeped in historical references, with several comments serving as a kind of *Vergangenheitsaufarbeitung* or coming to terms with the past, on both ends of the political spectrum. Some like @maulheldin, an avowed AfD supporter, saw the end of the ceremony as a break from history, and as such, a dangerous precedent. Other users, like the communications department of the Rosa Luxemburg Foundation (closely linked to the German Left Party (die Linke), a mix of German Democratic Republic era politicians and radical progressives) asked whether federal president Joachim Gauck, scheduled to speak in the Frauenskirche memorial assembly, was also going to speak to the role of the Saxon church in supporting the Nazis. Twitter became a place where critics might engage simultaneously with local and national memory formations.

In addition to the deployment of Twitter as a space for coming to terms with the past, there is also a palpable difference in constituents shaping the memory field the 2014 and 2020 streams. In 2014, the accounts with the most impact based on number of tweets and size of followers belonged to established media outlets (@Tagezwitscher, the Twitter arm of *die Tageszeitung,* @RadioDresden, and @mdr_online, for *Mitteldeutscher Rundfunk* or central German radio) confirming what Neumayer, Rossi, and Karlsson have shown about the role of media outlets in shaping protest frames online.[111] A mix of self-identified progressive, anarchist, pirate, and antifascist users like Green party delegate @JanAlbrecht, @FibsFreitag, and @Piratantifa rounded out the mix. By 2020, the top five most influential users were affirmed antifascist organizations like @DresdenNaziFrei, @DresdenRespekt, @Naziwatch, and @bergmannblog, with the Kulturburo Sachsen the only state institution. Since their founding in 2001, their purpose has been to serve as a mobile advisory bureau, promoting democracy.[112] In 2014, news outlets governed the mediatized memory landscape; by 2020, there was a palpable shift away from mainstream media toward civil society. While this might suggest that vernacular voices have enjoyed a victory in terms of how commemoration is framed within the city, even citizen tweets link to news stories as a citational way of underscoring legitimacy, suggesting that everyday people might not recognize their actions as being contextualized historically. It also speaks to the sense of urgency among these groups in tackling the challenge of the right and what they view is the city and state's appeasement of these forces whether in trading on what Dresden Nazifrei called in an October 2019 blog post "the eternal victim fable."[113]

As much as tweets conjure new spatialized memory formations in the translocal city, they also play with time. It is obvious that memorial spaces serve as crystallization points of memory and identity.[114] Less well-understood is that they are also meditations on time itself, specifically on the role of the past in shaping the present. Historians have long debated the differences between history and memory, with historians claiming distance through time as one of the defining markers of the discipline.[115] Different temporal structures of time, according to Gabrielle Spiegel, are the reasons history and memory should be kept apart. Memory can never do the work of history, because it refuses "to keep the past in the past."[116] While this sentiment holds weight in some parts of the field, increasingly scholars have questioned the "pastness" of the past, and the presumption that there is a singular flow of time, and that history, based around the notion of distance in time is somehow more truthful and pristine than memory, which is sullied by subjective witnessing.[117] The memory boom of the 1990s onward, with its emphasis on reparations for past injustices, begun with recognition of Holocaust crimes and extended into the twentieth century. These discussions of colonial and racist violence raised important questions about the presumptive break between past, present, and future. The presumptive power of history to deal objectively with the past also turns on the notion of progress, that past injustices, properly processed will lead to reparative futures. But as Chris Lorenz argues, with progress ever increasingly elusive in a world haunted by historical wounds, the past might never truly recede.[118] As long as past injustices continue to bubble up into the present, a hard and fast distinction between history and memory might remain elusive.

Conclusion

Connective memory complicates the ways in which historians have understood how memory functions. Although Pierre Nora charted new ground when he argued that whether memory was embodied in monuments, memorials, or even in city space, each generation makes and remakes anew the significance of these sites to contemporary society.[119] Nora recognized that memories are fluid, adaptive, changing, and multiple. They only become affixed, at select moments in time, to memory markers, usually physical spaces, that provide reference points for national and transnational conversation. Until the end of the Cold War upended cohesive memorial traditions, scholars like Aleida Assman argue that past, present, and future were more or less successfully united in the cultural memory landscape of an integrated Europe, with the history of the Holocaust (more so in the West than the East) serving as a warning against the perils of forgetting. Any belief in the inevitable march toward progress has been challenged by illiberalism and authoritarian regimes.[120] It has also been aided by the rise of network society where the uneven, synergistic force of globalization has reconfigured the experience and symbolic meaning of time and territory.[121] Networked individualism and self-curation have fractured the memory field, resulting in new, if splintered, spatial-temporal moorings of shared cultural reference points.[122] Adding the extra layer of mediatization into the mix, and the affordances of platform and algorithmic curation itself, we see that a territorialized sense of memory is tricky in the era of the multitude when in the digital environment of connective publics, networked memories are "all over the place, scattered yet simultaneous" with multiple beginnings and ends.[123]

Social media adds a new layer to long-standing debates around history and memory. While connectivity has certainly changed the state of play, it has not done away with earlier media and technological interventions and their role in shaping space, time, and experience. As much as Nora shattered the idea of a singular national consciousness organized around sites of memory, he still upheld the importance of anniversaries in commemoration, and we see that even in the era of mediatized Dresden marches, as with the tweet in Figure 24 from the Radio Dresden radio station that signals the yearly ringing of cathedral bells. Here, tweets might serve as a bridge to the putatively authentic experiences of the first night of bombing (Figure 24).[124]

Although the commemorations are calibrated to mirror the moments when bombers flew overhead, there is also a non-linear, neoteric, pluralization of timescapes in the Twitter stream that ushers in different forms of memorialization and protest.[125] One modality of time is connected to bourgeois civic space, wedded to the chronologies of work, labor, and consumption.[126] There is protest time, an intermedial amalgam of analog and digital framing that structures online activity and off.[127] There is connective time, which includes the various time series when the tweets themselves are typed into mobile technology and retweeted, which may be both simultaneous and non-simultaneous, depending on when they are issued, captured, archived, and reviewed. And there is network time and the patterns and predilections of the platform itself, which when subjected to visualization, showcase peak moments of user engagement and audience reach. In other words, the yearly commemorations showcase different, overlapping, rhythms of remembrance that sometimes coexist, while other times coming into conflict with established modes of memory.[128]

Radio Dresden ☑ @RadioDresden · Feb 13, 2014
Der emotionalste Moment heute: ab 21.45 Uhr läuten alle Glocken in #Dresden. 22.00 Uhr Nacht **der** Stille in **der** Frauenkirche. #13februar

♡   ↻ 10   ♡ 5   ⬆

Figure 24 Tweet by Radio Dresden about the ringing of the bells at the moment the first round of bombs dropped.

Our Twitter datasets reveal that these different rhythms can have the effect of reinforcing established memory formations, while at other times laying claim to new ways of acknowledging and working through the fraught history of the air war. Attention to the platform affordances of Twitter and its distinctive role in the mediatization of connective memory affords new insight into the changing course of commemoration in a fraught space like Dresden.

"Private Spaces/Public Interest: Facebook in the Digital Public Sphere"

In 2011, the UK-based nonpartisan think-tank Demos published a pamphlet on social media supporters of populist extremist parties across Europe. As part of its mandate to analyze the workings of digital technology as a tool of democracy, researchers opted to limit the scope to Facebook. What they found surprised them. Where nefarious ideas once lurked on the fringes of the dark web, on 4chan, 8chan, and Telegram, now far-right advocates appeared to be public facing on the platform, espousing their ideas brazenly and using the network for recruitment. Curiously, the tenor of the report was optimistic. At least the augmented presence of far-right voices online, they argued, had not translated into success at the ballot box.[1] In the wake of Brexit and its corrosive nativism, the election of Donald Trump, and the ascendance of nationalist governments in Eastern Europe, we would be hard-pressed to make similar arguments today. In a sense, the events of recent years have proven our point, that social media has the power to shape connective memory and historical consciousness, but not always in the best possible way. By drawing on and extending collective sentiment, it can have significant bearing on offline events, for better—but as these events also show sometimes also for worse.

This chapter continues with the question of the digitally mediated public sphere and asks how we might use Facebook to better understand populist impulses online and the antiracist activism that has mobilized against it. It explores the ways in which Facebook functions as part of a global participatory public, where, in Germany, broad-based if mediated communication has raised specters of far-right nationalism. It is a space where selves are formed, consent and support are manufactured, and motives for social action are framed, contested, and spread. Frequently, as we will see here, history plays a key role, especially in how users across the political spectrum think about and lay claim to a sense of the past to justify their platform in the present. A highly charged discursive environment, the digital public sphere needs to be thought about differently than conventionally constituted spaces of deliberative democracy, especially in relation to memory.[2] But how do we understand its function on its own terms and in comparison to other forms of communication and public dialogue? Corporate boosters promote platforms, devising community standards in lieu of regulating content, but how have scholars, activists, and NGOs navigated this terrain? As we have argued in this book, although media and communications scholars, sociologists, and historians have analyzed the relationship of new forms of discourse on class and identity formation, status, and authority, in the current terrain activist organizations, groups, and public intellectuals have played a considerable role both as participants in and analysts of social media. What can we learn from the actions of those battling hate in targeted campaigns? And what role does memory play in their actions?

As we have argued, any analysis of connective memory must consider vernacular knowledge producers and the way in which online communities help shape what circulates as fact, fiction, and even government policy in on- and offline realms. In places like Germany, where nativist parties have gained recognition at the ballot box in the wake of high-profile policies on migration, history, and memory of the nation's past are not an insignificant part of the discussion about how to consider social media as an arena of civic consciousness and direct action. As we will see, government did not set the agenda; antiracist NGOs led the charge. They commissioned studies of nationalist tropes in online discussion, provided datasets to scholars seeking to analyze their role in precipitating violence, and created programming for schools and youth organizations on how to counter hate speech online to buttress and protect democratic forms of discussion and debate. The prime motivator is the special responsibility Germans believe themselves to bear for meeting this challenge given the calamity of mid-twentieth-century history and how it shaped the legacy of two German states.[3] Lest there be any doubt, the stakes remain high. How this history is remembered online, how it animates contemporary government policy, opposition campaigns, and everyday acts of civil courage and opposition provides a poignant example of the precarious place of democratic expression in a mediatized environment.

Social media may provide a space where democratic communication forms are created, contested, and refined, but what role do the specific platforms play in how memory is evoked and instrumentalized in the service of strengthening the conditions of expression? As we will see here, when compared to other social media platforms, Facebook differs in critical ways. It remains a place where individual and collective users draw on and build shared as well as collective stories about the memory of the Third Reich. But Facebook-specific memory ecologies as Andrew Hoskins has called them—the different archival and representational strategies users use to narrate the "what, how, why and when of remembering and forgetting"—have significant bearing not just on how the crimes of midcentury are remembered in an age of post-memory but for how they function as sites of discussion and debate themselves around the scope and scale of responsibility and suffering and how best to represent democratic discourse in the diverse media environments of the current age.[4] How different is Facebook conversation from previous media forms, including the forms of communication it enables, and the memories generated and circumscribed there? How useful are mediatized memories in how the lessons of the Holocaust are made and remade, sometimes, in the service of "never forgetting" and other times in support of more nefarious forms of collective identity and action? How might we understand the intensity of the emotions generated there? Do they translate into real world action? To get at these questions, the chapter centers on three interrelated issues: the distinctiveness of networked publics in how historical consciousness manifests, specifically how online conversation relates to the fashioning of group identity, how discussion among users reinforces particular memory formations about the horror of Nazi crimes, and what these may tell us about the distinctiveness of the digital public sphere as an imperfect kind of *lieu de mémoire* of remembering and also forgetting certain aspects of the past.[5] It focuses on select Facebook group and discussion pages and evaluates the extent to which they create the conditions for what memory scholars see as cultural, communicative, and travelling memory, or whether an approach which centers the mediated, networked nature of online memory work is more apposite.[6] Our argument is that new media technologies must be taken seriously as essential—if circumscribed and fraught—spheres of debate that hold the potential to provide important new avenues of communicative action about the past and present.

Mediated Memories

As we've shown, new media technologies have led to the growth of new and diverse memory communities. On the one hand, this has helped democratize how the lessons of the Holocaust have been remembered and operationalized insofar as more and more members of society have gained access to the tools of debate and structure their ideas in public fora for purposes of mass consumption.[7]

On the other, it presents significant challenges for how to regulate what counts as fact and fiction in the public realm. These new memory entrepreneurs have shaped how public institutions like museums present history to their audience, using social media to bolster campaigns for a more ethical, responsible history of colonialism, for example, or the repatriation of artifacts to home countries. In this sense, civic activism helps spur new dialogue over difficult histories, allowing us to capture, catch, and recognize "fleeting memories."[8] Civic intervention of a more nefarious sort in the form of populist parties and organizations has changed the language of debate itself in newspaper editorials, in public policy, and on the floor of the *Bundestag* itself. This is not without its own share of problems; yet it need not be viewed solely as undermining truth about the past. The internet has not destroyed traditional forms of remembering.[9] So too, it is a stretch to say it promotes the banalization of history.[10] Rather, it has created new knowledge producers whose entry into the field forces us to ask new questions of the role of mediation, authority, and expertise in how history and memory are transmitted into policy and practice.

Here, too, as we have shown, this is not just a discursive performance. There is an embodied, real-world, spatial-temporal component as well.[11] The university lecture hall, the academic conference, and the peer-reviewed publication no longer dominate as the places where scholarship meets the public. Now, through a click of a mouse, and the sharing of a post, new actors interpolate with the past and with each other in a broad diversity of settings. Facebook does not just alter where and how users encounter historical events and arguments, but also helps organize how users experience historical time by archiving engagements with the past alongside events, birthdays, anniversaries, and family photography, and creating new relationships to self, other, and personal as well as collective pasts.[12] What is needed is an analysis of what emotions they stir and how this, too, functions as part of the networked public sphere. The absence of the Facebook Application Programming Interface (API), which before 2018 allowed researchers to harvest data with R so that it could be analyzed through sentiment analysis, requires that we assess our data through Facebook's own in-house analytics service. This allows us to explore who is using the platform, interrogate which causes garner support, and the emotional reactions evoked by participation. Our focus then shifts more directly to a series of anti-Nazi group initiatives to explore how users mobilize an opposition to these groups. This analysis unveils how the memory of war and genocide structures these individuals' own participation in the contemporary memory landscape.

Old and New

As with most media forms, Facebook contains a mix of old and new technologies. It began its life as a clever remediation of a paper catalogue of students and their photos like the one which Ivy League American schools had distributed to freshmen to help break through the anonymity of university life. Mark Zuckerberg took inspiration from these so-named "face books" and launched his online platform in 2004, together with fellow Harvard students Chris Hughes and Dustin Moskovitz. Initially limited to college students, not two years later it would be open to the world. Less well known is the fact that Facebook also adopted features from the 1970s "slam books"—spiral notebooks where junior high school students jotted down their friends' favorite quotes, bands, and movies. Indeed, Facebook did not come out of nowhere. It blended existing offline student and college subcultures with the possibilities of infinite, digitized network of friends and acquaintances.[13] Despite the amorphous nature of the platform, connecting old friends and fresh acquaintances, Facebook cut through the anonymity of the old-style Bulletin Boards or BBSs through its jaunty mix of images and text, personal stories, likes, and news. Encouraging users to capture their mood, to re-establish ties, mark birthdays and anniversaries, "like" favorite books and document outings, it played into a sense of nostalgia for "old times" and frustration with the anonymity of our quick-paced, everyday lives. Facebook provided a framework—part scrapbook, part archive—for how people might plot out, celebrate, and commemorate relationships, emotions, and intimacies. Overwhelmingly, people availed themselves of the opportunity. In 2005, when the Pew Research Center started tracking social media use, only 5 percent of American adults used one of the various platforms; today, over 2 billion people the world over has memberships to Facebook with 68 percent of Americans using it at any one time. The majority have a college education and fall into the age groups of eighteen to twenty-nine and thirty to forty-nine. At least in the United States, where we have the best data, Facebook use cuts across race, class, and gender. It truly represents a cross-section of society.[14]

While not entirely original, social online interaction was indeed transformative. It re-connected family and friends virtually, providing creative ways of sustaining bonds of intimacy over space and time. It allowed people to organize public pages and private groups, creating new public spheres of debate and the dissemination of ideas, and it collapsed time as people posted pictures of their teenaged selves or wedding photos alongside contemporary images of outings, parties, and events. Scholars have long noted how advances in technology heralded changes in spatial and temporal awareness. Changes in media technology have always had an impact in how social relationships are structured and experienced.[15] As the cultural historian of modernity Henri Lefebvre once noted, the media not only occupies days, but it also literally makes them.[16]

During the shift to industrial capitalism, urbanization, mass transportation, and the factory system, new technologies occasioned new forms of self-comportment and regulation to guide people through their increasingly routinized day. Mechanization challenged the Newtonian notion that time was something fixed, ordered, and external to social structures.[17] The quickened pace of modernity and the scientific management of the social world meant that time evolved into something layered and overlapping. Personal photography, diaries, clocks, calendars, even transit schedules brought with them huge perceptual changes in how people understood leisure and work time, the separation of the city and the countryside, and the rhythms and pace of everyday life.[18] The advent of mass media provided another case in point. Radio and television programming introduced the notion of simultaneity between public and private time. Scheduled programs meant the listener/viewer divided their days, months, and years around media offerings while news-programming, speeches, and special reports introduced common moments of shared national interests and concerns. Digital media took this multi-perceptual sense of time a step further still, monetizing the experience with the hope of marrying user activity online with profit making off.[19]

It is not coincidental that the commodification of space, time, and emotion through corporate control over mass media would be one of the major changes that Jürgen Habermas claims was heralded by the structural transformation of the public sphere from its origins in the eighteenth century through to modern age.[20] In his path-breaking analysis, grounded in the era of print-making, coffee shops and salons and the rise of the bourgeoisie, he argued that while communication networks once served the purpose of robust and open debate, market control meant modern media was always already sullied. There are good reasons why Habermas failed to appreciate the potential of mass media in transmitting progressive and critical forms of knowledge alongside the possibility for manipulation and promotion of problematic standpoints. Owing to the book's ideological moorings, linked as it was to the Frankfurt School's long-standing antipathy toward mass culture, it is far from surprising that Habermas emphasized technology's more coercive function, how it accentuates power differences and social control over freedom of address. Of course, not everyone espoused Habermas's assessment of the inability of mass media to radically transform the public sphere. Earlier in the century, Bertolt Brecht and Walter Benjamin saw much potential in what was then the new media of the day—particularly film and radio—and urged radical intellectuals to find creative new ways to "refunction" them as instruments of societal transformation.[21]

It almost looked as though Habermas had come around in 2006. In an oft-cited footnote to an article in *Communication Theory* on political communication in the digital age, he admitted that "the Internet has certainly re-activated the grassroots of an egalitarian public of writers and readers." However, the diffuse nature of the conversation, peppered throughout chat rooms, in social media, and in the comments pages of online newspapers has fragmented any would be mass audience into "a huge number of isolated issue publics."[22] The trouble with digitally mediated discourse is not just that it increased the number of voices in the mix, diluting opportunities for collective action, but the actual mode and operation of conversation in these networked publics "contributes independently to the diffuse alienation of citizens from politics."[23] How increased participation in alternative public spheres translates into alienation is left for the reader to figure out, but the takeaway is clear: the independent actions of the average person could never succeed in democratically transforming media, technology, and everyday life in such a way as to harness the power of communicative action in favor of social, technological, and political change. Habermas was not talking about 2018 reports that Facebook deliberately harvests and sells intimate user data, claims made in the wake of the Russian vote tampering probe which call into question the platform's usefulness as a democratic space. Nor was he referencing the literature on algorithmic curation, ever-increasingly personalized content, selective exposure to difficult ideas, filter bubbles, and echo chambers, which has questioned the free circulation of ideas online.[24] More important for his critique of electronic media was its ability to appeal to emotions, which inhibits online conversations from ever truly avoiding possible ideological exploitation. Communicative rationality, the essence of the bourgeois public sphere both created and sustained by print media in Habermas's formulation, is the purest form of civic dialogue, one that, pointed out by critics, was limited to narrow and select examples of past civic engagement.[25]

The current age of "fake news" and misinformation seems to confirm this reading. But even more troubling than the assault on conventional journalism, to say nothing of truth, knowledge, and expertise is the revelation that data collection and influence peddling are Facebook's stock and trade—and have been for some time now. Well before the Cambridge Analytica scandal ushered forth suggestions of a weaponized social mediascape with connections to white nationalists, antisemites, and the champion of the alt-right Steve Bannon, Facebook had weathered accusations of monetizing user privacy data. First there was the Beacon scandal in 2007, where contacts were automatically sent updates on purchases made through third-party sites, showcasing ways in which the site had allowed user data to be mined out for use in marketing algorithms. Then there were adjustments to user privacy controls, and finally psychometric testing apps like myPersonality culled user accounts for demographic, political, and situational data, with their consent, for use in academic research.[26] What is striking about these developments is not the extent to which privacy is breached—although that in and of itself is nothing short of shocking—but the involvement of users themselves in willingly turning over the controls to marketers, advertisers, information app makers, and now, security firms and influence peddlers. While it might be sobering to think that data gathering has been around since the invention of the punch card in the late nineteenth century, and of course, advertising execs have long understood the power of psychological profiling, there does seem to be a qualitative difference in this age of surveillance capitalism, whether the quickness of the pace or the extent of third-party collusion.[27] To some extent, this is Facebook's double bind: users pay for the breach in personal security through the illusion of control over shared intimacies. To riff on a *Time Magazine* article in 2010, the feelings we experience on Facebook may be heartfelt, but the data we are providing feed a bottom line.[28] Our desire for likes, for views, and for exposure has fueled and been fueled by corporate interest in building an "expository society" that brings with it new, convenient forms of surveillance, from which corporations and state interests benefit.[29] As sociologist Wolfgang Sofsky put it more directly in a manifesto written around the same time as the first wave of Facebook scandals, technology is not entirely to blame; rather, it is "the vulgar quest for short-lived prominence (that) is accelerating the destruction of privacy."[30]

Does this mean we throw the technological baby out with the bathwater? The truth of the matter is, like all forms of mass media, Facebook is complicated. Its privacy settings provide an excellent case in point. While privacy in the broad sense is increasingly illusory, Web 2.0 has succeeded in creating new spaces where actors on either side of the political spectrum can participate in virtual communities and promote group cohesion. Vilified for its willingness to allow access to private data, the social media giant has now gone in another direction completely, closing off access to researchers and safeguarding online chat spaces from preying eyes. Soon to be perfected end-to-end encryption of its Messenger service—a response to public pressure—will eliminate third-party access to conversations even in the event of crime, offering impunity to offenders under the pretense of privacy protection.[31] The same platform that breathed life into social movements in the Maidan, Turkey, Iran, and in New York's Wall Street will have greater power to shelter militias, white supremacists, and nativists the world over.[32] Even after the 2018 Cambridge Analytica revelations, Facebook remains one of the most difficult social media platforms for scholars to mine for data, especially for that which goes on in private group pages and internal messaging. Despite Mark Zuckerberg's repeated promises that Facebook must serve as a transparent, user-driven, collaborative space where the many wrests power from the few, the platform remains the least open model out there.[33]

Before Facebook dismantled its API in 2018, researchers were able to conduct large data grabs, effortlessly extracting and analyzing huge datasets from group pages, including likes, images, and comments. This allowed scholars like American Megan Squire to reproduce organizational networks, leadership hierarchies, crossover ideologies of hate, and the geo-spatial nature of a group's financial structure.[34] In the German context, political scientists and media scholars have had great success using polling data and cross-referencing it with data hauls from the Alternative für Deutschland's Facebook page to make arguments about the online appeal of the party to constituents around select hot-button issues. A smaller sample analysis of 1,000 Facebook pages from between 2015 and 2016 yielded important information about framing narratives in far-right worldviews. After 2018, even this level of analysis was out of reach unless a person collected screenshots of each individual page. Without this high level of data acquisition (one study culled 11 million user interactions with 78,667 posts with 101,147 external links), we lose the ability to forge overarching syntheses.[35] While freedom from invasive surveillance and privacy protection is a much-needed component of digital citizenship, one must ponder what is lost as well as gained when tech giants like Facebook limit access to research data.

Researchers have since had to rely on creative methodological strategies to acquire data. Facebook has no extant archive; its public pages are not housed in the Internet Archive (better known by its colloquial name, the Wayback Machine). Screen captures are one of the only options for researchers to access data, alongside data scraping individual pages, provided one has permission.[36] Researchers may still gain access to user preferences through web crawling, a method which pre-existed API, although this might go against the platform's Terms of Service. Another way to collect information is to design an app or place a survey in a particular group page through Python, although here too such querying requires the consent of the user. Digital ethnographers have managed to infiltrate select groups to gather information on the inside, but understandably this poses considerable ethical challenges for university researchers.[37] Social scientists have taken to creating their own archives of public-facing materials, conducting content analysis of comments and images.[38] Whichever method is used, it is important to remember that no data is pristine. It is a product of human intervention, culture bound, reflecting our own assumptions and stereotypes folded into the code and pulled out again with every search string and query we type in.[39]

Despite these more challenging conditions, for historians seeking to understand this moment of connectivity and media convergence, it bears looking at how we might use Facebook data—from before and after 2018—to think about the challenge at hand. This includes asking how historical events, like the crimes of the mid-twentieth century, have entered conversations around the online regulation of hate. In this next section, we consider the ways in which Facebook might be put to work to create a composite of those open to populist and right-wing narratives. By contextualizing the challenge and appeal of the far-right, we gain a better sense of the urgency of government policy and civic engagement in the arena of hate speech to build a foundation for "a democratic digital civil society."[40] Let's begin with the question of audience.

The Mediated Audience

In thinking about audience in the aggregate, short of creating our own archive of screen captures of public facing pages for future analysis, we are left with Facebook's own data-gathering program. Through its marketing software—Audience Insights—Facebook culls user information for demographic data including information about income, education, entertainment, and lifestyle, to job titles, family size, age, and political persuasion. This tool, though at the center of privacy debates for capitalizing on user interest, is nevertheless of tremendous help in piecing together one of the most elusive aspects of historical research—who is consuming content on Facebook. Historians can mine Audience Insights for country specific information, including the size of a given network. One search in March 2018 showed that there were roughly 5,000–6,000 German self-identified far-right supporters online. Audience Insights shows everything from the device used to connect to Facebook, the percentage of desktop versus smart phone users, to the gender of adherents as well as age, page likes, and frequency of use. If we read this program against the grain, we can create a social profile of users, preferences, and consumption patterns from several different settings.

As an example, the data on women users in Dresden, an important node in the far-right's network, point to an interesting development in party strategy. Historically, at least up until this latest wave of populism, women voters have lagged men in the polls. Indeed, across Europe, there is a significant gender gap; although not entirely absent, electoral support for radical right parties has overwhelmingly come from men.[41] Yet Facebook data show that the number of internet users self-identifying as open to far-right ideas are well represented by women. Indeed, support falls heavily between two generations: with 2 percent belonging to both the 25–35 and 45–55 age category. Another 13 percent of users are aged between 55 and 65 with half that in the 65+ category (Figure 25).

Men's participation mirrors women's up to a point, with 3 percent in the 25–35 age category and a steady drop off to as little as 6 percent over the age of 65. This data points to an important, new trend, that seems to have played out in the polling stations, that the far right's mix of conservative family politics and anti-migration holds significant appeal for female adherents, at least in places like Dresden, the home of the PEGIDA movement and yearly commemorative marches (Figure 26).

Aside from giving us a visual representation of support, this data helps us better understand why these parties, in recent years, have tactically adopted gender-dominated policy issues, especially but not limited to the wearing of the

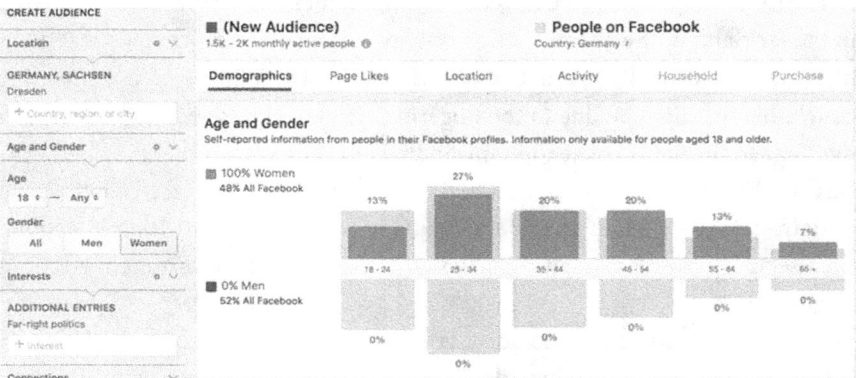

Figure 25 Facebook Audience Insights, March 30, 2018 Dresden.

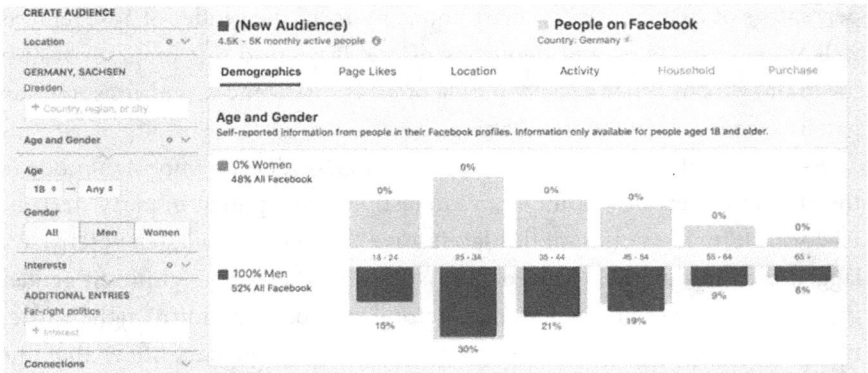

Figure 26 Facebook Audience Insights, March 30, 2018.

veil as both a security risk and threat to the secular state.[42] Facebook demographic data underscore the usefulness of broad populist tactics that, on the one hand, promote traditional family-focused agendas with hot-button issues like the veil, while on the other hand still adhere to the idea that women should be viewed as equal participants in the labour market.[43] It is as correct in 2018 as it was in 1997 when Herbert Kitschelt first made the observation in his now classic study of the far-right in Europe: gender plays a significant role in both ideology and strategy.[44]

When we pull back the lens to look at Germany as a whole, we see that roughly 45,000–50,000 people using far-right and right-wing identifiers (Figure 27).

Where we do see interesting patterns is in the location distribution, which confirms the prevalence of far-right attitudes in households in provinces like Saxony, Thuringia, and Brandenburg in the former East Germany. Yet, interestingly, while in Dresden older demographics show considerable interest in the far right, in the liberal Catholic city of Cologne, the percentage is actually higher for both the 25–34 and 55–64 age categories. While one is tempted to conclude this might be due to the lingering effect of the New Year's Eve attacks that fanned the flames of xenophobia in that city, forgotten is that the liberal city was also home to the Pro Cologne and Pro NDW movements, far-right citizens' initiatives that garnered considerable attention for their anti-Islamic actions, even securing over 5 percent of the votes in the local city government elections (Figure 28).[45]

A few other surprises include the predominance of men and women in the Berlin borough of Heinersdorf near Pankow, the increasingly gentrified neighbourhood to the northeast of Berlin's centre. Here, Facebook analytics

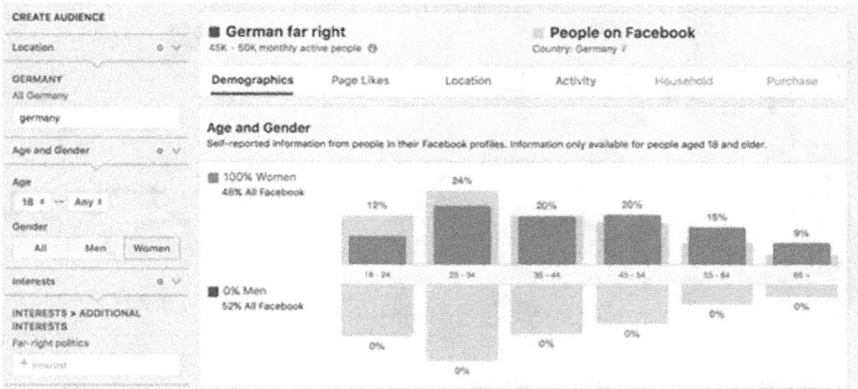

Figure 27 Facebook Audience Insights, March 30, 2018, data for all of Germany.

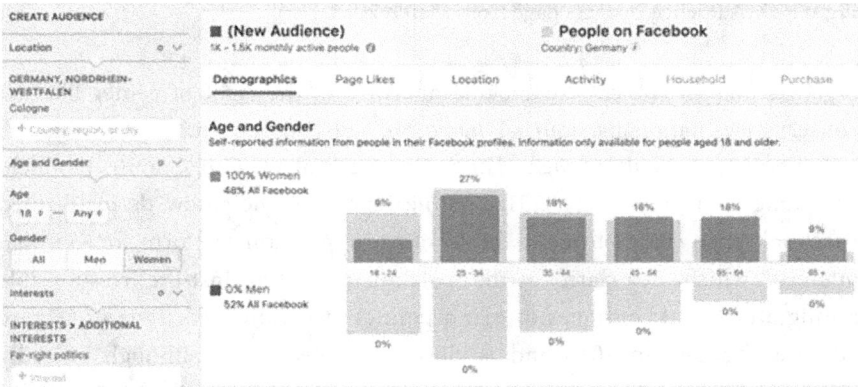

Figure 28 Facebook Audience Insights, March, 2018 data for Cologne.

confirm existing research on voting trends, that self-described populist adherents are increasingly well-established in left-leaning neighbourhoods in the former eastern districts of the city of Berlin.[46] Audience Insights also tracks page likes, identifying which public figures, groups, magazines, and political organizations attract followers. These provide important data into the kinds of materials that create "personal action frames" for populist connective organization (Figure 29).[47]

There is no surprise that among the self-identified adherents of the far-right the originally Eurosceptic but increasingly anti-migration *Alternative für Deutschland* (German Alternative) party is an audience favorite, considering parliamentary success in the 2017 election. Magazines and community

CREATE AUDIENCE

		■ (New Audience)			People on Facebook		
Location	○ ∨	150K - 200K monthly active people ⓘ			Country: Germany /		

GERMANY
All Germany

Demographics   **Page Likes**   Location   Activity   Household   Purchase

Top Categories

1	Non-Governmental Organization (NGO)	Identitäre Bewegurg - Deutschland
2	Political Party	AfD Sachsen-Anhal t · AfD Nürnberg · Alternative für Deutschland · AfD Köln
3	Community Organization	Ein Prozent für unser Land · Deutsch-Russische Bruderschaft
4	Newspaper	JUNGE FREIHEIT
5	Political Organization	AfD Baden-Württemberg · AfD Bayern · Fuck the EU
6	Personal Blog	Informationsschalter · Gegen den Strom
7	Nonprofit Organization	Wir für Deutschland WfD e.V · Campact e.V.
8	Public & Government Service	Angela Merkel Rücktritt jetzt
9	Books & Magazines	Kopp Verlag
10	Religious Organization	Germanische Götterwelt

Age and Gender ○ ∨
Age
18 ⬦ — Any ⬦
Gender
All Men Women
Interests ○ ∨
ADDITIONAL ENTRIES
Far-right politics
Connections ∨
Pages ∨
People Connected to

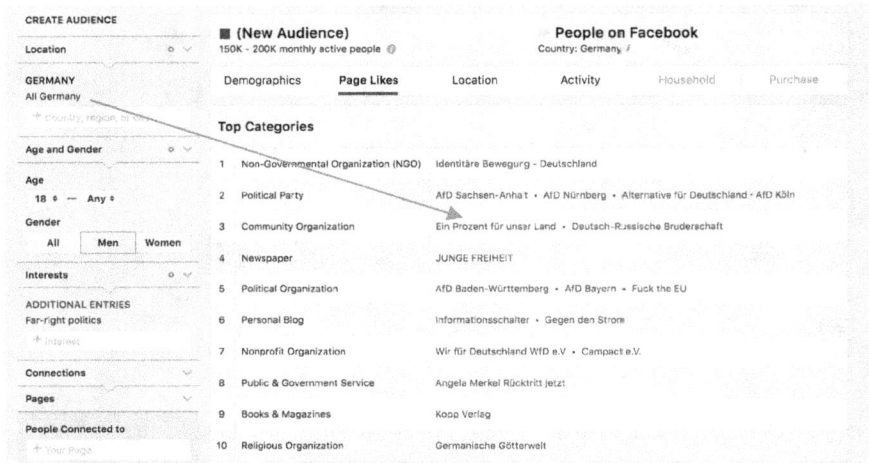

Figure 29 Audience Insights page from March 2018.

organizations of choice also include offerings to the right of center like the conservative, nationalist journal *Junge Freiheit* and the anti-asylum citizen's initiative *Ein Prozent für unser Land* (One Percent for Our Country), which, according to a January 24, 2018, online report on their now de-platformed Facebook page claims to be a "professional opposition platform for German interests" which they clarify as the "patriotic protest against the irresponsible immigration" that continues to mar a politics of reason.[48] *Ein Prozent* (Figure 30) was founded in 2015 and is closely affiliated with (although officially distanced from) the *Identitäre Bewegung* (Identity Movement), which is under surveillance by the Ministry for the Protection of the Constitution. Equal parts PR firm, crowdsourcing initiative, and media watch group, *Ein Prozent* uses a slick, techno-savvy frame to communicate its simple message: that a mere 1 percent of the population could radically change German policy. Financed by far-right publisher and ideologue Götz Kubitschek, founder of the "*Institut für Staatspolitik* (IfS)" (Institute for Domestic Politics), with deep connections to the AfD, *Ein Prozent* has recruited right-leaning business leaders, large and small, against what it sees as the "illegal immigration policy" of Angela Merkel's regime. As part of its general disposition—like much of the far-right and populist media—to discredit the elitism of the journalist and political mainstream, in 2018, it focused attention on training election monitors, using the suspicion of vote tampering as a way to legitimizing their claims of strengthening democracy by representing voices not always visible in traditional media and political parties.[49]

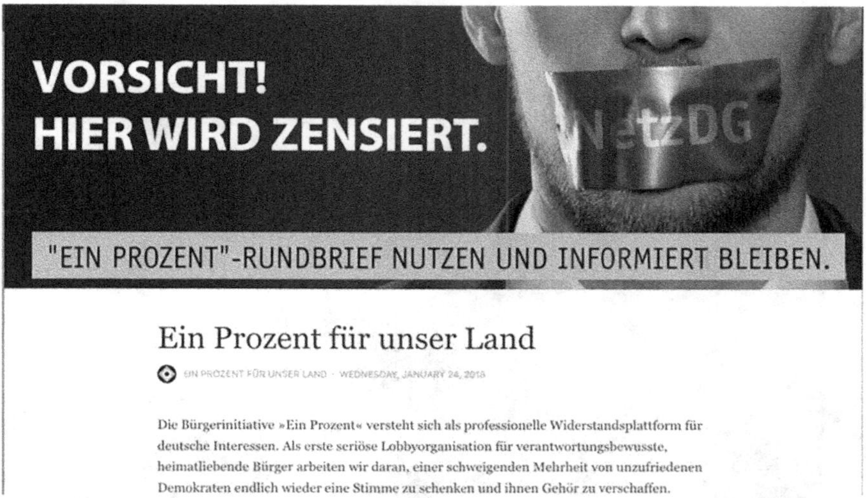
VORSICHT!
HIER WIRD ZENSIERT.
NetzDG
"EIN PROZENT"-RUNDBRIEF NUTZEN UND INFORMIERT BLEIBEN.
Ein Prozent für unser Land
EIN PROZENT FÜR UNSER LAND · WEDNESDAY, JANUARY 24, 2018
Die Bürgerinitiative »Ein Prozent« versteht sich als professionelle Widerstandsplattform für deutsche Interessen. Als erste seriöse Lobbyorganisation für verantwortungsbewusste, heimatliebende Bürger arbeiten wir daran, einer schweigenden Mehrheit von unzufriedenen Demokraten endlich wieder eine Stimme zu schenken und ihnen Gehör zu verschaffen.

Figure 30 Ein Prozent für Unser Land (One Percent for Our Country), January 24, 2018.

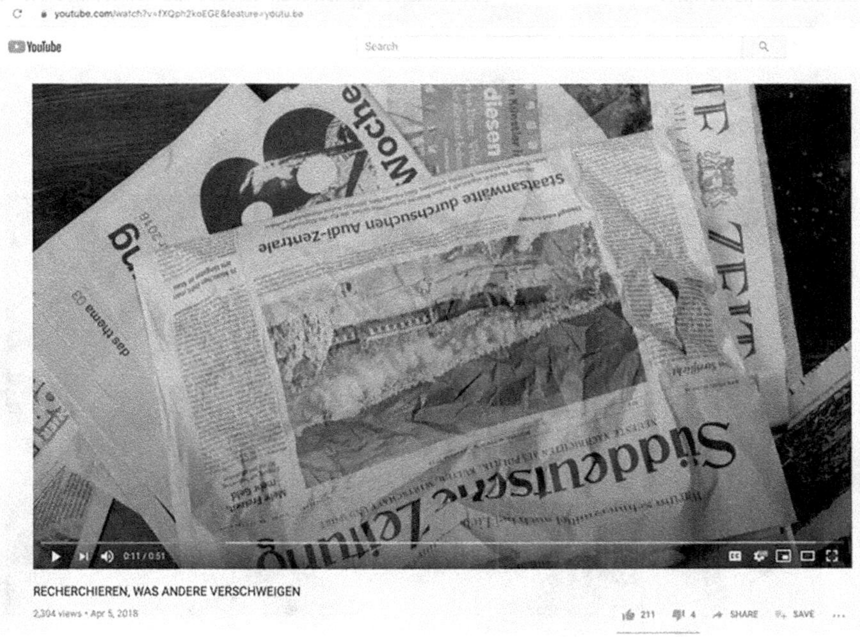
youtube.com/watch?v=fXQph2koEGE&feature=youtu.be
YouTube
Search
Woche
diesen
Staatsanwälte durchsuchen Audi-Zentrale
Süddeutsche Zeitung
DIE ZEIT
das thema
0:11 / 0:51
RECHERCHIEREN, WAS ANDERE VERSCHWEIGEN
2,304 views • Apr 5, 2018
211
4
SHARE
SAVE

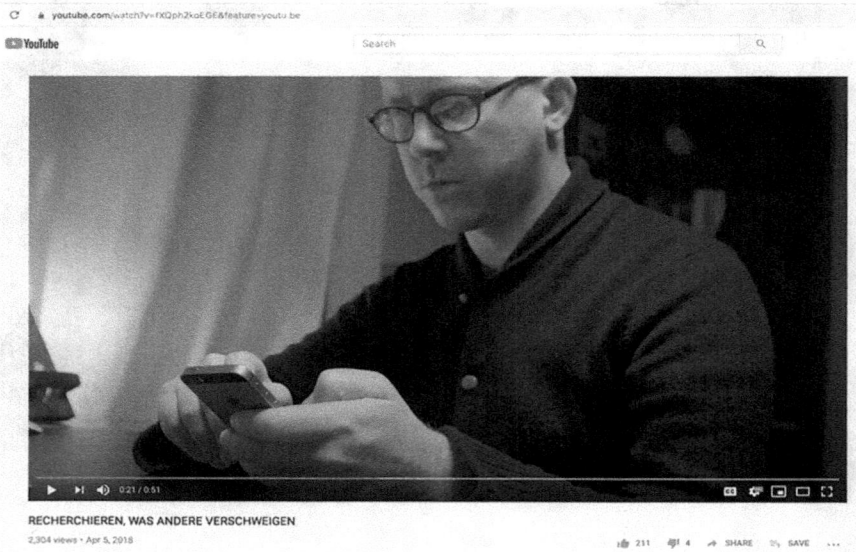

Figures 31, 32, 33 Still frames from former YouTube channel of "Ein Prozent für Deutschland" 2018.

A YouTube promotional video, promising to "go where traditional politics and media dare not go," puts this technical acumen to use. In a series of frames of a lone male researcher, searching through the daily newspapers for critical approaches to immigration policy, we see that the established press is worn and dog-eared, a metaphor for the outmoded ideas they pedal to readers. Our hero, young and bespectacled, tenaciously searches for the truth armed with notepaper and pen, cell phone, and computer database. His intrepid, hardnosed inquiry trumps what newsrooms of establishment journalists churn out day by day. Imagine what an army of individuals committed might accomplish (Figures 31–33)?

In addition to harnessing YouTube, the organizers of *Ein Prozent* were well aware of the power of Facebook both in appealing to adherents and also as a source of data.[50] By 2016, the organization had over 20,000 fans on Facebook, 2,600 followers on Twitter, and almost the same number of subscribers to their YouTube channel.[51] Unlike other far-right organizations, which take a more "we have nothing to hide" approach to their public-facing pages, *Ein Prozent* decided early on to block APIs from tracking groups they were connected to on their social networking site. This did not mean we could not piece together their orientation in other ways. Going through Twitter instead of Facebook, we can get a closer look at the composition of groups and causes they follow (Figure 34).

This data was collected using another publicly accessible marketing program, often used by advertisers aiming to target and understand their audiences.

ein prozent fur unser land 2016-2017

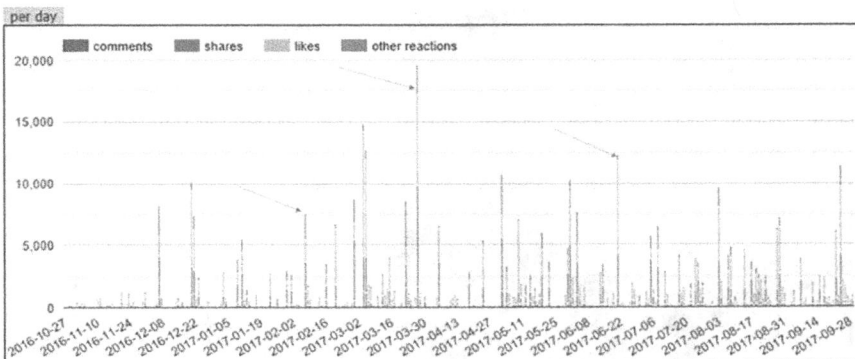

Figure 34 Twitter data for Ein Prozent für Unser Land account @EinProzent.de.

Netvizz gathers information regarding what is posted online, what is reposted, liked, and commented on. An analysis of tweets shows us that despite its claims to being a citizen's initiative for "freiheitliche Opposition" (independent opposition) to the "illegale Masseneinwanderung" (illegal mass migration), its supporters and posts betray a keener-than-usual interest in stories within a far-right orbit. Cross-referencing the peaks in the Twitterstream with the news archive of the *Süddeutsche Zeitung* reveals key moments in the far-right imaginary. One peak corresponds to the day AfD party co-chair Frauke Petry opted to step down on March 30, 2017. February 16th of that same year, the peek points to Björn Höcke's inflammatory comments on the embarrassment of the Holocaust Monument, a blight in Germany's national history. Another peak on June 22 corresponds to the Bundestag vote to exclude federal money for the NPD, while the August 31st peak references the Chemnitz riots. Another graph visualizes the nature of online discussion—size of circles represents amount of online conversation—interesting here is the actions against the building of a mosque in Erfurt, which saw supporters build crucifixes near the proposed building site, and online discussion coalescing around the idea that the silent majority did not want a mosque there (Figure 35).

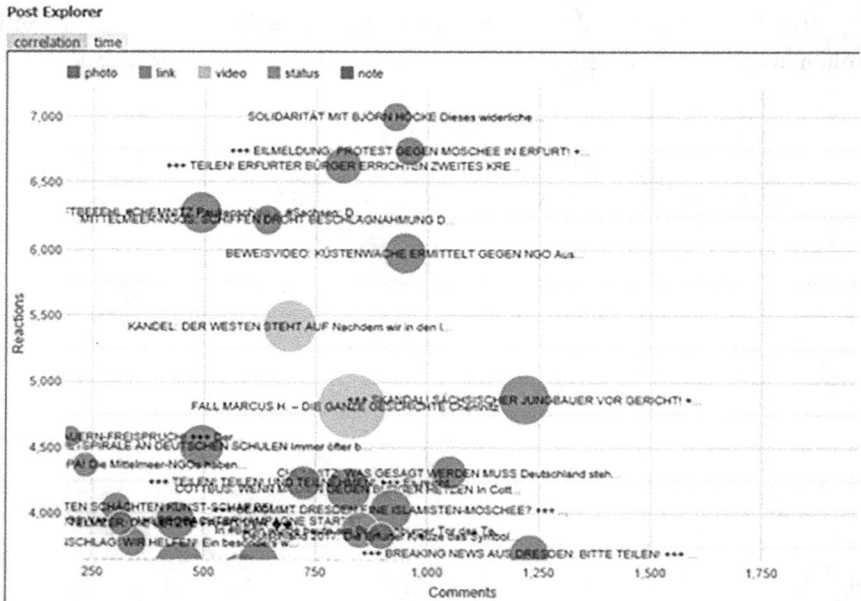

Figure 35 Graph generated from same set of data, Twitter.

Despite projecting themselves as any other citizen group, with no connections to neo-Nazis or the fascist past, the group's own Facebook and Twitter data stream confirmed what the antiracist Amadeu Antonio Foundation had argued all along that, that Ein Prozent is a conduit between the AfD, the New Right, and the extreme-right neo-Nazi scene (Figure 36).[52]

Although antiracist initiatives like *Belltower News* had been researching *Ein Prozent* for over a year, in 2017 the Bundesamt für Verfassungsschutz provided a formal response to the Bundestag about its own research into the linkages between the Identity Movement and the media-savvy citizens group. When queried by members of Die Linke party, the government went on record citing that key organizers of the Identity Movement, chiefly Martin Sellner, were also active in *Ein Prozent*.[53] In the wake of the Christchurch NZ shooter's rampage in 2019, when financial interactions between the assailant and Sellner became public record, Facebook and Instagram took the additional step of de-platforming *Ein Prozent,* citing contravention of its Community Standards on hate. *Ein Prozent* mounted a swift challenge, taking the social media giant to court for defamation. Dressed in the traditional colors of the Burschenschaften or fraternity movement, linked today to the radical nationalism of the far-right (indeed, many of the Austrian Identity Movement members come from fraternities), the coordinator of *Ein Prozent* Philip Stein appeared before the state court in the town of Görlitz to contest the first ever use of internet regulatory law against a purported "hate organization." *Ein Prozent*—and Stein by extension—

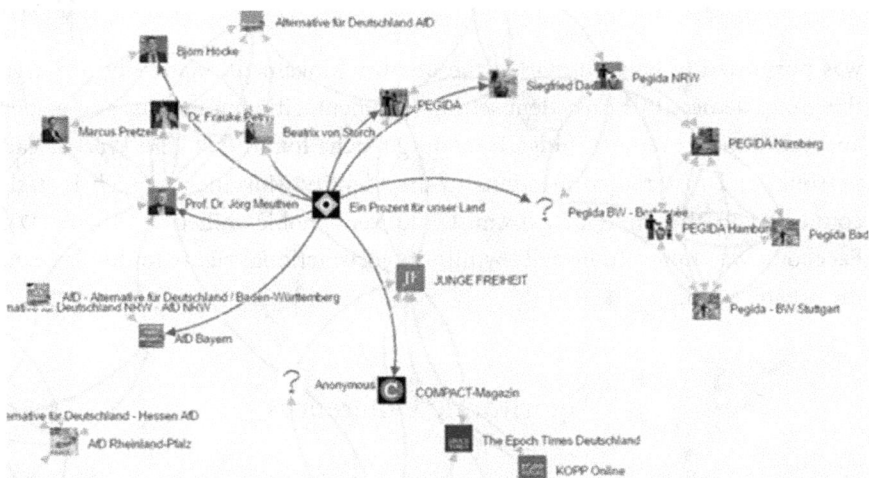

Figure 36 Simple network visualization from *Belltower News*, using Fanpagekarma.org.[54]

Figure 37 Twitter post from November 2016, retweeted in the context of the Facebook action.

was purported to have supported the Identity Movement financially, a charge the group denied. In a precedent setting judgment, citing numerous newspaper and social media reports, Judge Hans-Jörg Gocha found that "*Ein Prozent* had personal and material connections to the Identity Movement, which is itself connected to the far-right extremist and xenophobic milieu"[55] (Figure 37). Facebook was found to be fully within its jurisdictional rights to de-platform the organization.

Algorithmic Differences

The case against *Ein Prozent* illustrates that Audience Insights, together with Netvizz marketing software, can be repurposed to expose useful patterns in how groups present themselves for public consumption and how algorithmic archiving of likes might be used to create a social profile of a group and its members. When we key in the same search parameters for the United States, there are several significant differences. Perhaps it is unsurprising given the population difference that over 1–1.5 million people use the far-right designation per month. But there is another explanation still: according to a 2017 study by the German state television channels ARD and ZDF, although over 85 percent of all Germans are online, only half are active on social media.[56] Contrary to the image of the disaffected rural or working class, however, the bulk of American supporters—at least according to Audience Insights—are middle-to-high income earners from large metropolitan areas like New York, Boston, and Seattle. More men than women self-identify this way, but similar to and surpassing the situation in Germany, more women in their fifties and sixties—a full 22 and 23 percent—support far-right politics. Most shocking of all is the way in which the data contradicts popular perception. Respondents are overwhelmingly well-educated, with over 65 percent having attended college and 14 percent having served in the military. At the time of originally writing this chapter, page likes revealed that most respondents supported initiatives around gun ownership like the Oath Keepers, a nonprofit organization based out of Las Vegas, which claims to be a nonpartisan organization of current and past military, police, firefighters, and service men and women who have sworn oaths to protect the constitution.[57] A quick glance on its Facebook page shows over 500,000 likes. It is peppered with anti-Democratic Party attack memes and YouTube videos. Of course, in the intervening years, the Oath Keepers would prove itself to be more than a simple Fifth Amendment organization with key figures charged with sedition as participants in the Capitol Riot.

An interesting difference in the algorithmic curation is the fact that in Germany, the search terms "far right" bring up populist and anti-immigrant, new right public figures, and parties whereas when used in relation to the United States, these same search strings yield militia, gun enthusiasts, and defenders of free speech, many of whom pre-existed the 2000s. The difference is not just ideological, it is also temporal. History itself figures into their online identities. In this sample, American sites are nostalgic. They harken back to the Revolution, incorporating images of the nation's founding fathers. These "reactionary timescapes" as Alexandra Minna Stern calls them consciously evoke the notion of true patriots, linked in a righteous struggle across time.[58] They draw on symbols of the nation from the flag to historical paintings, even images of the constitution parchment itself. Whereas in Germany, the pages liked by most proponents of the self-proclaimed far-right are rooted in a more present past, in the migration crisis of 2015–16 and the politics of integration.

Even though the bulk of users are clustered in the former eastern states of the German Democratic Republic, and the argument has been made, repeatedly, that this region trends right and has a troubling history with neo-Nazism in the 1970s and 1980s, there is no sense of this anti-communist history, nor any overt connections to pre-1945 Germany. What they share, is the evocation of Western values under siege, an attack on the heartland, and a desire to return to a pristine European identity.[59]

Like other social media sources, Facebook's analytics uncover patterns that may be put to good use by researchers seeking to know more about reach, audience, and demographics. However, the program is not without its limits. Audience Insight provides rich data on the income and educational standing of far-right adherents, culled from, and cross-referenced with third-party sources. Aside from the ethical concerns about using this kind of material, another significant problem is that Facebook cannot provide this level of income data about non-US users. In other words, although we know that online media provides new visibility to marginalized actors, and that these actors, when brought together in conversation and cross-posting, help forge networked publics that shape the discourse of everyday politics, we are only privy to some of the demographic information, at any given time. Despite the illusion of greater reach and autonomy, Facebook remains bound by the power of the algorithm, the strength and reach of international privacy laws, and the yet still poorly understood scope of individual practices.

Radicalization

Despite legitimate concerns about the harvesting and selling of user information, Facebook goes some distance in protecting the privacy of its client base via the private group function and single or multi-party message service. However, as we saw in the wake of the Charlottesville Unite the Right rally in August 2017, private Messenger-like apps and group chat features have afforded neo-Nazis and far-right, populist groups a digital home to recruit new adherents and promote their particular brand of hate.[60] The only access researchers have to these sources is by archiving screen captures of public-facing, online conversations. It is perhaps surprising to note that although there now exists considerable material on connective organizing and protest politics, little systematic research has examined social media use and populist online organizing.[61] This is partly due to the chapter's previously outlined challenges regarding the limitations of Facebook's platform; the other is the scholarly and governmental emphasis on anti-establishment elites instead of on vernacular use.[62] While social media usage is commonly associated with the far-right, self-perception, organizing, and radicalization, Stier, Posch, Bleier, and Strohmaier argue that less research has actually gone into the tropes used, images drawn upon, and historical references made in the populist conceptualization of the historic struggle.[63]

A special issue of the journal *Information, Communication and Society* attempts to bridge the gap in what we know about online activity and the rise of populism in the early 2000s. Articles on adolescent online behavior suggest that populist groups are increasingly interested in teens at this crucial moment in their political and personality development. Add to this that successive generations of youths have turned to the internet as a news and information source, and it can hardly be surprising that social networks have become fertile ground for recruiting adherents.[64] While research from across Europe and the Americas confirms what we too have shown, that the overwhelming majority of users of participants in far-right populist movements are young and male, studies of online activity also suggest those that are susceptible possess certain personality traits as well. They are expressive online but not necessarily off, intellectually closed, and extraverted within select virtual circles, made manifestly easier, of course, under the cover of privacy settings.[65]

This research is mirrored in the anti-terrorism research of the German domestic intelligence service, the Ministry for the Protection of the Constitution (*Bundesamt für Verfassungschutz*, BfV). Established in 1950 with the express purpose of safeguarding the constitution, the BfV found that since 2014 far-right organizations use social media creatively, to circumvent police surveillance and party bans, and cultivate interest in already established online fora. For recruitment, there is no need for the lesser trod dark web discussions of Reddit and 4chan; a contact request or quick text is simply sent via a private Facebook group page and responded to by Instant Messenger. Once deleted, it leaves nary a trace or ripple.[66]

There is little doubt that there is a relationship between online activity, recruitment, and the increase of far-right, populist ideas the world over. However, it would be wrong to think that the hate purveyors' interest in the internet is new. Cyberspace is no terra incognita; it turns out, it had been on the right-wing radar since the early days. Well before Norwegian rightist Anders Breivik lauded Facebook as a space that nurtured the fight against multiculturalism, Stormfront had already exploited 1990s-era BBSs and bulletin boards.[67] It was not their cyber activism that got certain right-wing parties banned, it was their real-world activity. After a series of high profile and deadly attacks against asylum seekers in Germany, the Federal Republic undertook to monitor and then ban several neo-Nazi parties. By the late 1990s, there were roughly 50,000 right-wing activists agitating in unified Germany as compared to only 19,000 in 1982 with a full 20,000 members registered in the ultra-nationalist Republikaner Party. Although much concern was raised about the prevalence of right-wing ideology in the states of the former German Democratic Republic in the years following unification, West German racists felt very much at home in the established democracies of the FRG states.[68] Rightists had already been active in infiltrating other social organizations including German fraternities or Burschenschaften, exposing another 26,000 to right-wing ideas.[69] By the end of the 1990s, illegality failed to break the movement. If anything, it forced groups underground into "groupuscules," small, independent units like the now notorious comrade groups or *Kamaradschaften*, which still dominate street demonstrations today.[70]

Alongside the popularity and pervasiveness of social media has come the fear—not altogether unfounded—that Web 2.0 has been literally saturated by right-wing and populist groups. The far-right is not just organized, it is media-savvy.[71] A recent example from Germany's racistly named "Doner Kebap" killers, a group of three malcontents, two of whom committed suicide not before they killed nine immigrants and a policewoman, shows the importance of digital media in mounting right-wing opposition. The group's video manifesto was found on several DVDs in the embers of their burning apartment in Zwickau, already in envelopes addressed to the police. In them, they tell their audience they are the National Socialist Underground, a rightist riff on the notorious 1968 student group the Weather Underground. They boast that they are a "national network of comrades whose principle is to value action above words. If fundamental changes do not occur in politics, press and in freedom of opinion" they promised their actions would continue.[72]

To tackle this vexing problem of ever increasing far-right violence, the German federal government and Ministry of Justice, together with major newspapers, several activist groups, city and state governments, and NGOs, collaborated on a variety of initiatives to help prop up civil society.[73] With guidelines from the BfV and a mix of public and private money, initiatives like Netz-Gegen-Nazis (Network Against Nazis, renamed Belltower.News in 2017), Publikative.org, *Mut Gegen Rechte Gewalt* (Courage Against Right-Wing Violence), no-nazi.net and the social media wing of the Amadeu Antonio Foundation created programs to equip citizens with the tools to better recognize and combat online hate.[74] Facebook got involved as well, and together with the Online Civil Courage Initiative (OCCI), the Amadeu Antonio Foundation, London's Institute for Strategic Dialogue (ISD), and the International Centre for the Study of Radicalisation and Political Violence (ICSR) launched its own initiative to address online hate.[75] High on the agenda was to shore up other efforts at promoting civil courage, which unsurprisingly for Germans carries special, historical importance as related to the ineffective opposition of the German people to the eliminationist antisemitism of the Nazis.[76] This is made evident in the way in which each initiative makes specific appeals to history to solidify their efforts at building affective ties in both real and virtual antiracist communities.

Belltower.News, formerly Netz-Gegen-Nazis, styles itself as a clearing house of information regarding far-right internet and everyday activity. It is sponsored by the Amadeu Antonio Foundation, a not-for-profit organization founded in 1998, in response to the 1990 murder of an Angolan worker who had come to East Germany before the fall of the Berlin Wall, the first documented hate crime committed in reunified Germany. The organization supports grassroots memorial initiatives, funds studies of women in the neo-Nazi scene, and directs attention toward the ways in which neo-Nazism threatens democracy and pluralism, especially on the local level. One of their initiatives includes buttressing democratic digital civil society through educational programming like the Toxic Narratives Project which monitors and deconstructs the alternative, far-right media in terms of its narrative strategies, logic, and argumentation.[77]

It is in this spirit of creating a "digital civil society" that Belltower.News presents articles on far-right, extremist, and neo-Nazi activity online with the hopes of providing critical thinking skills to the reading, participatory public. Its focus is multi-pronged, but mainly the goal is to link digital literacy to consciousness raising and social activism. The page has several points of emphasis from a week by week press archive to issue specific themes. One area of particular interest is what organizers call Digital Streetwork, shorthand for rubber meets the road digital activism, in cyberspace and, critically, in everyday life. In addition to expository overviews of how social media is used by right-wing initiatives, Belltower's Digital Streetwork also provides concrete point-counterpoint suggestions for how to challenge nationalist and white supremacist narratives where they surface. Debunking "fake news" and false correlations is paramount; in this sense, proactive, issue-specific counterpoints to online position taking become a form of digital opposition, elements of which are made plain in an online brochure by Christina Heyken and Christina Dinar. At the heart of this activism is a pedagogical imperative to not let false facts and racist assertions stand, uncontested, in the public record. Active, formal, informed, and continued opposition is the only sure way to change the discourse toward a more "empirically based, factual, and solidarity-driven discussion."[78] Heyken and Dinar provide examples for how to go about supporting one's point by linking arguments to evidence drawn from trusted links, including newspaper articles and secondary literature. These efforts in digital literacy demonstrate once again that social media activism is a transmedial one, drawing examples across platforms and genres and weaving them together in the service of buttressing an argument. Here, there are elements of co-creation, of a shared form of authority, as subjective assertions align with objective evidence and the coexistence of old and new media forms. It is what media scholar Henry Jenkins refers to in *Convergence Culture* as a new participatory culture of activism, less a revolutionary shift away from what came before and more a fluid, overlapping form of media use and composition.[79] Crucially, it underscores the importance of average citizens as both creators and conduits of knowledge production.

Proactive digital communication is even more important in the era of misinformation, especially amidst defamation campaigns against progressive institutions and actors. It is here too that history occupies centre stage. Well before the term trolling became part of the vernacular, the Amadeu Antonio Foundation found itself in the crosshairs of several right-wing organizations, including the Identity Movement of Berlin and Brandenburg (*Identitäre Bewegung Berlin Brandenburg*), which, besides sending daily emails and hate mail, added the practice of leafleting and posting signs on their headquarters.[80] These defamation campaigns were personal, targeting select members of the foundation, especially its founder Anetta Kahane, who had been public about her erstwhile association with the East German secret police.

Those seeking to discredit Kahane draw on several themes, which speak to the way in which history is interwoven in the logic of the far right. In emails, poster campaigns, Facebook posts, and even YouTube videos, they launched a defamation campaign to slander the Moses Mendelssohn Award winner by pointing to her Stasi past, her supposed racism, and her Jewishness, underscoring in the process the way in which the Nazi and East German past conjoin in the way opponents of antiracist activism imagine their cause.[81] In microcosm, Kahane's life reflects the push and pull of twentieth-century German history.[82] She is the daughter of Jewish communists forced to flee the Third Reich for France and then Spain only to return in 1945 to support the nascent German Democratic Republic. Already at an early age, Kahane learned about the contradictions of socialist humanism, especially its blind spot toward antisemitism and the legacy of National Socialism. In the spirit of many activists, who use their own experiences to connect intersectionally to related causes, for Kahane, her anti-racist activism is also a deeply existential working through of National Socialist and East German past and the ruptures and ambivalences they continued to spawn in the evolving present. Just as she agitated for greater acceptance of Romani and Jewish migrants from eastern Europe in the early post-Cold War era, so now does she take up the issue of refugees from North Africa and the continued need to organize against home-spun racism against long-standing targets like Turkish Germans. In this way, her story is a reflection of the larger German one, a century-long battle over the nature of belonging during and after nationalism.[83] It is also a feature of mediatized memory more broadly. In linking the dangers of otherness in German history to today's struggles over integration, it symbolizes the ethical, if somewhat utopian potential of what historian Alison Landsberg has called prosthetic memory for the ways it creates empathy and social responsibility across difference.[84] At the same time, there are hard and fast limits to this ethical stance taking when it comes to left-leaning critiques of Israeli policies and how those are taken up in German public memory. In this regard, the foundation's targeting of the supposed antisemitism of the left has opened it to criticism that it has lost sight of the real and pressing danger of recurrent fascism and rising support for the AfD.

While Kahane's efforts for social change earned her recognition, her personal story was accompanied by unwanted attention. In her autobiography, she disclosed an uncomfortable truth, that like many East German citizens (a full 200,000 by the late 1970s according to one account), she found herself a pawn of the East German secret police, recruited while a student of Latin American studies to serve as an *Innofizielle Mitarbeiter*, an unofficial informant to monitor friends, school mates, and neighbors.[85] By her own account, initially she wasn't deemed politically engaged enough, "unzuverlässig" or politically unreliable, a result of which was a travel ban, meaning she could never take a foreign post or put her language skills to use. By the late 1970s, under the code name Victoria, she agreed to serve as an IM, impressed into the service after a friend had tried to flee the GDR, with her knowledge. Undergoing a crisis of conscience, she sought her release from duty, evoking her parents' struggle as German Jews, and the ambivalence of the state they helped build on matters of race and racism.[86] A noted expert in Stasi case files examined her records and found the authorities claimed that she was self-willed, obstinate, and not especially easy to direct. Any information she offered up did not seem to cause undue harm to third parties.[87]

To be fair, the far-right was not the first to land on Kahane's Stasi past. She was already in the crosshairs in the early 2000s when the then SPD-led federal government opposed her nomination on these grounds for the much-respected post of immigration and integrations commissioner (*Auslanderbeauftragte*). Despite her work in establishing a Berlin regional working group for foreigner affairs, anti-immigrant sentiment and the resurgence of neo-Nazism, especially in the eastern states together with her participation in the security apparatus cast doubt on her suitability for the post. At the same time, it provided fodder for ideological opponents to seize the opportunity to use her Stasi past to discredit her advocacy work. The remembering and forgetting of specific, overlapping pasts, lay at the heart of the campaign to silence Kahane. While her personal engagement with this history is also a selective working through of the past, emphasizing victimization over ambivalence, the defamation campaign is a brazen attempt to latch on to select aspects of these pasts, to revive ethnic nationalism and challenge the rights and protections of citizenship and belonging in liberal democracy. Amidst the threats of violence in these postering and email campaigns, there is the sense that Kahane is not only a fraud for hiding her Stasi past, but both a race traitor and racist for casting aspersions on white Germans chiefly but not solely in the eastern districts. One need only read the comments on YouTube attack videos to see that opponents barely hide their antisemitism, resurrecting that familiar trope of the Jew as a traitor to nation and race.[88]

Digital memory making through the use and reuse of anti-communist and antisemitic tropes was not limited to the arguments against Kahane. The migration "crisis" of 2015 and the success of far-right, populist parties like the AfD (Alternative für Deutschland) at the ballot box ignited Twitter feeds and Facebook group discussion boards with racist vitriol. This was certainly not the first time that united Germany bore witness to the vocalization of racially motivated sentiments. Yet it was precedent-setting that in 2017 an overtly nationalist party had secured entry into the Bundestag, normalizing the critique of cosmopolitanism and trading on nostalgia for the mono-ethnic state. In this sense, the success of the AfD was not owed to the internet, rather, it was buoyed by a history of race thinking that dated back to 1989, if not before.

The current discourse did connect with something new, however. In the winter of 2017–18, before the API was shut down, two scholars from the University of Warwick provided the missing link. In December 2017, they released a study, drawing on data provided by like the Amadeu Antonio Foundation and another human rights group, Pro-Asyl (or pro-asylum), that showed a correlation between social media posts and hate crimes. Karsten

Müller from the Warwick Business School and Carlo Schwarz, an economist, drew anti-refugee data from the AfD Facebook posts that they argued has had a triggering effect on real-time violence in municipalities with higher social media use. The AfD made it easy to make the correlation between discourse and practice. With over 300,000 likes, the third biggest party in parliament had the largest presence of all major parties online. Its populist orientation, which also meant they maintained an un-curated, unedited, open Facebook message board, without any rules of conduct regarding hateful comments, allowed the researchers access to "over 176,000 posts, more than 290,000 comments, and 500,000 likes by over 93,000 individual users."[89] They geo-tagged the user data from between January 2015 and January 2017, cross-referenced it with a general study of Facebook use, and analyzed both in tandem with local internet outages and geo-coded references to anti-refugee and immigrant crimes. They discovered that there was what appeared to be a propagation effect between social media use and hate crime. Facebook discourse itself did not cause violence to occur; rather, when combined with pre-existing, exogenous factors such as a history of right-wing ideology in certain milieus, numbers of immigrants, and decreased newspaper usage, anti-immigrant vitriol could instantiate a greater likelihood of hate crime. Interestingly, the obverse was also true; in moments of diminished Facebook use, there were also statistically fewer crimes registered.

There are two takeaways regarding the place of the internet and the culture of debate. One is that the authors did not find a similar correlation between antisemitic commentary online and anti-Jewish hate crimes, although municipalities with a history of racist thinking generally were more predisposed to anti-immigrant hate crimes, under appropriate conditions. History matters, but not as much as recent memory, which might tap into historical antisemitism with the focus remaining squarely on refugees. The second is that the subject of this report would be discussed by the parliamentary group organized under German Minister of Justice Heiko Mass as justification for a wide sweeping anti-online hate speech law brought into effect June 30, 2017, which threatened to charge Facebook and other social media providers with fines of up to 50 million Euros if they failed to remove "criminally harmful" content. Without data such as this, however, gleaned from the large-scale harvesting of online speech acts, the authors of the report argue that the dangers in our midst would remain unknowable. Simultaneously, they acknowledge that if the study is correct, regulation of social media means fewer possible hate crimes. Indeed, statistics show that there has been a decrease in local-level infractions in 2017, whether owing to the resettlement of recent immigrants and improved infrastructure, a newly enforced cap on migrants, or the enforcement of this law.[90] Stressing the ambivalent place of the law on freedom of thought and expression, both the authors of the report and Anetta Kahane and her organization are lukewarm about the anti-hate legislation, with the Amadeu Antonio Foundation taking an especially skeptical public stance.[91]

Kahane and the antiracist NGOs do not just want regulation, they wish to strengthen democratic debate through a robust internet culture. Together with various state and regional authorities, they have developed programs that emphasize the education of citizens to buttress deliberative democracy in the mediatized public sphere. Facebook is one of their prime focal points, and as we saw in the case against *Ein Prozent*, their work there has been largely successful. Of course, they are not alone in seeing their opponents as challenging freedom of expression. Many on the nativists right of the spectrum are quick to use this same argument against anti-hate legislation, and the fact that the law relies on a citizen initiative to flag offensive content.[92] But the law's motivation lies elsewhere. It is a direct response to fake news and reports such as Müller's and Schwarz's that affirm what German-Jewish philologist Viktor Klemperer wrote about the role of language in emboldening authoritarianism, that language alone is not the culprit but when taken up, ritualized, and thus rendered normative, words hold the potential to unmake democratic social structures in the most dangerous of ways.[93]

Conclusion

How does Facebook structure specific relationships of remembering and forgetting in the digital public sphere, and how might a critical analysis of this phenomenon help us better understand how certain memories become not only cultural or communicative memory, but wider claims to collective forms of remembrance? This chapter has illustrated the usefulness of thinking about social media as a site of contested memory formation. Social media is just that, social: its fluid, traveling, and medial nature means it is constantly being used to respond to the ebb and flow of conversations online and off.[94] It is not just mediated, or intermedial, to borrow from Astrid Erll, meaning it draws from, sometimes cuts across, and often extends other media forms.[95] It is a discursive and embodied process, one that gains expression and life online. Critically, even in its abstraction, as a mediated digital public, it has real implications for how policy is crafted and enforced, with online activity shaping offline action. In terms of actual memory formation, the digital public sphere constructs forms of memory that are as much recycled and reiterated as they are new.

Connective memory is mediated and remediated, in a constant state of flux, and yet, it also draws on culturally distinct mental, discursive, and habitual frameworks that have evolved historically over time.[96] It reflects ongoing societal concerns, while shaping the terms of debate and even language of engagement. Memory and the media, as José van Dijck has argued elsewhere, are intimately intertwined.[97]

Alongside creating a space for a broad range of opinion and emboldening new actors to contribute to the discussion, it cannot be denied that the social web has fundamentally changed the terms of discussion and debate, not always in the best of ways. Müller and Schwarz found online discussion polarizes debate, which, when combined with pre-existing local conditions, can have deleterious impact on vulnerable populations, hence the need for government regulation to ensure minimum standards of decorum especially around denial and hate speech. But despite bearing the brunt of intensive offline defamation campaigns and hate messaging, even the Amadeu Antonio Foundation argues that some forms of regulation are too interventionist, that there is merit to using digital tools to counter the misuse of history and reinforce civic mindedness through critical debate. Learning how to recognize hate, engaging deniers and racists and countering their assertions, and more importantly, analyzing the way in which their invective has permeated discourse offline is an essential part of a democratic digital civil society. Here, too, history is integral, both historical precedence and the lessons taken, especially in Germany, from past ways of seeing and knowing what comes from inaction.

What is different, then, about the participatory public sphere and Facebook's place in it? Unlike traditional forms of media, which historically, through elites, selectively amplified what counts as a nation's collective story, now this task has fallen to vernacular voices networked together in a more diffuse set of spaces and places.[98] Facebook, despite all its shortcomings, is one of those spaces. It bears asking, how different is social media in this regard? Aside from real concerns about privacy protection and data use and abuse by corporate interests, the distinction is its diffuseness. While traditional forms of authority and expertise are challenged by the emergence of new sites of memory making and archiving, spaces such as Facebook nevertheless provide possibilities for critical participation and activism. But as we have shown, this can be harnessed for good as well as evil. Depending on oversight, one that balances access to data with privacy protection, Facebook has great potential to be part of a more ethical model of civic discourse, one mindful of the lessons of the past.[99]

Conclusion—"Networked Knowledge and Digital Memory Activism"

It is easy to be persuaded by the argument that the right has capitalized most on the poorly regulated digital public sphere.[1] In 2016, alt-right message board chatter and tweets laid a foundation for Donald Trump's victory, while in 2018 "blast messages" hurled pro-Bolsonaro sloganeering to WhatsApp customers in Brazil, paving the way for election victory there.[2] Rightists have been brazen in trumpeting the fruits of their labor in getting "one of theirs" in the White House, while United States QAnon conspiracy theories have traversed the Atlantic, mobilizing thousands of Europeans—Germans especially—to take to the treats to protest COVID-19 health measures.[3] Worse, their venom has reached the mainstream. Through page views, likes, memes, video exchange, and retweets, online communities have become saturated with harmful speech, undermining what counts as evidence and expertise while also eroding faith in public institutions.[4] No longer simply informing self-narration and group identity, alt and far-right extremist vocabulary and conspiracy theories have emerged from the dark web to shape the transnational media landscape, creating alternative imaginings legitimized by strongmen and ideologues the world over.[5]

With social media conglomerates failing to adequately enforce hate policy, fake news continues to fester. The social web gives it life.[6] Yet, in the rush to find explanations for the tenacity of what Farkas, Schou, and Neumayer call "platformed antagonism"—including anti-Semitic, Islamophobic and nationalist sentiments online—we sometimes overlook the fact that despite its considerable shortcomings, social media has also facilitated networked opposition from consciousness-raising, organizing, or rubber-meets-the-road activism often at the hands of women and people from traditionally marginalized communities.[7] As we have shown in this book, it can foster memory formation, collective action, and outreach, creating affective communities that, in the words of Black Lives Matter organizers, help us "sharpen each other so that we all might rise."[8] By way of a hands-on, applied conclusion, we wish to revisit our core arguments via a brief discussion of the co-curated online project the *New Fascism Syllabus* (NFS, www.NewFascismSyllabus.com or Figure 39) to think about the way digital projects such as these help build opportunities for digital activism through the use of "connective memories"—in this case around the post-Holocaust memory as enlivened by the global threat of populism and authoritarianism in the last decade.

In the *New Fascism Syllabus,* the connective memories of past challenges to democracy serve as a common touchstone, binding users of both the web source repository and Facebook group page to the cause of opposing a new global authoritarian turn. They give succor to the creation of an online affective community, one that transcends place and binds people in a global knowledge network.[9] Picking up on themes in this volume, how might we think about the role of social media projects like this as a forum for scholarly debate, online curation, and digital activism in a globally mediated public sphere? What is the usefulness of something like the *New Fascism Syllabus* in mobilizing an activist agenda to combat misinformation and hate (Figure 38)? Guided by qualitative

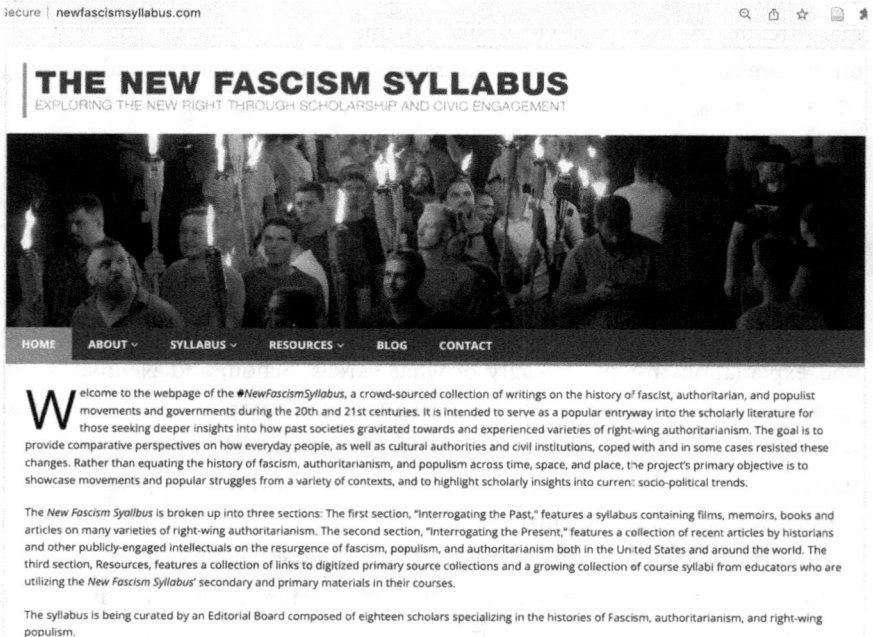

Figure 38 The landing page of the *New Fascism Syllabus.*

analyses of the social web for the way it conjures real possibilities for networked activism and community, initiatives such as the *New Fascism Syllabus* may be used to think about the possibilities and limits of critical history and memory mobilizations online.

As we have argued in this volume, connective memories of the history and function of fascism have the potential to mobilize knowledge communities as critical sites of education and debate. Algorithms certainly have earned their bad rap, but they also make information intelligible and curate it.[10] They shape publics of like-minded users, where relations develop "among strangers" through confrontation with ideas.[11] Even within echo chambers, groups are forced to navigate those issues, and the collective learning that goes into that process creates possibilities for common work toward a greater goal—what digital sociologist Noortje Marres calls "systematically caring for" an issue, subject, or thing.[12] The *New Fascism Syllabus*, both the web repository of online resources and the Facebook group itself, sheds light on the constraints of digital media in how knowledge is created, while also heralding the potential of "plural, partial and at times experimental methods" to help shore up a level of reflexivity, self-reflection, and learning that buttresses democratic social action.[13] Delimited by the particularities of each platform, with differing degrees of composition and reach, these rapidly-paced mediatized and networked publics require distinct methodologies to track, analyze, and make publicly tangible how they function.[14] As we have shown, repurposing corporatized media analytics offers one such way.

Always Already New

We have argued that the shift from analog to digital media leaves no doubt that online activity presents new and heightened forms of surveillance and regulation.[15] We have also shown that while there are legitimate concerns about the ways in which corporations mine user preferences to market products, goods, and services, there is the tendency to overstate the ways behavior manipulation through algorithms and influencing erode the possibility for autonomous thought, presuming that in the past there was a magical outside to mediatization from which moral judgment and critical thinking evolved pristine.[16] New media, like older media forms, present example after example of tangible opportunities for framing opposition, whether that is in archiving photographs of neo-Nazi demonstrations in Flickr or advertising the movement of far-right supporters in Dresden. Indeed, news sharing and consumption online and participation across a variety of digital networks can have a productive impact on political persuasion, strengthening the possibility for deliberative democracy and collective action. Yet, this is also tempered and mediated by corporate control.[17]

Still, there is no getting around the fact that new media technologies have played an indelible role in the spread of hate. But as our book has shown, participatory media has also aided in the formation of memory communities whose task it is to safeguard the historical record from misappropriation and denial, with Holocaust memorial museums among the quickest to capitalize on the popularity of the internet with in-house social media services set up to maintain the interest of visitors long after their trip to a site. Although the Auschwitz Memorial and Museum in Oświęcim Poland does not favor images of people in its Instagram feed, preferring to curate photographs of buildings and place, as we argued in Chapter 1, in regframing visitor photography and exchanging comments with the public, the museum enters into a relationship with its audience while still trying to control how memory should happen at its site.[18] In a similar fashion, it is now routine for local, regional, and national archives in North America and Europe to undertake collaborative crowdsourcing projects involving the public in acquisitions, cataloguing, and identifying actors in photographs, tagging metadata, and transcribing text.[19] On the one hand, this has helped democratize how the lessons of the past are curated for public consumption. On the other, it presents new challenges surrounding knowledge, truth, and expertise. Despite these concerns, new historical memory entrepreneurs have helped shape how public institutions and media reproduce vernacular knowledge for their various audiences.[20]

As we have seen, citizen activists have played a not insignificant role in the democratization of collections and memory formation by using social media campaigns to bolster calls for more ethical historical practices of sortation, from boycotting questionable exhibits to pushing for the repatriation of colonial artifacts to home countries. In this sense, civic involvement has helped spur new dialogue over difficult histories.[21] Civic intervention of a more nefarious kind of course, most notably the recent success of populist parties the world over, has also had a palpable impact on how people and nations conceive of and represent their sense of the past. We are slowly coming to appreciate what links online hate speech to offline violence, with social media blamed for normalizing extreme positions that turn on the misrepresentation of national histories.[22] But as Federico Finchelstein and Heidi Tworek have argued, "post-truth" media forms have had a long and dubious history in the analog era.[23] While there is certainly cause for concern, especially as end-to-end encryption makes it even more difficult to penetrate the private conversations of malcontents, the internet has not succeeded in completely destroying truth nor has it completely eroded critical discourse. Rather, it has created new knowledge producers whose entry into the fray has forced us to ask new questions of the role of mediation, authority, and expertise in how history and memory are transmitted into policy, practice, and everyday life.[24] It has challenged us to think more capaciously about how to harness online affordances for their democratic potential in how they might foster increased social responsibility beyond the particularism and malaise of authoritarian knowledge regimes.[25]

This is not simply about online activity. As we saw on Facebook in chapter five, there is an embodied, real-world, everyday spatial-temporal carryover to rubber-meets-the-road activism that productively challenges the spaces, places, and impact of intellectual debate in highly generative ways.[26] With the rise of online fora and the interconnectedness of social networks, the university lecture hall, the academic conference, and the peer-reviewed publication no longer dominate as where scholarship meets its publics. As the COVID-19 pandemic made patently clear, through a click of a mouse, virtually any space is affixed to the grid, allowing a range of actors to interpolate with the past and with each other in a broad diversity of settings sometimes for better, other times for worse. Sometimes platforms themselves stylize everyday life according to common temporalities, like Facebook's archiving affordances that curate posts alongside intimate events like birthdays, anniversaries, high school and family photography, creating new relationships of self to other and between our personal and collective pasts. Networked media and connective memories make the personal political in entirely new ways.

The New Fascism

Central to our book is the question of what is unique to social media constructions of the present past, as opposed to other forms of mediatized memory. The answer, we have shown, is both one of sentiment and mediatization; that is, the way media combined with historical situatedness has shaped how we lend expression to our thoughts online. If Russian novels and broadsheets measured the social barometer of modernity in the early twentieth century as having an air of melancholy, social media texts indicate people in the twenty-first century view the world through a prism of anxiety and despair.[27] For liberals and progressives in the United States, nothing was more demoralizing than the Trump victory in November 2016, which seemed to herald a startling new phase in the long history of racism in that country. Historians worked quickly to offer up their expertise on historical antecedents, analogies, and continuities in a wave of public intellectualism to counter what some observers decried as evidence of the new fascism. While scholars of fascism historically have varied in their understanding and definitions of the term and its valence for different historical and political settings, the rise of strong men and populist parties the world over gained new importance in the post-Trump moment. In a series of articles published in online journals and newspapers, scholars wondered aloud: might we indeed be seeing a revival of fascism and if so, what may be done? It was in this context that the *New Fascism Syllabus* was first conceived.

The phenomenon of the crowd-sourced syllabus itself began a few years earlier, in 2014, as a multi-platform response to the civil unrest in Ferguson, Missouri, following the outrageous shooting of Michael Brown, an unarmed black teen, by police. Georgetown professor Marcia Chatelaine appealed to colleagues on Twitter to use the medium in a restorative and productive way to gather and share resources in a single, curated list of critical studies of race, violence, and white supremacy in American history.[28] It was imagined as an act of solidarity and community building, bridging the divide between the university and everyday life. In an era of fake news and the denial of expertise, this was nothing short of a shot across the bow. In the weeks that followed, a string of such syllabi sprang up, each differing according to theme but united in the struggle to put critical scholarship into the hands of journalists, educators, and concerned citizens as quickly as possible.[29] These online initiatives built on a history of analog protest mobilizations from protest letter-writing to boycott campaigns. What was different was the way the digital affordances of the medium itself, including the rapidity of knowledge transfer, the amplification of emotion, and creation of new forms of copresence through acts of collaboration, developed new repertoires of contention and coalition, transforming otherwise arms-length academic knowledge networks into vibrant fora for activism and outreach through the curation and, where possible, open-source provision of scholarly material.[30]

The *New Fascism Syllabus* (NFS) was born digitally. Buoyed by the critical imperatives of the #FergusonSyllabus, the organizers decided to try something similar within their online academic communities. The NFS was originally conceptualized as a clearinghouse of contemporary articles for a course on 1933 at the University of Iowa offered in the semester following the inauguration. But following several Facebook Messenger exchanges (evidence again of the usefulness of privacy features along with its problems), Jennifer Evans and Lisa Heineman decided to build a two-fold crowd-sourced reading list offering informed perspective on this urgent contemporary problem alongside a compendium of texts on the history of authoritarianism, populism, and fascism. Unlike other online syllabi, we wanted our resource to capture the way colleagues used scholarly analysis and tools to shape public debate, drawing on analogies with the past to sharpen the focus on the present. As a result, we established the NFS in three locations: as an open Facebook page, a closed Facebook group, and a Twitter handle (Figure 39). They canvassed the support of our existing online networks and invited members to the Facebook page to post relevant newspaper and magazine articles, which we also tweeted out to the community at large with the hashtag #NewFascSyllabus. Members of the closed group then invited other possible members to join, and within weeks the forum grew to hundreds of participants.

Earliest attempts at outreach garnered immediate interest. The game changer was an email from an intrepid doctoral student in Italian history—Brian Griffith—who provided new considerations for what the project might entail. At his suggestion, and with the help of Meghan Lundrigan, we decided to use

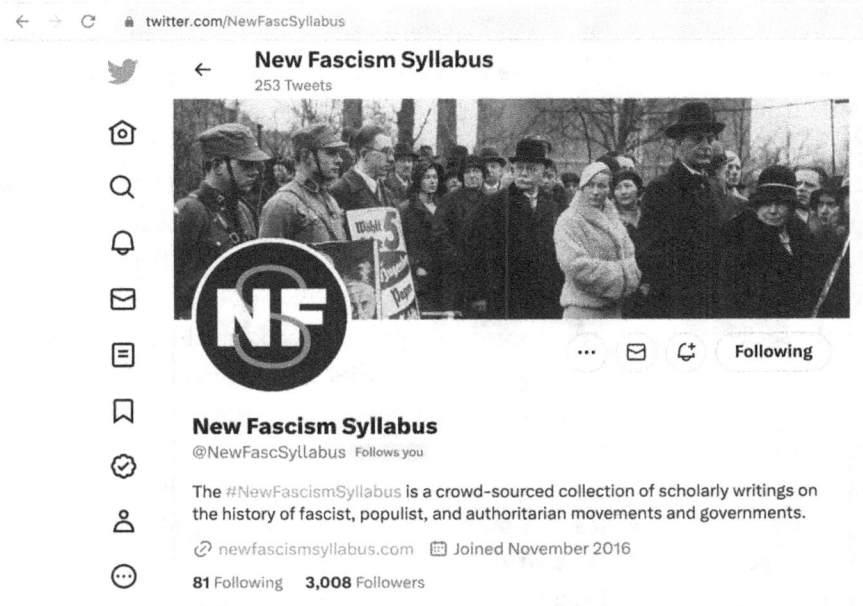

Figure 39 *New Fascism Syllabus* Twitter profile.

our audience and reach to craft a dedicated Wordpress website. There, we would house a variety of content options from the two bibliographies, "Interrogating the Past" and "Interrogating the Present," to invited submissions of real course syllabi, online primary source collections, and blogs. We divided the globe into regions, leaving the United States aside, and solicited what colleagues might consider the top texts in each field. Taking submissions back to the closed Facebook list for adjudication and suitability, which itself spawned even more discussion, they then populated the Wordpress site with guiding questions to be of use to the public in navigating the sources. In other words, as with other examples in this book, we used a multi-pronged methodology that reflected the sharing attributes of the platform itself. Although the Facebook page was originally imagined as a space to solicit and share these resources, it quickly emerged as a vibrant forum of discussion, which Evans, Heineman, Griffith, and Lundrigan decided was quickly becoming a generative originator of discourse and debate on its own. The ensuing collaborative, multi-platform conversation throughout the winter and spring of 2017, in an evolving and tense political moment, coalesced into one of Zizi Papacharissi's affective publics.[31] Unlike in the Dresden datasets, this time it was forged through sharing and remediation modalities of Facebook together with Twitter.

The closed Facebook page turned out to be the most dynamic of the three locations, eventually attracting around 800 members who together made several posts per week, most of which were links to articles in text-based digital media. Although galvanized by shared belief in the global threat of this "is it or isn't it" fascism, a network of this size is invariably heterogenous reflecting a diversity of opinions on and experiences with these themes. The sharing of common texts provided opportunity for argument and disagreement, while the movement of ideas across platforms, when Facebook posts were remediated to Twitter and vice versa, offered the possibility of engaging even more diverse, if parallel, audiences. While social media is often charged with creating echo chambers of selectivity and consensus, "blurred and porous boundaries between websites" create the possibility for inadvertent exposure to alternative perspectives or differences of persuasion if not ideological extremes.[32] We also must remember that progressive stances are, out of necessity, forged in interpellation with conservative ones, and vice versa. In other words, the sharing of resources within and beyond these knowledge networks possessed deliberative qualities by sparking debate and creating grounds for disagreement by degree, if not outright.

Initial canvassing of news articles challenged some pre-existing assumptions about the role of the US election in the use of historical references to fascism.

Interestingly, the first people to conjure the specter of Trump's emerging authoritarianism were not on the political left. Leaked Republican Party documents showed already in 2015 that there were rumors of Trump's fascist leanings a year before his election victory. In a senate committee memo that found its way to print in the *Washington Post*, Republic Party officials likened the reality TV star and presidential nominee to Wendell Wilkie, a 1940s businessman with far-right leanings.[33] These concerns took on a crescendo effect after the executive orders on immigration, and observers of European history became especially interested in questioning the relevance of the term for how to understand the current moment. Of particular interest were comparisons to Nazi Germany and Adolf Hitler. Was Trump's ascendance America's "Reichstag moment" as Masha Gessen argued, referring to the moment when Hitler used fear-mongering as a context for the Enabling Act, executive orders initiated in the wake of the Reichstag fire that effectively unmade the Weimar Republic, Germany's fledgling twelve-year experiment in constitutional democracy?[34] Were attacks on the free press and the judiciary the stuff of tyranny, As Yale professor Timothy Snyder put it in his November 16, 2016 Facebook post (which later evolved into a series of YouTube Lectures and a short book on the same subject) one of many such missives by academics hoping to shape the discourse in the public sphere?[35]

Surveying the public mood through articles in newspapers and online magazines, we see this public writing did not always agree on how and whether fascism was the appropriate lens through which to analyze the current moment. Germanists held a certain pride of place as suddenly there was great interest in the last days of the fragility of the liberal democracy, but they were not alone in answering calls from journalists. Coterminous conversations around populism, authoritarianism, and nationalism meant that there was a lot of definitional work in press, and our page became a clearinghouse for such conversations beyond the headlines. Scholars were not the only ones making analogies; if Google trends are any indication, there was heightened interest generally among members of the public. Although we cannot know precisely what guided their keystrokes, Boolean searches for Trump AND Nazism, fascism, populism, and authoritarianism dominated the fall and winter of 2016 and 2017 (Figures 40 and 41). It is perhaps not surprising, then, given the headlines, that scholars of Nazism, fascism, and the Holocaust were particularly well represented in the first 100 days of Trump's reign.[36]

Whereas fascism as an historical category had once held little contemporary valence, suddenly it seemed to be on everyone's tongue. Historians and political

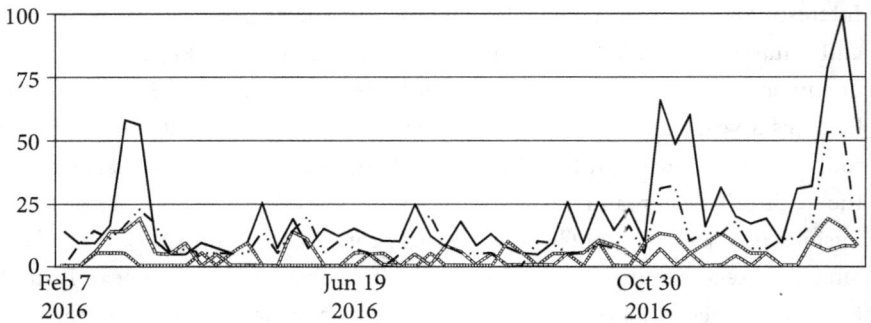

Figure 40 Bold line: Trump AND Nazism. Broken line with dots and dashes: fascism. Remaining: authoritarianism. Major aligned peaks Super Tuesday, election, and Auschwitz anniversary.

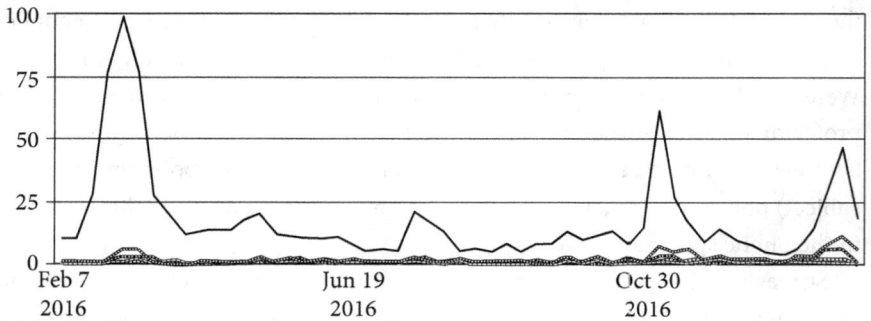

Figure 41 Bold line: Trump AND Hitler.

scientists were in high demand to help make sense of it all. Evans and Heineman saw it as motivation to capture some of that conversation and make it available to the wider public in the syllabus.

Crowdsourced Knowledge

Audre Lorde's famous dictum—that we cannot use the master's tools to dismantle the master's house—is a stark reminder of the perils and pitfalls of trying to do progressive work on a platform whose primary purpose is to create affective relationships shoring up consumer citizenship. What can the NFS Facebook page—both its make-up and impact—tell us about the unique online community that emerged in the year following the election and its potential for shaping the terms of debate? it helps to consider the different form and function of this particular participatory public sphere.

1) What can we interpret about the audience and reach of the NFS Facebook page?
2) What does this tell us about NFS as a social media forum?
3) What is its potential?

Audience

As we've shown throughout our chapters, the first point is both the easiest to answer and the hardest. Facebook has the widest use of all social media platforms. And yet, it is the least understood of all social networks for the simple fact that it is one of the most challenging to work with in terms of harvesting usable data. Furthermore, its modalities differ in critical ways from Twitter, Instagram, Tumblr, and Flickr, both in how it tackles the thorny issue of privacy protection and also the specific opportunities it makes available for deliberation, collective sentiment, and action.[37] Chief among the differences is the fact that it does not operate with hashtags, so cannot be searched across networks or within according to theme. Second, it has no archive in the traditional sense. Even its public pages are not housed in the internet archive better known by its colloquial name, the *Wayback Machine*. Perhaps most vexing, page owners and administrators can't simply download a list of all the posts made to a private group, nor can they access data on top contributors further than sixty days in the past. These attributes place tangible limits on how to interpret Facebook a source.

Despite the storied Cambridge Analytica breach, Facebook's privacy protections and general software make it difficult to impossible for scholars to scrape the platform pages for information. This has led researchers to employ creative strategies to gain access to viable datasets, like collecting screen captures in real time for analysis later. Were we researching Twitter or Instagram, we might use a program like Tweet Archivist or Martin Hawksey's open source program TAGS, which pulls up entries organized by hashtag or keyword.[38] Access to their metadata would then be analyzed in a variety of different ways through topic modeling—the production of in and out groups and an ordering of most to least popular terms—network analysis, and visualization techniques. We might even use sentiment analysis, an algorithm that gauges a post's emotional range. If the data is good, one can even analyze change over time according to audience and reach.

As we saw in the Facebook chapter, wide sweeping changes in the name of privacy protection meant key APIs were disabled, discontinuing access to core datasets. Even efforts to provide data to scholars directly from Facebook central through collaboration with research bodies like the Social Science Research Council's Social Data Initiative ultimately folded—at Facebook's behest—in a ham-handed process that saw many researchers allocated grants only to learn that their datasets were not forthcoming.[39] These challenges notwithstanding, and they are important issues in need of unpacking in their own right, Facebook's platform-level sharing applications are also double edged. On the one hand they facilitate conversation, but they also provide cover for all sorts of potentially nefarious relations. This is especially palpable when considering its in-program chat, page, and group privacy functions. As computer scientist Megan Squire has shown, private Facebook groups provide refuge for hate groups of all stripes to build their communities unaffected by the platform's Community Standards policy. And yet, these same features that nurture the cultivation of misinformation can also buttress strategies for users to counter these same "economies of hate."[40] Scholars have the possibility of infiltrating a group to gather data, but this methodology would scarcely pass most university ethics boards. Like the Janus face of modernity, which spawned these mass media forms, Facebook holds the power to protect malcontents while stymying progressives. How we think about this dual role of information gathering and sharing requires a reconceptualization of how the mediatized public sphere works in relation to the tenor, shape, and pace of information exchange within democracies and the tensions that pre-existed new media while now giving it life.

NFS as a Social Media Forum?

How *can* we get access to the material needed to make any arguments and observations, let alone historical ones? We've discussed the difficulties of conducting research with social media datasets, from the perspective of access and scale. Work with this medium requires a broad skill set as well as patience. Screen captures are one option, as is joining a group and cursoring down page by page, doing good old-fashioned content analysis. We can take the analysis down to the level of code as feminist scholars have done to analyze the rigidity of the program in recognizing a broad spectrum of gender pronouns despite proclamations to the contrary. In the past, researchers have gained access to user preferences, sometimes in questionable ways. It bears recalling that the Cambridge Analytica scandal drew on the myPersonality research project of two scholars—one at Cambridge, the other at Stanford—who had users fill out personality tests while simultaneously acquiring their consent to harvest their Facebook user data; although this was not as clear as it could have been to most users and the project was, understandably, shuttered.[41] Another approach is to place a survey on a particular group page, as the UK think tank Demos has done with right-wing Facebook groups.[42] And finally, one could, as we do here, use existing marketing programs to generate specific demographic information about users and their situatedness in relation to the far-right. Regardless of the path chosen, it bears keeping in mind what media scholar Lisa Nakamura reminds us, that no data is in fact pristine. It must be always viewed as a product of human intervention, culture-bound, reflecting our own assumptions and stereotypes. These are folded into the code and pulled out again with every keystroke, every search string and query we type.[43]

Like relationship statuses, in other words, "it is complicated" working with social media platforms and texts, and Facebook is especially challenging. To analyze our group, one needs a mix of old and new approaches to harvest data, scrape and organize user patterns, and interpret the results. One of the most intriguing resources is Facebook's own analytics program, which revealed some surprising information about our page and its users for the first year of data from our site. Even using the embedded Facebook Group Insights API, however, Facebook does not present any data any further back than July 15, 2017, even though our posts date back to the 2016 election.

What we do know is that among the 800 or so subscribers to our page, the bulk are perhaps unsurprisingly located in North America and Europe, in cities aligned with universities. This fact parallels social media use more broadly, which is more concentrated in North America than Europe, and our early membership drive meant that our users overwhelmingly (though not exclusively) came from the academic community, mobilized by the Trump election. One might read into this a bit further still, along with the membership list, and hazard some guesses about the areas of specialization of member-contributors. This is a closed group. Admission is by member referral at which time the editors evaluate whether a person is suitable for admission. Administrator have indeed had to turn away applicants who seemingly thought the group's purpose was to celebrate the global right-wing turn instead of critiquing it. Luckily, adherents to these ideologies tend to telegraph their stances by their "original" profile names and iconography (Figure 42).

As these maps show (Figures 43 and 44), users are dispersed across the globe. When we cull data from the NFS Facebook page with the program

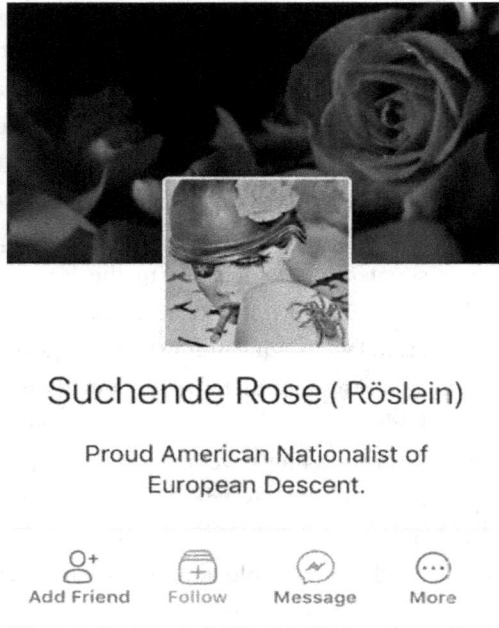

Suchende Rose (Röslein)

Proud American Nationalist of European Descent.

Add Friend   Follow   Message   More

Figure 42 People seeking membership with other intentions, June 29, 2018.

Figure 43 Membership according to population. NodeXL.

Figure 44 Membership according to latitude and longitude. NodeXL.

NodeXL, which generates an Excel spreadsheet that ranks cities and countries in terms of number of members, the map reveals the breakdown of members from August 28, 2017 to August 30, 2018. Although this is not a dedicated network analysis, it does show the importance of the co-curators of the page in generating adherents to the Facebook group through personal networks and affiliations. From this list of users, Facebook Analytics tells us that there were around 35 posts per month, 429 total, with 601 comments and 2,043 other reactions such as likes (Figure 45). A total of 611 of these members are labeled as "active" with 50 percent of users identified as women, 48.7 percent men, and 1.3 percent where gender is not specified.

What is interesting in our Facebook groups demographics is the sizeable participation of women, which at first glance seems to buttress the utopian claims of knowledge networks within social media, that it levels the playing field, removes social barriers, and destabilizes traditional power structures in favor of vernacular voices. There's only one problem: our data does not bear this out. Part of the issue is that the analytics fail to differentiate adequately between the quality of posts, that is, the differences among posting, liking, and offering commentary. Women may participate at roughly the same level as men, and yet, when we peel back the layers to explore the kinds of actions men and women perform on our page, we are confronted with a different picture indeed. Our own qualitative examination of user activity revealed that in most cases, barring Lisa and me, with few exceptions most women "liked" the comments while men

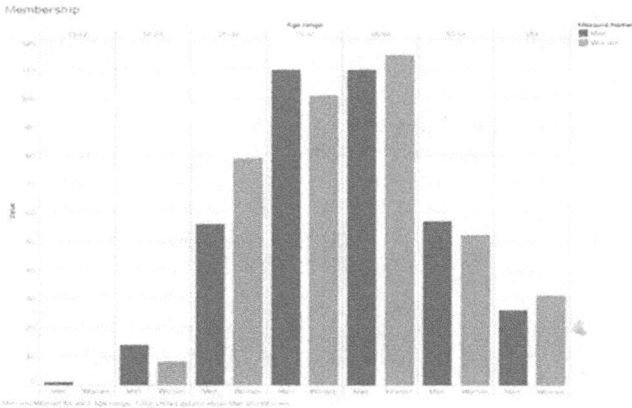

Figure 45 Membership according to Facebook Audience Insights.

tended to begin discussion threads and weigh in greater detail on existing ones and in greater numbers. While women have been present in the technological revolution in variety of important ways, from content creation to social organizing online, our findings support what Letitia Bode has discovered in her own study of political discussion online, that women typically engage in less visible acts of participation, suggesting the need for greater attention to gender, representation, and political participation in the modern media environment.[44]

What Is Its Potential?

Just how transformative was the NFS page in shaping academic discussion and public opinion? The algorithms tell us when people post and how many view a news story. But they don't tell us who is an academic and who is following our site out of pure interest. The list of cities suggests that most followers are more than likely clustered in major cities or in university or college towns (Figure 46). Intriguing as outliers is the number of followers in Japan and India (Figure 47). Similarly, one might surmise from this data that users are primarily interested in European and US developments, which is indeed born out in which posts, which themes, and even which days generated the most commentary on our site. Mixing Facebook's own analytics software with a qualitative method of simply cursoring back through the posts, we came up with the following data:

Top locations (with top cities)

- United States: 465
    - ○ New York: 42
    - ○ Washington, DC: 23
    - ○ Chicago: 15
    - ○ Iowa City: 13
    - ○ Los Angeles: 12
    - ○ Ann Arbor: 12
- Canada: 115
    - ○ Ottawa: 48
    - ○ Toronto: 19
- Germany: 58
    - ○ Berlin: 36
- United Kingdom: 44
    - ○ London: 18
- France: 16
- Netherlands: 11
- Finland: 7
- Austria: 6
- India: 6
- Japan: 5

Figure 46 Breakdown of locations where members post.

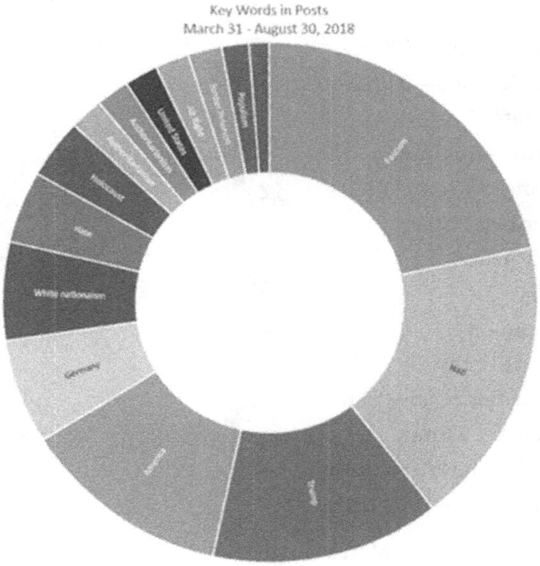

Figure 47 Keywords mapped March 30 to August 30, 2018.

While we know the gender of users and where people are located when they post, and we may speculate based on patterns in the data about who they might be demographically, what can we know about the posts themselves, which themes were considered popular, and which ones garnered the most attention? We can come at this several ways. A content analysis of post topics and themes presents us with the following keywords graphed according to frequency of use (Figure 47).

How did we get these? After scrolling back through five months of posts, we conducted a simple keyword search using the in-browser search function. It is important to note that each "hit" represents one time that term was used, whether in the member's post, the title of the article, the URL, or the comments on the post. This thematic breakdown does not represent the number of posts, but rather, the number of times each term was mentioned over the course of five months, or roughly 400 individual posts. It is not a huge dataset by most standards; however, it does allow us to make some observations about this group and how it responded to the challenge of the early Trump years.

If we were to quantify the number of posts organized according to keyword and divide it against the others listed in those months, this would be the breakdown (Figure 48):

- Trump—34 times (26%)
- Jordan Peterson—5 times
- Alt Right—5
- Germany—16 times
- Fascism—53 times (39%)
- America—31 times
- United States—5
- Canada—3
- Populism—4
- Hate—11 times
- White nationalism—15 times
- Holocaust—9 times
- Authoritarianism—5 times
- Authoritarian—16 times

Figure 48 Number of posts, March–August 2018.

Sources of Posts (pulled from 59% of all posts from March 31 - August 30, 2018)

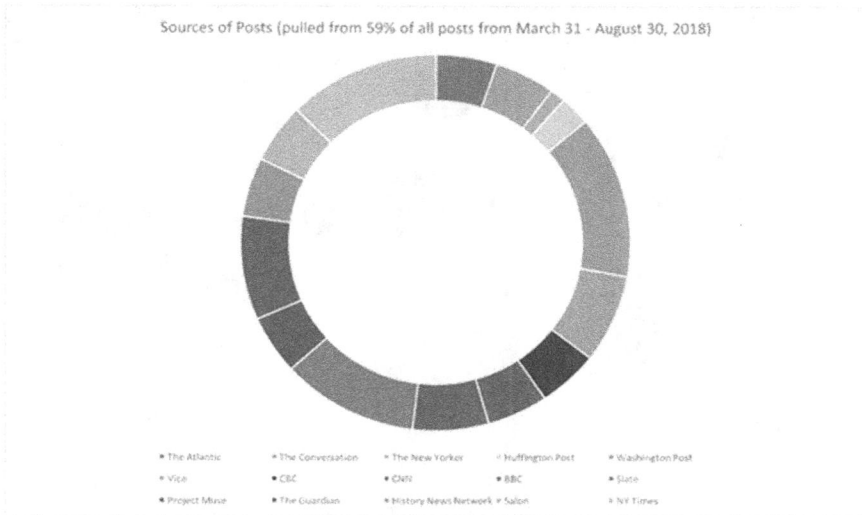

● The Atlantic ● The Conversation ● The New Yorker ● Huffington Post ● Washington Post
● Vice ● CBC ● CNN ● BBC ● Slate
● Project Muse ● The Guardian ● History News Network ● Salon ● NY Times

Figure 49 Sources of posts, March–August 2018.

Figure 49 demonstrates which publications these posts drew upon. This is interesting insofar as it reveals the changing places and spaces of historical analysis and debate, from traditional news sources to niche blogs like *The Conversation* and *Slate*. When we look more deeply at the articles themselves, we see that memories of "what came before" continue to motivate analyses of "where we find ourselves today." The data suggests that while this is geared toward historians, there is an interdisciplinary aspect to the page that appeals to scholars keen on finding ways of meeting our audiences where they reside, in quotidian media outlets, as users try to make sense of the election and its implications as part of a larger authoritarian moment.

Another way into the matter of scope and reach is to use the Facebook API itself. It tells us through raw hits from a five-month span, that certain posts solicited more attention than others (Figure 50).

Cursoring back to explore what these topics were that motivated the discussion on these days and cross-referencing them with the general news cycle, the events of the day, and any other contributing factors helps contextualize audience interest.

To take an example: the spikes around July 11 to 17 all coalesced around the theme of comparative fascisms. On July 11, there was a post on our page about Portuguese monuments, then July 12 Richard Evans's interview with *Slate* entitled "Democracy Dies in a Variety of Ways," followed by Waitman Beorn's Op/Ed in the *Washington Post* comparing Trump's America to the

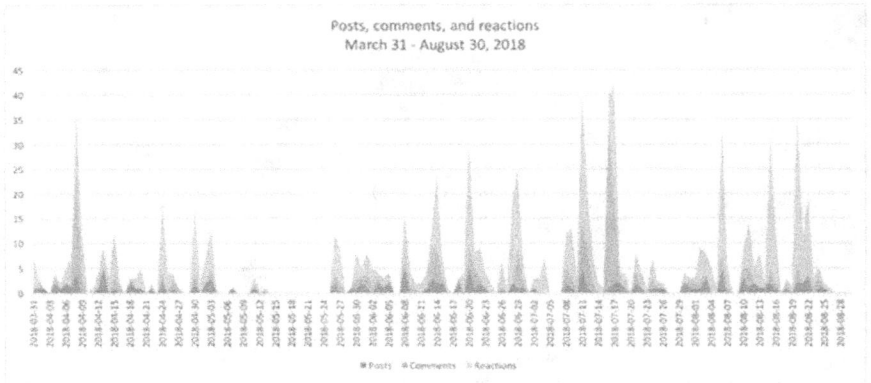

Figure 50 Bar graph of posts, comments, reactions March to August 2018.

Holocaust.[45] We may not be able to explain what motivated the individual responses, but taken in the aggregate over time, our data can map out subtle shifts and changes in the discourse and which actors are fueling discussion versus reacting to it.

As with all social media sites, what we have demonstrated here are some of the challenges at getting at audience and reach given the technology-specific modalities of Facebook. To ascertain impact is even more difficult still. One option is to rely on qualitative data so as to sketch out a rudimentary survey of our page's usefulness. In the leadup to a keynote address on the NFS at the 2017 German Studies Association annual meeting, users commented that they had benefited from the page's function as a repository of information. Some mentioned that posted materials had made their way into course syllabi, while others said they found the online discussion deeply enriching. The NFS Facebook page had become a kind of go-to space for international news coverage especially given that most newspapers allowed access via so-called leaky paywalls when articles were remediated from user's who had subscriptions. Respondents were laypeople as well as educators, journalists alongside professors.

But what are the metrics of gauging the importance of this mediated knowledge network? In the humanities, scholars generally balk at the notion that bibliometric indicators alone are a marker of an idea's salience.[46] Emphasis, instead, is on putting it out in the world. Fora such as the NFS chart audience engagement and allow us to visualize the mobility of a set of ideas. This interplay between on and offline worlds can be hard to navigate. Online conversations are frenetic and mobile. They migrate between spaces and places in the network.

Once they surface, they are quickly trafficked offline, to classroom discussions, book clubs, kitchen table conversations, and into the news. Once made visible, we can then attempt to chart these movements, tracking the tenacity of a set of ideas in each moment.

The *New Fascism Syllabus*, which began as a humble attempt to meet the challenge of the day, had a similarly migratory on- and offline life. It was featured on CBC radio, represented on an American Historical Association roundtable, it formed the stuff of a keynote address at our annual meeting of Germanists, and helped germinate research in the German Studies Association on digital history and the far-right. Users have used the forum to initiate letters of protest for controversial events. In September 2018, it served as a conduit of information and activism around Polish Holocaust revisionism at the University of Ottawa and a 2019 letter by scholars of European history and German Studies to the United States Holocaust Memorial Museum expressing outrage at the museum's condemnation of analogy in thinking about the history of concentration camps. In the summer 2021, it played host to a major memory debate among German historians and historians of colonialism. Termed the Catechism Debate for the way it coalesced around the genocide scholar Dirk Moses's polemic in which he argued contemporary German memory culture failed to create a space for comparative thinking around the history of colonialism and continuities in anti-foreigner sentiment.[47] This debate, like many of the examples explored in this book, quickly jumped platforms from the NFS webpage to its Facebook group page and over to Twitter.[48] It also garnered the attention of legacy media in Germany, as major newspapers like the *Frankfurter Allgemeine Zeitung* and *Zeit* published responses to pieces in the Syllabus. The NFS was not solely responsible for this convergence of interests, but it did serve as a galvanizing presence for those seeking tangible ways to contribute to the dialogue.

The NFS suggests that the combination of platforms and interfaces, Wordpress, Facebook, and Twitter helped spawn affective attachments that galvanized responsiveness to these hot-button issues. As we've shown, there's are important arguments about digital spaces serving as affective sites of self-care, support, and activism. As silly and superfluous as Facebook may seem, its site-specific affective ecologies, from the different curatorial, rhetorical, and representational ways users have intervened on the page around the "what, how, why and when of remembering" and forgetting to the urgency of the debate around historical fascisms, have created fungible scholarly activist regimes.[49] The crowdsourced nature of the NFS site, alongside the co-curators' own expertise in intersectional feminist history, resulted in a diverse mix of users and interests. Through these different pathways, all converging around the memory and legacy fascism and racial injustice, users came together as an online community, ready to mobilize where necessary. The need for such mobilization became apparent in response to a series of posts to an online news story featuring the *New Fascism Syllabus* at Carleton University, shared to the NFS Facebook group page. Two critics of the project called the undertaking to task in no uncertain terms. One saw this as little more than a vanguard attack on the right, which "just seeks to maintain some semblance of order, sanity, and historical continuity." In defense of the NFS, one commentator countered by questioning whether such continuities worthy of protection included "genocide, slavery, colonialism, the usurpation of power to exploit natural landscapes and resources and the historical continuities and those isms sexism, antisemitism, racism and more?" Two historians of genocide, one at the United States Memorial Holocaust Museum, weighed in on the intellectual merits of the NFS, while an independent scholar wrote:

> I have been studying right-wing social and political movements for over 30 years, and have written essays for daily newspapers and articles in academic books and journals. And yet the New Fascism Syllabus continuously amazes me with materials of which I had been unaware, and points of view that teach me that although nearing 70 years of age I am never too old to learn.[50]

This one small example shows how attempts to besmirch the work of this networked knowledge community mobilized support immediately, in defense of critical pedagogy and historical evidence.

Conclusion

So, what *does* this initiative—and those we have addressed in this book—tell us about how social media sites function in the digital public sphere, and how might a critical analysis of our group page help us better understand social media as a site of activism around crowdsourced knowledge communities? This is, of course, too big of a question to answer fully here. Let us offer a few ideas in broad strokes. 1) Social media is just that, social: its fluid, traveling, and medial nature means it is constantly being used to respond to the ebb and flow of conversations online and offline. This is often seen as its downfall, but as our group page shows, it can also be its benefit for understanding how knowledge migrates between media. 2) Networked communities are not just mediated, they are also intermedial, to borrow from memory scholar Astrid Erll, meaning they draw from, sometimes cut across, and often extend other media conversations and forms, from the past as well as in the present.[51] In this respect, what goes on in a Facebook group like our own is not original. Nor is it entirely unique. What is new is the way users deploy the mediated conversation for mobilization, public writing, and simple reflection. At minimum, the group page emerged as a touchstone for sharing and commenting on news material, which even in the era before COVID-19 created spaces of scholarly exchange not always in supply on the university campus. In this sense, it re-spatialized knowledge production, broadening the places and spaces where engagement happens. 3) The group page has a discursive component, an emotional one, occasionally a self-promotional one (it *is* dominated by academics after all), and also a collegial one. Emanating out of these differently sized networks and in overlapping, interconnected publics, there is great potential to reach the wider world.[52]

We saw evidence in the NFS page of discussion that evolved online being taken up by individual readers and users. It carried over into other networked conversations, and in some instances bubbled up in emotional responses and vitriolic debate. More tangibly, conversations born on the NFS Facebook and Wordpress page influenced the writing and sharing of op/eds in several major newspapers, which were then remediated back to the group page upon publication. These news stories and conversations informed coursework and symposia, sharpened research questions, and formed the basis of grant applications on populism, hate, and the far-right. In Kansas City, the NFS syllabus was even the jumping off material for a weekly salon that cut across faculty and lay lines. In other words, the NFS as both a phenomenon and a thing were discursive and virtual but also material and real, with online activity shaping offline action. 4) Finally, it is not simply a site of conversation and politics, but a site of memory contestation as well. Connective memory, in a constant state of flux, draws on culturally distinct mental, discursive, and habitual frameworks that have evolved historically over time. Cataloguing news stories, marking one's day by reading articles, and responding in various fora, here, online is one example of the way in which memories of historical fascism galvanized contemporary views of the Trump moment. Page posts reflect ongoing societal concerns, while shaping the terms of debate and language of engagement. In this way, connective memory and the platform's affordances, as José van Dijck has argued elsewhere, are intimately intertwined.[53]

What is different, then, about the participatory public sphere and the role of history and memory in it? Unlike traditional forms of media, which historically, through elites, selectively chose what counts as a nation's collective story, now this task has fallen to vernacular voices networked together in a more diffuse set of spaces and places. Social media platforms, as strange as it may sound, are one of the spaces. Even before the advent of new media, Maurice Halbwachs recognized the intermedial nature of collective memory formation.[54] It bears asking then, how different is social media in this regard? Aside from real concerns about privacy protection and data use and abuse by corporate interests, the distinction is its diffuseness. While traditional forms of authority and expertise are challenged by the emergence of new sites of memory making and archiving, social media spaces of memory co-curation nevertheless provide possibilities for critical participation and activism. Beholden to the networked nature of the conversation and the affinities it constructs, groups such as the *New Fascism Syllabus* page are examples of connective memory activism that transcend borders and boundaries as part of a globalized form of digital communication, providing an ethical model of civic discourse to meet the challenge of this moment of danger.[55] Social media scripts in other words have their place in the post-Holocaust memory field, but understanding them requires that we treat them with attention and care, drawing from across disciplines, ever mindful of the technological underpinnings of our everyday interactions with technology.

Notes

Introduction

1   Tobias Ebbrecht-Hartmann and Lital Henig, "I-Memory: Selfies and Self-Witnessing in #Uploading_Holocaust (2016)," in *Digital Holocaust Memory, Education and Research*, ed. Victoria Grace Walden (Cham: Springer International Publishing, 2021), 213–35, https://doi.org/10.1007/978-3-030-83496-8_9.

2   Andrew Hoskins and Huw Halstead, "The New Grey of Memory: Andrew Hoskins in Conversation with Huw Halstead," *Memory Studies* 14, no. 3 (2021): 675–85, https://doi.org/10.1177/17506980211010936.

3   Andreas Huyssen, *Present Pasts: Urban Palimpsests and the Politics of Memory*, Cultural Memory in the Present (Stanford, CA: Stanford University Press, 2003), 18.

4   Maurice Halbwachs, *The Collective Memory*, Harper Colophon books; CN/800 (New York: Harper & Row, 1980); Jan Assmann, "Communicative and Cultural Memory," in *Cultural Memories: The Geographical Point of View*, ed. Peter Meusburger, Michael Heffernan, and Edgar Wunder, Knowledge and Space (Dordrecht: Springer Netherlands, 2011), 15–27, https://doi.org/10.1007/978-90-481-8945-8_2.

5   Wulf Kansteiner, "Transnational Holocaust Memory, Digital Culture and the End of Reception Studies," in *The Twentieth Century in European Memory*, ed. Tea Sindbæk Andersen and Barbara Törnquist-Plewa, Transcultural Mediation and Reception (Brill, 2017), 305–44, http://www.jstor.org/stable/10.1163/j.ctt1w8h377.18; "Touching Virtual Trauma: Performative Empathics in Second Life—Bryoni Trezise, 2012," https://journals-sagepub-com.proxy.library.carleton.ca/doi/full/10.1177/1750698011426355 (accessed March 24, 2022). Mark Deuze, "Media Life," *Media, Culture & Society* 33, no. 1 (2011): 137–48.

6   Victoria Grace Walden, "What Is 'Virtual Holocaust Memory'?," *Memory Studies* (November 22, 2019).

7   Joanne Garde-Hansen, Andrew Hoskins, and Anna Reading, *Save As ... Digital Memories* (Basingstoke: Palgrave Macmillan, 2009), 1.

8   Paul O'Connor, "The Unanchored Past: Three Modes of Collective Memory," *Memory Studies*, December 17, 2019, 1750698019894694, https://doi.org/10.1177/1750698019894694; Stefania Manca, "Bridging Cultural Studies and Learning Science: An Investigation of Social Media Use for Holocaust Memory and

Education in the Digital Age," *Review of Education, Pedagogy, and Cultural Studies* 43, no. 3 (May 27, 2021): 226–53, https://doi.org/10.1080/10714413.2020.1862582.

9   Ann Rigney, "The Dynamics of Remembrance: Texts between Monumentality and Morphing," in *Cultural Memory Studies: An International and Interdisciplinary Handbook*, ed. Astrid Erll and Ansgar Nunning (Berlin and New York: de Gruyter, 2008), 345–53.

10   Astrid Erll, "Travelling Memory," *Parallax (Leeds, England)* 17, no. 4 (2011): 4–18, https://doi.org/10.1080/13534645.2011.605570; Astrid Erll and Ann Rigney, *Mediation, Remediation, and the Dynamics of Cultural Memory*, Media and Cultural Memory = Medien Und Kulturelle Erinnerung (New York: Walter de Gruyter, 2009). See also Aleida Assmann and Sebastian Conrad, *Memory in a Global Age: Discourses, Practices and Trajectories*, Palgrave Macmillan Memory Studies (Basingstoke: Palgrave Macmillan, 2010).

11   Susannah Radstone, "What Place Is This? Transcultural Memory and the Locations of Memory Studies," *Parallax* 17, no. 4 (November 1, 2011): 109–23, https://doi.org/10.1080/13534645.2011.605585.

12   Aleida Assmann, "Transnational Memories," *European Review* 22, no. 4 (October 2014): 546–56, http://dx.doi.org.proxy.library.carleton.ca/10.1017/S1062798714000337.

13   Marianne Hirsch, *The Generation of Postmemory: Writing and Visual Culture after the Holocaust* (New York: Columbia University Press, 2012), 32.

14   Victoria Walden, *Digital Holocaust Memory, Education and Research* (Basingstoke: Palgrave Macmillan, 2021).

15   Hoskins and Halstead, "The New Grey of Memory."

16   Kenneth Neil Cukier and Viktor Mayer-Schönberger, "The Rise of Big Data," June 28, 2021, https://www.foreignaffairs.com/articles/2013-04-03/rise-big-data.

17   Wolfgang Ernst, *Digital Memory and the Archive*, Electronic Mediations ; v. 39 (Minneapolis: University of Minnesota Press, 2013).

18   Ceilyn Boyd, "Use of Optional Data Curation Features by Users of Harvard Dataverse Repository," *Journal of Escience Librarianship* 10, no. 2 (2021): e1191–, https://doi.org/10.7191/jeslib.2021.1191.

19   Yifat Gutman and Jenny Wüstenberg, "Challenging the Meaning of the Past from Below: A Typology for Comparative Research on Memory Activists," *Memory Studies*, October 10, 2021, 1070–86, https://doi.org/10.1177/17506980211044696.

20   Andrew Hoskins, "The Right to Be Forgotten in Post-Scarcity," in *The Ethics of Memory in a Digital Age: Interrogating the Right to Be Forgotten*, ed. Alessia Ghezzi et al. (New York: Palgrave Macmillian, 2014), 50–64, 60; see Also Andrew Hoskins, "Digital Network Memory," in *Mediation, Remediation and the Dynamic of Cultural Memory*, ed. Astrid Erll and Ann Rigney (Berlin: De Gruyter, 2009), 91–106.

21 Jean Burgess, "Remediating Vernacular Creativity: Photography and Cultural Citizenship in the Flickr Photo-Sharing Network," in *Spaces of Vernacular Creativity: Rethinking the Cultural Economy*, ed. Tim Edensor, Routledge Studies in Human Geography (London and New York: Routledge, 2010), 116–26.

22 Andrew Hoskins, "The Memory of the Multitude. The End of Collective Memory," in *Digital Memory Studies. Media Pasts in Transition*, ed. Andrew Hoskins (New York: Routledge, 2018), 85–109.

23 Saul Friedländer, "History, Memory, and the Historian: Dilemmas and Responsibilities," *New German Critique*, no. 80 (2000): 3–15, https://doi.org/10.2307/488629.

24 Wulf Kansteiner, *Transnational Holocaust Memory, Digital Culture and the End of Reception Studies* (Brill, 2017), https://doi.org/10.1163/9789004352353_014; *Antisemitism on Social Media* ed. Monika Hübscher and Sabine von Mehring (New York: Routledge, 2022).

25 Anne Kelly Knowles et al., *Geographies of the Holocaust*, Spatial Humanities (Bloomington, IN: Indiana University Press, 2014); Todd Presner, "The Ethics of the Algorithm: Close and Distant Listening to the Shoah Foundation Visual History Archive," in *Probing the Ethics of Holocaust Culture,* ed. Claudio Fogu, Wulf Kansteiner, and Todd Presner (Cambridge, MA: Harvard University Press, 2016), 175–202; Todd Presner, "The Humanities—Bigger and Bolder," *Seminar: A Journal of Germanic Studies* 50, no. 2 (2014): 154–60.

26 Wulf Kansteiner, "The Holocaust in the Twenty-first Century," in *Digital Memory Studies. Media Pasts in Transition*, ed. Andrew Hoskins (Routledge, 2018), 114. Kansteiner has in mind here specifically Anne Kelly Knowles et al., *Geographies of the Holocaust*, Spatial Humanities (Bloomington, IN: Indiana University Press, 2014); Claudio Fogu, Wulf Kansteiner, and Todd Presner, *Probing the Ethics of Holocaust Culture* (Cambridge, MA: Harvard University Press, 2016), 175–202. See also "Interview with Anne Knowles, Tim Cole, Alberto Giordano, and Paul B. Jaskot, Contributing Authors to *Geographies of the Holocaust*," in Fogu, Kansteiner, and Presner, *Probing the Ethics of Holocaust Culture*, 240–56.

27 Wulf Kansteiner, "The Holocaust in the Twenty-first Century," in *Digital Memory Studies. Media Pasts in Transition*, ed. Andrew Hoskins (New York: Routledge, 2018), 114.

28 Wulf Kansteiner, "Transnational Holocaust Memory, Digital Culture and the End of Reception Studies," in *The Twentieth Century in European Memory*, ed. Tea Sindbæk Andersen and Barbara Törnquist-Plewa (Leiden: Brill, 2017), 321. See also Anna Cento Bull and Hans Lauge Hansen, "On Agonistic Memory," *Memory Studies* 9, no. 4 (October 1, 2016): 390–404.

29 Claudio Fogu, "A Spatial Turn in Holocaust Studies," in Kansteiner and Presner, *Probing the Ethics of Holocaust Culture*, 218–39.

30 Alison Landsberg, *Prosthetic Memory the Transformation of American Remembrance in the Age of Mass Culture* (New York: Columbia University Press, 2004); Michael

Rothberg, *The Implicated Subject: Beyond Victims and Perpetrators, Cultural Memory in the Present* (Stanford, CA: Stanford University Press, 2019).

31 Geoffrey Batchen, *Burning with Desire: The Conception of Photography* (The MIT Press, 1999); John Berger, *Ways of Seeing*, Pelican Originals (London: British Broadcasting Corporation, 1972); Elizabeth Edwards, "Photography and the Material Performance of the Past," *History and Theory* 48, no. 4 (2009): 130–50, https://doi.org/10.1111/j.1468-2303.2009.00523.x.

32 Ariella Azoulay, *The Civil Contract of Photography* (New York: Zone Books, 2008); Sharon Sliwinski, *Human Rights In Camera* (University Of Chicago Press, 2011); Susie Linfield, *The Cruel Radiance: Photography and Political Violence* (Chicago: University of Chicago Press, 2010); Jennifer V. Evans, Paul Betts, and Stefan-Ludwig Hoffmann, *The Ethics of Seeing: Photography and Twentieth-Century German History* , Studies in German History, vol. 21 (New York: Berghahn, 2018). There is a vast literature on photography and the Holocaust that comes at the issue from diverse perspectives. Three recent examples providing an overview of the issues for historians include Daniel Magilow and Lisa Silverman, "The Boy in the Warsaw Ghetto (photograph, 1943): What Do Iconic Photographs Tell Us about the Holocaust?" in *Holocaust Representations in History: An Introduction* (London: Bloomsbury, 2019), 17–18; Elissa Mailander, "Making Sense of a Rape Photograph: Sexual Violence as Social Performance on the Eastern Front, 1939–1944," *Journal of the History of Sexuality* 26, no. 3 (2017): 489–520; David Shneer, "The Elusive Search for Evidence: Evgenii Khaldei's Budapest Ghetto, Images of Rape, and Soviet Holocaust Photography," *Slavic Review* 76, no. 1 (2017): 80–9, Wendy Lower, *The Ravine: A Family, a Photograph, a Holocaust Massacre Revealed* (Boston: Houghton Mifflin Harcourt, 2021).

33 Elizabeth Edwards, "Photography and the Material Performance of the Past," *History and Theory* 48, no. 4 (2009): 130–50.

34 Nadav Hochman and Lev Manovich, "Zooming into an Instagram City: Reading the Local through Social Media," *First Monday*, June 17, 2013, https://doi.org/10.5210/fm.v18i7.4711.

35 On this specifically, see "Pictures of Life, Living Pictures" in José van Dijck's *Mediated Memories in the Digital Age*, Cultural Memory in the Present (Stanford, CA: Stanford University Press, 2007), 98–121.

36 William K. Carroll and Robert A. Hackett, "Democratic Media Activism through the Lens of Social Movement Theory," *Media, Culture & Society* (January 2006); Luke Goode, "Social News, Citizen Journalism and Democracy," *New Media & Society* 11, no. 8 (January 12, 2009): 1287–305, https://doi.org/10.1177/1461444809341393; Thomas Poell and Erik Borra, "Twitter, YouTube, and Flickr as Platforms of Alternative Journalism: The Social Media Account of the 2010 Toronto G20 Protests," *Journalism* 13, no. 8 (2011): 1–19, https://doi.org/10.1177/1464884911431533.

37 Halbwachs, *The Collective Memory*.

38 Merlyna Lim, "Algorithmic Enclaves: Affective Politics and Algorithms in the Neoliberal Social Media Landscape," in *Affective Politics of Digital Media: Propaganda by Other Means*, ed. M. Boler and E. Davis (New York and London: Routledge, 2020), 186–203.

39 Bruno Latour, *Pandora's Hope: Essays on the Reality of Science Studies* (Cambridge, MA: Harvard University Press, 1999), 304.

40 Lim, "Algorithmic Enclaves." Spohr, "Fake News and Ideological Polarization: Filter Bubbles and Selective Exposure on Social Media," *Business Information Review*, 2017; Petter Törnberg, "Echo Chambers and Viral Misinformation: Modeling Fake News as Complex Contagion," *PLoS ONE* 13, no. 9 (September 20, 2018), https://doi.org/10.1371/journal.pone.0203958.

41 Sharon Macdonald, "Is 'Difficult Heritage' Still 'Difficult'?," *Museum International* 67, no. 1–4 (January 1, 2015): 6–22, https://doi.org/10.1111/muse.12078.

42 Martin Pogačar, "Museums and Memorials in Social Media," in *Media Archaeologies, Micro-Archives and Storytelling: Re-Presencing the Past*, ed. Martin Pogačar, Palgrave Macmillan Memory Studies (London: Palgrave Macmillan UK, 2016), 87–113, https://doi.org/10.1057/978-1-137-52580-2_4; Christoph Bareither, "Difficult Heritage and Digital Media: 'Selfie Culture' and Emotional Practices at the Memorial to the Murdered Jews of Europe," *International Journal of Heritage Studies: IJHS* 27, no. 1 (2021): 57–72, https://doi.org/10.1080/1352725 8.2020.1768578.

43 Dijck, *Mediated Memories in the Digital Age*, 10; Joanne Garde-Hansen, *Media and Memory*, Media Topics (Edinburgh: Edinburgh University Press, 2011).

44 See the United States Holocaust Memorial Museum (@holocaustmuseum) on Instagram. http://www.instagram.com/holocaustmuseum.

45 Auschwitz-Birkenau Memorial and Museum (@auschwitzmemorial). https://www.instagram.com/p/BU7VXssF2JO/?taken-by=auschwitzmemorial.

46 Eli Pariser, *The Filter Bubble: What the Internet Is Hiding from You* (New York: Penguin Press, 2011); Landsberg, *Prosthetic Memory the Transformation of American Remembrance in the Age of Mass Culture*.

47 Anna Reading, "Seeing Red: A Political Economy of Digital Memory," *Media, Culture & Society* 36, no. 6 (September 1, 2014): 748–60, https://doi.org/10.1177/0163443714532980.

48 Megan Boler and Elizabeth Davis, "The Affective Politics of the 'Post-Truth' Era: Feeling Rules and Networked Subjectivity," *Emotion, Space and Society* 27 (May 1, 2018): 75–85, https://doi.org/10.1016/j.emospa.2018.03.002.

49 Bruno Latour, "Why Has Critique Run Out of Steam? From Matters of Fact to Matters of Concern," *Critical Inquiry* 30, no. 2 (2004): 225–48, https://doi.org/10.1086/421123.

50 Bareither, "Difficult Heritage and Digital Media."

51 Boler and Davis, "The Affective Politics of the 'Post-Truth' Era," 81.

52 Sara Ahmed, "Affective Economies," *Social Text* 22, no. 2 (2004): 117–39, https://doi.org/10.1215/01642472-22-2_79-117.

53 Sara Jones, "Mediated Immediacy: Constructing Authentic Testimony in Audiovisual Media," *Rethinking History* 21, no. 2 (2017): 135–53. On these ethical communities, see Geoffrey Hartman, "Memory.com: Tele-suffering and Testimony in the Dot Com Era," *Raritan: A Quarterly Review* 19, no. 3 (2000): 1–18; Marianne Hirsch, "The Generation of Postmemory," *Poetics Today* 29, no. 1 (2008): 103–28.

54 Gary Weissman, *Fantasies of Witnessing: Postwar Efforts to Experience the Holocaust* (Ithaca and London: Cornell University Press, 2004); Landsberg, *Prosthetic Memory the Transformation of American Remembrance in the Age of Mass Culture*; Hirsch, *The Generation of Postmemory*.

55 Dorota Golańska, "Bodily Collisions: Toward a New Materialist Account of Memorial Art," *Memory Studies* 13, no. 1 (February 1, 2020): 74–89, https://doi.org/10.1177/1750698017741928.

56 Eloise Florence, "Entangled Memories: Complicating the Memory of Area Bombing through the Haunted Ruins of Anhalter Bahnhof," *Cultural Studies ↔ Critical Methodologies* 21, no. 3 (June 2021): 251–63, https://doi.org/10.1177/1532708621997584.

57 Jacques Ellul, *Propaganda: The Formation of Men's Attitudes*, Vintage Books edn. (New York: Vintage Books, 1973), 75.

Chapter 1

1 See Meghan Lundrigan, "People, Places, Things: Considering the Role of Visitor Photography at the United States Holocaust Memorial Museum," in *Lessons and Legacies XIV: The Holocaust in the Twenty-First Century; Relevance and Challenges in the Digital Age,* ed. Tim Cole and Simone Gigliotti (Evanston, IL: Northwestern University Press, 2020), 263–86; and Meghan Lundrigan, "#Holocaust #Auschwitz: Performing Holocaust Memory on Social Media," in *A Companion to the Holocaust,* ed. Simone Gigliotti and Hilary Earl (Hoboken, NJ: John Wiley & Sons, Inc. 2020), 639–56; Imogen Dalziel, "Romantic Auschwitz: Examples and Perceptions of Contemporary Visitor Photography at the Auschwitz-Birkenau State Museum," *Holocaust Studies* 22, no. 2–3 (2016): 187–207; Gemma Commane and Rebekah Potton, "Instagram and Auschwitz: A Critical Assessment of the Impact Social Media Has on Holocaust Representation," *Holocaust Studies: A Journal of Culture and History* 25, no. 1–2 (2019): 151–81.

2 Nicholas Mirzoeff, *An Introduction to Visual Culture* (London and New York: Routledge, 1999), 13.

3   Wulf Kansteiner and Todd Presner, "Introduction: The Field of Holocaust Studies and the Global Emergence of Holocaust Culture," in *Probing the Ethics of Holocaust Culture*, ed. Claudio Fogu, Wulf Kansteiner, and Todd Presner (Cambridge, MA: Harvard University Press, 2016), 33–4.

4   Tobias Ebbrecht-Hartmann and Tom Divon, "Hashtagging the Holocaust: How COVID Gave Death Camps New Life Online," *Haaretz*, https://www.haaretz.com/world-news/2021-01-27/ty-article-opinion/.premium/hashtagging-the-holocaust-how-covid-gave-death-camps-new-life-online/0000017f-e199-d9aa-afff-f9d964d70000 (accessed September 3, 2022).

5   Eva Pfanzelter, "At the Crossroads with Public History: Mediating the Holocaust on the Internet," *Holocaust Studies* 21, no. 4 (2015): 250–71.

6   James E. Young, *The Texture of Memory: Holocaust Memorials and Meanings* (New Haven and London, 1993), 2. For more on multidirectional memory, see Michael Rothberg, *Multidirectional Memory: Remembering the Holocaust in the Age of Decolonization* (Stanford: Stanford University Press, 2009).

7   Mike Robinson and David Picard, "Moments, Magic, and Memories: Photographing Tourists, Tourist Photographs and Making Worlds," in *The Framed World: Tourism, Tourists, and Photography*, ed. Mike Robinson and David Picard (England: Ashgate Publishing Ltd., 2009), 1.

8   Ibid., 10.

9   Jack Kugelmass' assessment of the Auschwitz visit as a secular ritual is also incorporated in Stier's assessment of tourism and ritual. See Jack Kugelmass, "Why We Go to Poland: Holocaust Tourism as Secular Ritual," in *The Art of Memory: Holocaust Memorials in History*, ed. James E. Young (New York: Prestel, 1994), 175–83; and Oren Baruch Stier, *Committed to Memory: Cultural Mediations of the Holocaust* (Amherst and Boston: University of Massachusetts Press, 2015).

10 Marianne Hirsch, *Family Frames: Photography, Narrative, and Post-memory* (Cambridge, MA: Harvard University Press, 1997).

11 The list is long here. See Janina Struk, *Photographing the Holocaust: Interpretations of Evidence* (London and New York: I.B. Tauris, 2004) and Astrid Erll, *Astrid Memory in Culture* (New York: Palgrave Macmillan, 2011).

12 Dalziel, "Romantic Auschwitz," 188.

13 Roland Barthes, *Camera Lucida: Reflections on Photography*, trans. Richard Howard (New York: Hill and Wang, 1981), 76–81.

14 James E. Young, *The Stages of Memory: Reflections on Memorial Art, Loss, and the Spaces Between* (Amherst: University of Massachusetts Press, 2016), 16.

15 Wulf Kansteiner, "Genocide Memory, Digital Cultures, and the Aesthetization of Violence," *Memory Studies* 7, no. 4 (2014): 405.

16 For a very comprehensive discussion of the development of Holocaust archives and their transformation into information processing systems in the early 2000s (as well as the challenges they face in the digital age), see Presner, "The Ethics of the Algorithm."

17 For more on hashtag usage across platforms, see Jean Burgess and Ariadna Matamoros-Fernández, "Mapping Sociocultural Controversies across Digital Media Platforms: One Week of #Gamergate on Twitter, YouTube, and Tumblr," *Communication Research and Practice* 2, no. 1 (2016): 76–96.

18 Michele Zappavigna, "Ambient Affiliation: A Linguistic Perspective on Twitter," *New Media and Society* 13, no. 5 (2011).

19 The research conducted for this chapter was developed by cross-referencing prominent Holocaust hashtags, such as #holocaust, #holocaustmuseum, #holocaustmemorial, and #auschwitz, starting first with #auschwitz, and then through the tracking of other popular hashtags, such as #nofilter and #blackandwhite.

20 See the United States Holocaust Memorial Museum (@holocaustmuseum) on Instagram. http://www.instagram.com/holocaustmuseum (accessed September 2, 2022).

21 On the Auschwitz-Birkenau Memorial and Museum's Instagram profile (@auschwitzmemorial), a "like = remember." http://www.instagram.com/auschwitzmemorial (accessed September 2, 2022). The Neuengamme Holocaust Memorial also has a very active social media presence—especially on Instagram.

22 See @auschwitzmemorial's 2016 retrospective image on Instagram. https://www.instagram.com/p/BOpAQ6qgIqR/ (accessed September 2, 2022).

23 Auschwitz Memorial and Museum (Instagram user @auschwitzmemorial), June 17, 2017, https://www.instagram.com/p/BVcugThltRe/ (accessed September 2, 2022).

24 User @craigcohenhistory in response to user @unmanageablehairdontcare, June 17, 2017, https://www.instagram.com/p/BVcugThltRe/ (accessed September 2, 2022).

25 See Marianne Hirsch and Leo Spitzer, "Incongruous Images: Before, during, and after the Holocaust," *History and Theory* 48, no. 4 (2009): 9–25.

26 This is easy to see with a quick hashtag search on Instagram. https://www.instagram.com/explore/tags/auschwitz/ (accessed September 2, 2022).

27 Cornelia Brink, "Secular Icons: Looking at Photographs from Nazi Concentration Camps," *History & Memory* 12, no. 1 (2000): 136.

28 Marita Sturken, "Memory, Consumerism and Media: Reflections on the Emergence of the Field," *Memory Studies* 1, no. 1 (2008): 75.

29 Auschwitz Memorial and Museum (Instagram user @auschwitzmemorial), June 17, 2022, https://www.instagram.com/p/BVcugThltRe/ (accessed September 2, 2022).

30 Auschwitz Birkenau Memorial 2007 Annual Report, 7. For a complete list of museum reports, see Auschwitz Birkenau Museum and Memorial, "Museum Reports," http://auschwitz.org/en/museum/museum-reports/ (accessed September 2, 2022).

31 Pawel Sawicki, Auschwitz Memorial and Museum (@auschwitzmemorial), November 25, 2019, https://www.instagram.com/p/B5Sr0DHpQKH/. (accessed September 2, 2022).

32 Gemma Commane and Rebekah Potton, "Instagram and Auschwitz: A critical assessment of the impact social media has on Holocaust representation," *Holocaust Studies* (2018): 20.

33 Piotr M.A. Cywiński, *Auschwitz Birkenau Memorial 2009 Annual Report* (Państwowe Muzeum Auschwitz-Birkenau w Oświęcimiu, 2010), 5.

34 Self-photography, at its most basic level, is the act of capturing oneself on camera. Typically, these photos are taken alone, at arms-length. Selfies can be group efforts, but the act of taking a photo always lies in the hands of one person. The selfie always features some part of the human body of the person who has snapped the photo, and preferably includes partial or full pictures of the individual's face. Due to the proximity of the camera to the face of the individual, their facial features are always the predominant subject within the frame. Selfies have received a great deal of scholarly and popular attention. See Lev Manovich, "Selfiecity: Exploring Photography and Self-Fashioning in Social Media," in *Postdigital Aesthetics: Art, Computation and Design*, ed. David M. Berry and Michael Dieter (Palgrave Macmillan: 2015), 109–22.

35 Maskellharry's review of Auschwitz-Birkenau on TripAdvisor, October 28, 2018. http://bit.ly/maskellharry (accessed September 2, 2022).

36 Samantha Mitschke, "The Sacred, the Profane, and the Space in Between: Site-Specific Performance at Auschwitz," *Holocaust Studies* 22, no. 2–3 (2016): 228–43.

37 Imogen Dalziel, "Becoming the 'Holocaust Police'? The Auschwitz-Birkenau State Museum's Authority on Social Media," in *Digital holocaust Memory, Education and Research,* ed. Victoria Grade Walden (Switzerland: Palgrave Macmillan, 2021).

38 The United States Holocaust Memorial Digital Encyclopedia features an entire media essay on the process of receiving a tattoo at Auschwitz. "Receiving Tattoos at Auschwitz," *The United States Holocaust Memorial Museum Digital Encyclopedia*, https://encyclopedia.ushmm.org/content/en/gallery/receiving-tattoos-at-auschwitz (accessed September 2, 2022).

39 Dora Apel, "The Tattooed Jew," in *Visual Culture and the Holocaust*, ed. Barbie Zelizer (New Brunswick, NJ: Rutgers University Press, 2000), 302.

40 Nicholas Chare, *Auschwitz and Afterimages: Abjection, Witnessing and Representation* (London and New York: I.B. Tauris, 2011), 93.

41 This can also be linked to a consideration of the yellow Star of David, as well as other visual markings (though not irreversible) which victims of the Holocaust were forced to wear as identifying visual aids. When considering these early visual signifiers of the Holocaust experience, the politics of gaze must also be investigated. For more on the gaze of the victim/perpetrator, see Struk, *Photographing the Holocaust* and Marianne Hirsch, "Surviving Images: Holocaust Photographs

and the Work of Post-memory," in *Visual Culture and the Holocaust*, ed. Barbie Zelizer (New Brunswick, NJ: Rutger's University Press, 2000), and Susan A. Crane, "Choosing Not to Look: Representation, Repatriation, and Holocaust Atrocity Photography," *History and Theory* 47 (2009): 315–16.

42 The act of receiving a tattoo as an embodiment of post-memory has become popular and not uncommon amongst third-generation Israeli Holocaust survivors. See Jodi Rudoren, "Proudly Bearing Elders' Scars, Their Skin Says 'Never Forget,'" *The New York Times*, September 30, 2012, https://www.nytimes.com/2012/10/01/ world/middleeast/with-tattoos-young-israelis-bear-holocaust-scars-of-relatives. html (accessed September 2, 2022).

43 Tim Cole, *Selling the Holocaust: From Auschwitz to Schindler, How History Is Bought, Packaged, and Sold* (New York: Routledge, 2000), 3.

44 @auschwitzmemorial, October 8, 2017, https://www.instagram.com/p/BZ-yBkLFhW7/ (accessed September 2, 2022).

45 @auschwitzmemorial, October 8, 2017, https://www.instagram.com/p/BZ-yBkLFhW7/ (accessed September 2, 2022).

46 "Prisoners Photos," the Auschwitz-Birkenau Memorial and Museum, Prisoners photos / About the available data / Museum / Auschwitz-Birkenau, https://www. auschwitz.org/en/museum/about-the-available-data/prisoners-photos/ (accessed September 2, 2022).

47 Struk, *Photographing the Holocaust,* 216.

48 Susan A. Crane, "Choosing Not to Look: Representation, Repatriation, and Holocaust Atrocity Photography," *History and Theory* 47 (2008): 309–30.

49 Julia Adenay Thomas, "Hope Flies, Death Dances: Moving toward an Ethics of Seeing," in *The Ethics of Seeing: Photography and 20th Century German History* (New York: Berghahn Press, 2018), 276.

50 Kate Douglas, "Youth, Trauma, and Memorialisation: The Selfie as Witnessing," *Memory Studies* 13, no. 4 (2017): 3.

51 Ibid., 4.

52 Ebbrecht-Hartmann and Henig, "I-Memory." See Chapter 3 for an in-depth discussion of #Uploading_Holocaust in relation to vlogging practices on YouTube.

53 Nicholas Mirzoeff, *How to See the World: An Introduction to Images, from Self-Portraits to Selfies, Maps to Movies, and More* (New York: Basic Books, 2016), 30.

54 Elisa Serafinelli's discussion of Belting's work is also particularly useful here. Serafinelli extends Belting's analysis to argue for a networked memory in the age of digital media. See Elisa Serafinelli, *Digital Life on Instagram: New Social Communication of Photography* (Bingley: Emerald Publishing Limited, 2018), 26–7.

55 Hans Belting, "Image, Medium, Body: A New Approach to Iconology," *Critical Inquiry* 31, no. 2 (2005): 302–18; see also Hans Belting and Thomas Dunlap, *An Anthropology of Images: Picture, Medium, Body* (Princeton: Princeton University Press, 2011).

56 Belting, "Image, Medium, Body," 302–3.

57 Serafinelli, *Digital Life on Instagram,* 26.

58 Visual anthropologist Elizabeth Edwards considers the intersection of class and gender as they relate to amateur survey photography in Great Britain at the turn of the twentieth century. See Elizabeth Edwards, *The Camera as Historian: Amateur Photographers and the Historical Imagination, 1885–1918* (Durham and London: Duke University Press, 2012). Mirzoeff also traces the history of the self-portrait in the context of visual culture and visuality in *How to See the World,* 29–69.

59 See Irit Dekel, *Mediation at the Holocaust Memorial in Berlin* (Basingstoke, Hampshire: Palgrave Macmillan, 2013), "Jews and Other Others at the Holocaust Memorial in Berlin," *Anthropological Journal of European Cultures* 23, no. 2 (2014): 71–84, and "Ways of Looking: Observation and Transformation at the Holocaust Memorial, Berlin," *Memory Studies* 2, no. 1 (2009): 71–86.

60 Dekel, "Ways of Looking," 72.

61 The relationship between memorials, the body, and historical memory transference constitutes an entire field. Many scholars trace their analysis of memory to Plato, Aristotle, Halbwachs, Descartes, Derrida, and Kant. For a time, many scholars relied on an analysis of Pierre Nora's *Lieux de mémoire* to best explain the relationship between history, memory, and memorialization. However, in recent years, historians and memory scholars have moved away from Nora, re-considering the transmission of memory in contexts beyond that of the historical monument. Here, it is important to mention Paul Ricouer 's landmark contribution, *Memory, History, Forgetting,* trans. Kathleen Blamey and David Pellauer (Chicago: University of Chicago Press, 2004). For a historical overview of the philosophical understanding of memory, see Dmitri Nikulin, *Memory: A History* (Oxford: Oxford University Press, 2015); see also Susannah Radstone and Bill Schwarz's edited volume, *Memory: Histories, Theories, and Debates* (New York: Fordham University Press, 2010), as it provides an excellent cross-section of theoretical debates and practical contemporary applications in the fields of both history and philosophy.

62 Peter Rigny, "A Visit to the Memorial," *PBS: Frontline,* May 31, 2005, http://www.pbs.org/wgbh/pages/frontline/shows/germans/memorial/visit.html (accessed April 10, 2014).

63 James E. Young expands on this sentiment in *At Memory's Edge: After-Images of the Holocaust in Contemporary Art and Architecture* (New Haven: Yale University Press, 2000).

64 Nicholas Mirzoeff in Jeanette Vigliotti, "The Double Sighted: Visibility, Identity, and Photographs on Facebook" (Master's Thesis, University of North Florida, 2014), 6.

65 Dekel, "Ways of Looking," 72–3.

66 The selfie received a great deal of media attention after it went viral in June 2014. The controversy prompted a number of public debates over the appropriate forms

of behavior at solemn sites. See Caitlin Dewey's analysis of the selfie's context and Breanna's personal motivations. See Caitlin Dewey, "The Other Side of the Infamous 'Auschwitz Selfie'," *The Washington Post*, July 22, 2014, https://www. washingtonpost.com/news/the-intersect/wp/2014/07/22/the-other-side-of-the-infamous-auschwitz-selfie/ (accessed September 2, 2022).

67   Dewey, "The Other Side of the Infamous 'Auschwitz Selfie.'"

68   Here, we refer specifically the use of multiple hashtags. Some Instagram images use only a single hashtag, but if an image bears several hashtags it will be even more visible in different image feeds. For example, many images at the Holocaust memorial in Berlin feature the tags #holocaust, #holocaustmemorial, #history, and sometimes even #auschwitz—long-considered the ultimate symbol of the Holocaust in the age of post-memory.

69   Shahak Shapira, "YOLOCAUST," https://yolocaust.de/ (accessed September 2, 2022).

70   Marianne Hirsch, "Nazi Photographs in Post-Holocaust Art: Gender as an Idiom of Memorialization," in *Phototextualities: Intersections of Photography and Narrative*, ed. Alex Hughes and Andrea Noble (Albuquerque: University of New Mexico Press, 2003), 26.

71   For more on the ways in which cities are reconstituted through social media photography, see Jon D. Boy and Justus Uitermark, "Reassembling the City through Instagram," *Transactions of the Institute of British Geographers* 42 (2017): 612–24.

72   On the contrary: underneath the Memorial to the Murdered Jews of Europe there is a well-developed museum and interpretation center to help visitors understand the history of the Holocaust and its visual representation. See "Information Centre under the Field of Stelae," https://www.stiftung-denkmal. de/en/exhibitions/information-centre.html. Eisenman's words are from Joel Gunter's "How Should You Behave at a Holocaust Memorial?" *BBC News*, January 20, 2017, http://www.bbc.com/news/world-europe-38675835 (accessed September 2, 2022).

73   It is worth clarifying that archival Holocaust imagery isn't accessible at the street level of the Berlin memorial, though you can choose to visit the exhibit below the memorial. That being said, aside from minimal signage, not everyone who visits the memorial is aware of the exhibit space below.

74   For more on the construction of recent Holocaust memorials, see Erin Donnelly, "The Tricky Business of Designing a Holocaust Memorial in 2017," *Azure Magazine*, February 15, 2017, http://www.azuremagazine.com/article/challenges-of-designing-a-holocaust-memorial-in-2017/ (accessed May 4, 2017). See Rebecca Clare Dolgoy and Jerzy Elzanowski, "Working through the Limits of Multidirectional Memory: Ottawa's Memorial to the Victims of Communism and National Holocaust Monument," *Citizenship Studies* 22, no. 4 (2018): 433–51.

75   Hirsch, *Family Frames*, 15.

76   Instagram user @leeannelouise, June 4, 2017, https://www.instagram.com/p/
     BU7cL0jFQyz/.

77   Instagram user @lorajayne15, June 4, 2017, https://www.instagram.com/p/
     BU7OYrQD9XH/.

78   Interview with Raisa Galofre, Berlin, July 25, 2016.

79   Instagram image by @rotemzo, July 10, 2017, https://www.instagram.com/p/
     BWXVtyxn8ss/.

80   Instagram image by @meetmelbee, December 12, 2018, https://www.instagram.
     com/p/BrTiPNOHZSZ/ (accessed September 2, 2022).

81   Visitor comments from the United States Holocaust Memorial Museum,
     Institutional Fonds, July 29, 2015.

82   "What you do matters: The choices we as individuals make are critical to making
     a more just and humane world," caption by @caitcomber, April 24, 2017, https://
     www.instagram.com/p/BTRMiixD78q/.

83   Visitor comments from the United States Memorial Holocaust Museum,
     Institutional Fonds, September 11, 2003.

84   Visitor comments from the United States Holocaust Memorial Museum,
     Institutional Fonds, October 2, 2002.

85   Sometimes, the presence of the victim's body or face is certainly more personal
     for the visitor. A visitor commented, "When I Was [at Auschwitz] I saw a woman
     crying in the hallway … She had found her Grandma's pic [*sic*] on the wall
     [of prisoners]." Comment by @alanbcourt on @auschwitzmemorial's image,
     October 8, 2017, https://www.instagram.com/p/BZ-yBkLFhW7/ (accessed
     September 2, 2022).

86   Instagram image by @gresaismaili, December 26, 2018, https://www.instagram.
     com/p/BrdWZJXnHfX/ (accessed September 2, 2022).

87   Caption copyright @courtney_dunbar_84, June 3, 2018. The entire caption reads:
     "I have been compelled to understand the Holocaust for much of my life. I've
     read countless books, watched countless documentaries, and still cannot accept a
     peace in understanding why this horrific genocide occurred. While going through
     the trip pictures Addison sent home today, I immediately landed on this picture.
     It was imperative to me that she truly absorb their visit to Dachau today. Albeit
     a reflection, do you see how she fades in and melds to this prisoner's uniform?
     The person who wore this uniform was human … just like Addison. This person
     had family, friends, and a purpose for being … just like all of us. This person, and
     the millions subject to the tyranny and barbarism of the Nazis were people just
     like us. I am thankful for this photographic gift from my child today. It's been
     of such importance to me over the years that she understand why I've spent so
     many hours learning what I can about Nazi genocide and the persecution of the
     Jews, specifically. I know that, today, she witnessed and felt what I so hoped she
     would … #neverforget #holocaust #dachauconcentrationcamp."

88   To date, the New Fascism Syllabus Facebook group hosts 900 members. Home—
     The New Fascism Syllabus (accessed September 2, 2022).

89   Taylor Lorenz, "Instagram Is teeming with Antisemitism," *The Atlantic*,
     October 30, 2018, https://www.theatlantic.com/technology/archive/2018/10/
     instagram-ignored-crazyjewishmom-harassment/574450/

90   The Conference on Jewish Material Claims against Germany, "Holocaust
     Knowledge and Awareness Study," *Schoen Consulting*, February 23–27, 2018,
     http://www.claimscon.org/study/ (accessed September 2, 2022). For a concise
     summary of the findings of the study, see *Schoen Consulting*, "Holocaust
     Knowledge and Awareness Study," April 18, 2019, http://www.claimscon.org/
     wp-content/uploads/2018/04/Holocaust-Knowledge-Awareness-Study_Executive-
     Summary-2018.pdf (accessed September 2, 2022).

91   *Schoen Consulting* "Holocaust Knowledge and Awareness Study: Executive
     Summary," 7, http://www.claimscon.org/wp-content/uploads/2018/04/Holocaust-
     Knowledge-Awareness-Study_Executive-Summary-2018.pdf.

92   United States Holocaust Memorial Museum, "Days of Remembrance: More Ways
     to Remember," https://www.ushmm.org/remember/days-of-remembrance/more
     (accessed September 2, 2022).

93   Ibid.

94   See Taylor Lorenz's "Instagram Has a Massive Harassment Problem," *The Atlantic*,
     October 15, 2018, https://www.theatlantic.com/technology/archive/2018/10/
     instagram-has-massive-harassment-problem/572890/ (accessed September 2,
     2022).

95   See Gavriel Rosenfeld, *Hi Hitler! How the Nazi Past Is Being Normalized in
     Contemporary Culture* (Cambridge: Cambridge University Press, 2014).

96   See Michael Bernard-Donals, *Figures of Memory: The Rhetoric of Displacement at
     the United States Holocaust Memorial Museum* (Albany, NY: State University of
     New York, 2016).

97   See, for example, Deborah Lipstadt's writing on this comparison. Lipstadt,
     "It's Not the Holocaust," *The Atlantic*, June 22, 2018, https://www.theatlantic.
     com/ideas/archive/2018/06/holocaust-family-separation/563480/ (accessed
     September 2, 2022).

98   Sarah Harmer, "Going Visual: Holocaust Representation and Historical Method,"
     The American Historical Review 115, no. 1 (2010): 115–22.

99   Hirsch and Spitzer, "Incongruous Images 'before, during, and after' the Holocaust."

100 See Rebecca Jinks, *Representing Genocide: The Holocaust as Paradigm?* (London:
     Bloomsbury, 2016).

101 W. J. T. Mitchell, *What Do Pictures Want? The Lives and Loves of Images* (Chicago:
     The University of Chicago Press, 2005), 3.

102 Mirzoeff, *How to See the World*.

Chapter 2

1   Jacques Derrida, *Archive Fever. A Freudian Impression* (Chicago: University of Chicago Press, 1995).

2   Boeseralterman https://www.flickr.com/photos/boeseraltermannberlin/; PM Cheung (https://www.flickr.com/photos/pm_cheung/); Thomas Rassloff (https://www.flickr.com/photos/rassloff/)

3   This chapter does not employ Bruno Latour's now infamous actor-network-theory, yet it goes without saying his ideas have animated much of the work in digital humanities since his book was published in 2005. Bruno Latour, *Reassembling the Social: An Introduction to Actor-Network-Theory* (Oxford: Oxford University Press 2005).

4   In our case, we used several different tools to narrow down our empirical field, including Voyant and Mallet http://mallet.cs.umass.edu/topics.php. This will be discussed later on in the chapter.

5   The term "glocal" helps us understand the concerns of a local site or locality within larger global processes. See R. Robertson, "Globalisation or Glocalization?" *The Journal of International Communication* 1, no. 1 (1993): 33–52. See Also Victor Roudometof, *Glocalization: A Critical Introduction* (New York: Routledge, 2016).

6   José van Dijck, "Flickr and the Culture of Connectivity: Sharing Views, Experiences, Memories," *Memory Studies* 4, no. 4 (2011): 401–15.

7   Paul Levinson, *Cellphone: The Story of the World's Most Mobile Medium and How It Has Transformed Everything!* (2004). See also Nancy Martha West, *Kodak and the Lens of Nostalgia* (2000).

8   Paul Duguid, "Material Matters: Aspects of the Past and the Futurology of the Book," in *The Future of the Book*, ed. Geoffrey Nunberg (Stanford: University of California Press, 1996), 63–92; Robert Darnton, "What Is the History of Books" *Daedalus* (1993): 65–83.

9   *Online Collective Action: Dynamics of the Crowd in Social Media*, ed. Nitin Agarwal, Merlyna Lim, and Rolf T. Wigand (2014).

10 Zeynep Tufekci, "Capabilities of Movements and Affordances of Digital Media: Paradoxes of Empowerment" *dmlcentral. Digital Media+Learning: The Power of Participation*, http://dmlcentral.net/blog/zeynep-tufekci/capabilities-movements-and-affordances-digital-media-paradoxes-empowerment; Charles Tilly, *Stories, Identities, and Political* Change (2002), 188.

11 Zizi Pararacharissi, *Affective Publics. Sentiment, Technology, and Politics* (Oxford: Oxford University Press 2015), 7.

12 José van Dijck, *The Culture of Connectivity.*

13 Jamie Bartlett, Caterina Froio, Mark Littler, and Duncan McDonnell, *"Social Media Is Changing Politics across Europe": New Political Actors in Europe. Beppe Grillo and the M5S* (2013). See also "Social Media Powers Youth Participation in Politics,"

Science Daily, June 26 2012, www.sciencedaily.com/releases/012/06/120626121043.
htm (accessed June 25, 2014).

14 W. Lance Bennett and Alexandra Segerberg, "The Logic of Connective Action.
Digital Media and the Personalization of Contentious Politics," *Information,
Communication, and Society* 15, no. 5 (June 2012): 739–68.

15 In 2010, *New Yorker* columnist Malcolm Gladwell mounted a challenge
against so-called cyber-utopians who argue that online activism is an effective
form of political mobilization. See "Small Change: Why the Revolution Will
Not Be Tweeted," *New Yorker*, October 4, 2010, http://www.newyorker.com/
magazine/2010/10/04/small-change-3?currentPage=all Former Open Society
fellow and media commentator Evgeny Morozov made a similar argument in *The
Net Delusion. The Dark Side of Internet Freedom* (2011). Academics on the other
hand, especially those working on new media and social protest, see valuable
links between on and offline activism. See Merlyna Lim, "Clicks, Cabs, and Coffee
Houses: Social Media and Oppositional Movements in Egypt, 2004–2011," *Journal
of Communication* 62 (2012), especially the argument on page 231.

16 Steven Lovell, *Russia in the Microphone Age: A History of Soviet Radio, 1919–1970*
(2015).

17 Andrew Chadwick, "Web 2.0: New Challenges for the Study of E-Democracy
in an Era of Information Exuberance," *I/S: A Journal of Law and Policy for the
Information Society* 5, no. 1 (2008): 3–29.

18 Benedict Anderson, *Imagined Communities. Reflections on the Origin and Spread of
Nationalism* (London: Verso, 1983).

19 On this way digital communication alters notions of place, see Kazys Varnelis and
Anne Friedberg, "Place: The Networking of Public Space" in *Networked Publics*,
ed. Kazys Varnelis (2012), 17.

20 Jürgen Osterhammel and Niels P. Pietersson, *Globalization: A Short History* (2005),
69.

21 Karen Mossberger, Caroline J. Tolbert, and Ramona S. McNeal, *Digital Citizenship.
The Internet, Society, and Participation* (2008); Manuel Castells, *The Rise of the
Network Society* (1996). See also Nicole M. Rishel, "Digitizing Deliberation:
Normative Concerns for the Use of Social Media in Deliberative Democracy,"
Administrative Theory & Praxis 33, no. 3 (2011): 411–32. On the role of print media
in fostering a sense of bourgeois identity as linked to conceptualizations of the
nation state, see again iconic text by Benedict Anderson, *Imagined Communities*.

22 Tim Highfield and Tama Leaver, "Instagrammatics and Digital Methods: Studying
Visual Social Media, from Selfies and GIFS to Memes and Emoji," *Communication
Research and Practice* 2, no. 1 (2016): 47–62; Nadav Hochman and Lev Manovich,
"Reading the Local through Social Media," *First Monday* (2013), https://
firstmonday.org/ojs/index.php/fm/article/view/4711/3698; Ming-Hsiang Tsou,

"Visualization of Social Media Seeing a mirage or message?" *Cartography and Geographic Information Science* 40, no. 2 (April 2013): 55–60.

23 Susan Murray, "New Media and Vernacular Photography," in *The Photographic Image in Digital Culture,* ed. Martin Lister (London: Routledge, 2013), 167.

24 Scott McQuire, "Photography's Afterlife: Documentary Images and the Operational Archive," *Journal of Material Culture* 18, no. 3 (2013): 223–4. See also Nicholas Mirzoeff, *An Introduction to Visual Culture* (London: Routledge, 1999), 86.

25 Anna Reading, "The Mobile Family Gallery? Gender, Memory and the Cameraphone?" *Trames: Journal of the Humanities and Social Sciences* 12 (3) (2008): 355–65; Daniel Rubinstein and Katrina Sluis, "A Life More Photographic: Mapping the Networked Image," *Photographies* 1, no. 1 (2008): 9–28.

26 danah boyd [*sic*], "Social Network Sites as Networked Publics," 47.

27 Damian Sutton, "Immanent Images," 314. The literature on this is vast. A good overview may be found in Lynn Hunt Vanessa Schwartz, "The History Issue," *Journal of Visual Culture* 9, no. 3 (December 2010).

28 Julia Adenay Thomas, "Hope Flies, Death Dances: Moving toward an Ethics of Seeing," in *The Ethics of Seeing: Photography and Twentieth Century German History,* ed. Jennifer V. Evans, Paul Betts and Stefan-Ludwig Hoffmann (New York: Berghahn Press, 2018), 274–86.

29 Arielle Azoulay, *Civil Imagination: A Political Ontology of Photography* (2012). The University of Toronto-based photography group The Photographic Situation has explored Azoulay's framework for the historical study of affect and photography. See http://www.torontophotographyseminar.org/project/photographic-situation-project

30 Here, we are thinking of the term in two ways, primarily as a way of denoting what falls within and outside a photo's own frame. However, we are also hinting at the notion of framing as a sociological phenomenon. For a cogent overview in relation to collective action, see *Frames of Protest. Social Movements and the Framing Perspective,* ed. Hank Johnston and John A. Noakes (2005).

31 Susan Murray, "New Media and Vernacular Photography: Revisiting Flickr," in *The Photographic Image in Digital Culture* ed. Martin Lister (London: Routledge, 2013), 167.

32 Jean Burgess, "Hearing Ordinary Voices: Cultural Studies, Vernacular Creativity, and Digital Storytelling," *Journal of Media and Cultural Studies* 20, no. 2 (2006): 201–14.

33 Interview with Thomas Rassloff, Berlin, July 14, 2014. On camera clubs, see Pierre Bourdieu, *Photography: A Middle-Brow Art* (1996[1965]) and Edwards, *The Camera as Historian. Amateur Photographs and the Historical Imagination, 1885–1918.* See also Merlyna Lim and Mark E. Kann, "Politics: Deliberation,

Mobilization, and Networked Practices of Agitation," in *Networked Publics*, ed. Kazys Varnelis (2008), 70–108.

34 Sandra Robinson, "Platform Multiverse: Discontent and Disconnection among Alt-Rights," *Canadian Journal of Communication* 47, no. 1 (February 15, 2022): 197–218.

35 There is even a group devoted to Flickr hacks: https://www.flickr.com/groups/flickrhacks/

36 Jean Burgess, "Remediating Vernacular Creativity: Photography and Cultural Citizenship in the Flickr Photo-sharing Network," in *Spaces of Vernacular Creativity: Rethinking the Cultural Economy,* ed. Tim Edensor et al. (2010): 116–26.

37 Zanny Begg, "Recasting Subjectivity," *Third Text* 19, no. 6 (November 2005): 625–36; Steve Edwards, "The Commons and the Crowd: Figuring Photography from Above and Below," *Third Text* 23, no. 4 (July 2009), 447–64; and Benjamin Young, "On Strike: Allan Sekula's *Waiting for Tear Gas*," in *Sensible Politics: The Visual Culture of Nongovernmental Action*, ed. Yates McKee and Meg McLagan (New York, 2012), 148–81.

38 Allan Sekula's photographs from Seattle, which were mounted in an exhibition and set into a film, are also included in the volume he co-edited with Alexander Cockburn and Jeffrey St. Clair, *Five Days that Shook the World: Seattle and Beyond* (2000). Also discussed in Kaja Silverman, "Disassembled Movies," *Synopsis 3: Testimonies: Between Fact and Fiction* (2003).

39 Jacques Rancière, *Aux bords du politique* (1998), 177.

40 Timothy Scott Brown, *West Germany in the Global Sixties* (2013); *1968. Ein Handbuch zur Kultur und Mediengeschichte,* ed. Martin Klimke and Joachim Sharloth (2013); Joachim Sharloth, *1968 Eine Kommunikationsgeschichte* (2011).

41 Geoffrey Pleyers, *Alter-globalization: Becoming Actors in the Global Age* (2010). See also Charles Tilly and Lesley D. Wood, *Social Movements, 1768–2012* (2012).

42 Jan A. van Dijk, "One Europe, Digitally Divided" in Routledge Handbook of Internet Politics, ed. Andrew Chadwick and Philip N. Howard. (New York: Routledge, 2009). 288–304.

43 On digital memory, see *Save As … Digital Memory*, ed. Joanne Garde-Hansen, Andrew Hoskins, and Anna Reading (2009) and José van Dijck, "Digital Photography: Communication, Identity, Memory," *Visual Communication* 7, no. 1 (2008): 57–76. See also "Flickr and the Culture of Connectivity: Sharing Views, Experiences, Memories," *Memory Studies* 4, no. 4: 404.

44 Roland Barthes, *Camera Lucida: Reflections on Photography* (1982); Paul Levinson, *The Soft Edge: A Natural History and Future of the Information Revolution* (1997), W.T. Mitchell, *Picture Theory* (1994), and Susan Sontag, *On Photography* (1977).

45 Andrew Hoskins, "Introduction," in *Save As ... Digital Memory*, ed. Joanne Garde-Hansen, Andrew Hoskins, and Anna Reading (2009): 7. See too Nigel Thrift, "Remembering the Technological Unconscious by Foregrounding Knowledges of Position," in *Knowing Capitalism* (2005), 212–16. Also useful on this point is Henry Jenkins, *Spreadable Media: Creating Value and Meaning in a Networked Culture* (2013). Nicholas Carr, of course, suggested that these otherwise benign acts actually have the capacity to change cognition itself, changing our attention spans (for the worse), impeding judgment, and inhibiting probing analysis. See Nicholas Carr, *The Shallows: What the Internet Is Doing to Our Brains* (2011).

46 Jonathan Crary argues that the nineteenth-century observer was radically different than that which came before, based around new optical and epistemological imperatives and demands. Jonathan Crary, *Techniques of the Observer: On Vision and Modernity in the Nineteenth Century* (1990): 137.

47 Marianne Hirsch, *Family Frames: Photography, Narrative and Postmemory* (1997).

48 José van Dijck, "Flickr and the Culture of Connectivity," 401.

49 Lev Manovich, *The Language of New Media* (2001).

50 J. David Bolter and Richard A. Grusin, *Remediation: Understanding New Media* (1999). For a slightly different approach, see Lisa Gitelman, *Paper Knowledge: Toward a Media History of Documents* (2014).

51 On the relationship between aesthetics and subjectivity, Bolter and Grusin draw from the work of Stanley Cavell, *The World Viewed: Reflections on the Ontology of the Cinema* (1979), 21.

52 Michael Moss, "Memory Institutions, the Archive, and Digital Disruption?" in *Digital Memory Studies. Media Pasts in Transition*, ed. Andrew Hoskins (London: Routledge, 2018), 253–79.

53 Bolter and Grusin, *Remediation*, 234–5. On subjectivity and the self in the internet age see Sherry Turkle, *Life on the Screen: Identity in the Age of the Internet* (1995).

54 Manuel Castells, "Communication, Power and Counter-power," *International Journal of Communication* 1, no. 1 (February 2007): 249.

55 Susan Murray, "Digital Images, Photo-Sharing, and Our Shifting Notions of Everyday Aesthetics," *Journal of Visual Culture* 7, no. 2 (2008): 147–63.

56 Emma Angus, David Stuart, and Mike Thelwall, "Flickr's Potential as an Academic Image Resource: An Exploratory Study," *Journal of Librarianship and Information Science* 42, no. 4 (2010): 268.

57 Jean Burgess, "Remediating Vernacular Creativity: Photography and Cultural Citizenship in the Flickr Photo-Sharing Network," in *Spaces of Vernacular Creativity: Rethinking the Cultural Economy*, ed. Tim Edensor et al. (2010), 116–26; Cristina Garduño Freeman, "Photosharing on Flickr: Intangible Heritage and Emergent Publics," *International Journal of Heritage Studies* 16, no. 4–5 (2010): 355;

Zizi A. Papacharissi, *A Private Sphere: Democracy in a Digital Age* (2010); Malcolm R. Parks, "Social Network Sites as Virtual Communities," in *A Networked Self: Identity, Community, and Culture on Social Network Sites*, ed. Zizi Papacharissi (2011), 105–23; José van Dijck, "Digital Photography: Communication, Identity, Memory," *Visual Communication* 7, no. 1 (2008): 57–76; José van Dijck, "Flickr and the Culture of Connectivity: Sharing Views, Experiences, Memories," *Memory Studies* 4, no. 4 (2011): 401–15; Nancy A. Van House, "Collocated Photosharing, Story-telling, and the Performance of Self," *International Journal of Human— Computer Studies* 67 no. 12 (2009): 1073–86.

58 W. Lance Bennett, "Communicating Global Activism. Strengths and Vulnerabilities of Networked Politics," in *Cyberprotest. New Media, Citizens, and Social Movements*, ed. Wim van de Donk, Brian D. Loader, Paul G. Nixon, and Dieter Rucht (2004), 123–46. And W. Lance Bennett and A. Segerberg, "Digital Media and the Personalization of Collective Action," *Information, Communication & Society* 14, no. 6 (2004): 770–99; Donatella Della Porta, "Multiple Belongings, Flexible Identities and the Construction of 'Another Politics': Between the European Social Forum and the Local Social Fora," in *Transnational Protest and Global Activism,* ed. Donatella Della Porta, Sidney Tarrow, and W. Lance Bennett (2004), 175–202.

59 Susan Neiman, *Learning from Germans: Race and the Memory of Evil* (New York: Farrar Giroux, 2019).

60 For neo-Nazi symbols see Horst Uberhorst, "Feste, Fahnen, Feiern: die Bedeutung politischer Symbole und Rituale im Nationalsozialismus" in *Politik der Symbole: Symbole der Politik,* ed. Rüdiger Voigt (1989), 157–78. On the use of symbols as a means of group representation in public, see Benjamin Ziemann, "Situating Peace Movements in the Political Culture of the Cold War," in *Peace Movements in Western Europe, Japan, and the USA during the Cold War,* ed. Benjamin Ziemann (2007), 25. On the so-called Vermummungsverbot or the ban on face coverings, see Jörg Meyer, "Vom Recht auf Anonymität," *Neues Deutschland*, June 28, 2010, http://www.neues-deutschland.de/artikel/174046.vom-recht-auf-anonymitaet.html.

61 Interview with Thomas Rassloff, Berlin, July 14, 2014.

62 See *1968. Ein Handbuch zur Kultur—und Mediengeschichte,* with Joachim Scharloth (Stuttgart: Metzler Verlag, 2007; new edition 2008). Frank Biess, "'Everybody Has a Chance': Civil Defense. Nuclear Angst, and the History of Emotions in Postwar Germany," *German History* 27, no. 2 (2009): 215–43; Belinda Davis, "What's Left? Popular and Democratic Political Participation in Postwar Europe," *American Historical Review* 113, no. 2 (April 2008): 363–90; Geoff Eley, *Forging Democracy: The History of the Left in Europe, 1850–2000* (2002); Karin Hanshew, *Terror and Democracy in West Germany* (2012); Martin Klimke, *The Other Alliance: Student Protest in West Germany and the United States in the Global Sixties* (2010); Carla Macdougall, "We Too Are Berliners: Protest, Symbolism, and the City in Cold War

Germany," in *Changing the World, Changing Oneself. Political Protest and Collective Identities in West Germany and the US in the 1960s and 1970s*, ed. Belinda Davis, Wilfried Mausbach, Martin Klimke, and Carla MacDougall (2010), 83–104. On Kanak Attak, see Fatima El-Tayeb, *European Others: Queering Ethnicity in Postnational Europe* (Minneapolis, MN: University of Minnesota Press, 2011).

63   Christina von Hodenberg, "Mass Media and the Generation of Conflict. West Germany's Long Sixties and the Formation of a Critical Public Sphere," *Central European History,* 15, no. 3 (August 2006): 367–5. See also the essays in Martin Klimke and Joachim Scharloth, eds., 1968. *Handbuch zur Kultur—und Mediengeschichte der Studentenbewegung* (Stuttgart: J. B. Metzler, 2007).

64   Wulf Kansteiner, "Finding Meaning in Memory: A Methodological Critique of Collective Memory Studies," *History and Theory*, 41 (2002): 179–97.

65   Joanne Garde-Hansen, *Media and Memory*, 105.

66   Hal Foster, "An Archive without Museums" *October* 77 (Summer 1996): 97–119.

67   "Serie: 'Neue deutsche Nazis,'" *Die Zeit*, March 3–May 16, 2012 http://www.zeit.de/serie/neue-deutsche-nazis (accessed May 17, 2012).

68   W. Chen and B. Wellman, "Minding the Cyber-Gap: The Internet and Social Inequality," in *The Blackwell Companion to Social* Inequalities, ed. M. Romero and E. Margolis (2005), 523–45.

69   See https://www.flickr.com/photos/pm_cheung/6110669070/in/faves-boeseraltermannberlin/ and http://www.flickr.com/photos/rassloff/

70   Zanny Begg, "Recasting Subjectivity," *Third Text* 19, no. 6 (November 2005): 627.

71   https://www.flickr.com/photos/rassloff/

72   Thomas Rassloff, http://www.rasslof.info/contact.php, (accessed June 23, 2014).

73   https://www.theguardian.com/world/2013/jan/29/syrian-rebels-bodies-aleppo-canal; https://www.bostonglobe.com/news/world/2013/01/30/scores-bodies-found-suburb-syrian-city/KKG1CYp5fiC95YmpM6gMAP/story.html; https://www.thetimes.co.uk/article/syrias-river-of-death-68-men-found-executed-6xz8r8drd2c (accessed August 22, 2023).

74   "People of Bustan Al Qasr Recall the River Massacre," *Enab Baladi,* January 30, 2016, https://english.enabbaladi.net/archives/2016/01/bustan-al-qasr-people-recall-the-river-massacre-in-aleppo/

75   Thomas Rassloff, Flickr album Syrien Aleppo Jeser Al Sendean, January 29, 2013, IMG_6911, https://www.flickr.com/photos/rassloff/19737702852/in/album-72157632640499030/; https://www.readingthepictures.org/2013/01/i-feel-it-would-be-wrong-not-to-stop-and-take-note-of-this-photo-from-aleppo/

76   José van Dijck, "Flickr and the Culture of Connectivity," 410.

77   Andrew Jenkins, *Convergence Culture: Where Old and New Media Collide* (New York: New York University Press, 2006).

78	Interview with Thomas Rassloff, Berlin, July 10, 2014.

79	Andrew Hoskins, "Introduction to Digital Memory and Media," *Digital Memory Studies. Media Pasts in Transition,* ed. Andrew Hoskins (London: Routledge Press, 2018), 4.

80	André H. Caron and Letitia Caronia, *Moving Cultures: Mobile Communication in Everyday Life* (Kingston, ON: McGill-Queens University Press, 2007); and Jay David Bolter and Richard Grusin, *Remediation: Understanding New Media* (Cambridge, MA: MIT Press, 2000).

81	Anna Reading, "The London Bombings: Mobile Witnessing, Mortal Bodies, and Globital Time," *Memory Studies* 4, no. 3 (2011): 299.

82	Anna Reading, "The London Bombings," 306.

83	Interview with Thomas Rassloff, Berlin, July 10, 2014.

84	Nancy K. Van House and Elizabeth Churchill, "Technologies of Memory: Key Issues and Critical Perspectives," *Memory Studies* 1, no. 3 (2008): 306.

85	Luciano Floridi, *The Ethics of Information* (Oxford: Oxford University Press, 2013).

86	Andrew Hoskins, 2018, 3.

87	Stearns, *Encyclopedia of Social History.*

88	Kansteiner, *Finding Meaning in Memory.*

89	Ulli Linke, "The Language of Resistance: Political Rhetoric and Symbols of Popular Protest in Germany," *City & Society: The Journal of the Society for Urban Anthropology* 2, no. 2 (1988): 127–33.

90	Jeffrey Juris, "Violence Performed and Imagined: Militant Action, the Black Bloc and the Mass Media in Genoa," *Critique of Anthropology* 25, no. 4 (December 2004): 413–32. See also *Passionate Politics: Emotions and Social Movements,* ed. Jeff Goodwin, James M. Jasper, and Francesca Polletta (2001).

91	Ruud Wouters, "From the Street to the Screen: Characteristics of Protest Events as Determinants of Television News Coverage" *Mobilization: An International Quarterly* 18, no. 1 (2013): 83–105. Reinhold Lütgemeier-Davin, Holger Nehring Karlheinz Lipp, *Frieden und Friedensbewegungen in Deutschland 1892–1992* (2010); Leif Jerram, *Streetlife: The Untold Story of Europe's Twentieth Century* (2010).

92	Earlier media like radio performed a similar function only it didn't provide opportunities to log ones ideas and shape the discourse. See Karl Christian Führer and Corey Ross, "Mass Media, Culture and Society in Twentieth-Century Germany: An Introduction," in *Mass Media, Culture, and Society in Twentieth-Century Germany,* ed. Karl Christian Führer and Corey Ross (2007), 9; Sven Reichhardt and Detlef Siegfried, *Das Alternative Milieu: Antibürgerlicher Lebensstil und linke Politik in der Bundesrepublik Deutschland und Europa 1968–1983* (2010).

93	Merlyna Lim, "Seeing Spatially: People, Networks, and Movements in Digital and Urban Space," *IDPR* 36, no. 1 (2014): 56.

94	Michael Warner, *Publics and Counterpublics* (2002).

95 David Harvey, *Spaces of Hope* (2000). Zizi Papacharissi is critical of the notion that this represents a true Habermasian public sphere. See Zizi Papacharissi, "The Virtual Sphere 2.0: The Internet, the Public Sphere, and Beyond," *Routledge Handbook of Internet Politics*, ed. Andrew Chadwick and Philip N. Howard (New York: Routledge, 2009), 230–45.

96 See Timothy Scott Brown, *West Germany and the Global Sixties: The Antiauthoritarian Revolt, 1962–1978 (2013)*, especially the chapter "Vision." See Also Joachem Haeberlen, *The Emotional Politics of the Alternative Left. West Germany, 1968–1984* (Cambridge, MA: Cambridge University Press, 2018).

97 Sara Blaylock coined the term in her discussion of the visual politics of the alternative left in *the Politics of Authenticity: Countercultures and Radical Movements across the Iron Curtain, 1968–1989*, ed. Joachim Haeberlen, Mark Keck-Szajbel, and Kate Mahoney (New York: Berghahn Press, 2018), 283. See also Massimo Perinelli, "Longing, Lust, Violence, and Liberation: Discourses on Sexuality on the Radical Left, 1969–72," in *After the History of Sexuality: German Genealogies with and Beyond Foucault*, ed. Scott Spector, Helmut Puff, and Dagmar Herzog (2012), 248–81.

98 Joachim Haeberlen, Mark Keck-Szajbel, and Kate Mahoney, *The Politics of Authenticity.*

99 Martin Klimke and Laura Stapane, "From Artists for Peace to the Green Caterpillar: Cultural Activism and Electoral Politics in 1980s West Germany," in *Accidental Armageddons: The Nuclear Crisis and the Culture of the Cold War in the 1980s,* ed. Eckart Conze, Martin Klimke, and Jeremy Varon (Cambridge, MA: Cambridge University Press, 2016), 116–41.

100 Kenney, *A Carnival of Revolution. Eastern Europe 1989* (2002).

101 Bakhtin, *Rabelais and His World* (1941).

102 Paul Routledge, "Sensuous Solidarities: Emotion, Politics and Performance in the Clandestine Insurgent Rebel Clown Army," *Antipode*, 44, no. 2 (2012): 428–52. See also Jeffrey D. Juris and Geoffrey Henri Pleyers, "Alter-activism: Emerging Cultures of Participation among Young Global Justice Activists," *Journal of Youth Studies* 12, no. 1 (February 2009): 57–75.

103 Radu-Andrei Negoescu and Daniel Gatica-Perez, "Analyzing Flickr Groups" CIVR'08: Proceedings of the 2008 International Conference on Content-based image and video retrieval (July 2008): 417–26.

104 P.M. Cheung, "Neuruppin bleibt bunt," July 2011, https://www.flickr.com/photos/pm_cheung/5919047049/in/photostream/ (accessed June 23, 2014).

105 Rassloff's Neuruppin album is here: https://www.flickr.com/photos/rassloff/albums/72157627153782450

106 PM Cheung's photoalbum is here: https://www.flickr.com/photos/pm_cheung/albums/72157627030634351

107 "Behörden haben wohl bewusst Journalisten durchsucht," February 3, 2013, https://
www.tagesspiegel.de/berlin/polizei-justiz/nach-razzia-bei-fotografen-behoerden-
haben-wohl-bewusst-journalisten-durchsucht/7742288.html

108 Thomas Rassloff, "Leipzig Nazidemo und Antifa Gegenprotest," May 1, 2005
https://www.flickr.com/photos/rassloff/6437795761/in/album-72157628237451683/
(accessed July 15, 2015).

109 Alan Dundes, *Life Is Like a Chicken Coop Ladder. A Portrait of German Culture
through Folklore* (1984). For a contemporary link between feces and National
Socialism, see the scene involving SA youths defecating in a shop. Günter Grass,
The Tin Drum (2009), pg. 202. Of course, one of the most horrifying accounts
of feces as linked to Nazi humiliation tactics may be found in Terence des Pres,
"Excremental Assault," in *The Survivor: An Anatomy of Life in the Death Camps*
(1977). On the GDR peace movement see Steven Pfaff, "The Politics of Peace in the
GDR: The Independent Peace Movement, the Church, and the Original of the East
German Opposition," *Peace and Change* 26, no. 3 (July 2001): 280–300.

110 Freddie Rokem, *Performing History: Theatrical Representations of the Past in
Contemporary Theatre*, ed. Thomas Postlewait, Studies in Theatre History &
Culture (2000).

111 Hassan Masum and Mark Tovey, *The Reputation Society: How Online Opinions Are
Shaping the Offline World* (2012).

112 Martin Klimke has taken some important first steps here with his application
of cultural studies methodologies to the history of protest. See Martin Klimke
and Laura Stapane's forthcoming chapter "From Artists for Peace to the Green
Caterpillar: Cultural Activism and Electoral Politics in 1980s West Germany."

113 Belinda Davis, "What's Left? Popular and Democratic Political Participation
in Postwar Europe," *The American Historical Review* 113, no. 2 (April 2008):
390; Timothy Brown and Lorena Anton, eds., *Between the Avant-Garde and the
Everyday: Subversive Politics in Europe from 1957 to the Present*, vol. 6, Protest,
Culture & Society (2011): 1.

114 Evgenii Morozov, *The Net Delusion: The Dark Side of Internet Freedom* (New York:
Public Affairs, 2012).

115 Ariella Azoulay, *Civil Imagination. A Political Ontology of Photography* (2012),
69–70.

116 Geoffrey Pleyers, *Alter-globalization: Becoming Actors in the Global Age* (2010);
Charles Tilly and Lesley D. Wood, *Social Movements, 1768–2012* (2012).

117 Jean Burgess, "Remediating Vernacular Creativity: Photography and Cultural
Citizenship in the Flickr Photo-sharing Network," in *Spaces of Vernacular
Creativity: Rethinking the Cultural Economy*, ed. Tim Edensor et al. (2010):
116–26.

Chapter 3

1 Wulf Kansteiner, "Finding Meaning in Memory: A Methodological Critique of Collective Memory Studies," *History and Theory* 41, no. 2 (2002): 179–98.
2 Maggie Griffith and Zizi Papacharissi, "Looking for You: An Analysis of Video Blogs," *First Monday*, 2010, https://doi.org/10.5210/fm.v15i1.2769.
3 Jean Burgess, *YouTube: Online Video and Participatory Culture*, 2nd edn., Digital Media and Society Press (Cambridge, UK: Politya, 2018), see especially Chapter 5.
4 Burgess, *YouTube*, 3.
5 "About," YouTube.com, http://www.youtube.com/about (accessed December 2012). After YouTube was acquired by Google for $1.65 billion on October 9, 2006, in one of the "most talked about web acquisitions to date," YouTube has become the fastest-growing site in the history of the internet and remains the default site for uploading and sharing video. Snickars and Vonderau claim that "posting the clip 'A Message from Chad and Steve' in many ways became a performative web 2.0 act. […] The apparently coincidental recording demonstrated how video could be used as an unobtrusive channel of communication to address the community that had built up YouTube as a proprietary platform in the first place." The YouTube Reader, ed. Pelle Snickars and Patrick Vonderau (Lithuania: Logotipas, 2009), 9.
6 Chris Welch, "YouTube Users Now Upload 100 Hours of Video Every Minute," *The Verge*, May 19, 2013 https://www.theverge.com/2013/5/19/4345514/youtube-users-upload-100-hours-video-every-minute (accessed August 24, 2022).
7 Rhys Blakely, "BBC's Flagship Site to Be Toppled in the Charts by YouTube," *The Times*, June 21, 2007, https://www.thetimes.co.uk/article/bbcs-flagship-site-to-be-toppled-in-the-charts-by-youtube-v33xj2jkkpr (accessed August 25, 2022).
8 "Google to Acquire YouTube for $1.65 Billion—The New York Times," https://www.nytimes.com/2006/10/09/business/09cnd-deal.html (accessed August 25, 2022).
9 Joanne Garde-Hansen, *Media and Memory*, Media Topics (Edinburgh: University Press, 2011).
10 Gehl highlights these issues in "YouTube as Archive," *International Journal of Cultural Studies* 12, no. 1 (2009): 43–60, as well as in "The Archive and the Processor: The Internal Logic of Web 2.0," *New Media & Society* 13, no. 8 (2011): 1228–44.
11 Joan M. Schwartz and Terry Cook, among many others, have commented on the archive as a site of power and memory construction, and there is no shortage of analysis of the modern archive and issues of neutrality and power. They note, "Archives as institutions and records as documents are generally seen by academic and other users, and by society generally, as passive resources to be exploited for various historical and cultural purposes. […] Yet archives are established by

the powerful to protect or enhance their position in society. [...] This represents enormous power over memory and identity, over the fundamental ways in which society seeks evidence of what its core values are and have been, where it has come from, and where it is going." "Archives, Records, and Power: The Making of Modern Memory," *Archival Science* 2 (2002): 1. YouTube does not escape this lack of neutrality; indeed, one of the many issues involved with viewing YouTube as an archive is the glaringly obvious question: who is the archivist?

12 Britta T. Knudsen and Carsten Stage, "Online War Memorials: YouTube as a Democratic Space of Commemoration Exemplified through Video Tributes to Fallen Danish Soldiers," *Memory Studies* 6, no. 4 (2013): 432.

13 David F. Crew, *Bodies and Ruins: Imagining the Bombing of Germany, 1945 to the Present*, Social History, Popular Culture, and Politics in Germany (Ann Arbor: University of Michigan Press, 2017).

14 Yasmin Ibrahim, "Accounting the 'Self': From Diarization to Life Vlogs," *Convergence* 27, no. 2 (April 1, 2021): 330–42, https://doi.org/10.1177/1354856520947618.

15 "The State of the Live Web, April 2007," David Sifry, http://www.sifry.com/alerts/2007/04/the-state-of-the-live-web-april-2007 (accessed August 27, 2022).

16 Ibrahim, "Accounting the 'Self'," 342.

17 Erving Goffman, *The Presentation of Self in Everyday Life*, Anchor books edn., Doubleday Anchor Books (Garden City: Doubleday & Company, 1959).

18 Griffith and Papacharissi, "Looking for You."

19 Michael Strangelove, *Watching YouTube: Extraordinary Videos by Ordinary People* (Toronto: University of Toronto Press, 2010), 4.

20 Such ideas have also been explored by Geoffrey Bowker, who agrees that "what is stored in the archives is not facts, but disaggregated classifications that can at will be reassembled to take the form of facts about the world." Geoffrey Bowker, *Memory Practices in the Sciences* (Cambridge: MIT Press, 2005), 18.

21 S. Banjali and D. Buckingham, *The Civic Web: Young People, the Internet, and Civic Participation* Cambridge: MIT Press, 2013.

22 E. R. Halverson, "Film as Identity Exploration: A Multimodal Analysis of Youth-produced Films," *Teachers College Record* 112, no. 9 (2010): 2352–78.

23 We used Bertopic https://maartengr.github.io/BERTopic/algorithm/algorithm.html

24 Peter Dahlgren, "Tracking the Civic Subject in the Media Landscape: Versions of the Democratic Ideal," *Television and New Media* 14, no. 1 (2013): 71–88.

25 "My Best Present | Anne Frank video diary | Episode 1 | Anne Frank House," https://youtu.be/ZWFjgWGI_YE (accessed August 28, 2022).

26 A common script for a scraper can be found here: https://github.com/MAN1986/LearningOrbis/blob/master/scrapeCommentsWithReplies.gs

27 Anne Frank House, "Anne Frank Video Diary," https://www.youtube.com/watch?v=ilXx0rdRfPk&list=PLDwwb2V397Q6192UeDFpcNuSoK8uS1cgz (accessed August 31, 2022).

28 *Annual Report 2020*, Anne Frank House, 1.

29 Anne Frank House project description, https://www.annefrank.org/en/museum/web-and-digital/video-diary/ (accessed August 29, 2022).

30 Nina Siegal, "The (Video) Diary of Anne Frank," *The New York Times*, April 22, 2020, sec. Arts, https://www.nytimes.com/2020/04/22/arts/anne-frank-video-diary.html.

31 "In a World in Lockdown, Anne Frank Is the Latest Social Media Influencer—World News—Haaretz.Com," https://www.haaretz.com/world-news/2020-04-20/ty-article-magazine/.premium/how-anne-frank-became-the-latest-social-media-influencer/0000017f-f798-d47e-a37f-ffbcb2510000 (accessed August 29, 2022).

32 "Anne Frank: Famous Diary Turned into a Vlog for Museum YouTube Channel—CBBC Newsround," https://www.bbc.co.uk/newsround/52184019 (accessed August 29, 2022).

33 More details on the Anne Frank House, their mandate and mission can be found in their 2020 Annual Report: jaarverslag_en_jaarrekening_2020_engels.pdf (annefrank.freetls.fastly.net).

34 Tim Cole, *Selling the Holocaust: From Auschwitz to Schindler, How History Is Bought, Packaged, and Sold* (1999), 23.

35 Cole, *Selling the Holocaust,* 29.

36 More details on the Anne Frank House, their mandate and mission can be found in their 2020 Annual Report: jaarverslag_en_jaarrekening_2020_engels.pdf (annefrank.freetls.fastly.net).

37 *Annual Report 2020*, Anne Frank House, 1.

38 Anne Frank House, "Anne Frank Video Diary." View the series here: Video diary series | Anne Frank House (accessed September 3, 2022).

39 Comment on "Utterly Terrified | Anne Frank video diary | Episode 4 | Anne Frank House," https://youtu.be/jGPj-GwEGvM (accessed August 31, 2022).

40 Donald Horton and R. Richard Wohl, "Mass Communication and Para-Social Interaction," *Psychiatry: Interpersonal and Biological Processes* 19, no. 3 (1956): 215–29.

41 Comment on "D-Day! | Anne Frank video diary | Episode 9 | Anne Frank House," https://youtu.be/kiC18W4twUM (accessed August 28, 2022).

42 Comment on "Utterly Terrified | Anne Frank video diary | Episode 4 | Anne Frank House," https://youtu.be/jGPj-GwEGvM (accessed August 28, 2022).

43 "A Jaw-Dropping Anne Frank Video Diary," The Jerusalem Post | JPost.com, https://www.jpost.com/israel-news/culture/a-jaw-dropping-anne-frank-video-diary-625377 (accessed August 31, 2022).

44 See https://www.insider.com/canadian-newspaper-compared-lockdown-to-anne-franks-hiding-from-nazis-2021-3 (accessed August 30, 2022) and https://www.mynewsdesk.com/be/aenetworks/pressreleases/the-history-channel-highlights-march-2021-3069289 (accessed August 30, 2022).

45 Comments from "My Best Present | Anne Frank video diary | Episode 1 | Anne Frank House," https://youtu.be/ZWFjgWGI_YE (accessed September 3, 2022).

46 Ibid.

47 Ibid.

48 Ibid.

49 Ibid.

50 Comments from "'Hatred of the Jews' | Anne Frank video diary | Episode 7 | Anne Frank House," https://www.youtube.com/watch?v=YNaqzAOoYUc (accessed August 31, 2022).

51 Chris Jones et al., "Net Generation or Digital Natives: Is There a Distinct New Generation Entering University?" *Computers & Education*, Learning in Digital Worlds: Selected Contributions from the CAL 09 Conference, 54, no. 3 (April 1, 2010): 722–32.

52 Comments from "My Best Present | Anne Frank video diary | Episode 1 | Anne Frank House," https://youtu.be/ZWFjgWGI_YE (accessed September 3, 2022).

53 Comments from "Hatred of the Jews | Anne Frank video diary | Episode 7 | Anne Frank House," https://youtu.be/YNaqzAOoYUc (accessed September 3, 2022).

54 Comment from "Discovered | Anne Frank video diary | Episode 15 | Anne Frank House," https://youtu.be/a4lxDhPC8gY (accessed September 3, 2022).

55 Episode 1| Diary of a young girl | Anne Frank | June 12, 1942–June 24, 1942, https://www.youtube.com/watch?v=L8ixMqb26H0&t=0s (accessed August 31, 2022).

56 Thomas Łysak, "Vlogging Auschwitz: New Players in Holocaust Commemoration," *Holocaust Studies: A Journal of Culture and History* 28, no. 3 (2022): 397 (377–402).

57 "#Uploading_Holocaust: Documentary," Documentary | #uploading_holocaust (uploading-holocaust.com), accessed September 1, 2022.

58 #Uploading_Holocaust (2016), dir. Bornstein and Nir, 00:01:15.

59 #Uploading_Holocuast (2016), dir. Sagi Bornstein and Udi Nir, 00:01:48. See also Jackie Feldman, "Nationalising Personal Trauma, Personalising National Redemption: Performing Testimony at Auschwitz-Birkenau," in *Remembering Violence: Anthropological Perspectives on Intergenerational Transmission*, ed. N. Argenti and K. Schramm (Berghahn Books, 2009), 104. For more on the intersection between Holocaust memory and Israeli national identity, see Jackie Feldman's *Above the Death Pits, Beneath the Flag: Youth Voyages to Poland and the Performance of Israeli National Identity* (Berghahn Books, 2008).

60 Comment on "D-Day! | Anne Frank video diary | Episode 9 | Anne Frank House," https://youtu.be/kiC18W4twUM (accessed August 29, 2022).

61 Ebbrecht-Hartmann and Henig, "i-Memory."

62 Ibid., 223.

63 Łysak, "Vlogging Auschwitz," 396.

64 #Uploading_Holocaust (2016), 00:03:15.

65 #Uploading_Holocaust (2016), 00:23:41. The individual filming is referencing the crematorium.

66 #Uploading_Holocaust (2016), 00:27:50.

67 #Uploading_Holocaust (2016), 00:40:53.

68 #Uploading_Holocaust (2016), 00:11:26.

69 #Uploading_Holocaust (2016), 00:10:15.

70 Ebbrecht-Hartmann and Henig, "i-Memory," 219.

71 #Uploading_Holocaust (2016), 00:17:00 and 00:19:35, respectively. On the contested space of the train car in memorial museums, see Simone Gigliotti, *The Train Journey: Transit, Captivity and Witnessing in the Holocaust* (Basingstoke: Palgrave Macmillan, 2009).

72 #Uploading_Holocaust (2016), 00:28:09 and 00:28:26.

73 #Uploading_Holocaust (2016), 00:31:55.

74 Ebbrecht-Hartmann and Henig, "i-Memory," 214.

75 Ibrahim, "Accounting the 'Self'," 331.

76 #Uploading_Holocaust (2016), 00:23:20.

77 #Uploading_Holocaust (2016), 00:39:11.

78 #Uploading_Holocaust (2016), 00:05:48.

79 #Uploading_Holocaust (2016), 00:58:17.

80 #Uploading_Holocaust (2016), 00:40:49.

81 #Uploading_Holocaust (2016), 00:40:19.

82 #Uploading_Holoucast (2016), 00:38:45.

83 #Uploading_Holocaust (2016), 00:39:28.

84 Ebbrecht-Hartmann and Henig, "i-Memory," 232.

85 Andrew Hoskins, "The Mediatisation of Memory," in *Save As … Digital Memories*, ed. Joanne Garde-Hansen, Andrew Hoskins, and Anna Reading (Basingstoke: Palgrave Macmillan, 2009), 27.

86 Ebbrect-Hartmann does not delineate between what serves as memorial and what does not, but arguably Auschwitz Memorial and Museum and numerous other memorials have long been engaged in the usage of social media to promote memory-making practices. Tobias Ebbrecht-Hartmann, "Commemorating from a Distance: The Digital Transformation of Holocaust Memory in Times of COVID-19," *Media, Culture & Society* 43, no. 6 (2021): 1.

87 Ibrahim, "Accounting the 'Self'," 331.

88 Ibid.

89 Lital Henig and Tobias Ebbrecht-Hartmann, "Witnessing Eva Stories: Media Witnessing and Self-Inscription in Social Media Memory," *New Media & Society* 24, no. 1 (2020): 220.

90 Jan Grabowski and Shira Klein, "Wikipedia's Intentional Distortion of the History of the Holocaust," *The Journal of Holocaust Research* (February 9, 2023): 1–58, https://doi.org/10.1080/25785648.2023.2168939.

Chapter 4

1   Tetyana Lokot, *Beyond the Protest Square: Digital Media and Augmented Dissent* (London: Rowman & Littlefield Publishers, 2021).

2   Sonia Livingstone, "Foreword: Coming to Terms with Mediatization," in *Mediatization: Concepts, Changes, Consequences*, ed. Knut Lundby (New York: Peter Lang, 2009), ix–xii; Knut Hickethier,"Mediatisierung und Medialisierung der Kultur," in *Die Mediatisierung der Alltagswelt*, ed. Maren Hartmann and Andreas Hepp (Wiesbaden: VS-Verlag, 2010), 85–96; Knut Lundby, *Mediatization of Communication* (Berlin: De Gruyter Mouton, 2014); Ulrich Sarcinelli, "Mediatisierung," in *Politische Kommunikation in der demokratischen Gesellschaft*, ed. Otfried Jarren, Ulrich Sarcinelli, and Ulrich Saxer (Opladen: Westdeutscher Verlag, 1998), 678–79; Jesper Strömbäck and Frank Esser, "Introduction," *Journalism Practice* 8, no. 3 (2014): 245–57.

3   Michael Warner, *Publics and Counterpublics* (Boston: MIT Press, 2002).

4   Nick Couldry and Andreas Hepp, "Conceptualizing Mediatization: Contexts, Traditions, Arguments," *Communication Theory* 23, no. 3 (2013): 191–202; Stig Hjarvard, "The Mediatization of Society. A Theory of the Media as Agents of Social and Cultural Change," *Nordicom Review* 29, no. 2 (2008): 105–34 and also *The Mediatization of Culture and Society* (London: Routledge, 2013); Winfried Schulz, "Reconstructing Mediatization as an Analytical Concept," *European Journal of Communication* 19, no. 1 (2004): 87–101.

5   Andreas Hepp, *Cultures of Mediatization* (Cambridge: Polity Press, 2013), 618.

6   Knut Lundby, *Mediatization of Communication*, 11.

7   Andre Jansson, "Mediatization and Social Space: Reconstructing Mediatization for the Transmedia Age," *Communication Theory* 23 (2013): 279–96.

8   Piotr Celinski, "Mediatization and Memory Policies in the Urban Context," *Analecta Política* 8, no. 15 (July–December 2018): 282.

9   Karin Fast, Emilia Ljungberg, and Lotta Braunerhielm, "On the Social Construction of Geomedia Technologies," *Communication and the Public* 4, no. 2 (2019): 89–99.

10 José van Dijck and Thomas Poelle, "Social Media and the Transformation of Public Space," *Social Media + Society* (July–December 2015): 1–5; Andreas Hepp, Stig Hjarvard, and Knut Lundby, "Mediatization: Theorizing the Interplay between Media, Culture and Society," *Media, Culture, and Society* 37, no. 2 (2015): 324.

11 Bernard Harcourt, *Exposed: Desire and Disobedience in the Digital Age* (Cambridge, MA: Harvard University Press, 2015).

12 José van Dijck, *The Culture of Connectivity. A Critical History of Social Media* (Oxford: Oxford University Press, 2013).

13 Andrew Hoskins, "The Mediatisation of Memory," in *Save As … Digital Memories*, ed. Joanne Garde-Hansen, Andrew Hoskins, and Anna Reading (London: Palgrave Macmillan UK, 2009), 672.

14 Hoskins and Halstead, "The New Grey of Memory."

15 Aleida Assmann, "Texts, Traces, Trash: The Changing Media of Cultural Memory," *Representations* 56 (1996): 126. See also Lokot, *Beyond the Protest Square*.

16 Conversation between Thomas Rudert, provenance expert of Staatliche Kunstsammlungen Dresden and Murry Teitel, "Revisiting the Bombing of Dresden," *Canadian Jewish News*, February 12, 2020, https://www.cjnews.com/news/international/revisiting-the-bombing-of-dresden.

17 Far from disconnected from the war effort, despite postwar mythmaking, Dresden was circled by factories like the Zeiss-Ikon concern outside the city limits employing 14,000 workers, many of them forced laborers, that crafted lenses and fuses for the military. They weren't the initial targets, however, at least not until the Americans followed suit with targeted precision campaigns. See *Historical Analysis of the February 14–15, 1945 Bombings of Dresden*, prepared by the USAF Historical Division, Research Studies Institute, 1945.

18 Barbie Zelizer, "Memory as Foreground, Journalism as Background," in *Journalism and Memory*, ed. B. Zelizer and K. Tenenboim-Weinblatt (Basingstoke: Palgrave Macmillan, 2014), 32–49.

19 Anne Fuchs, *After the Dresden Bombing: Pathways of Memory 1945 to the Present* (Basingstoke: Palgrave Macmillan, 2012), 32.

20 Dietmar Suess, *Tod aus der Luft. Kriegsgesellschaft und Luftkrieg in Deutschland und England* (München: Siedler Verlag, 2011).

21 Jennifer V. Evans, *Life Among the Ruins: Cityscape and Sexuality in Cold War Berlin, 1949–1961* (Basingstoke: Palgrave Macmillan, 2011).

22 Matthias Neuntzner, "Vom Anklagen zum Erinnern. Die Erzaehlung vom 13. Februar," in *Das rote Leuchten. Dresden und das Bombenkrieg*, ed. Oliver Reinhard, Matthias Neutzner, and Wolfgang Hesse (Dresden: Edition Saechsische Zeitung, 2005), 144–6.

23 Richard J. Evans, *Lying About Hitler. History, Holocaust and the David Irving Trial* (London: Basic Books, 2002).

24 Svenska Dagbladet, February 17, 1945.

25 Roland Barthes, *Camera Lucida*.

26 Hirsch, "Surviving Images," 224.

27 Tina M. Campt, *Listening to Images* (Durham, NC: Duke University Press, 2017).

28 Steven Hoelscher, "'Dresden, a Camera Accuses': Rubble Photography and the Politics of Memory in a Divided Germany," *History of Photography* 26, no. 3 (August 2012): 288–305.

29 James E. Young, *The Texture of Memory. Holocaust Memorials and Meaning* (Yale University Press, 1993); Edwards, *The Camera as Historian. Amateur Photographers and Historical Imagination*, 7.

30 Dagmar Barnouw, *Germany 1945: Views of War and Violence* (Bloomington: Indiana University Press, 2008).

31　Stefan-Ludwig Hoffmann, "Gazing at Ruins: German Defeat as Visual Experience," in *The Ethics of Seeing: Photography and Twentieth Century German Photography Reconsidered*, ed. Jennifer Evans, Paul Betts, and Stefan-Ludwig Hoffmann (New York: Berghahn Press, 2018), 144.

32　August Sander, *Die Zerstörung Kölns: Photographien 1945–1946* (Munich: Schirmer/Mosel, 1985); Friedrich Seidenstücker, *Von Weimar bis zum Ende: Fotografien aus bewegter Zeit* (Dortmund: Harenberg, 1980).

33　Robert Moeller, "War Stories: The Search for a Usable Past in the Federal Republic of Germany," *American Historical Review* 101, no. 4 (October 1996): 1012–13.

34　Crew, *Bodies and Ruins*.

35　Ibid., 10.

36　Kurt Schaarshuch, *Bilddokument Dresden, 1933–1945* (Dresden: Rat der Stadt Dresden, 1945).

37　David Crew argues that there is also an implicit emphasis on the city's resolve to survive and rebuild, that also takes emphasis away from the underlying reasons for the city's destruction in the first place. See Crew, *Bodies and Ruins,* 148–9.

38　Neuntzner, "Vom Anklagen zum Erinnern," 146.

39　Marita Sturken, *Tangled Memories: The Vietnam War, the Aids Epidemic, and the Politics of Remembering* (Berkeley: University of California Press, 1997).

40　Crew, *Bodies and Ruins,* 149.

41　Patrizia McBride, *The Chatter and the Visible: Montage and Narrative in Weimar Germany* (Ann Arbor: University of Michigan Press, 2016).

42　Thomas, "Hope Flies," 275.

43　Crew, *Bodies and Ruins,* 149.

44　Ibid.

45　Jörg Colberg, "The Curious Case of a Photobook," https://medium.com/@jmcolberg/a-curious-tale-of-a-photobook-64e1529fa7c4 (accessed June 15, 2020); Lokot, *Beyond the Protest Square*; C. Neumayer and G. Stald, "The Mobile Phone in Street Protest: Texting, Tweeting, Tracking, and Tracing," *Mobile Media & Communication* 2, no. 2 (2014): 117–33; Dan Mercea, "Digital Prefigurative Participation: The Entwinement of Online Communication and Offline Participation in Protest Events," *New Media & Society* 14, no. 1 (February 2012): 153–69; Thomas Poell and Erik Borra, "Twitter, YouTube, and Flickr as Platforms of Alternative Journalism: The Social Media Account of the 2010 Toronto G20 Protests," *Journalism* 13, no. 8 (2011): 1–19.

46　See Mary Nolan, "Air Wars, Memory Wars," *Central European History* 38, no. 1 (2005): 7–40 and Malte Thießen, "Gemeinsame Erinnerungen im geteilten Deutschland: Der Luftkrieg im '"kommunalen Gedäächtnis"' der Bundesrepublik und DDR," *Deutschland Archiv* 41, no. 2 (2008): 226–32. For the relevance of the bombing to postwar East and West German memory formation, see Gilad Margalit,

"Der Luftangriff aus Dresden: seine Bedeutung für die Erinnerungspolitik der DDR und für die Herauskristallisierung einer historischen Kriegserinnerung im Westen," in *Narrative der Shoah: Repräsentationen der Vergangenheit in Historiographie, Kunst und Politik*, ed. Susanne Düwell and Matthias Schmidt (Paderborn: Schöningh 2002), 189–207; "Dresden and Hamburg: Official Memory and Commemoration of the Victims of Allied Air Raids in the Two Germanies," in *A Nation of Victims?: Representations of German Wartime Suffering from 1945 to the Present*, ed. Helmut Schmitz (Amsterdam: Rodopi 2007), 125–40.

47 *Photobook Lust: Brad Feuerhelm on Richard Peter's Ein Kamera klagt an* https:// aperture.org/pbr/photobook-lust-brad-feuerhelm-richard-peter-dresden-eine-kamera-klagt/.

48 Crew, *Bodies and Ruins*, 151.

49 Eli Rubin, *Amnesiopolis: Modernity, Space, and Memory in East Germany* (London: Oxford University Press, 2016).

50 Sara Ahmed, "Affective Economy," *Social Text* 22, no. 2 (Summer 2004): 117–39 and Fabian Virchow, "Performance, Emotion and Ideology—On the Creation of "Collectives of Emotion" and World View in the Contemporary German Far Right" *Journal of Contemporary Ethnography* 36, no. 2 (2007): 147–64.

51 Crew, *Bodies and Ruins*, 160.

52 Neuntzer, *Vom Anklagen zur Errinerung in das rote Leuchten.*

53 Susanne Vees-Gulani, "The Politics of New Beginnings. The Continued Exclusion of the Nazi Past in Dresden's Cityscape," in *Beyond Berlin. Twelve German Cities Confront the Nazi Past*, ed. Paul B. Jaskot and Gavriel D. Rosenfeld (Ann Arbor: University of Michigan Press, 2008), 43.

54 Gerard Braunthal, *Right-Wing Extremism in Contemporary Germany* (Basingstoke: Palgrave Macmillan, 2009).

55 Harry Waibel, *Rechtsextremismus in der DDR bis 1989* (Köln: Papyrossa Verlag, 1996).

56 Groger Griffin, "From Slime Mould to Rhizome: An Introduction to the Groupuscular Right," *Patterns of Prejudice* 37, no. 1 (2003): 27–50. Uwe Backes and Cas Mudde, "Germany: Extremism without Successful Parties," *Parliamentary Affairs* 53, no. 3 (2000): 457–468.

57 Mudde, "Germany," 464, and Jan Schadtler, "The Devil in Disguise: Action Repertoire, Visual Performance and Collective Identity of the Autonomous Nationalists," *Nations and Nationalism* 20, no. 2 (April 2014): 242.

58 Sven Reichardt, "Praxeologie und Faschismus. Gewalt und Gemeinschaft als Elemente eines praxeologischen Faschismusbegriffs," in *Doing Culture. Neue Positionen zum Verhältnis von Kultur und sozialer Praxis*, ed. K. Hörning and J. Reuter (Bielefeld: Transcript, 2004).

59 See "A Framework for Remembrance," https://www.dresden.de/en/city/07/03/Remembrance.php.

60 Schedler, 241, and Kathrin Fahlenbrach, "Protest-Räume—Medien-Räume," *Straße als kultureller Aktionsraum*, ed. Geschke S.M. (VS Verlag für Sozialwissenschaften), 88–110.

61 Ahmed, "Affective Economies," 120; Hoelscher, "'Dresden, a Camera Accuses'," 288–305.

62 See David Crew "After the Cold War: The Multimedia Bombing War since the 1990s," 169–212.

63 A Framework for Remembrance, https://www.dresden.de/en/city/07/03/Remembrance.php.

64 Martin Clemens Winter, "Luftkrieg. Akteure und Deutungen des Gedenkens seit 1945," in *Erringerungsorte der extremen Rechten*, ed. Martin Langebach and Michael Sturm (Wiesbaden: Springer Fachmedien, 2015), 197–212.

65 The literature is vast. See the special issue of *Information, Communication and Society* from 2015 for one prominent example.

66 Friedrich Krotz, "The Metaprocess 'Mediatization' as a Conceptual Frame," *Global Media and Communication* 3, no. 3 (2007): 256–60.

67 Marshall McLuhan, *Understanding Media: The Extensions of Man* (New York: McGraw Hill, 1964).

68 Raymond Williams, *Television. Technology and Culture Form* (New York: Schocken Pres, 1974), 140 and Lisa Nakamura, *Cybertypes: Race, Ethnicity, and Identity on the Internet* (New York: Routledge 2002).

69 Andrew Hoskins, "Television and the Collapse of Memory," *Time & Society* 13, no. 1 (March 1, 2004): 109–27.

70 Maria Mast, "Gedenken muss wie Schmerz sein, es kann nicht beruhigen," *Die Zeit*, February 13, 2020, https://www.zeit.de/wissen/geschichte/2020-02/luftangriffe-dresden-1945-gedenken-75-jahrestag-instrumentalisierung (accessed June 8, 2020).

71 Stefan Reinicke, "Der Himmel uber Dresden," *Der Tageszeitung*, February 13, 2015, https://taz.de/Jahrestag-der-Bombardierung/!5020188&s=dresden+bombenkrieg/.

72 Mattias Berek, "Transfer Zones: German and Global Suffering in Dresden," in *Local Memories in a Nationalizing and Globalizing World*, ed. Marnix Beyer and Brecht Deseure (Palgrave Macmillan, 2014), 78. http://www.dnn-online.de/dresden/web/regional/politik/detail/-/specific/DNN-Barometer-Mehrheit-der-Dresdner-befuerwortet-friedliche-Blockadenvon-Nazi-Demos-797623438.

73 Berek, "Transfer Zones," 77. See also Swen Steinberg, "From Memorial Space to Learning Place. Present and Prospective (Hi)story Telling at the Dresden Heidefriedhof/Heath Cemetery," *Abolish Commemoration, Critique of the Discourse Relating to the Bombing of Dresden in 1945*, ed. Dissonanz author collective (Berlin: Verbrecher Verlag, 2014), 189–213.

74 danah boyd, *It's Complicated: The Social Lives of Networked Teens* (New Haven: Yale University Press, 2014), 8.

75 Ibid., 11–13.

76 Nancy Fraser, "Rethinking the Public Sphere: A Contribution to the Critique of Actually Existing Democracy," Social Text no. 25/26 (1990), 68.

77 Andrew Chadwick, "Explaining the Failure of an Online Citizen Engagement Initiative: The Role of Internal Institutional Variables" Journal of Information Technology and Politics 8 no. 1 (2011), 21–40. Manuel Castells, Communication Power (Oxford: Oxford University Press, 2009).

78 Kate Crawford, "What's Happening? Banality and Intimacy in Mobile and Social Media" Humanities Australia no. 1 (2010): 64–71. Vincent Miller, "New Media, Networking and Phatic Culture," Convergence: The International Journal into New Media Technologies" 14, no. 4 (2008): 387–400.

79 Thompson, 2008.

80 Alice E. Marwick and Danah Boyd [*sic*], "I Tweet Honestly, I Tweet Passionately: Twitter Users, Context Collapse, and the Imagined Audience," *New Media & Society* 13, no. 1 (2010): 118.

81 Christina Neumayer and Bjarki Valtysson, "Tweet against Nazis? Twitter, power and networked publics in anti-fascist protests," MedieKultur: Journal of Media and Communication Research vol 55 (2013), 4.

82 Antifa Recherche Team Dresden (ART), "Dresden Calls. How One of the Biggest Nazi Parades Came to Be," in *Abolish Commemoration: Critique of the Discourse Rleaint to the Bombing of Dresden in 1945,* ed. Dissonanz author collective (Berlin: Verbrecher Verlag, 2015), 249.

83 Gruzd et al., 2011.

84 Tweets with #dresdennazifrei numbered sometimes in only the hundreds, rather than the thousands.

85 Christina Neumayer and Bjarki Valtysson, "Tweet against Nazis? Twitter, Power, and Networked Publics in Anti-Fascist Protests," *MedieKultur. Journal of Media and Communication Research* 55 (2013): 9.

86 #13Februar 2014 Twitter dataset.

87 Johan Farkas, Jannick Schou, and Christina Neumayer, "Platformed Antagonism: Racist Discourses on Fake Muslim Facebook Pages," *Critical Discourse Studies* 15, no. 5 (2018): 463–80. https://doi.org/10.1080/17405904.2018.1450276.

88 Please consult the Populist Publics datasets available as part of the Carleton University Dataverse collection: https://borealisdata.ca/dataverse/carleton.

89 "10,000 Teilnehmer bei Menschkette," *Radio Dresden*, February 13, 2014, https://www.radiodresden.de/beitrag/11-000-teilnehmer-bei-menschenkette-410751/.

90 Michelle Zappavigna, "Searable Talk: The Linguistic Functions of Hashtags," *Social Semiotics* 25, no. 3 (2015).

91 "Eine solidarische Kritik am "Aufruf 13. Februar 2020: Nazis stören!" January 20, 2020, https://www.addn.me/antifa/darfs-ein-bisschen-mehr-sein/.

92   Aufruf 13. Februar: Nazis stören!" https://dresden-nazifrei.com/aufruf2020/.

93   Bürgel was originally invited to city hall by AfD officials, but the city cancelled the room reservation. Bürgel's two lectures were livestreamed and recorded for the AfD-Dresden YouTube channel. https://www.youtube.com/watch?v=TnvuZSq81zQ. For more on Bürgel's claims see https://www.welt.de/geschichte/zweiter-weltkrieg/article113572177/Dossier-berichtet-ueber-Tiefflieger-Angriffe-auf-Dresden.html.

94   As but one example, see https://twitter.com/ezoderwitz/status/1226583916653481985. The exhibition itself is available here https://weiterdenken.de/de/neunzehn-namen-aus-neunzehntausend.

95   Swen Steinberg, "Nicht Gedenkort, sondern Lernort. Was der Heidefriedhof erzählt, und erzählen könnte," in *Gendenken abschaffen. Kritik am Diskurs zu Bombadierung Dresdens 1945*, ed. Autor_innenkollektiv Dissonanz (Berlin: Verbrecher Verlag, 2013), 105–16.

96   Quoted in Maria Mast, "Gedenken muss wie Schmerz sein, es kann nicht beruhigen," *Die Zeit*, February 13, 2020, https://www.zeit.de/wissen/geschichte/2020-02/luftangriffe-dresden-1945-gedenken-75-jahrestag-instrumentalisierung (accessed June 8, 2020).

97   Astrid Erll, "Travelling Memory," *Parallax* 17, no. 4 (2011): 4–18; E. Keightley, "From Immediacy to Intermediacy: The Mediation of Lived Time," *Time & Society* 22 no. 1 (2013): 55–75.

98   Paul Virilio, *Open Sky* (London: Verso, 1997), 24.

99   Andrew Hoskins, "Mediatization of Memory," in *Mediatization of Communication*, ed. Knut Lundby (De Gruyter, 2004), 661.

100 Samuel Merrill and Johan Pries, "Translocalising and Relocasing Antifascist Struggles: From #KämpaShowan to #KämpaMalmö," *Antipode* 51, no. 1 (2019): 259.

101 Andrew Hoskins, "Mediatization of Memory," 676.

102 Merrill and Pries, "Translocalising and Relocasing Antifascist Struggles."

103 David Abernathy, *Using Geodata and Geolocation in the Social Sciences: Mapping Our Connected World* (London: Sage, 2016), 129.

104 See Ned Richardson-Little and Samuel Merrill, "Who Is the Volk? PEGIDA and the Contested Memory of 1989 on Social Media," in Samuel Merrill, *Social Movements, Cultural Memory, and Digital Media: Mobilising Mediated Remembrance* (Palgrave Macmillan, 2020), 72.

105 https://www.bbc.com/news/uk-england-tyne-31657167.

106 Göttinger Institut für Demokratieforschung (2016), 24.

107 On February 12, 2015, @Pegidizer links to the news article in *Die Tagesszeitung* on http://t.co/7dyVtNR5jd and http://t.co/uyePlv8DXZ and also in "Die Welt Die Trauer um die Toten kommt in Dresden zu kurz," February 13, 2015), https://www.welt.de/politik/deutschland/article137444761/Die-Trauer-um-die-Toten-kommt-in-Dresden-zu-kurz.html. @Pegidizer's posts are ambivalent, however. They are an

attempt to catalogue news coverage of #PEGIDA and include posts both critical and supportive of the movement. In 2019, it was banned.

108 "Sachsens fatale Strategie im Umgang mit Pegida," *Die Tagesspiegel*, March 3, 2020, https://www.tagesspiegel.de/politik/wegschauen-gewaehren-lassen-verharmlosen-sachsens-fatale-strategie-im-umgang-mit-pegida/25640572.html.

109 E. Keightley and P. Schlesinger, "Digital Media—Social Memory: Remembering in Digitally Networked Times," *Media, Culture and Society* 36, no. 6 (2014): 745–7.

110 "Die Nacht in der Dresden unterging," *Hannoverische Zeitung*, February 13, 2015, https://www.haz.de/Nachrichten/Panorama/Uebersicht/Bombenangriff-vor-70-Jahren-Die-Nacht-in-der-Dresden-unterging.

111 Christina Neumayer, Luca Rossi, and Björn Karlsson, "Contested Hashtags: Blockupy Frankfurt in Social Media," *International Journal of Communication* 10 (2016): 5558–79.

112 https://twitter.com/KBSachsen.

113 "Das Ewige Dresden Märchen," October 9, 2019, https://dresden-nazifrei.com/2019/10/04/dresden-das-ewige-trauermaerchen/.

114 Etienne François and Hagen Schulze, "Einleitung," in *Erinnerungsorte*, ed. Etienne François and Hagen Schulze (München: C.H Beck, 2001), 9–24.

115 There is a large literature on this. For an overview of the faultlines, see Claudio Fogu and Wulf Kansteiner, "The Politics of Memory and the Poetics of History," in *The Politics of Memory in Postwar Europe*, ed. Richard Ned Lebow, Wulf Kansteiner, Claudio Fogu (Duke: Duke University Press, 2006), 286 and Chris Lorenz, "Unstuck in Time. Or: The Sudden Presence of the Past," in *Performing the Past. Memory, History and Identity in Modern Europe*, ed. Karin Tilmans, Frank van Vree, and Jay Winter (Amsterdam: Amsterdam University Press, 2010), 67–105.

116 Gabrielle Spiegel, "Memory and History: Liturgical Time and Historical Time," *History and Theory* XLI (2002): 149–62.

117 Aleida Assmann, "History and Memory," *International Encyclopedia of the Social and Behavioral Sciences* (2002), 6822–9; M. Sabrow and N. Frei, eds., *Die Geburt des Zeitzeugen nach 1945* (Göttingen: Wallstein, 2012). On historical distance, see Mark Salber Phillips, *On Historical Distance* (Yale: Yale University Press, 2013).

118 Chris Lorenz, "Blurred Lines History, Memory and the Experience of Time," *International Journal for History, Culture and Modernity* 2, no. 1: 43–62.

119 Raphael Samuel, *Theatres of Memory. Past and Present in Contemporary Culture* (London: Verso, 1994), 10. Wolf Kansteiner warns against assumptions around generational thinking as always emphasizing change over moments of homogeneity and continuity. See Wulf Kansteiner, "Moral Pitfalls of Memory Studies: The Concept of Political Generations," *Memory Studies* 5, no. 2 (2012): 111–13.

120 Aleida Assman, "Europe: A Community of Memory?" *Bulletin of the German Historical Association* 40, no. 1 (2007): 11–25. See Also Andreas Huyysen, *Present Pasts: Urban Palimpsests and the Politics of Memory* (Stanford: Stanford University Press, 2003), 12.

121 Anna Reading, "Globital Time," in *Time, Media, and Modernity,* ed. Emily Kneightley (Basingstoke: Palgrave Macmillan, 2012), 144.

122 Michael Rothberg, "Introduction: Between Memory and Memory—From Lieux de mémoire to Noeuds de mémoire," *Yale French Studies* 118–19 (2010): 10. See also W. Lance Bennett and Anne Segerberg, "Digital Media and the Personalization of Collective Action: Social Technology and the Organization of Protests against the Global Economic Crisis," *Information, Communication & Society,* 14 (2011): 770–99.

123 Andrew Hoskins, "Memory of the Multitude: The End of Collective Memory," in *Digital Memory Studies: Media Pasts in Transition,* ed. Andrew Hoskins (New York: Routledge, 2017), 85–109.

124 Frank Ankersmith, "Commemoration and National Identity," *Textos De História,* 10, no. 1–2 (2002): 15–39.

125 Preston King, *Thinking Past a Problem. Essays in the History of Ideas* (London: Routledge, 2000), 25–68.

126 Maiken Umbach, *German Cities and Bourgeois Modernism, 1890–1924* (Oxford: Oxford University Press, 2009).

127 Merlyna Lim, "Seeing Spatially: People, Networks, and Movements in Digital and Urban Spaces," *International Development Planning Review* 36, no. 1 (2014): 54–5. See Manual Castells, *Networks of Outrage and Hope. Social Movements in the Internet Age* (Cambridge: Polity Press, 2012).

128 Henri Lefebvre, *Rhythmanalysis: Space, Time and Everyday Life* (Trowbridge: Continuum, 1992).

Chapter 5

1 Jamie Bartlett, Jonathan Birdwell, and Mark Littler, *The New Face of Digital Populism* (London: Demos, 2011).

2 Douglas Kellner, "Habermas, the Public Sphere, and Democracy," in *Re-Imaging Public Space: The Frankfurt School in the 21st Century,* ed. Diana Boros and James Glass (Basingstoke: Palgrave Macmillan, 2011), 19–43.

3 Susan Neiman, *Learning from the Germans: Confronting Race and the Memory of Evil* (London: Allen Lane, 2019).

4 Andrew Hoskins, "Anachronisms of Media, Anachronisms of Memory: From Collective Memory to a New Memory Ecology," in *On Media Memory: Collective Memory in a New Media Age,* ed. Motti Neiger, Oren Meyers, and Eyal Zandberg (Basingstoke: Palgrave Macmillan, 2011), 278–88.

5 See Gunnþórunn Guðmundsdóttir, "The Online Self: Memory and Forgetting in the Digital Age," *European Journal of Life Writing* 3 (2014): 42–54.

6 We side with José van Dijck, *The Culture of Connectivity. A Critical History of Social Media* (Oxford, UK: Oxford University Press, 2013).

7   Sara Jones has done this with victim memories in online chat groups. See Sara Jones, "Catching Fleeting Memories: Victim Forums as Mediated Remembering Communities," *Memory Studies* 6, no. 4 (August 2013): 390–403.

8   Julia Rose, *Difficult History at Museums and Historic Sites* (London: Rowman and Littlefield Publishers, 2016).

9   Joanne Garde-Hansen, Andrew Hoskins, and Anna Reading, eds., "Introduction," in *Save As … Digital Memories* (Basingstoke: Palgrave Macmillan, 2009), 1–21.

10 Rosenfeld, *Hi Hitler? How the Nazi Past Is Being Normalized in Contemporary Culture.*

11 Chris Berry, Soyoung Kim, and Lynn Spigel, *Electronic Elsewhere: Media Technology and the Experience of Social Space* (Minneapolis: University of Minnesota Press, 2010).

12 Anne Kaun and Fredrik Stiernstedt, "Facebook Time: Technological and Institutional Affordances for Media Memories," *New Media and Society* 16, no. 7 (July 2014): 1154–68.

13 E.J. Westlake, "Friend Me if You Facebook: Generation Y and Performative Surveillance," *TDR: The Drama Review* 52, no. 4 (Winter 2008): 21–40.

14 Aaron Smith and Monica Anderson, "Social Media Use in 2018," PEW Research Center, March 1, 2018, http://www.pewinternet.org/2018/03/01/social-media-use-in-2018/ (accessed March 7, 2018). See also Social Media Fact Sheet, PEW Research Center, February 5, 2018, http://www.pewinternet.org/fact-sheet/social-media/ (accessed March 7, 2018). On the German side, for a case study of use from before the Facebook API was dismantled, see Sebastian Stier et al., "When Populists Become Popular: Comparing Facebook Use by the Right-Wing Movement Pegida and German Political Parties," *Information, Communication & Society* 20, no. 9 (September 2, 2017): 1365–88, https://doi.org/10.1080/1369118X.2017.1328519.

15 Klaus Beck, *Computervermittelte Kommunikation im Internet Lehr—und Handbücher der Kommunikationswissenschaft* (Oldenbourg: Oldenbourg Verlag, 2006), 169.

16 Henri Lefebvre, *Rhythmanalysis* (London: Continuum, 2004).

17 John Urry, "Time, Complexity, and the Global," in *Social Conceptions of Time. Structure and Process in Work and Everyday*, ed. Graham Crow and Sue Heath (Basingstoke: Palgrave Macmillan, 2002), 12.

18 Peter Bailey, "Adventures in Space: Victorian Railway Erotics or Taking Alienation for a Ride," *Journal of Victorian Culture* 9, no. 1 (2004): 1–21; E.P. Thompson, "Time, Work-Discipline and Industrial Capitalism," *Past and Present* no. 38 (December 1967): 56–97; M.D. Peters, "Calendar, Clock, Tower," in *Deus in Machina: Religion and Technology in Historical Perspective*, ed. J. Stolow (New York: Fordham University Press, 2013), 25–42.

19 Christian Fuchs, "Digital Prosumption Labour on Social Media in the Context of the Capitalist Regime of Time," *Time and Society* 23, no. 1 (2014): 97–123.

20 Jürgen Habermas, *The Structural Transformation of the Public Sphere* (Cambridge, MA: MIT Press, 1991).

21 Kellner, "Habermas, the Public Sphere, and Democracy," 36. Of course, Benjamin was also wary of the power of mass media, especially photography, and the way in which it might be co-opted through propaganda. See Jennifer V. Evans, "Photography as an Ethics of Seeing," in *The Ethics of Seeing: Photography and Twentieth Century German History*, ed. Jennifer V. Evans, Paul Betts, and Stefan-Ludwig Hoffmann (New York: Berghahn Books, 2018), 1–22.

22 See footnote 3 of Jürgen Habermas, "Political Communication in Media Society: Does Democracy Still Enjoy an Epistemic Dimension? The Impact of Normative Theory on Empirical Research," *Communication Theory* 16, no. 4 (November 2006): 411–26.

23 Habermas, "Political Communication in Media Society," 422.

24 Pablo Barberá, Richard Bonneau, and John T. Jost, "Tweeting from Left to Right: Is Online Political Communication More Than an Echo Chamber?" *Psychological Science* 26 (2015): 1531–42; R.K. Garrett, "Echo Chambers Online? Politically Motivated Selective Exposure among Internet News Users" *Journal of Computer-mediated Communication* 14 (2009): 265–85; Paulo Gerbaudo, "Populism 2.0: Social Media Activism, the Generic Internet User and Interactive Direct Democracy," in *Social Media, Politics and the State: Protests, Revolutions, Riots, Crime and Policing in the Age of Facebook, Twitter and Youtube*, ed. D. Trottier and C. Fuchs (New York: Routledge, 2009), 67–87.

25 Craig Calhoun, "Introduction: Habermas and the Public Sphere," in *Habermas and the Public Sphere,* ed. Craig Calhoun (Cambridge, MA: MIT Press, 1992); Nancy Fraser, "What's Critical about Critical Theory? The Case of Habermas and Gender," in *Feminism and Critique,* ed. Seyla Benhabib and Drucilla Cornell (Cambridge, MA: Polity Press, 1987), 31–56; Michael Warner, "Publics and Counterpublics," *Public Culture* 14, no. 1 (Winter 2002): 49–90.

26 The myPersonality project has acquired the data of over 10 million people since the app was created in 2007. It is governed by ethics review and the data is made public, only anonymized. Access to personal material is only possible with an ethics clearance. See Michal Kosinsk, Sandra C. Matz, Samuel D. Gosling, Vesselin Popov, and David Stillwell, "Facebook as a Research Tool for the Social Sciences. Opportunities, Challenges, Ethical Considerations, and Practical Guidelines," *American Psychologist* 70, no. 6 (September 2015): 543–56.

27 John Naughton, "The New Surveillance Capitalism," *Prospect Magazine*, January 19, 2018, https://www.prospectmagazine.co.uk/magazine/how-the-internet-controls-you (accessed March 20, 2018).

28 Dan Fletcher, "How Facebook is Redefining Privacy," *Time Magazine*, March 18, 2018, http://content.time.com/time/magazine/article/0,9171,1990798,00.html (accessed March 19, 2018).

29 Bernard E. Harcourt, *Exposed. Desire and Disobedience in the Digital Age* (Cambridge, MA: Harvard University Press, 2015). These concerns are echoed in Morozov, *The Net Delusion*.

30 Wolfgang Sofsky, *Privacy—a Manifesto* (Princeton: Princeton University Press, 2008).

31 David S. Wall and Roberto Musotto, "Facebook's Push for End-to-End Encryption Is Good News for User Privacy, as Well as Terrorists and Paedophiles," *The Conversation*, http://theconversation.com/facebooks-push-for-end-to-end-encryption-is-good-news-for-user-privacy-as-well-as-terrorists-and-paedophiles-128782 (accessed July 22, 2020). See also aughton, "Facebook's New Encrypted Network Will Give Criminals the Privacy They Crave | John Naughton," *The Guardian*, March 17, 2019, sec. Opinion, https://www.theguardian.com/commentisfree/2019/mar/17/facebook-encrypted-network-gives-criminals-privacy-they-crave-john-naughton.

32 John T. Jost et al., "How Social Media Facilitates Political Protest: Information, Motivation, and Social Networks," *Political Psychology* 39, no. S1 (2018): 85–118, https://doi.org/10.1111/pops.12478; "The Boogaloo Movement Is Not What You Think," *bellingcat*, May 27, 2020, https://www.bellingcat.com/news/2020/05/27/the-boogaloo-movement-is-not-what-you-think/; Farkas, Schou, and Neumayer, "Platformed Antagonism," 463–80.

33 Lev Grossmann, "Mark Zuckerberg. Person of the Year 2010," *Time*, December 15, 2010, http://content.time.com/time/specials/packages/article/0,28804,2036683_2037183_2037185-5,00.html (accessed June 30, 2016).

34 Megan Squire, "Understanding Gray Networks—Megan's Blog," https://megansquire.com/understanding-gray-networks/ (accessed May 7, 2020); Megan Squire, "Network Analysis of Anti-Muslim Groups on Facebook: 10th International Conference, SocInfo 2018, St. Petersburg, Russia, September 25–28, 2018, Proceedings, Part I," 2018, 403–19, https://doi.org/10.1007/978-3-030-01129-1_25.

35 Johannes Baldauf and Amadeu Antonio Stiftung, *Toxische Narrative: Monitoring Rechts-Alternativer Akteure* (Berlin: Amadeu Antonio Stiftung, 2017), 8–9.

36 Deen Freelon, "Computational Research in the Post-API Age," *Political Communication* 35, no. 4 (October 2018): 665–8, https://doi.org/10.1080/10584609.2018.1477506.

37 Christine Hine, *Ethnography for the Internet: Embedded, Embodied and Everyday* (London: Taylor & Francis, 2015); Anja Bechmann and Peter Bjerregaard Vahlstrup, "Studying Facebook and Instagram Data: The Digital Footprints Software," *First Monday*, December 15, 2015, https://doi.org/10.5210/fm.v20i12.5968.

38 Stier et al., "When Populists Become Popular."

39 Lisa Nakamura, *Cybertypes: Race, Ethnicity, and Identity on the Internet* (London: Routledge, 2002).

40 "Hate Speech," *Amadeu Antonio Stiftung* (blog), https://www.amadeu-antonio-stiftung.de/en/hate-speech/ (accessed July 22, 2020).

41 Terri E. Givens, "The Radical Right Gender Gap," *Comparative Political Studies* 37, no. 1 (2004): 30–54; Pippa Norris, *Radical Right: Voters and Parties in the Electoral Market* (Cambridge: Cambridge University Press 2005), 145. See also Eelco Harteveld, Wouter Van Der Brug, Stefan Dahlberg, and Andrej Kokkonen, "The Gender Gap in Populist Radical-right Voting: Examining the Demand Side in Western and Eastern Europe," *Patterns of Prejudice* 49, no. 1–2 (2015): 103–34.

42 Joan Scott, *The Politics of the Veil* (Princeton, NJ: Princeton University Press, 2007) and also Joan Scott, *Secularism* (Princeton, NJ: Princeton University Press, 2017). See Also Roman Kuhar and David Paternotte, eds., *Gender Campaigns in Europe. Mobilizing against Equality* (London: Rowan and Littlefield, 2017).

43 Tjitske Akkerman, "Gender and the Radical Right in Western Europe. A Comparative Analysis of Policy Agendas," *Patterns of Prejudice* 49, no. 1–2 (2015): 37–60.

44 Herbert Kitschelt with Anthony J. McGann, T*he Radical Right in Western Europe: A Comparative Analysis* (Ann Arbor: University of Michigan Press 1997), 20.

45 Official result of the 2009 city election, Cologne municipality, http://www.stadt-koeln.de/wahlen/kommunalwahl/2009/wahlpraesentation/index.html?ansicht=7.

46 Berlin in Wahlen results for 2017 Bundestag Election. Amt für Statistik Berlin-Brandenburg https://www.wahlen-berlin.de/wahlen/BU2017/AFSPRAES/uebersicht_wahlkreis-76-berlin-pankow_gesamt.html. AfD support was logged at roughly 13%.

47 W. Lance Bennett and Alexandra Segerberg, "The Logic of Connective Action: Digital Media and the Personalization of Contentious Politics" *Information, Communication & Society* 15, no. 5 (2012): 739–68.

48 "Ein Prozent für Unseres Land," January 24, 2018. https://www.facebook.com/einprozentfuerunserland/ (accessed March 22, 2018).

49 Christian Fuchs and Paul Middelhoff, "Die Wutmacher," *Die Zeit*, March 13, 2019, https://www.zeit.de/2019/12/ein-prozent-verein-neue-rechte/komplettansicht. See also Stefan Lauer Belltower News, August 30, 2019, https://www.belltower.news/landtagswahlen-wie-eine-rechtsradikale-ngo-das-vertrauen-in-die-demokratie-untergraebt-90493/.

50 "Recherchieren was die Anderen verschweigen," YouTube video, April 5, 2018, https://youtu.be/fXQph2koEGE.

51 "NGO der neuen Rechten," *Belltower News*, May 31, 2016, https://www.belltower.news/ein-prozent-fuer-unser-land-ngo-der-neuen-rechten-42110/.

52 https://www.idz-jena.de/wsddet/ein-prozent-eine-extrem-rechte-organisation-im-kampf-um-kulturelle-hegemonie/.

53 Antwort der Bundesregierung auf die Kleine Anfrage der Abgeordneten Ulla Jelpke, Frank Trempel, Katrin Kunert, weiterer Abgeordneter und der Fraktion Die Linke—Druksache 18/11963, May 8, 2017, 2.

54 "NGO der neuen Rechten," *Belltower News,* https://www.belltower.news/ein-prozent-fuer-unser-land-ngo-der-neuen-rechten-42110/.

55 Alexander Bischoff, "Rechte Klagen gegen Facebook-Sperre: 'Ein Prozent' Will keine Hass-Organisation Sein," *Tag 24,* November 12, 2019, https://www.tag24.de/nachrichten/landgericht-goerlitz-dresden-sachsen-rechte-klagen-gegen-facebook-sperre-ein-prozent-hass-organisation-1282624.

56 Ergebnisse aus der Studienreihe „Medien und ihr Publikum" (MiP) ARD/ZDF-Onlinestudie 2017, October 11, 2017. http://www.ard-zdf-onlinestudie.de/ardzdf-onlinestudie-2017/, (accessed March 28, 2018).

57 Oath Keepers, https://www.facebook.com/OKNational/ (accessed March 28, 2018).

58 Alexandra Minna Stein, *Proud Boys and the White Ethnostate. How the Alt-Right is Warping the American Imagination* (Boston: Beacon Press, 2019).

59 Paul Taggart, "Populism and Representative Politics in Contemporary Europe," *Journal of Political Ideologies* 9, no. 3 (2004): 269–88.

60 Kevin Roose, "This Was the Alt-Right's Favourite Chat App. Then Came Charlottesville," *New York Times,* https://www.nytimes.com/2017/08/15/technology/discord-chat-app-alt-right.html (accessed June 29, 2018). See also "LEAKED: Violent Racists Use Facebook to Plan "Unite the Right 2," https://www.unicornriot.ninja/2018/leaked-violent-racists-use-facebook-chat-to-plan-unite-the-right-2/ (accessed June 29, 2018).

61 Raffael Heiss and Jörg Matthes, "Who 'likes' Populists? Characteristics of Adolescents Following Right-Wing Populist Actors on Facebook," *Information, Communication, and Society* 20, no. 9 (September 2017): 1408–24.

62 P. Gerbaudo, "Populism 2.0," in *Social Media, Politics and the State. Protests, Revolutions, Riots, Crime and Policing in the Age of Facebook, Twitter and YouTube,* ed. D. Trottier and C. Fuchs (New York: Routledge), 16–67.

63 Stier et al., "When Populists Become Popular."

64 Andrew Chadwick, *The Hybrid Media System: Politics and Power* (Oxford: Oxford University Press, 2013). See also Cynthia Miller-Idriss, *Hate in the Homeland: The New Global Far Right* (Princeton, NJ: Princeton University Press, 2020).

65 Heiss and Matthes, "Who 'likes' Populists?" 1408–24.

66 Cynthia Muller-Idriss, *The Extreme Gone Mainstream* (Princeton, NJ: Princeton University Press, 2018).

67 Jamie Bartlet, "From Hope to Hate: How the Early Internet Fed the Far-Right Movement," *The Guardian,* https://www.theguardian.com/world/2017/aug/31/far-right-alt-right-white-supremacists-rise-online.

68 Rand C. Lewis, *The Neo-Nazis and German Unification* (New York: Praeger, 1996).

69 Steinmetz, 342.

70 See *Handbuch deutscher Rechtsextremismus,* ed. Jens Mecklenburg (Berlin: Espresso Verlag 1996); *Rechtsextremismus in der Bundesrepublik Deutschland: eine*

Bilanz, ed. Wilfried Schubarth and Richard Stöss (2001); Fabian Virchow, "The Groupuscularization of Neo-Nazism in Germany. The Case of the Aktionsbüro Norddeutschland," *Patterns of Prejudice* 38, no. 1 (2004): 56–70; Fabian Virchow, "Extreme Right Marches in Germany Today," in *The Street as Stage. Protest Marches and Public Rallies since the Nineteenth Century*, ed. Matthias Reiss (2007), 295–310.

71 A mixed media history of German political culture is only in its infancy. See Vittoria Borso, Christiane Liermann, Patrick Merziger, eds., *Die Macht des Populären: Politik und populäre Kultur im 20. Jahrhundert* (2010); Martin Klimke and Laura Stapane, "From Artists for Peace to the Green Caterpillar: Cultural Activism and Electoral Politics in 1980s West Germany," in *Accidental Armageddons: The Nuclear Crisis and the Culture of the Cold War in the 1980s*, ed. Eckart Conze, Martin Klimke, and Jeremy Varon (forthcoming); Michael Rauhut, *Schalmei und Lederjacke: Rock und Politik in der DDR der achtziger Jahre* (2002); Detlef Siegfried, *Time Is on My Side: Konsum und Politik in der westdeutschen Jugendkultur der 60er Jahre* (2006).

72 "Neo-Nazi Video: Suspects Appear to Claim Responsibility for Murders 11/14/2011," Spiegel Online, http://www.spiegel.de/video/video-1161229.html and "Neo-Nazis in Brandenburg have even resorted to the use of Sesame Street characters for recruitment." See *International Business Times*, April 14, 2014, http://www.ibtimes.co.uk/german-neo-nazis-using-cookie-monster-recruit-children-1443716.

73 Bartlett, Birdwell, Littler, *The New Face of Digital Populism*. See also "Cyber-nationalism: The Brave New World of E-Hatred," *The Economist*, January 19, 2011; Chris Atton, "Far-right Media on the Internet: Culture, Discourse and Power," *New Media and Society* 8, no. 4 (August 2006): 573–87; T. K. Kim, "Electronic Storm— Stormfront Grows a Thriving Neo-Nazi Community," *Intelligence Report* no. 118 (July 2004); Ruud Koopmans and Susan Olzak, "Discursive Opportunities and the Evolution of Right-Wing Violence in Germany," *The American Journal of Sociology* 110, no. 1 (July 2004): 198–230.

74 Die Braune Falle, Eine rechstextremistische "Karriere" Bundesamt für Verfassungsschutz (2010).

75 Marie-Teresa Weber, "Greeting," in *Hate Speech and Radicalization Online. The OCCI Research Report*, ed. Johannes Baldauf, Julia Ebner, and Jakob Guhl (London: ISD Press, 2019), 4.

76 Jean Burgess, *YouTube: Online Video and Participatory Culture* (2009); Barbara Perry and Patrik Olsson, "Cyberhate: the Globalization of Hate," *Information & Communications Technology Law* 18, no. 2 (2009): 185–99; Lacy G. McNamee, Brittany L. Peterson, and Jorge Pena, "A Call to Educate, Particpate, Invoke and Indict: Understanding the Communication of Online Hate Groups," *Communication Monographs* 77, no. 2 (2010): 257–80.

77 "Toxic Narratives. Monitoring Alternative Right Actors." https://www.amadeu-antonio-stiftung.de/w/files/englisch/monitoring-2017-englisch-int.pdf (accessed June 26, 2018).

78 "Debunking—Vom Entlarven Falscher Tatsachen," http://www.belltower.news/artikel/debunking-%E2%80%93-vom-entlarven-falscher-tatsachen-13713 (accessed June 28, 2018).

79 Henry Jenkins, *Convergence Culture. Where Old and New Media Collide* (New York: New York University, 2006).

80 "Rechtsextremekampagne gegen die Amadeu Antonio Stiftung," April 25, 2016, http://www.belltower.news/artikel/rechtsextreme-bedrohungskampagne-28917.

81 "Moses Mendelssohn-Preis 2002 an Anette Kahane," https://www.berlin.de/rbmskzl/aktuelles/pressemitteilungen/2002/pressemitteilung.46477.php.

82 See the two chapters written by Kahane in Enrico Heitzer et al., eds., *Nach Auschwitz: schwieriges Erbe DDR: Plädoyer für einen Paradigmenwechsel in der DDR-Zeitgeschichtsforschung, 1.* Auflage, Wochenschau Wissenschaft (Frankfurt/M: Wochenschau Verlag, 2018).

83 See Helmut W. Smith, *Germany: A Nation in Its Time. Before, During, and After Nationalism, 1500–2000* (New York: W. W. Norton, 2020).

84 Alison Landsberg, *Prosthetic Memory: The Transformation of American Memory in the Age of Mass Culture* (New York: Columbia University Press, 2004). Similar to this approach is Michael Rothberg's notion of multidirectional memory. See Michael Rothberg, *Multidirectional Memory. Remembering the Holocaust in the Age of Decolonization* (Stanford: Stanford University Press, 2009).

85 Helmut Müller-Enbergs, *Die inoffiziellen Mitarbeiter* (MfS-Handbuch) (Berlin: BStU, 2008), 36. For a ground level, everyday life approach to how the Stasi operated, see Gary Bruce, *The Firm. The Inside Story of the Stasi* (New York: Oxford University Press, 2010).

86 Interview, Anette Kahane, Vorsitende Amadeu Antonio Stiftung, April 24, 2014. https://www.ardmediathek.de/tv/alpha-Forum/Anetta-Kahane-Vorsitzende-Amadeu-Antoni/ARD-alpha/Video?bcastId=14912942&documentId=20973696.

87 See the statement provided by Prof. Helmut Müller-Enberg, upon analysis of her case file. https://www.amadeu-antonio-stiftung.de/w/files/pdfs/gutachten-anetta-kahane.pdf.

88 Interestingly, new allegations surfaced against Kahane in 2016 when the director of the Hohenschönhausen memorial in Berlin, Hubertus Knabe, revived criticism of Kahane as another example of the failure of reunified Germany to tackle with the legacy of East German crimes. Notably, he made mention of the fact that Kahane's Stasi past had not tarnished her reputation with the governing CDU party, who supports many of the initiatives of the Amadeu Antonio Foundation. See Mathias

Meisner, "Streit um die Stasi-Vergangenheit von Anetta Kahane," https://www. tagesspiegel.de/politik/amadeu-antonio-stiftung-streit-um-die-stasi-vergangenheit-von-anetta-kahane/14966422.html (accessed July 22, 2020).

89 Karsten Müller and Carlo Schwarz, "Fanning the Flames of Hate: Social media and Hate Crime," https://ssrn.com/abstract=3082972 or http://dx.doi.org/10.2139/ ssrn.3082972.

90 Ben Knight, "New Study Shows AfD Facebook Posts Spur Anti-refugee Attacks," *Deutsche Welle*, December 29, 2017, https://www.dw.com/en/new-study-shows-afd-facebook-posts-spur-anti-refugee-attacks/a-41972992.

91 See especially their articles on hate speech and efforts to strengthen democratic conversation. http://www.belltower.news/category/lexikon/hate-speech.

92 "Germany Is Silencing Hate Speech but Cannot Define It," *The Economist*, January 13, 2018, https://www.economist.com/europe/2018/01/13/germany-is-silencing-hate-speech-but-cannot-define-it.

93 Victor Klemperer, *LTI—Lingua Tertii Imperii: Notizbuch eines Philologen*, 24th ed. (Stuttgart: Reclam, 2010).

94 Astrid Erll and Ann Rigney, *Memory in a Mediated World: Remembrance and Reconstruction,* ed. Andrea Hajek, Christine Lohmeier, and Christian Pentzold (New York: Routledge, 2015).

95 Astrid Erll, "Traveling Memory," *Parallax* 17, no. 4 (2011): 4–18.

96 Ibid., 5.

97 José van Dijck, *Mediated Memories. Personal Memory in the Digital Age* (Stanford: Stanford University Press, 2007).

98 Konrad Jarausch and Michael Geyer, *Shattered Pasts: Reconstructing German Histories* (Princeton: Princeton University Press, 2003), 322–3.

99 Andreas Huyssen, *Present Pasts: Palimpsests and the Politics of Memory* (Stanford: Stanford University Press, 2003).

Conclusion

1 Regulatory provisions have often failed to curtail the incivility, hate propaganda, and white supremacy circulating online and the major social media companies have historically been indifferent to regulating conduct. But this has recently changed. Facebook and Twitter and other social platforms are increasingly imposing regulation via moderation by censoring accounts, removing questionable content, blocking spurious and hateful content and de-platforming. In addition to these practices, there are other forms of regulation via cyber-law provisions, laws by national legislative bodies, and corporate self-regulation (terms and conditions and privacy policies, etc). Critics are not convinced of their efficacy.

2   "Opinion | Did WhatsApp Help Bolsonaro Win the Brazilian Presidency?—
    The Washington Post," https://www.washingtonpost.com/news/theworldpost/
    wp/2018/11/01/whatsapp-2/ (accessed March 20, 2022). Stern, *Proud Boys and the
    White Ethnostate*.

3   "'We Actually Elected a Meme as President': How 4chan Celebrated Trump's
    Victory," *The Washington Post*, https://www.washingtonpost.com/news/the-
    intersect/wp/2016/11/09/we-actually-elected-a-meme-as-president-how-4chan-
    celebrated-trumps-victory/ (accessed March 20, 2022).

4   Chris Tenove, Heidi Tworek, and Fenwick McKelvey, "Poisoning Democracy. What
    Can Be Done about Harmful Speech Online?," *Public Policy Forum Online*, 2018,
    https://ppforum.ca/publications/poisoning-democracy-what-can-be-done-about-.

5   Martin Kessler and Meghna Chakrabarti, "What the 'Strongmen' of History
    Reveal about Modern Politics," *On Point*, WBUR, November 12, 2020, https://
    www.wbur.org/onpoint/2020/11/12/what-the-strongmen-of-history-reveal-about-
    modern-politics; "Strongmen: Mussolini to the Present—Ruth Ben-Ghiat—Google
    Books," (New York: W. W. Norton, 2020), https://books-google-ca.proxy.library.
    carleton.ca/books?hl=en&lr=&id=tDbtDwAAQBAJ&oi=fnd&pg=PT3&dq=info
    :qzam82Jp1ZQJ:scholar.google.com&ots=Td1TvFLgjO&sig=2k14QZKgmvSe1-
    BOCSb13u7Uxv8&redir_esc=y#v=onepage&q&f=false (accessed March 20, 2022).

6   Philip M Napoli, "What if More Speech Is No Longer the Solution? First
    Amendment Theory Meets Fake News and the Filter Bubble," no. 1 (n.d.): 50;
    Stephanie Alice Baker, "The Mediated Crowd: New Social Media and New Forms of
    Rioting," *Sociological Research Online* 16, no. 4 (2011): 21; Vian Bakir and Andrew
    McStay, "Fake News and the Economy of Emotions: Problems, Causes, Solutions,"
    Digital Journalism 6, no. 2 (February 7, 2018): 154–75, https://doi.org/10.1080/2167
    0811.2017.1345645.

7   Farkas, Schou, and Neumayer, "Platformed Antagonism," 463–80, https://doi.org/1
    0.1080/17405904.2018.1450276.

8   *An Interview with the Founders of Black Lives Matter. TEDTalks, Alicia Garza,
    Patrisse Cullors, and Opal Tometi*, TED, 2018.

9   Ahmed, "Affective Economies," 117–39; Merlyna Lim, "Clicks, Cabs, Coffee Houses:
    Social Media and the Oppositional Movements in Egypt (2004–2011)," *Journal of
    Communication* 62 (April 2, 2012): 231–48. Merlyna Lim, "Roots, Routes, Routers:
    Communications and Media of Contemporary Social Movements," *Journalism &
    Communication Monographs Series* 20, no. 2 (2018): 92–136.

10 Tarleton Gillespie, *Custodians of the Internet* (New Haven, CT: Yale University
    Press, 2018), https://yalebooks.yale.edu/book/9780300173130/custodians-internet.

11 Michael Warner, *Publics and Counterpublics* (New York: Zone Books,
    2002); Noortje Marres, *Digital Sociology: The Reinvention of Social*

Research (London: Polity Press, 2017), https://www.wiley.com/en-ru/ Digital+Sociology%3A+The+Reinvention+of+Social+Research-p-9780745684789.

12 Noortje Marres, "Front-Staging Non-Humans: The Politics of 'Green' Things and the Constraint of Publicity," in *The Stuff of Politics*, ed. Bruce Braun and Sarah J. Whatmore (Minneapolis: University of Minnesota Press, 2008), 177–210.

13 Tenove, Tworek, and McKelvey, "Poisoning Democracy. What Can Be Done about Harmful Speech Online?."

14 Dijck, *The Culture of Connectivity*; Zizi Papacharissi, "Affective Publics and Structures of Storytelling: Sentiment, Events and Mediality," *Information, Communication & Society* 19 (2015): 307–24.

15 Bernard Harcourt, *Exposed. Desire and Disobedience in the Digital Age* (Boston, MA: Harvard University Press, 2018); Shoshana Zuboff, *The Age of Surveillance Capitalism. The Fight for a Human Future at the Frontier of Power* (New York: Public Affairs, 2019).

16 Heidi Tworek, *News from Germany: The Competition to Control World Communications, 1900–1945* (Boston, MA: Harvard University Press, 2018).

17 Gavriel D. Rosenfeld, "The Rise of Illiberal Memory," *Memory Studies*, February 15, 2021, https://doi.org/10.1177/1750698020988771.

18 "Rubber Duck Photo at Auschwitz Sparks Criticism and a Conversation about Photo Ethics—The Washington Post," https://www.washingtonpost.com/ travel/2019/11/12/an-instagram-rubber-duck-auschwitz-starts-conversation-about-photo-ethics-again/ (accessed March 21, 2022).

19 Jones, "Catching Fleeting Memories," 390–403.

20 Burgess, "Remediating Vernacular Creativity," 116–26.

21 Rose, *Difficult History at Museums and Historic Sites*.

22 Karsten Müller and Carlo Schwarz, "Fanning the Flames of Hate: Social Media and Hate Crime," SSRN Scholarly Paper (Rochester, NY: Social Science Research Network, June 5, 2020), https://doi.org/10.2139/ssrn.3082972; Rosenfeld, "The Rise of Illiberal Memory."

23 Tworek, *News from Germany: The Competition to Control World Communications, 1900–1945*; Federico Finchelstein, *From Fascism to Populism in History* (Berkeley, CA: University of California Press, 2017).

24 See the introduction to Garde-Hansen, Hoskins, and Reading, *Save As … Digital Memories*.

25 Landsberg, *Prosthetic Memory the Transformation of American Remembrance in the Age of Mass Culture*.

26 Berry, Chris, Soyoung Kim, and Lynn Spiegel, eds. *Electronic Elsewheres: Media Technology and the Experience of Social Space* (Minneapolis: University of Minnesota Press, 2010), 92–136.

27 Mark D. Steinberg, "Melancholy and Modernity: Emotions and Social Life in Russia Between the Revolutions," *Journal of Social History* 41, no. 4 (2008): 813–41.

28   Marcia Chatelaine, "Teaching the #FergusonSyllabus," November 28, 2014, https://www.dissentmagazine.org/blog/teaching-ferguson-syllabus.

29   See Trump 2.0; The Immigration Syllabus, https://editions.lib.umn.edu/immigrationsyllabus/; The Standing Rock Syllabus, https://nycstandswithstandingrock.wordpress.com/standingrocksyllabus/; The Charlottesville Syllabus, https://medium.com/@UVAGSC/the-charlottesville-syllabus-9e01573419d0.

30   Jennifer Earl and Katrina Kimport, *Digitally Enabled Social Change: Activism in the Internet Age*, 1st ed. (Boston: MIT Press, 2011).

31   Zizi Papacharissi, *Affective Publics: Sentiment, Technology, and Politics* (Oxford, UK: Oxford University Press, 2017).

32   Walter Quattrociocchi, Antonio Scala, and Cass R. Sunstein, "Echo Chambers on Facebook," SSRN Scholarly Paper (Rochester, NY: Social Science Research Network, June 13, 2016), https://papers.ssrn.com/abstract=2795110.

33   Dana Millbank, "Donald Trump: America's Modern Mussolini," *Washington Post*, December 8, 2015.

34   Masha Gessen, "Donald Trump's Fascist Performance," *The New Yorker*, June 3, 2020, https://www.newyorker.com/news/our-columnists/donald-trumps-fascist-performance.

35   Timothy Snyder, *On Tyranny* (New York: Penguin, 2017).

36   Jane Caplan, "Trump and Fascism. A View from the Past." *History Workshop: Histories of the Present*, November 17, 2016, https://www.historyworkshop.org.uk/trump-and-fascism-a-view-from-the-past/; Sean Illing, "Comparing the Alt-right to Nazism May Be Hyperbolic—But It's Not Ridiculous," *Vox*, December 6, 2016, http://www.vox.com/policy-and-politics/2016/12/6/13807056/altright-donald-trump-hitler-nazism-christopher-browning-ideology?platform=hootsuite.

37   Kellner, "Habermas, the Public Sphere, and Democracy," 19–43.

38   Martin Hawksey, https://tags.hawksey.info/ CC-BY 4.0 mhawksey and Tweet Archivist www.tweetarchivist.com.

39   Jeffrey Mervis, "Privacy Concerns Could De-Rail Unprecedented Plan to Use Facebook Data in Study of Elections," *Science*, September 24, 2019, https://www.sciencemag.org/news/2019/09/privacy-concerns-could-derail-unprecedented-plan-use-Facebook-data-study-elections.

40   Ahmed, "Affective Economies."

41   Carole Cadwalladr and Duncan Campbell, "Revealed: Facebook's Global Lobbying against Data Privacy Laws," *The Observer*, March 2, 2019, sec. Technology, https://www.theguardian.com/technology/2019/mar/02/facebook-global-lobbying-campaign-against-data-privacy-laws-investment.

42   "Engendering Hate: The Contours of State-Aligned Gendered Disinformation Online," Demos, https://demos.co.uk/project/engendering-hate-the-contours-of-state-aligned-gendered-disinformation-online/ (accessed October 26, 2020).

43 Lisa Nakamura, *Cybertypes: Race, Ethnicity, and Identity on the Internet* (New York: Routledge, 2014).

44 Leticia Bode, "Closing the Gap: Gender Parity in Political Engagement on Social Media," *Information, Communication & Society* 20, no. 4 (2017): 587–603.

45 Isaac Chotiner interview with Richard Evans, "Democracy Dies in a Variety of Ways," *Slate*, July 12, 2018; van Dijck, *Mediated Memories in the Digital Age*; Waitman Wade Beorn, "Its Not Wrong to Compare Trump's America to the Holocaust. And Here's Why," *Washington Post*, July 16, 2018, https://www. washingtonpost.com/news/posteverything/wp/2018/07/16/its-not-wrong-to-compare-trumps-america-to-the-holocaust-heres-why/.

46 Mike Thelwell and Maria Delgado, "Arts and Humanities Research Evaluation: No Metrics Please, Just Data," *Journal of Documentation* 71, no. 4 (2005): 817–33.

47 A. Dirk Moses, "The German Catechism," *Geschichte der Gegenwart*, May 23, 2021, https://geschichtedergegenwart.ch/the-german-catechism/.

48 *The New Fascism Syllabus Catechism Debate*, http://newfascismsyllabus.com/category/opinions/the-catechism-debate/.

49 Hoskins, "Anachronisms of Media, Anachronisms of Memory," 278.

50 Nick Ward, "The Fog of Our New Political Reality," October 27, 2017, https://carleton.ca/fass/2017/studying-history-take-new-fascism-prof-jennifer-evans/.

51 Erll, "Traveling Memory," 4–18.

52 John Kean, "Structural Transformations of the Public Sphere," in *Digital Democracy: Issues of Theory and Practice*, ed. Kenneth L. Hacker and Jan van Dijk (London: Sage, 2000), 70–89.

53 Dijck, *Mediated Memories in the Digital Age*.

54 Halbwachs was quite emphatic that collective memories did not originate in contemporary journalism. They could very easily be drawn from books and film, with certain strands amplified or downplayed in print media, while others might remain marginally important or even forgotten. See Maurice Halbwachs, *La Mémoire Collective* (Paris: Presses Universitaire de France, 1950), 44.

55 Neil Levi and Michael Rothberg, "Memory Studies in a Moment of Danger: Fascism, Postfascism, and the Contemporary Political Imaginary," *Memory Studies* 11, no. 3 (2018): 355–67.

Bibliography

Abernathy, David. *Using Geodata and Geolocation in the Social Sciences: Mapping Our Connected World*. London: Sage, 2016.

Ahmed, Sara. "Affective Economies," *Social Text* 22, no. 2 (2004): 117–39.

An Interview with the Founders of Black Lives Matter. TEDTalks, Alicia Garza, Patrisse Cullors, and Opal Tometi. TED, 2018.

Anderson, Benedict. *Imagined Communities. Reflections on the Origin and Spread of Nationalism*. London: Verso, 1983.

Angus, Emma, David Stuart, and Mike Thelwall. "Flickr's Potential as an Academic Image Resource: An Exploratory Study," *Journal of Librarianship and Information Science* 42, no. 4 (2010): 268.

Ankersmith, Frank. "Commemoration and National Identity," *Textos De História* 10, nos. 1–2 (2002): 15–39.

Anne, Kelly Knowles et al. *Geographies of the Holocaust, Spatial Humanities*. Bloomington, IN: Indiana University Press, 2014.

Antifa Recherche Team Dresden (ART). "Dresden Calls. How One of the biggest Nazi Parades Came to Be," in *Abolish Commemoration: Critique of the Discourse Rleaint to the Bombing of Dresden in 1945*, ed. Dissonanz author collective. Berlin: Verbrecher Verlag, 2015, 249.

Apel, Dora. "The Tattooed Jew," in *Visual Culture and the Holocaust*, ed. Barbie Zelizer. New Brunswick, NJ: Rutgers University Press, 2000, 302.

Assman, Aleida. "Europe: A Community of Memory?" *Bulletin of the German Historical Association* 40, no. 1 (2007): 11–25.

Assmann, Aleida. "History and Memory," *International Encyclopedia of the Social and Behavioral Sciences* (2002): 6822–9.

Assmann, Aleida. "Texts, Traces, Trash: The Changing Media of Cultural Memory," *Representations* 56 (1996): 126.

Assmann, Aleida. "Transnational Memories," *European Review* 22, no. 4 (October 2014): 546–56.

Assmann, Aleida and Sebastian Conrad. *Memory in a Global Age: Discourses, Practices and Trajectories*. Basingstoke: Palgrave Macmillan, 2010.

Assmann, Jan. "Communicative and Cultural Memory," in *Cultural Memories: The Geographical Point of View*, ed. Peter Meusburger, Michael Heffernan, and Edgar Wunder. Dordrecht: Springer Netherlands, 2011, 15–27.

Aufruf 13. "Februar: Nazis stören!" https://dresden-nazifrei.com/aufruf2020/.

Auschwitz Birkenau Memorial. Annual Report (2007), 7. For a complete list of museum reports, see Auschwitz Birkenau Museum and Memorial, "Museum Reports." http://auschwitz.org/en/museum/museum-reports/ (accessed May 12, 2018).

Auschwitz Memorial and Museum (Instagram user @auschwitzmemorial), June 17, 2017. https://www.instagram.com/p/BVcugThltRe/ (accessed January 17, 2017).

Azoulay, Ariella. *The Civil Contract of Photography*. New York: Zone Books, 2008.

Azoulay, Ariella. *Civil Imagination: A Political Ontology of Photography*, trans. Louise Bethlehem. English-language edn. London: Verso, 2012.

Backes, Uwe and Cas Mudde. "Germany: Extremism without Successful Parties," *Parliamentary Affairs* 53, no. 3 (2000): 457–68.

Baker, Stephanie Alice. "The Mediated Crowd: New Social Media and New Forms of Rioting," *Sociological Research Online* 16, no. 4 (2011): 21.

Bakhtin, M.M. (Mikhail Mikhaĭlovich). *Rabelais and His World*. 1st Midland book edn. Bloomington: Indiana University Press, 1984.

Bakir, Vian and Andrew McStay. "Fake News and The Economy of Emotions: Problems, Causes, Solutions," *Digital Journalism* 6, no. 2 (February 7, 2018): 154–75.

Baladi, Enab. "People of Bustan Al Qasr Recall the River Massacre," January 30, 2016. https://english.enabbaladi.net/archives/2016/01/bustan-al-qasr-people-recall-the-river-massacre-in-aleppo/.

Bareither, Christoph. "Difficult Heritage and Digital Media: 'Selfie Culture' and Emotional Practices at the Memorial to the Murdered Jews of Europe," *International Journal of Heritage Studies: IJHS* 27, no. 1 (2021): 57–72.

Barnouw, Dagmar. *Germany 1945: Views of War and Violence*. Bloomington: Indiana University Press, 2008.

Barthes, Roland. *Camera Lucida: Reflections on Photography*. 1st American pbk. edn. New York: Hill and Wang, 1982.

Bartlett, Jamie, Caterina Froio, Mark Littler and Duncan McDonnell. *Social Media Is Changing Politics across Europe: New Political Actors in Europe: Beppe Grillo and the M5S*. 2013. https://www.demos.co.uk/files/Beppe_Grillo_and_the_M5S_-_Demos_web_version.pdf.

Batchen, Geoffrey. *Burning with Desire: The Conception of Photography*. Cambridge, MA: The MIT Press, 1999.

Begg, Zanny. "Recasting Subjectivity," *Third Text* 19, no. 6 (November 2005).

Belting, Hans. "Image, Medium, Body: A New Approach to Iconology," *Critical Inquiry* 31, no. 2 (2005): 302–18.

Belting, Hans and Thomas Dunlap. *An Anthropology of Images: Picture, Medium, Body*. Princeton: Princeton University Press, 2011.

Bennett, W. Lance. "Communicating Global Activism. Strengths and Vulnerabilities of Networked Politics," in *Cyberprotest. New Media, Citizens, and Social Movements*, ed. Wim van de Donk, Brian D. Loader, Paul G. Nixon, and Dieter Rucht. London: Routledge, 2004, 123–46.

Bennett, W. Lance and Anne Segerberg. "Digital Media and the Personalization of Collective Action: Social Technology and the Organization of Protests against the Global Economic Crisis," *Information, Communication & Society* 14 (2011): 770–99.

Bennett, W. Lance and Alexandra Segerberg. "The Logic of Connective Action: Digital Media and the Personalization of Contentious Politics," *Information, Communication, and Society* 15, no. 5 (June 2012): 739–68.

Berek, Mattias. "Transfer Zones: German and Global Suffering in Dresden," in *Local Memories in a Nationalizing and Globalizing World*, ed. Marnix Beyer and Brecht Deseure. Houndmills, Basingstoke, Hampshire: Palgrave Macmillan, 2015.

Berger, John. *Ways of Seeing, Pelican Originals*. London: British Broadcasting Corporation, 1972.

Bernard-Donals, Michael. *Figures of Memory: The Rhetoric of Displacement at the United States Holocaust Memorial Museum*. Albany, NY: State University of New York, 2016.

Berry, Chris, Chris Kim and Lynn Spigel. *Electronic Elsewhere: Media Technology and the Experience of Social Space*. Minneapolis: University of Minnesota Press, 2010.

Biess, Frank. "'Everybody Has a Chance.' Civil Defense. Nuclear Angst, and the History of Emotions in Postwar Germany," *German History* 27, no. 2 (2009): 215–43.

Blaylock, Sara. *Politics of Authenticity: Countercultures and Radical Movements across the Iron Curtain, 1968–1989*, ed. Joachim Haeberlen, Mark Keck-Szajbel, and Kate Mahoney. New York: Berghahn Press, 2018.

Bode, Leticia. "Closing the Gap: Gender Parity in Political Engagement on Social Media," *Information, Communication & Society* 20, no. 4 (2017): 587–603.

Boler, M. and E. Davis. "The Affective Politics of the 'Post-Truth' Era: Feeling Rules and Networked Subjectivity," *Emotion, Space and Society* 27 (2018): 75–85.

Bolter, J. David, Grusin Richard and A. Grusin Richard. *Remediation: Understanding New Media*. Cambridge, MA: MIT Press, 1999.

Bolter, J. David and Richard Grusin. *Remediation: Understanding New Media*. Cambridge, MA: MIT Press, 1999.

Boy, D. and Justus Uitermark. "Reassembling the City through Instagram," *Transactions of the Institute of British Geographers* 42 (2017): 612–24.

Boyd, Ceilyn. "Use of Optional Data Curation Features by Users of Harvard Dataverse Repository," *Journal of Escience Librarianship* 10, no. 2 (2021): 1–20.

boyd, danah *It's Complicated: The Social Lives of Networked Teens*. New Haven: Yale University Press, 2014.

boyd, danah. "Social Network Sites as Networked Publics: Affordances, Dynamics, and Implications," in *Networked Self: Identity, Community, and Culture on Social Network Sites*, ed. Zizi Papacharissi. New York: Routledge, 2011, 39–58.

Braunthal, Gerard. *Right-Wing Extremism in Contemporary Germany*. Basingstoke: Palgrave Macmillan, 2009.

Brink, Cornelia. "Secular Icons: Looking at Photographs from Nazi Concentration Camps," *History & Memory* 12, no. 1 (2000): 136.

Brown, Timothy Scott. *West Germany and the Global Sixties: The Antiauthoritarian Revolt, 1962–1978*. Cambridge, UK: Cambridge University Press, 2013.

Brown, Timothy Scott. *West Germany in the Global Sixties*. Cambridge, UK: Cambridge University Press, 2013.

Brown, Timothy Scott and Lorena Anton, eds. *Between the Avant-Garde and the Everyday Subversive Politics in Europe from 1957 to the Present*. New York: Berghahn Books, 2011.

Bull, Anna Cento and Hans Lauge Hansen. "On Agonistic Memory," *Memory Studies* 9, no. 4 (October 1, 2016): 390–404.

Burgess, Jean. "Hearing Ordinary Voices: Cultural Studies, Vernacular Creativity, and Digital Storytelling," *Journal of Media and Cultural Studies* 20, no. 2 (2006): 201–14.

Burgess, Jean. "Remediating Vernacular Creativity: Photography and Cultural Citizenship in the *Flickr Photo-Sharing Network*," in *Spaces of Vernacular Creativity: Rethinking the Cultural Economy*, ed. Tim Edensor, Routledge Studies in Human Geography 30. London: Routledge, 2010, 116–26.

Burgess, Jean and Ariadna Matamoros-Fernández. "Mapping Sociocultural Controversies across Digital Media Platforms: One Week of #Gamergate on Twitter, YouTube, and Tumblr," *Communication Research and Practice* 2, no. 1 (2016): 76–96.

Cadwalladr, Carole and Duncan Campbell. "Revealed: Facebook's Global Lobbying against Data Privacy Laws," *The Observer*, March 2, 2019, sec. Technology. https://www.theguardian.com/technology/2019/mar/02/facebook-global-lobbying-campaign-against-data-privacy-laws-investment.

Campt, Tina. *Listening to Images*. Durham: Duke University Press, 2017.

Caplan, Jane. "Trump and Fascism: A View from the Past," *History Workshop: Histories of the Present*, November 17, 2016. https://www.historyworkshop.org.uk/trump-and-fascism-a-view-from-the-past/.

Caron, André H. and Letitia Caronia. *Moving Cultures: Mobile Communication in Everyday Life*. Kingston, ON: McGill-Queens University Press, 2007.

Carr, Nicholas G. *The Shallows: What the Internet Is Doing to Our Brains*, 1st edn. New York: W. W. Norton, 2011.

Carroll, William K. and Robert A. Hackett. "Democratic Media Activism through the Lens of Social Movement Theory," *Media, Culture & Society* 28, no. 1 (2006): 83–104.

Castells, Manuel. "Communication, Power and Counter-power," *International Journal of Communication* 1, no. 1 (February 2007): 249.

Castells, Manual. *Networks of Outrage and Hope. Social Movements in the Internet Age*. Cambridge, MA: Polity Press, 2012.

Castells, Manuel. *The Rise of the Network Society*. Cambridge, MA: Blackwell Publishers, 1996.

Cavell, Stanley. *The World Viewed: Reflections on the Ontology of Film*. Cambridge, MA: Harvard University Press, 1979.

Celinski, Piotr. "Mediatization and Memory Policies in the Urban Context," *Analecta Política* 8, no. 15 (July–December 2018): 282.

Chadwick, Andrew. "Web 2.0: New Challenges for the Study of E-Democracy in an Era of Information Exuberance," I/S, *A Journal of Law and Policy for the Information Society* 5, no. 1 (2008): 3–29.

Chare, Nicholas. *Auschwitz and Afterimages: Abjection, Witnessing and Representation.* London and New York: I.B. Tauris, 2011.

Chen, W. and B. Wellman. "Minding the Cyber-Gap: The Internet and Social Inequality," in *The Blackwell Companion to Social Inequalities*, ed. M. Romero and E. Margolis. Williston: Wiley, 2008, 523–45.

Chulov, Martin and Mona Mahmood. "Syrian Rebels Recover Scores of Bodies from Aleppo River as Floodwaters Recede," *The Guardian.* Guardian News and Media, January 29, 2013. https://www.theguardian.com/world/2013/jan/29/syrian-rebels-bodies-aleppo-canal.

Cole, Tim. *Selling the Holocaust: From Auschwitz to Schindler, How History Is Bought, Packaged, and Sold.* New York: Routledge, 2000.

Commane, Gemma and Rebekah Potton. "Instagram and Auschwitz: A Critical Assessment of the Impact Social Media Has on Holocaust Representation," *Holocaust Studies* 25, nos. 1–2 (2018): 158–81.

The Conference on Jewish Material Claims against Germany. "Holocaust Knowledge and Awareness Study," *Schoen Consulting*, February 23–27, 2018. http://www.claimscon.org/study/. (accessed September 30, 2018).

Conversation between Thomas Rudert, provenance expert of Staatliche Kunstsammlungen Dresden and Murry Teitel. "Revisiting the Bombing of Dresden," *Canadian Jewish News*, February 12, 2020. https://www.cjnews.com/news/international/revisiting-the-bombing-of-dresden.

Couldry, Nick and Andreas Hepp. "Conceptualizing Mediatization: Contexts, Traditions, Arguments," *Communication Theory* 23, no. 3 (2013): 191–202.

Crane, Susan A. "Choosing Not to Look: Representation, Repatriation, and Holocaust Atrocity Photography," *History and Theory* 47 (2009): 315–16.

Crary, Jonathan. *Techniques of the Observer: On Vision and Modernity in the Nineteenth Century.* Cambridge, MA: MIT Press, 1990.

Crew, David. *Bodies and Ruins. Imagining the Bombing of Germany 1945 to the Present.* Ann Arbor: University of Michigan Press, 2017.

Cukier, Kenneth Neil and Viktor Mayer-Schönberger. "The Rise of Big Data," *Foreign Affairs*, June 28, 2021. https://www.foreignaffairs.com/articles/2013-04-03/rise-big-data.

Cywiński, Piotr M.A. Auschwitz Birkenau Memorial 2009 Annual Report. Państwowe Muzeum Auschwitz-Birkenau w Oświęcimiu, 2010.

Dalziel, Imogen. "Becoming the 'Holocaust Police?': The Auschwitz Birkenau State Museum's Authority on Social Media," in *Digital Holocaust Memory, Education and Research*, ed. Victoria Grace Walden. Basingstoke: Palgrave Macmillan, 2021.

Darnton, Robert. "What Is the History of Books," *Daedalus* 111, no. 3 (1993): 65–83.

Davis, Belinda. "What's Left? Popular and Democratic Political Participation in Postwar Europe," *American Historical Review* 113, no. 2 (April 2008): 363–90.

Dekel, Irit. "Jews and Other Others at the Holocaust Memorial in Berlin," *Anthropological Journal of European Cultures* 23, no. 2 (2014): 71–84.

Dekel, Irit. *Mediation at the Holocaust Memorial in Berlin*. Basingstoke, Hampshire: Palgrave Macmillan, 2013.

Dekel, Irit. "Ways of Looking: Observation and Transformation at the Holocaust Memorial, Berlin," *Memory Studies* 2, no. 1 (2009): 71–86.

Della Porta, Donatella. "Multiple Belongings, Flexible Identities and the Construction of 'Another Politics': Between the European Social Forum and the Local Social Fora," in *Transnational Protest and Global Activism*, ed. Donatella Della Porta. Sidney Tarrow and W. Lance Bennett. Lanham, MD: Rowman & Littlefield, 2005, 175–202.

Derrida, Jacques. *Archive Fever: A Freudian Impression*. Chicago: University of Chicago Press, 1995.

Des Pres, Terrence. *The Survivor: An Anatomy of Life in the Death Camps*. New York: Oxford University Press, 1980.

Deuze, Mark. "Media Life," *Media, Culture & Society* 33, no. 1 (2011): 137–48.

Dewey, Caitlin. "The Other Side of the Infamous 'Auschwitz Selfie'," *The Washington Post*, July 22, 2014. https://www.washingtonpost.com/news/the-intersect/wp/2014/07/22/the-other-side-of-the-infamous-auschwitz-selfie/ (accessed December 10, 2018).

Didi-Huberman, Georges. *Invention of Hysteria. Charcot and the Photographic Iconography of Salpetriere*. Boston: MIT Press, 2003.

Dolgoy, Rebecca Clare and Jerzy Elzanowski. "Working through the Limits of Multidirectional Memory: Ottawa's Memorial to the Victims of Communism and National Holocaust Monument," *Citizenship Studies* 22, no. 4 (2018): 433–51.

Douglas, Kate. "Youth, Trauma, and Memorialisation: The Selfie as Witnessing," *Memory Studies* 13 (2017): 3.

Duguid, Paul. "Material Matters: Aspects of the Past and the Futurology of the Book," in *The Future of the Book*, ed. Geoffrey Nunberg. Stanford: University of California Press, 1996, 63–92.

Dundes, Alan. *Life Is Like a Chicken Coop Ladder: A Portrait of German Culture through Folklore*. New York: Columbia University Press, 1984.

Earl, Jennifer and Katrina Kimport. *Digitally Enabled Social Change: Activism in the Internet Age*, 1st edn. Boston: MIT Press, 2011.

Ebbrecht-Hartmann, Tobias and Lital Henig. "I-Memory: Selfies and Self-Witnessing in #Uploading_Holocaust (2016)," in *Digital Holocaust Memory, Education and Research*, ed. Victoria Grace Walden. Cham: Springer International Publishing, 2021, 213–35.

Edwards, Elizabeth. *The Camera as Historian: Amateur Photographers and the Historical Imagination, 1885–1918*. Durham and London: Duke University Press, 2012.

Edwards, Elizabeth. "Photography and the Material Performance of the Past," *History and Theory* 48, no. 4 (2009): 130–50.

Edwards, Steve. "The Commons and the Crowd: Figuring Photography from Above and Below," *Third Text* 23, no. 4 (July 2009): 447–64.

Eley, Geoff. *Forging Democracy the History of the Left in Europe, 1850–2000.* Oxford: Oxford University Press, 2002.

Ellul, Jacques. *Propaganda: The Formation of Men's Attitudes,* Vintage Books edn. New York: Vintage Books, 1973, 75.

El-Tayeb, Fatima. *European Others Queering Ethnicity in Postnational Europe.* Minneapolis, MN: University of Minnesota Press, 2011.

Epstein, Kayla. "An Instagram of a Rubber Duck at Auschwitz Starts a Conversation about Photo Ethics—Again," *The Washington Post.* WP Company, November 12, 2019. https://www.washingtonpost.com/travel/2019/11/12/an-instagram-rubber-duck-auschwitz-starts-conversation-about-photo-ethics-again/.

Erll, Astrid. "Traveling Memory," *Parallax* 17, no. 4 (2011): 4–18.

Erll, Astrid and Ann Rigney. *Mediation, Remediation, and the Dynamics of Cultural Memory, Media, and Cultural Memory.* New York: Walter de Gruyter, 2009.

Ernst, Wolfgang. *Digital Memory and the Archive, Electronic Mediations,* vol. 39. Minneapolis: University of Minnesota Press, 2013.

Evans, Jennifer V. *Life among the Ruins: Cityscape and Sexuality in Cold War Berlin.* Basingstoke, UK: Palgrave Macmillan, 2011.

Evans, Jennifer V., Paul Betts and Stefan-Ludwig Hoffmann, *The Ethics of Seeing: Photography and Twentieth-Century German History.* New York: Berghahn, 2018.

Evans, Richard J. *Lying about Hitler: History, Holocaust, and the David Irving Trial.* New York: Basic Books, 2001.

Fahlenbrach, Kathrin. "Protest-Räume—Medien-Räume," in Straße als kultureller Aktionsraum. VS Verlag für Sozialwissenschaften, ed. S.M. Geschke. Wiesbaden: VS Verlag, 2009, 98–110.

Farkas, Johan, Jannick Schou and Christina Neumayer. "Platformed Antagonism: Racist Discourses on Fake Muslim Facebook Pages," *Critical Discourse Studies* 15, no. 5 (October 20, 2018): 463–80.

Fast, Karin, Emilia Ljungberg and Lotta Braunerhielm. "On the Social Construction of Geomedia Technologies," *Communication and the Public* 4, no. 2 (2019): 89–99.

Finchelstein, Frederico. *From Fascism to Populism in History.* Oakland, California: University of California Press, 2017.

Florence, Eloise. "Entangled Memories: Complicating the Memory of Area Bombing through the Haunted Ruins of Anhalter Bahnhof," *Cultural Studies ↔ Critical Methodologies* 21, no. 3 (June 2021): 251–63.

Floridi, Luciano. *The Ethics of Information.* Oxford: Oxford University Press, 2013.

Fogu, Claudio and Wulf Kansteiner. "The Politics of Memory and the Poetics of History," in *The Politics of Memory in Postwar Europe,* ed. Richard Ned Lebow, Wulf Kansteiner, and Claudio Fogu. Duke: Duke University Press, 2006, 286.

Foster, Hal. "An Archive Without Museums," *October* 77 (Summer 1996): 97–119.

François, Etienne and Hagen Schulze. *Erinnerungsorte*. München: C.H Beck, 2001, 9–24.

Freeman, Cristina Garduño. "Photosharing on Flickr: Intangible Heritage and Emergent Publics," *International Journal of Heritage Studies* 16, no. 4–5 (2010): 355.

Friedländer, Saul. "History, Memory, and the Historian: Dilemmas and Responsibilities," *New German Critique* 80, no. 80 (2000): 3–15.

Fuchs, Anne. *After the Dresden Bombing: Pathways of Memory 1945 to the Present*. Basingstoke: Palgrave Macmillan, 2012, 32.

Führer, Karl Christian and Corey Ross. *Mass Media, Culture and Society in Twentieth-Century Germany*. Basingstoke: Palgrave Macmillan, 2006.

Garde-Hansen, Joanne. *Media and Memory*. Edinburgh: Edinburgh University Press, 2011, 72.

Garde-Hansen, Joan, Andrew Hoskins and Anna Reading. *Save as ... Digital Memories*. Basingstoke: Palgrave Macmillan, 2009.

Gillespie, Tarleton. *Custodians of the Internet: Platforms, Content Moderation, and the Hidden Decisions That Shape Social Media*. New Haven, CT: Yale University Press, 2018.

Gitelman, Lisa. *Paper Knowledge: Toward a Media History of Documents*. Durham: Duke University Press, 2014.

Golańska, Dorota. "Bodily Collisions: Toward a New Materialist Account of Memorial Art," *Memory Studies* 13, no. 1 (February 1, 2020): 74–89.

Goode, Luke. "Social News, Citizen Journalism and Democracy," *New Media & Society* 11, no. 8 (January 12, 2009): 1287–305.

Grabowski, Jan and Shira Klein. "Wikipedia's Intentional Distortion of the History of the Holocaust," *The Journal of Holocaust Research* (February 9, 2023): 1–58. https://doi.org/10.1080/25785648.2023.2168939.

Griffin, Groger. "From Slime mould to Rhizome: An Introduction to the Groupuscular Right," *Patterns of Prejudice* 37, no. 1 (2003): 27–50.

Gutman, Yifat and Jenny Wüstenberg. "Challenging the Meaning of the Past from Below: A Typology for Comparative Research on Memory Activists," *Memory Studies* 15, no. 6 (October 10, 2022): 1070–86.

Häberlen, Joachim C., Mark Keck-Szajbel and Kate Mahoney. *The Politics of Authenticity: Countercultures and Radical Movements Across the Iron Curtain (1968-1989)*, ed. Joachim C. Häberlen, Mark Keck-Szajbel, and Kate Mahoney. New York: Berghahn, 2019.

Haeberlen, Joachem. *The Emotional Politics of the Alternative Left. West Germany, 1968-1984*. Cambridge, MA: Cambridge University Press, 2018.

Halbwachs, Maurice. *La Mémoire Collective Presses Universitaire de France* (1950): 44.

Halbwachs, Maurice. *The Collective Memory*. New York: Harper & Row, 1980.

Hanshew, Karrin. *Terror and Democracy in West Germany*. Cambridge, MA: Cambridge University Press, 2012.

Harcourt, Bernard. *Exposed: Desire and Disobedience in the Digital Age*. Cambridge, MA: Harvard University Press, 2015.

Harmer, Sarah. "Going Visual: Holocaust Representation and Historical Method," *The American Historical Review* 115, no. 1 (2010): 115–22.

Hartman, Geoffrey. "Memory.com: Tele-suffering and Testimony in the Dot Com Era," *Raritan: A Quarterly Review* 19, no. 3 (2000): 1–18.

Harvey, David. *Spaces of Hope*. Edinburgh: Edinburgh University Press, 2000.

Hepp, Andreas. *Cultures of Mediatization*. Cambridge, MA: Polity Press, 2013, 618.

Hepp, Andreas, Stig Hjarvard and Knut Lundby. "Mediatization: Theorizing the Interplay between *Media, Culture and Society*," Media, Culture, and Society 37, no. 2 (2015): 324.

Hickethier, Knut. "Mediatisierung und Medialisierung der Kultur," in *Die Mediatisierung der Alltagswelt*, ed. Maren Hartmann and Andreas Hepp. Wiesbaden: VS-Verlag, 2010, 85–96.

Highfield, Tim and Tama Leaver. "Instagrammatics and Digital Methods: Studying Visual Social Media, from Selfies and GIFs to Memes and Emoji," *Communication Research and Practice* 2, no. 1 (2016): 47–62.

Hirsch, Marianne. *Family Frames: Photography, Narrative, and Postmemory*. Cambridge, MA: Harvard University Press, 1997, 15.

Hirsch, Marianne. *The Generation of Postmemory: Writing and Visual Culture After the Holocaust*. New York: Columbia University Press, 2012, 32.

Hirsch, Marianne. "Nazi Photographs in Post-Holocaust Art: Gender as an Idiom of Memorialization," in *Phototextualities: Intersections of Photography and Narrative*, ed. Alex Hughes and Andrea Noble. Albuquerque: University of New Mexico Press, 2003, 26.

Hirsch, Marianne. "Surviving Images: Holocaust Photographs and the Work of Postmemory," in *Visual Culture and the Holocaust*, ed. Barbie Zelizer. New Brunswick, NJ: Rutger's University Press, 2000, 215–46.

Hirsch, Marianne and Leo Spitzer. "Incongruous Images: Before, during, and after the Holocaust," *History and Theory* 48, no. 4 (2009): 9–25.

Hjarvard, Stig. *The Mediatization of Culture and Society*. London: Routledge, 2013.

Hjarvard, Stig. "The Mediatization of Society. A Theory of the Media as Agents of Social and Cultural Change," *Nordicom Review* 29, no. 2 (2008): 105–34.

Hochman, Nadav and Lev Manovich. "Reading the Local through Social Media," *First Monday*, 2013. https://firstmonday.org/ojs/index.php/fm/article/view/4711/3698.

Hochman, Nadav and Lev Manovich. "Zooming into an Instagram City: Reading the Local through Social Media," *First Monday*, June 17, 2013.

Hoelscher, Steven. "'Dresden, a Camera Accuses': Rubble Photography and the Politics of Memory in a Divided Germany," *History of Photography* 36, no. 3 (August 2012): 288–305.

Hoffmann, Stefan-Ludwig. "Gazing at Ruins: German Defeat as Visual Experience," in *The Ethics of Seeing: Photography and Twentieth Century German Photography*

Reconsidered, ed. Jennifer Evans, Paul Betts, and Stefan-Ludwig Hoffmann. New York: Berghahn Press, 2018, 144.

Hoskins, Andrew. "Anachronisms of Media, Anachronisms of Memory: From Collective Memory to a New Memory Ecology," in *On Media Memory: Collective Memory in a New Media Age*, ed. Motti Neiger, Oren Meyers, and Eyal Zandberg. Basingstoke: Palgrave Macmillan, 2011.

Hoskins, Andrew. "Digital Network Memory," in *Mediation, Remediation and the Dynamic of Cultural Memory*, ed. Astrid Erll and Ann Rigney. Berlin: De Gruyter, 2009, 91–106.

Hoskins, Andrew. "Introduction to Digital Memory and Media," in *Digital Memory Studies*. Media Pasts in Transition, ed. Andrew Hoskins. London: Routledge Press, 2018.

Hoskins, Andrew. "Introduction," in *Save As … Digital Memory,* ed. Joanne Garde-Hansen, Andrew Hoskins, and Anna Reading. Basingstoke: Palgrave Macmillan, 2009.

Hoskins, Andrew. "The Mediatisation of Memory," in *Save As … Digital Memories*, ed. Joanne Garde-Hansen, Andrew Hoskins, and Anna Reading. London: Palgrave Macmillan UK, 2009, 672.

Hoskins, Andrew. "Mediatization of Memory," in *Mediatization of Communication*, ed. Knut Lundby. Berlin; Boston: De Gruyter Mouton, 2004.

Hoskins, Andrew. "Memory of the Multitude: The End of Collective Memory," in *Digital Memory Studies: Media Pasts in Transition*, ed. Andrew Hoskins. New York: Routledge, 2017, 85–109.

Hoskins, Andrew. "The Right to Be Forgotten in Post-Scarcity," in *The Ethics of Memory in a Digital Age: Interrogating the Right to Be forgotten*, ed. Alessia Ghezzi et al. New York: Palgrave Macmillan, 2014, 50–64, 60.

Hoskins, Andrew. "Television and the Collapse of Memory," *Time & Society* 13, no. 1 (March 1, 2004): 109–27.

Hoskins, Andrew and Huw Halstead. "The New Grey of Memory: Andrew Hoskins in Conversation with Huw Halstead," *Memory Studies* 14, no. 3 (2021): 675–85.

Hübscher, Monika and Sabine von Mehring, eds. *Antisemitism on Social Media*. New York: Routledge, 2022.

Huyssen, Andreas. *Present Pasts: Urban Palimpsests and the Politics of Memory, Cultural Memory in the Present*. Stanford, CA: Stanford University Press, 2003.

Illing, Sean. "Comparing the Alt-Right to Nazism May Be Hyperbolic—but It's Not Ridiculous," *Vox*, December 6, 2016. http://www.vox.com/policy-and-politics/2016/12/6/13807056/altright-donald-trump-hitler-nazism-christopher-browning-ideology?platform=hootsuite.

Isaac Chotiner interview with Richard Evans. "Democracy Dies in a Variety of Ways," *Slate*, July 12, 2018.

Jansson, Andre. "Mediatization and Social Space: Reconstructing Mediatization for the Transmedia Age," *Communication Theory* 23 (2013): 279–96.

Jenkins, Andrew. *Convergence Culture: Where Old and New Media Collide*. New York: NYU Press, 2006.

Jenkins, Henry, Sam Ford, and Joshua Green. *Spreadable Media: Creating Value and Meaning in a Networked Culture*. New York: New York University Press, 2013.

Jerram, Leif. *Streetlife: The Untold Story of Europe's Twentieth Century*. Oxford: Oxford University Press, 2011.

Jinks, Rebecca. *Representing Genocide: The Holocaust as Paradigm?* London: Bloomsbury, 2016.

Jones, Sara. "Mediated Immediacy: Constructing Authentic Testimony in Audiovisual Media," *Rethinking History* 21, no. 2 (2017): 135–53.

Judson, Ellen, Asli Atay, Alex Krasodomski-Jones, Rose Lasko-Skinner, and Josh Smith. "Engendering Hate: The Contours of State-Aligned Gendered Disinformation Online," *Demos*. https://demos.co.uk/project/engendering-hate-the-contours-of-state-aligned-gendered-disinformation-online/ (accessed October 26, 2020).

Juris, Jeffrey. "Violence Performed and Imagined: Militant Action, the Black Bloc and the Mass Media in Genoa," *Critique of Anthropology* 25, no. 4 (December 2004): 413–32.

Juris, Jeffrey D. and Geoffrey Henri Pleyers, "Alter-activism: Emerging Cultures of Participation among Young Global Justice Activists," *Journal of Youth Studies* 12, no. 1 (February 2009): 57–75.

Kansteiner, Wulf. "Finding Meaning in Memory: A Methodological Critique of Collective Memory Studies," *History and Theory* 41 (2002): 179–97.

Kansteiner, Wulf. "The Holocaust in the Twenty-First Century," in *Digital Memory Studies. Media Pasts in Transition*, ed. Andrew Hoskins. New York: Routledge, 2018.

Kansteiner, Wulf. "Moral Pitfalls of Memory Studies: The Concept of Political Generations," *Memory Studies* 5, no. 2 (2012): 111–13.

Kansteiner, Wulf. *Transnational Holocaust Memory, Digital Culture and the End of Reception Studies* Brill, 2017.

Kansteiner, Wulf. "Transnational Holocaust Memory, Digital Culture and the End of Reception Studies," in *The Twentieth Century in European Memory*, ed. Tea Sindbæk Andersen and Barbara Törnquist-Plewa, Transcultural Mediation and Reception. London: Brill, 2017, 305–44.

Kansteiner, Wulf and Todd Presner, "Introduction: The Field of Holocaust Studies and the Global Emergence of Holocaust Culture," in *Probing the Ethics of Holocaust Culture*, ed. Claudio Fogu, Wulf Kansteiner, and Todd Presner. Cambridge, MA: Harvard University Press, 2016, 33–4.

Kean, John. "Structural Transformations of the Public Sphere," in *Digital Democracy: Issues of Theory and Practice*, ed. Kenneth L. Hacker and Jan van Dijk. London: Sage, 2000, 70–89.

Keightley, E. "From Immediacy to Intermediacy: The Mediation of Lived Time," *Time & Society* 22, no. 1 (2013): 55–75.

Keightley, E. and P. Schlesinger. "Digital Media—Social Memory: Remembering in Digitally Networked Times," *Media, Culture and Society* 36, no. 6 (2014): 745–7.

Kellner, Douglas. "Habermas, the Public Sphere, and Democracy," in *Re-Imaging Public Space: The Frankfurt School in the 21st Century*, ed. Diana Boros and James Glass. Basingstoke: Palgrave Macmillan, 2011, 19–43.

Kenney, Padraic. *A Carnival of Revolution Central Europe 1989*. Woodstock: Princeton University Press, 2003.

King, Preston. *Thinking Past a Problem. Essays in the History of Ideas*. London: Routledge, 2000, 25–68.

Klimke, Martin. *The Other Alliance Student Protest in West Germany and the United States in the Global Sixties*. Princeton, NJ: Princeton University Press, 2010.

Klimke, Martin and Joachim Scharloth, eds., *1968. Handbuch zur Kultur- und Mediengeschichte der Studentenbewegung*. Stuttgart: J.B. Metzler, 2007.

Klimke, Martin and Laura Stapane. "From Artists for Peace to the Green Caterpillar: Cultural Activism and Electoral Politics in 1980s West Germany," in *Accidental Armageddons: The Nuclear Crisis and the Culture of the Cold War in the 1980s* ed. Eckart Conze, Martin Klimke, and Jeremy Varon. Cambridge, MA: Cambridge University Press, 2016, 116–41.

Krotz, Friedrich. "The Metaprocess "Mediatization" as a Conceptual Frame," *Global Media and Communication* 3, no. 3 (2007): 256–60.

Kugelmass, Jack. "Why We Go to Poland: Holocaust Tourism as Secular Ritual," in *The Art of Memory: Holocaust Memorials in History*, ed. James E. Young. New York: Prestel, 1994, 175–83.

Landsberg, Alison. *Prosthetic Memory the Transformation of American Remembrance in the Age of Mass Culture*. New York: Columbia University Press, 2004.

Latour, Bruno. *Pandora's Hope: Essays on the Reality of Science Studies*. Cambridge, MA: Harvard University Press, 1999.

Latour, Bruno. *Reassembling the Social an Introduction to Actor-Network-Theory*. Oxford: University Press, 2005.

Latour, Bruno. "Why Has Critique Run out of Steam? From Matters of Fact to Matters of Concern," *Critical Inquiry* 30, no. 2 (2004): 225–48.

Lefebvre, Henri. *Rhythmanalysis: Space, Time and Everyday Life*. Trowbridge: Continuum, 1992.

Levi, Neil and Michael Rothberg. "Memory Studies in a Moment of Danger: Fascism, Postfascism, and the Contemporary Political Imaginary," *Memory Studies* 11, no. 3 (2018): 355–67.

Levinson, Paul. *Cellphone: The Story of the World's Most Mobile Medium and How It Has Transformed Everything!* (2004).

Levinson, Paul. *The Soft Edge: A Natural History and Future of the Information Revolution.* London: Routledge, 1997.

Lim, Merlyna. "Algorithmic Enclaves: Affective Politics and Algorithms in the Neoliberal Social Media Landscape," in *Affective Politics of Digital Media: Propaganda by Other Means*, ed. M. Boler and E. Davis. New York and London: Routledge, 2020, 186–203.

Lim, Merlyna. "Clicks, Cabs, and Coffee Houses: Social Media and Oppositional Movements in Egypt, 2004–2011," *Journal of Communication* 62 (2012): 231–48.

Lim, Merlyna. "Roots, Routes, Routers: Communications and Media of Contemporary Social Movements," *Journalism & Communication Monographs Series* 20, no. 2 (2018): 92–136.

Lim, Merlyna. "Seeing Spatially: People, Networks, and Movements in Digital and Urban Spaces," *International Development Planning Review* 36, no. 1 (2014): 51–72.

Lim, Merlyna, and Mark E. Kann. "Politics: Deliberation, Mobilization, and Networked Practices of Agitation," in *Networked Publics*, ed. Kazys Varnelis. Cambridge, MA: MIT Press, 2008, 70–108.

Linfield, Susie. *The Cruel Radiance: Photography and Political Violence.* Chicago: University of Chicago Press, 2010.

Linke, Ulli. "The Language of Resistance: Political Rhetoric and Symbols of Popular Protest in Germany," *City & Society: The Journal of the Society for Urban Anthropology* 2, no. 2 (1988): 127–33.

Livingstone, Sonia. "Foreword: Coming to Terms with Mediatization," in *Mediatization: Concepts, Changes, Consequences*, ed. Knut Lundby. New York: Peter Lang, 2009, ix–xii.

Lokot, Tetyana. *Beyond the Protest Square: Digital Media and Augmented Dissent.* London: Rowman & Littlefield Publishers, 2021.

Lorenz, Chris. "Blurred Lines History, Memory and the Experience of Time," *International Journal for History, Culture and Modernity* 2, no. 1 (2014): 43–62.

Lorenz, Chris. "Unstuck in Time. Or: The Sudden Presence of the Past," in *Performing the Past. Memory, History and Identity in Modern Europe*, ed. Karin Tilmans, Frank van Vree, and Jay Winter. Amsterdam: Amsterdam University Press, 2010, 67–105.

Lower, Wendy. *The Ravine: A Family, a Photograph, a Holocaust Massacre Revealed.* Boston: Houghton Mifflin Harcourt, 2021.

Lundby, Knut. *Mediatization of Communication.* Berlin: De Gruyter Mouton, 2014.

Lundrigan, Meghan. "People, Places, Things: Considering the Role of Visitor Photography at the United States Holocaust Memorial Museum," in *The Holocaust in the Twenty-First Century: Relevance and Challenges in the Digital Age (Lessons and Legacies XIV)*, ed. Tim Cole and Simone Gigliotti. Evanston, IL: Northwestern University Press, 2021, 263–86.

Lundrigan, Meghan. "#Holocaust #Auschwitz: Performing Holocaust Memory on Social Media," in *A Companion to the Holocaust*, ed. Simone Gigliotti and Hilary Earl. Hoboken, NJ: John Wiley & Sons, Inc., 2020, 639–56.

Macdonald, Sharon. "Is 'Difficult Heritage' Still 'Difficult'?" *Museum International* 67, nos. 1–4 (January 1, 2015): 6–22.

Macdougall, Carla. "We Too Are Berliners: Protest, Symbolism, and the City in Cold War Germany," in *Changing the World, Changing Oneself. Political Protest and Collective Identities in West Germany and the US in the 1960s and 1970s*, ed. Belinda Davis, Wilfried Mausbach, Martin Klimke, and Carla MacDougall. New York: Berghahn Books, 2010, 83–104.

Magilow, Daniel and Lisa Silverman. "The Boy in the Warsaw Ghetto (Photograph, 1943): What Do Iconic Photographs Tell Us about the Holocaust?" in *Holocaust Representations in History: An Introduction*. London: Bloomsbury, 2019.

Mailander, Elissa. "Making Sense of a Rape Photograph: Sexual Violence as Social Performance on the Eastern Front, 1939–1944," *Journal of the History of Sexuality* 26, no. 3 (2017): 489–520.

Manca, Stefania. "Bridging Cultural Studies and Learning Science: An Investigation of Social Media Use for Holocaust Memory and Education in the Digital Age," *Review of Education, Pedagogy, and Cultural Studies* 43, no. 3 (May 27, 2021): 226–53.

Manovich, Lev. *The Language of New Media*. Cambridge, MA: MIT Press, 2001.

Manovich, Lev. "Selfiecity: Exploring Photography and Self-Fashioning in Social Media," in *Postdigital Aesthetics: Art, Computation and Design*, ed. David M. Berry and Michael Dieter. Palgrave Macmillan, 2015, 109–22.

Margalit, Gilad. "Der Luftangriff aus Dresden: seine Bedeutung für die Erinnerungspolitik der DDR und für die Herauskristallisierung einer historischen Kriegserinnerung im Westen," in *Narrative der Shoah: Repräsentationen der Vergangenheit in Historiographie, Kunst und Politik*, ed. Susanne Düwell and Matthias Schmidt. Paderborn: Schöningh 2002, 189–207.

Marres, Noortje. *Digital Sociology: The Reinvention of Social Research*. London: Polity Press, 2017.

Marwick, Alice E. and danah boyd [*sic*]. "I Tweet Honestly, I Tweet Passionately: Twitter Users, Context Collapse, and the Imagined Audience," *New Media & Society* 13, no. 1 (2010): 114–33.

Masum, Hassan and Mark Tovey. *The Reputation Society: How Online Opinions Are Reshaping the Offline World*, ed. Hassan Masum and Mark Tovey. Cambridge, MA: MIT Press, 2012.

McBride, Patrizia. *The Chatter and the Visible: Montage and Narrative in Weimar Germany*. Ann Arbor, Michigan: University of Michigan Press, 2016.

McLuhan, Marshall. *Understanding Media: The Extensions of Man*. New York: McGraw Hill, 1964.

McQuire, Scott. "Photography's Afterlife: Documentary Images and the Operational Archive," *Journal of Material Culture* 18, no. 3 (2013): 223–4.

Mercea, Dan. "Digital Prefigurative Participation: The Entwinement of Online Communication and Offline Participation in Protest Events," *New Media & Society* 14, no. 1 (February 2012): 153–69.

Merrill, Samuel and Johan Pries. "Translocalising and Relocasing Antifascist Struggles: From #KämpaShowan to #KämpaMalmö," *Antipode* 51, no. 1 (2019): 259.

Millbank, Dana. "Donald Trump: America's Modern Mussolini," *Washington Post* December 8, 2015.

Mirzoeff, Nicholas. *An Introduction to Visual Culture.* London: Routledge, 1999.

Mirzoeff, Nicholas. *How to See the World: An Introduction to Images, from Self-Portraits to Selfies, Maps to Movies, and More.* New York: Basic Books, 2016.

Mitchell, W.J.T. *Picture Theory: Essays on Verbal and Visual Representation.* Chicago: University of Chicago Press, 1994.

Mitchell, W.J.T. *What Do Pictures Want? The Lives and Loves of Images.* Chicago: The University of Chicago Press, 2005.

Mitschke, Samantha. "Sacred, the Profane, and the Space in Between: Site-Specific Performance at Auschwitz." *Holocaust Studies* 22, nos. 2–3 (2016): 228–43.

Moeller, Robert. "War Stories: The Search for a Usable Past in the Federal Republic of Germany," *American Historical Review* 101, no. 4 (October 1996): 1012–13.

Morozov, Evgeny. *The Net Delusion: The Dark Side of Internet Freedom,* 1st edn. New York: Public Affairs, 2011.

Moses, Dirk. "The German Catechism," *Geschichte der Gegenwart,* May 23, 2021. https://geschichtedergegenwart.ch/the-german-catechism/.

Moss, Michael. "Memory Institutions, the Archive, and Digital Disruption?" in *Digital Memory Studies. Media Pasts in Transition,* ed. Andrew Hoskins (London: Routledge, 2018), 253–79.

Mossberger, Karen, Caroline J. Tolbert and Ramona S. McNeal, *Digital Citizenship the Internet, Society, and Participation.* Cambridge, MA: MIT Press, 2008.

Müller, Karsten and Carlo Schwarz. "Fanning the Flames of Hate: Social Media and Hate Crime," in *SSRN Scholarly Paper.* Rochester, NY: Social Science Research Network, June 5, 2020.

Murray, Susan. "Digital Images, Photo-Sharing, and Our Shifting Notions of Everyday Aesthetics," *Journal of Visual Culture* 7, no. 2 (2008): 147–63.

Murray, Susan. "New Media and Vernacular Photography: Revisiting Flickr," in *The Photographic Image in Digital Culture,* ed. Martin Lister. London: Routledge, 2013, 165–82.

Nakamura, Lisa. *Cybertypes: Race, Ethnicity, and Identity on the Internet.* New York: Routledge, 2014.

Napoli, Philip M. "What If More Speech Is No Longer the Solution? First Amendment Theory Meets Fake News and the Filter Bubble," *Federal Communications Law Journal* 70, no. 1 (2018): 55–108.

Negoescu, Radu-Andrei and Daniel Gatica-Perez. "Analyzing Flickr Groups" CIVR'08: Proceedings of the 2008 International Conference on Content-based image and video retrieval (July 2008): 417–26.

Neiman, Susan. *Learning from the Germans: Race and the Memory of Evil*, 1st edn. New York: Farrar, Straus and Giroux, 2019.

Neumayer, Christina and G. Stald. "The Mobile Phone in Street Protest: Texting, Tweeting, Tracking, and Tracing," *Mobile Media & Communication* 2, no. 2 (2014): 117–33.

Neumayer, Christina and Bjarki Valtysson. "Tweet against Nazis? Twitter, Power, and Networked Publics in Anti-fascist Protests." *Journal of Media and Communication Research* 55 (2013): 9.

Neumayer, Christina, Luca Rossi, and Björn Karlsson. "Contested Hashtags: Blockupy Frankfurt in Social Media," *International Journal of Communication* 10 (2016): 5558–79.

Neuntzner, Matthias. "Vom Anklagen zum Erinnern. Die Erzaehlung vom 13. Februar," in *Das rote Leuchten. Dresden und das Bombenkrieg*, ed. Oliver Reinhard, Matthias Neutzner, and Wolfgang Hesse. Dresden: Edition Saechsische Zeitung, 2005.

Nikulin, Dmitri. *Memory: A History*. Oxford: Oxford University Press, 2015.

Nolan, Mary. "Air Wars, Memory Wars," *Central European History* 38, no. 1 (2005).

The New Fascism Syllabus Catechism Debate. http://newfascismsyllabus.com/category/opinions/the-catechism-debate/.

Noortje, Marres. "Front-Staging Non-Humans: The Politics of 'Green' Things and the Constraint of Publicity," in *The Stuff of Politics*, ed. Bruce Braun and Sarah J. Whatmore. United States: University of Minnesota Press, 2008, 177–210.

O'Connor, Paul. "The Unanchored Past: Three Modes of Collective Memory," *Memory Studies* 15, no. 4 (2022): 634–49.

Online Collective Action: Dynamics of the Crowd in Social Media, ed. Nitin Agarwal, Merlyna Lim, and Rolf T. Wigand. Vienna: Springer Vienna, 2014.

Osterhammel, Jürgen and Niels P. Petersson. *Globalization: A Short History*. Princeton, NJ: Princeton University Press, 2005.

Papacharissi, Zizi. "Affective Publics and Structures of Storytelling: Sentiment, Events and Mediality," *Information, Communication & Society* 19 (2015): 307–24.

Papacharissi, Zizi. *Affective Publics: Sentiment, Technology, and Politics*. New York: Oxford University Press, 2014.

Papacharissi, Zizi. *A Private Sphere: Democracy in a Digital Age*. Cambridge, UK: Polity, 2010.

Pariser, Eli. *The Filter Bubble: What the Internet Is Hiding from You*. New York: Penguin Press, 2011.

Parks, Malcolm R. "Social Network Sites as Virtual Communities," in *A Networked Self: Identity, Community and Culture on Social Network Sites*, ed. Zizi Papacharissi. New York: Routledge, 2011, 105–23.

Passionate Politics: Emotions and Social Movements, ed. Jeff Goodwin, James M. Jasper, and Francesca Polletta. Chicago: University of Chicago Press, 2001.

Perinelli, Massimo. "Longing, Lust, Violence, and Liberation: Discourses on Sexuality on the Radical Left, 1969–72," in *After the History of Sexuality: German Genealogies with and Beyond Foucault*, ed. Scott Spector, Helmut Puff, and Dagmar Herzog. New York: Berghahn Press, 2012.

Pfanzelter, Eva. "At the Crossroads with Public History: Mediating the Holocaust on the Internet," *Holocaust Studies* 21, no. 4 (2015): 250–71.

Pfaff, Steven. "The Politics of Peace in the GDR: The Independent Peace Movement, the Church, and the Original of the East German Opposition," *Peace and Change* 26, no. 3 (July 2001): 280–300.

Phillips, Mark Salber. *On Historical Distance*. Yale: Yale University Press, 2013.

Photobook Lust: Brad Feuerhelm on Richard Peter's Ein Kamera klagt an. https://aperture. org/pbr/photobook-lust-brad-feuerhelm-richard-peter-dresden-eine-kamera-klagt/.

Pleyers, Geoffrey. *Alter-Globalization: Becoming Actors in the Global Age*. Cambridge, UK: Polity, 2010.

Poell, Thomas and Erik Borra. "Twitter, YouTube, and Flickr as Platforms of Alternative Journalism: The Social Media Account of the 2010 Toronto G20 Protests," *Journalism* 13, no. 8 (2011): 1–19.

Pogačar, Martin. "Museums and Memorials in Social Media," in *Media Archaeologies, Micro-Archives and Storytelling: Re-Presencing the Past*, ed. Martin Pogačar, Palgrave Macmillan Memory Studies. London: Palgrave Macmillan UK, 2016, 87–113.

Presner, Todd. "The Ethics of the Algorithm: Close and Distant Listening to the Shoah Foundation Visual History Archive," in *Probing the Ethics of Holocaust Culture*, ed. Claudio Fogu, Wulf Kansteiner, and Todd Presner. Cambridge, MA: Harvard University Press, 2016, 175–202.

Presner, Todd. "The Humanities—Bigger and Bolder," *Seminar: A Journal of Germanic Studies* 50, no. 2 (2014): 154–60.

Presner, Todd Samuel, Wulf Kansteiner and Claudio Fogu. *Probing the Ethics of Holocaust Culture*, ed. Todd Samuel Presner, Wulf Kansteiner, and Claudio Fogu. Cambridge, MA: Harvard University Press, 2016.

Quattrociocchi, Walter, Antonio Scala and Cass R. Sunstein. "Echo Chambers on Facebook," *SSRN Scholarly Paper*. Rochester, NY: Social Science Research Network, June 13, 2016. https://papers.ssrn.com/abstract=2795110.

Rancière, Jacques. *Aux bords du politique*. Paris: Gallimard, 1998.

Radstone, Susannah. "What Place Is This? Transcultural Memory and the Locations of Memory Studies," *Parallax* 17, no. 4 (November 1, 2011): 109–23.

Radstone, Susannah and Bill Schwarz's edited volume. *Memory: Histories, Theories, and Debates*. New York: Fordham University Press, 2010.

Reading, Anna. "Globital Time," in *Emily Kneightley, Time, Media, and Modernity*. Basingstoke: Palgrave Macmillan, 2012, 144.

Reading, Anna. "The London Bombings: Mobile Witnessing, Mortal Bodies, and Globital Time," *Memory Studies* 4, no. 3 (2011): 299.

Reading, Anna. "The Mobile Family Gallery? Gender, Memory and the Cameraphone?" *Trames: Journal of the Humanities and Social Sciences* 12, no. 3 (2008): 355–65.

Reading, Anna. "Seeing Red: A Political Economy of Digital Memory," *Media, Culture & Society* 36, no. 6 (September 1, 2014): 748–60.

Reichardt, Sven. "Praxeologie und Faschismus. Gewalt und Gemeinschaft als Elemente eines praxeologischen Faschismusbegriffs," in *Doing Culture. Neue Positionen zum Verhältnis von Kultur und sozialer Praxis,* ed. K. Hörning and J. Reuter. Bielefeld: Transcript, 2004.

Reichhardt, Sven and Detlef Siegfried. *Das Alternative Milieu: Antibürgerlicher Lebensstil und linke Politik in der Bundesrepublik Deutschland und Europa 1968–1983* Berlin: deGruyter, 2010.

Reinhold Lütgemeier-Davin, Holger Nehring Karlheinz Lipp. *Frieden und Friedensbewegungen in Deutschland 1892–1992.* Essen: Klartext Verlage, 2010.

Richardson-Little, Ned and Samuel Merrill. "Who Is the Volk? PEGIDA and the Contested Memory of 1989 on Social Media," in *Social Movements, Cultural Memory, and Digital Media: Mobilising Mediated Remembrance,* ed. Samuel Merrill, Emily Keightley, and Priska Daphi. Palgrave Macmillan, 2020, 59–84.

Ricouer, Paul. *Memory, History, Forgetting,* trans. Kathleen Blamey and David Pellauer. Chicago: University of Chicago Press, 2004.

Rigney, Ann. "The Dynamics of Remembrance: Texts between Monumentality and Morphing," in *Cultural Memory Studies: An International and Interdisciplinary Handbook,* ed. Astrid Erll and Ansgar Nunning. Berlin and New York: de Gruyter, 2008, 345–53.

Rishel, Nicole M. "Digitizing Deliberation: Normative Concerns for the Use of Social Media in Deliberative Democracy," *Administrative Theory & Praxis* 33, no. 3 (2011): 411–32.

Robertson, Roland. "Globalisation or Glocalization?" *The Journal of International Communication* 1, no. 1 (1993): 33–52.

Robinson, Mike and David Picard. "Moments, Magic, and Memories: Photographing Tourists, Tourist Photographs and Making Worlds," in *The Framed World: Tourism, Tourists, and Photography,* ed. Mike Robinson and David Picard. England: Ashgate Publishing Ltd., 2009, 1.

Robinson, Sandra. "Platform Multiverse: Discontent and Disconnection among Alt-Rights," *Canadian Journal of Communication* 47, no. 1 (2022): 197–218.

Rokem, Freddie. "Performing History: Theatrical Representations of the Past in Contemporary Theatre," *Studies in Theatre History & Culture,* ed. Thomas Postlewait (2000).

Rose, Julia. *Difficult History at Museums and Historic Sites.* London: Rowman and Littlefield, 2016.

Rosenfeld, Gavriel D. "The Rise of Illiberal Memory," *Memory Studies* 16, no. 3 (2021): 1–18.

Rosenfeld, Gavriel D. *Hi Hitler! How the Nazi Past Is Being Normalized in Contemporary Culture.* Cambridge, MA: Cambridge University Press, 2014.

Rothberg, Michael. *The Implicated Subject: Beyond Victims and Perpetrators, Cultural Memory in the Present*, Stanford, CA: Stanford University Press, 2019.

Rothberg, Michael. "Introduction: Between Memory and Memory—From Lieux de mémoire to Noeuds de mémoire," *Yale French Studies*, no. 118–19 (2010): 10.

Rothberg, Michael. *Multidirectional Memory: Remembering the Holocaust in the Age of Decolonization*. Stanford: Stanford University Press, 2009.

Roudometof, Victor. *Glocalization: A Critical Introduction*. New York: Routledge, 2016.

Routledge, Paul. "Sensuous Solidarities: Emotion, Politics and Performance in the Clandestine Insurgent Rebel Clown Army," *Antipode* 44, no. 2 (2012): 428–52.

Rubin, Eli. *Amnesiopolis: Modernity, Space, and Memory in East Germany*. Oxford: Oxford University Press, 2016.

Rubinstein, Daniel and Katrina Sluis. "A Life More Photographic: Mapping the Networked Image," *Photographies* 1, no. 1 (2008): 9–28.

Sabrow, M. and N. Frei, eds. *Die Geburt des Zeitzeugen nach 1945*. Göttingen: Wallstein, 2012.

Samuel, Raphael. *Theatres of Memory. Past and Present in Contemporary Culture*. London: Verso, 1994, 10.

Sander, August. *Die Zerstörung Kölns: Photographien 1945–1946*. Munich: Schirmer/Mosel, 1985.

Sarcinelli, Ulrich. "Mediatisierung," in *Politische Kommunikation in der demokratischen Gesellschaft*, ed. Otfried Jarren, Ulrich Sarcinelli, and Ulrich Saxer. Opladen: Westdeutscher Verlag, 1998, 678–9.

Schadtler, Jan. "The Devil in Disguise: Action Repertoire, Visual Performance and Collective Identity of the Autonomous Nationalists," *Nations and Nationalism* 20, no. 22 (April 2014): 242.

Schoen Consulting. "Holocaust Knowledge and Awareness Study: Executive Summary," 7. http://www.claimscon.org/wp-content/uploads/2018/04/Holocaust-Knowledge-Awareness-Study_Executive-Summary-2018.pdf (accessed January 25, 2019).

Schulz, Winfried. "Reconstructing Mediatization as an Analytical Concept," *European Journal of Communication* 19, no. 1 (2004): 87–101.

Seidenstücker, Friedrich. *Von Weimar bis zum Ende: Fotografien aus bewegter Zeit*. Dortmund: Harenberg, 1980.

Sekula, Alan. *Photography against the Grain. Essays and Photoworks 1973–1983*. Halifax: Press of the Noval Scotia College of Art and Design, 1984.

Serafinelli, Elisa. *Digital Life on Instagram: New Social Communication of Photography*. Bingley: Emerald Publishing Limited, 2018, 26–7.

Sharon, Sliwinski. *Human Rights in Camera*. Chicago: University of Chicago Press, 2011.

Shneer, David. "The Elusive Search for Evidence: Evgenii Khaldei's Budapest Ghetto, Images of Rape, and Soviet Holocaust Photography," *Slavic Review* 76, no. 1 (2017): 80–9.

Silverman, Kaja. "Disassembled Movies," in *Synopsis III: Fiction and Reality*. Athens: National Museum of Contemporary Art, 2003.

Snyder, Timothy. *On Tyranny*. New York: Penguin, 2017.

Sontag, Susan. *On Photography*. London: Penguin Books, 1977.

Spiegel, Gabrielle. "Memory and History: Liturgical Time and Historical Time," *History and Theory* XLI (2002): 149–62.

Spohr, Dominic. "Fake News and Ideological Polarization: Filter Bubbles and Selective Exposure on Social Media," *Business Information Review* 34, no. 3 (2017): 150–160.

Stearns, Peter N. *Encyclopedia of Social History*. New York: Garland, 1994.

Steinberg, Mark D. "Melancholy and Modernity: Emotions and Social Life in Russia between the Revolutions," *Journal of Social History* 41, no. 4 (2008): 813–41.

Steinberg, Sven. "From Memorial Space to Learning Place. Present and Prospective (hi)story Telling at the Dresden Heidefriedhof/Heath Cemetery," in *Abolish Commemoration, Critique of the Discourse Relating to the Bombing of Dresden in 1945*, ed. Dissonanz author collective. Verbrecher Verlag, 2014, 189–213.

Steinberg, Sven. "Nicht Gedenkort, sondern Lernort. Was der Heidefriedhof erzählt, und erzählen könnte," in *Gendenken abschaffen. Kritik am Diskurs zu Bombadierung Dresdens 1945*, ed. Autor_innenkollektiv Dissonanz. Berlin: Verbrecher Verlag, 2013, 105–16.

Stephen, Lovell. *Russia in the Microphone Age: A History of Soviet Radio, 1919–1970*, 1st edn. Oxford: Oxford University Press, 2015.

Stern, Alexandra. *Proud Boys and the White Ethnostate: How the Alt-Right Is Warping the American Imagination*. Boston, MA: Beacon Press, 2019.

Stier, Oren Baruch. *Committed to Memory: Cultural Mediations of the Holocaust*. Amherst and Boston: University of Massachusetts Press, 2015.

Strömbäck, Jesper and Frank Esser. "Introduction," *Journalism Practice* 8, no. 3 (2014): 245–57.

Struk, Janina. *Photographing the Holocaust: Interpretations of Evidence*. London and New York: I.B. Tauris, 2004.

Sturken, Marita. "Memory, Consumerism and Media: Reflections on the Emergence of the Field," *Memory Studies* 1, no. 1 (2008): 75.

Sturken, Marita. *Tangled Memories: The Vietnam War, the Aids Epidemic, and the Politics of Remembering*. Berkeley: University of California Press 1997.

Sutton, Damian. "Immanent Images: Photography after Mobility," in *Afterimages of Gilles Deleuze's Film Philosophy*, ed. D.N. Rodowick. Minneapolis, MN: University of Minnesota Press, 2009.

Tagg, John. *The Burden of Representation. Essays on Photographies and Histories*. Minneapolis: University of Minnesota Press, 1988.

Tenove, Chris, Heidi Tworek, and Fenwick McKelvey. "Poisoning Democracy. What Can Be Done about Harmful Speech Online?" *Public Policy Forum Online*, 2018. https://ppforum.ca/publications/poisoning-democracy-what-can-be-done-about-.

Thelwell, Mike and Maria Delgado. "Arts and Humanities Research Evaluation: No Metrics Please, Just Data," *Journal of Documentation* 71, no. 4 (2005): 817–33.

Thießen, Malte. "Gemeinsame Erinnerungen im geteilten Deutschland: Der Luftkrieg im 'kommunalen Gedaächtnis' der Bundesrepublik und DDR," *Deutschland Archiv* 41, no. 2 (2008): 226–32.

Thomas, Julia Adeney. "Hope Flies; Death Dances," in *The Ethics of Seeing: Photography and Twentieth-Century History*, ed. Jennifer Evans, Paul Betts, and Stefan-Ludwig Hoffmann. New York: Berghahn Books, 2018, 274–86.

Thrift, Nigel. "Remembering the Technological Unconscious by Foregrounding Knowledges of Position," in *Knowing Capitalism*. London: Sage, 2005, 212–26.

Tilly, Charles. *Stories, Identities, and Political Change*. Lanham, MD: Rowman & Littlefield, 2002.

Tilly, Charles and Lesley D. Wood. *Social Movements, 1768–2012*, London: Routledge, 2013.

Törnberg, Petter. "Echo Chambers and Viral Misinformation: Modeling Fake News as Complex Contagion," *PLoS ONE* 13, no. 9 (September 20, 2018).

Trezise, Bryoni. "Touching Virtual Trauma: Performative Empathics in Second Life," *Memory Studies* 5, no. 4 (2011): 392–409.

Tsou, Ming-Hsiang and Michael Leitner. "Visualization of Social Media: Seeing a Mirage or a Message?" *Cartography and Geographic Information Science* 40, no. 2 (2013): 55–60.

Tufekci, Zeynep. "Capabilities of Movements and Affordances of Digital Media: Paradoxes of Empowerment. dmlcentral." *Digital Media+Learning: The Power of Participation*. http://dmlcentral.net/blog/zeynep-tufekci/capabilities-movements-and-affordances-digital-media-paradoxes-empowerment.

Turkle, Sherry. *Life on the Screen: Identity in the Age of the Internet*. New York: Simon & Schuster, 1995.

Tworek, Heidi. *News from Germany: The Competition to Control World Communications, 1900–1945*. Cambridge, MA: Harvard University Press, 2019.

Uberhorst, Horst. "Feste, Fahnen, Feiern: die Bedeutung politischer Symbole und Rituale im Nationalsozialismus," in *Politik der Symbole: Symbole der Politik*, ed. Rüdiger Voigt. VS Verlag für Sozialwissenschaften, 1989, 157–78.

Umbach, Maiken. *German Cities and Bourgeois Modernism, 1890–1924*. Oxford: Oxford University Press, 2009.

United States Holocaust Memorial Museum (@holocaustmuseum) on Instagram and Twitter. http://www.instagram.com/holocaustmuseum.

United States Holocaust Memorial Museum. "Days of Remembrance: More Ways to Remember." https://www.ushmm.org/remember/days-of-remembrance/more.

United States Holocaust Memorial Museum. "Receiving Tattoos at Auschwitz," the United States Holocaust Memorial Museum Digital Encyclopedia. https://encyclopedia.ushmm.org/content/en/gallery/receiving-tattoos-at-auschwitz (accessed December 16, 2018).

van Dijck, Jose. *Mediated Memories in the Digital Age, Cultural Memory in the Present.* Stanford, CA: Stanford University Press, 2007.

van Dijck, José. "Digital Photography: Communication, Identity, Memory," *Visual Communication 7*, no. 1 (2008): 57–76.

van Dijck, Jan A. "One Europe, Digitally Divided" in Routledge Handbook of Internet Politics, ed. Andrew Chadwick and Philip N. Howard. (New York: Routledge, 2009). 288–304.

van Dijck, José. "Flickr and the Culture of Connectivity: Sharing Views, Experiences, Memories," *Memory Studies* 4, no. 4 (2011): 401–15.

van Dijck, José. *The Culture of Connectivity. A Critical History of Social Media.* Oxford: Oxford University Press, 2013.

van Dijck, José and Thomas Poelle. "Social Media and the Transformation of Public Space," *Social Media + Society* 1, no. 2 (July–December 2015): 1–5.

Van House, Nancy A. "Collocated Photosharing, Story-telling, and the Performance of Self," *International Journal of Human—Computer Studies* 67, no. 12 (2009): 1073–86.

Van House, Nancy K. and Elizabeth Churchill. "Technologies of Memory: Key Issues and Critical Perspectives," *Memory Studies* 1, no. 3 (2008): 306.

Varnelis, Kazys and Anne Friedberg. "*Place: The Networking of Public Space*," in *Networked Publics*, ed. Kazys Varnelis. Cambridge, MA: MIT Press, 2012, 17.

Vees-Gulani, Susanne. "The Politics of New Beginnings. The Continued Exclusion of the Nazi Past in Dresden's Cityscape," in *Beyond Berlin: Twelve German Cities Confront the Nazi Past,* ed. Paul B. Jaskot and Gavriel D. Rosenfeld. Ann Arbor: University of Michigan Press, 2008, 43.

Virchow, Fabian. "Performance, Emotion and Ideology—On the Creation of 'Collectives of Emotion' and World View in the Contemporary German Far Right," *Journal of Contemporary Ethnography* 36, no. 2 (2007): 147–64.

Virilio, Paul. *Open Sky*. London: Verso, 1997.

Visitor comments from the United States Holocaust Memorial Museum, Institutional Fonds, July 29, 2015.

Visitor comments from the United States Holocaust Memorial Museum, Institutional Fonds, October 2, 2002.

Visitor comments from the United States Memorial Holocaust Museum, Institutional Fonds, September 11, 2003.

von Hodenberg, Christina. "Mass Media and the Generation of Conflict. West Germany's Long Sixties and the Formation of a Critical Public Sphere," *Central European History* 15, no. 3 (August 2006): 367–95.

Voyant and Mallet. http://mallet.cs.umass.edu/topics.php.

Waibel, Harry. *Rechtsextremismus in der DDR bis 1989*. Köln: Papyrossa Verlag, 1996.

Walden, Victoria. *Digital Holocaust Memory, Education and Research*. Basingstoke: Palgrave Macmillan, 2021.

Walden, Victoria Grace. "What Is 'Virtual Holocaust Memory'?" *Memory Studies* 15, no. 4 (November 22, 2019): 1–13.

Warner, Michael. *Publics and Counterpublics*. Boston: MIT Press, 2002.

Weissman, Gary. *Fantasies of Witnessing: Postwar Efforts to Experience the Holocaust*. Ithaca/London: Cornell University Press, 2004.

West, Nancy Martha. *Kodak and the Lens of Nostalgia*. Charlottesville: University Press of Virginia, 2000.

Williams, Raymond. *Television, Technology and Culture Form*. New York: Schocken Press, 1974.

Winter, Martin Clemens. "Luftkrieg. Akteure und Deutungen des Gedenkens seit 1945," in *Erringerungsorte der extremen Rechten*, ed. Martin Langebach and Michael Sturm. Wiesbaden: Springer Fachmedien, 2015, 197–212.

Wouters, Ruud. "From the Street to the Screen: Characteristics of Protest Events as Determinants of Television News Coverage." *Mobilization: An International Quarterly* 18, no. 1 (2013): 83–105.

Young, Benjamin. "On Strike: Allan Sekula's Waiting for Tear Gas," in *Sensible Politics: The Visual Culture of Nongovernmental Action*, ed. Yates McKee and Meg McLagan. New York: Zone Books, 2012, 148–81.

Young, James E. *At Memory's Edge: After-Images of the Holocaust in Contemporary Art and Architecture*. New Haven: Yale University Press, 2000.

Young, James E. *Stages of Memory: Reflections on Memorial Art, Loss, and the Spaces Between*. Amherst: University of Massachusetts Press, 2016.

Young, James E. *The Texture of Memory: Holocaust Memorials and Meaning*. New Haven, CT: Yale University Press, 1993.

YouTube channel. https://www.youtube.com/watch?v=TnvuZSq81zQ. For more on Bürgel's claims see https://www.welt.de/geschichte/zweiter-weltkrieg/article113572177/Dossier-berichtet-ueber-Tiefflieger-Angriffe-auf-Dresden.html.

Zappavigna, Michele. "Ambient Affiliation: A Linguistic Perspective on Twitter," *New Media and Society* 13, no. 5 (2011).

Zappavigna, Michelle. "Searable Talk: The Linguistic Functions of Hashtags," *Social Semiotics* 25, no. 3 (2015).

Zelizer, Barbie. "Memory as Foreground, Journalism as Background," in *Journalism and Memory*, ed. B. Zelizer and K. Tenenboim-Weinblatt. Basingstoke: Palgrave Macmillan, 2014, 32–49.

Ziemann, Benjamin. *Peace Movements in Western Europe, Japan, and the USA during the Cold War*. Essen: Klartext, 2008.

Index

www.ingramcontent.com/pod-product-compliance
Lightning Source LLC
Chambersburg PA
CBHW071844270326
41929CB00013B/2103